Integrated Series in Information Systems

Series Editors

For further volumes:
http://www.springer.com/series/6157

Kweku-Muata Osei-Bryson
Gunjan Mansingh • Lila Rao
Editors

Knowledge Management for Development

Domains, Strategies and Technologies for Developing Countries

Springer

Editors
Kweku-Muata Osei-Bryson
Department of Information Systems
Virginia Commonwealth University
Richmond, VA, USA

Gunjan Mansingh
Department of Computing
University of the West Indies
Mona Campus, Jamaica

Lila Rao
Mona School of Business and Management,
The University of the West Indies
Mona Campus, Jamaica

ISSN 1571-0270 ISSN 2197-7968 (electronic)
ISBN 978-1-4899-7391-7 ISBN 978-1-4899-7392-4 (eBook)
DOI 10.1007/978-1-4899-7392-4
Springer New York Heidelberg Dordrecht London

Library of Congress Control Number: 2013957135

Printed on acid-free paper

Springer is part of Springer Science+Business Media (www.springer.com)

We dedicate this book to our parents

Jeremiah and Pilarcita Bryson

Vijay and Rachna Srivastava
Ajai and Laxmi Mansingh

Bhaskar and Judy Rao

Foreword

In today's increasingly digital world, the importance of extracting knowledge out of the continuous production of different types and forms of stored data residing across functional areas in organizations to facilitate optimized and efficient decision making, necessitates effective and efficient knowledge infrastructures and knowledge management. The readiness, competence, and agility of organizations to manage and align diverse knowledge assets inter- and intra-organizations and to extract embedded knowledge to improve the processes, agility, and efficiency of the value chain across the organization as well as smart decision making and policies for continuous problem solving and innovation is the only surety of their sustainability and resilience of organizations. This is particularly true in developing countries where the challenges to solve problems and provide innovations that will propel the economic engines are huge and continuous.

Thus, the need for developing countries to develop innovative processes and structures and redesign organizational architectures to smarter and more agile forms, motivated by the contextual realities both at the public and private institution levels, is urgent and important. However, the ability of these countries to address all their social and economic needs efficiently is continuously challenged by huge resource constraints. These include a limited stock of adequate and efficient human capital to create, share, and manage knowledge as well as limited access to or the availability of adequate financial resources to yield maximum impact and efficient decision making and policy instruments.

Thus, the importance to developing countries of building and implementing knowledge management infrastructures and capabilities across organizations, both public and private, grounded and guided by effective knowledge management principles cannot be overemphasized. This volume addresses these issues and challenges with contributions from many developing countries including case studies with insights on strategies and technologies relevant to several sectors, including health care, agriculture, education, and disaster management.

It is therefore pivotal for organizations in developing countries to master the art of integrating disparate sources of knowledge. Managing knowledge in developing countries requires an understanding of the complex combination of new tools, intellectual capital, processes, cultural and environmental contexts, and strategies, and their integration into and coexistence with the existing infrastructure. Although knowledge management (KM) implementation in developing countries may be at its infancy and does appear relatively risky and overwhelming, it starts with a few steps and requires assistance from inside and outside the organization. The current situation is that most actors and agents do not have an appreciation or knowledge of the management infrastructure or the capacity or competence in knowledge management to foresee its importance and centrality to the socioeconomic ecosystem of public and private organizations and as a potential enabler in the rejuvenation and acceleration of the economies of developing countries. Therefore, it is important for organizations in developing countries to incorporate knowledge management as the core of their organizational structure, aligned with and integral to their ICT infrastructure. Thus, the included chapters focus on mechanisms to improve existing KM capability in organizations, domains, and developing countries with emphasis on technologies and knowledge sharing.

While the debate on the utility of information and communication technologies (ICTs) and the use of knowledge for development in developing countries has largely been won, the challenge of how best to use ICTs and KM for poverty reduction and economic growth and development remains. Although the link between economic growth, knowledge utilization, and ICTs has been well established, the exact process of how ICTs and KM can be used for development in developing countries needs exploration. In particular, there are few if any theoretical explanations as to how knowledge management strategies and technologies can assist in development in a developing country setting. This volume does just that, offering insights on implementation of KM technologies in disaster management and agriculture in Mexico, Jamaica, and sub-Saharan African countries, as well as informing readers on the need for and development of ontologies which are a key component in development and use of KMS.

In addition, this volume on knowledge management and development highlights relevant issues and challenges in critical economic sectors including agriculture, health care, disaster recovery management, and the development of the private sector, especially, small and medium enterprises, and identifies KM strategies and technologies which can be applied to areas that are critical to the economic growth of developing countries.

Knowledge management is aimed at improving the productivity and efficiency of economic sectors and organizations in developing countries; however, there is lack of knowledge infrastructure and KM capacity and a lack of understanding, building, and adopting relevant KM strategies and technologies. Thus, consideration must be given to the unique context and social norms of developing countries to ensure that KM results in stimulating economic growth and production efficiency. ICTs will facilitate the building of human and social capital through increasing flows of information, building on endogenous knowledge and human capacity for poverty reduction and enhancing efficiencies of organizational processes and thus lead to economic gains across sectors and organizations. These ICTs can be used to facilitate the appropriate adoption of KM with KM processes, solutions, and strategies that will provide unparalleled opportunities for the management of sectors, policy making, and quality decision making in developing countries thereby contributing to economic development.

Knowledge and effective KM strategies and technologies in organizations governing economic activity in developing countries are central to poverty alleviation and economic development. Without a KM infrastructure, processes and strategies applied to enhance policy and decision making in sectors, knowledge as an enabler to enhance economic activity, growth, and development will be less than optimal and will not yield the requisite value for development. The chapters in the book highlight the importance and opportunities of knowledge and knowledge management for the health care, agriculture, disaster recovery management, and small and medium size enterprise development for developing countries.

Knowledge management, when implemented in sectors and organizations in developing countries, will enhance productivity and quality decision making and empower individuals and organizations to problem solve efficiently and manage resources optimally to yield maximum value. The book also highlights the contribution of knowledge management perspectives in developing countries and provides a deeper understanding of the role of knowledge and how it assists social capital formation in a development situation. Effective implementation of KM in sectors and organizations in developing countries will facilitate access to knowledge that ICTs enable which can lead to the formation of human and social capital and, in turn, contribute to economic growth and development.

This volume shares with us a diversity of approaches in the implementation of KM from a dynamic capabilities perspective and conveys a needed normative framework on which organizations in developing countries can build the requisite knowledge infrastructure and knowledge management capability to be in a position to embark on the path towards successful KM implementation as core to all organization processes. For developing countries, the utility of an adaptable and sustainable knowledge management framework is that it can guide efforts to manage knowledge, drawing practical recommendations from all actors and agents including managers and policy makers, and enabling them to develop their organizations in the increasingly digital and global knowledge economy. Effective and efficient knowledge management will invigorate the efficiency and productivity of both public and private organizations in developing countries and enhance the quality of policy and decision making which will result in economic efficiencies, growth, and development.

Although an understanding of the value of knowledge may not be new in the developing world, managing it and leveraging it for competitive advantage is increasingly being recognized as important and even necessary for survival in the global marketplace and is influencing the outpacing of countries' economic growth and development. This is not the case in most developing countries. The chapters of the book attempt, in a diversity of perspectives, to shed light on and underscore the urgency and importance for developing countries to build knowledge infrastructures and adopt and make knowledge management a key to organizational development to enhance the quality of decision and policy making. This undoubtedly is argued in the chapters of the book to facilitate efficient management of resources which will yield for developing countries substantive and efficient process improvements that will result in accelerated economic growth and development. The included chapters establish this through case studies illustrating insights on strategies and technologies in vital areas key to development. These chapters further highlight issues with knowledge sharing in developing countries across the world with specific examples from Jamaica, India, and Indonesia.

This volume attempts to contribute to knowledge management research in developing countries by providing insights into KM implementation in various sectors in developing countries based on the dynamic capabilities approach. The chapters share insights that focus on assessing and setting targets for building the organizational and technological infrastructures a company needs before KM processes can be adopted and implemented.

It is important to note that successful KM implementation in organizations and sectors in developing countries requires them to identify, evaluate, and alter their existing capabilities that can support knowledge management (Gold, Malhotra, & Segar, 2001). It is equally important to radically change the culture and value of the ownership of knowledge, the creation, and sharing of knowledge and the use of knowledge as key to decision and policy making. Further, the revamping, revising, and realigning of the entire functional and organizational processes will be required as a prerequisite to the development of knowledge infrastructure and knowledge management as an important and core component of all organizations. When this is rooted fully in organizations and sectors in developing countries and becomes part of the institutional culture and actors and agents in these organizations adopt knowledge management principles, approaches, and methods, this will undoubtedly enhance organizational efficiencies and productivity which will have positive spillover effects influencing the economy with positive gains that will result in economic growth and development. The included chapters focus on implementations of KM technologies in the sectors of agriculture and disaster management in Jamaica, Mexico, and sub-Saharan Africa.

Readers will find from this volume that most organizations and sectors seek the key benefits of KM. These benefits are capturing and sharing best practices, providing and improving KM capacity, effective implementation of KM technologies, community-focused initiatives essential for the development of community leadership and projects, and development of ontologies for KMS; managing the citizenry or societal stakeholders; and delivering competitive intelligence to enhance the quality of judgment for policy and decision making. Readers will also find that the advantages of successful KM implementation include fewer mistakes, less redundancy, quicker problem solving, better decision making, reduced research development costs, increased worker independence, enhanced customer and stakeholder relations, and improved service and enhanced decision making and organization productivity.

It is gathered from the chapters in this volume that knowledge and its effective utilization and management is key to sector development. However, it is important for the reader to be clear what knowledge is. Knowledge can be either explicit or tacit in nature (Davenport, De Long, & Beers, 1998). Explicit knowledge is information that can be easily articulated and shared with others, while tacit knowledge is personal knowledge residing in an individual's head; and it is very difficult to codify (Gupta & McDaniel, 2002). A key objective of KM is to ensure that the right knowledge is available to the right person at the right time in a manner that enables timely decision making (Hariharan, 2002). The contributed chapters through the case studies shed additional light on the effective utilization of knowledge.

Although KM has achieved a level of popularity among many organizations globally, it has no unique or standardized definition (Nonaka, 1994) and the same can be said to be the case in developing countries. Nonaka and Takeuchi (1995) define knowledge as a true justified belief. Tuomi (1999) questions this definition, claiming that we know the world in the same way as facts, through socially constructed and historically developed distinctions. Leonard and Sensipar (1998) define knowledge as information that is relevant, actionable, and based partially on experience. O'Dell and Grayson (1998) define it as what people in organizations know about their products, customers, processes, mistakes, and success. Furthermore, Davenport and Prusak (1998) define knowledge as a fluid mix of framed experience, values, contextual information, and expert insight that provide a framework for evaluating and incorporating new experiences and information. KM is also conceived as the process of opening communication channels and fostering knowledge flow in the firm through teamwork so that it can be used, enhanced, and built upon to leverage the performance of individuals and consequently the whole organization or sector (LaMonica, 2001). In other places in the literature, KM is defined as the process of capturing and organizing individual and organizational knowledge within its context and making it accessible to everyone in the company. Thus, KM enables companies to optimize the use of their collective knowledge to achieve business goals and acquire a sustainable competitive advantage (Davenport et al., 1998). These concepts are highlighted and discussed adequately in various chapters of the volume and highlighted in the included case studies.

There are virtually an unlimited number of KM-related activities that an organization and sector can implement. These are grouped into four main categories: knowledge creation (generation), conversion (codification and storage), transfer (access and absorption), and application (use). Knowledge creation processes or acquisition processes means doing both capturing outside knowledge and developing new knowledge from existing content (Davenport, Jarvenpaa, & Beers, 1996). Knowledge is created as a product of socialization. For instance, new tacit knowledge can be created out of existing tacit knowledge through shared expertise and creative problem solving, (Leonard-Barton, 1995). Davenport and Prusak (1998) identified five modes of knowledge generation; they are acquisition and rental from outside sources, use of dedicated resources such as R&D facilities, fusion of different perspectives, adaptation to avoid core rigidities (also see Leonard-Barton, 1995), and the establishment of formal and informal networks of knowers.

Knowledge conversion or codification processes include locating knowledge, evaluating it for usefulness and relevance, and eventually codifying it (Leonard-Barton, 1995). The purpose here is to store and reapply knowledge and workable solutions as procedures that can be used instead of replicating the work every time a problem occurs (Alavi & Leidner, 2001). Hence, knowledge codification organizes knowledge and makes it explicit, portable, accessible, and applicable to everyone who needs it in the organization or sector. IT plays a key role in storing this codified information and making it available when needed.

Many entities are involved in transferring knowledge in an organization. For instance, knowledge is transferred between individuals, individuals and explicit sources, people and groups, multiple groups, and from groups to the whole organization or sector (Alavi & Leidner, 2001). Knowledge transfer is driven by communication processes and information flows within the company and among its partners. Effective knowledge transfer depends on three main factors: (1) mutual willingness of knowledge supplier and receiver to exchange knowledge, (2) existence and quality of transfer channels, and (3) absorptive capacity of the recipient. Although the availability of transfer channels is vital to achieving effective knowledge transfer, they are of no value if the recipient does nothing with the transmitted knowledge. Knowledge transfer could also be inhibited or slowed down by factors such as lack of trust, lack of a common language, lack of time and meeting places (Davenport & Prusak, 1998), and lack of absorptive capacity of the recipient (Cohen & Levinthal, 1990).

The principal source of an organization's or sector's competitive advantage resides in the application of knowledge rather than in the knowledge itself (Alavi & Leidner, 2001). Application of knowledge refers to the commercial application of knowledge to achieve organizational objectives (Lane & Lubatkin, 1998). Grant (1996) identified three primary mechanisms for the integration of knowledge:

1. Directives (rules and standards developed for efficient communication to nonspecialists)
2. Organizational routines
3. The creation of self-contained task teams for problems with high uncertainty and complexity (Alavi & Leidner, 2001)

Specific organizational, sectoral, and technological infrastructures are prerequisites to ensure smooth KM implementation. Most KM projects rely on IT as an important enabler to support the activities of knowledge creation, codification, transfer, and application. For instance, at the creation stage, IT can be used for active and continuous learning and hence the generation of new knowledge.

Technologies such as data warehousing and mining, broad knowledge repositories, software agents, and intranets can facilitate the creation of a virtual place or space, which is at the heart of knowledge creation. Other technologies can include information systems designed to support collaboration, coordination, and communication to facilitate teamwork, thereby increasing contact with others (Alavi & Leidner, 2001). KM technologies could also be used to augment knowledge storage and retrieval through the use of computer storage technologies and sophisticated retrieval techniques such as query languages, multimedia databases, and database management systems. These tools increase the speed at which organizational knowledge could be accessed.

Meanwhile, document management technologies can be used for storing explicit knowledge that is dispersed among the different units in an organization. However, for rich tacit knowledge, cloud computing technologies, mobile technologies, multimedia technologies such as videoconferencing can be used to transfer this type of knowledge to remote locations. ICTs can also contribute to the effective application of knowledge by embedding knowledge into organizational routines and procedures. Such technologies include decision support systems, expert systems and artificial intelligence, constraint-based systems, and workflow automation systems that automate the routing of work-related documents, rules, and information (Alavi & Leidner, 2001).

These highlighted technologies are effective tools for storing vast amounts of data and information and promoting the processes of knowledge creation, storage/retrieval, transfer, and application. However, these technologies lack the ability to codify or create tacit knowledge. Therefore, they fail to duplicate or codify human intelligence, intuition, and experience. Another shortcoming of KM technologies is their inability to ensure that the knowledge available in repositories will be accessed and used effectively. Readers are adequately provided with insights and examples illustrated through case studies in the chapters on KM technologies in disaster management and agriculture in Mexico, Jamaica, and sub-Saharan Africa.

In addition to the urgent need for effective, efficient managerial systems and management capacity for organizations, sector management and leadership in developing countries, the values and norms of organizational culture act as screening mechanisms that filter the "what and how" aspects of knowledge (Sbarcea, 1998). A learning environment is needed in organizations and sectors in developing countries, in which individuals are respected, failure is tolerated, and the management is open to new ideas and innovations, supports KM. A crucial organizational value in a KM firm is the commitment of upper management to the continuous support of knowledge codification and sharing. This commitment would result in the formation of productive formal and informal communication networks important for transferring tacit and explicit knowledge (Birkinshaw, 2001). Such organizational values and norms also facilitate and promote the establishment of a system and an environment of knowledge sharing, as opposed to knowledge hoarding. Knowledge hoarding is a problematic phenomenon in developing countries that hinders the effective use of knowledge for development.

The chapters in this volume suggest that to implement KM in an organization or sector, internal and external competencies should be integrated, built, and reconfigured to respond to a changing environment. Certain capabilities, namely organizational and technological infrastructures, should be developed to facilitate successful implementation and integration of KM into an organization or sector in developing countries. These infrastructures evolve along certain evolutionary paths that comprise business processes, which in turn interact and support the various KM initiatives (Teece, Pisano, & Shuen, 1997). Thus, it is gathered from the chapters in the volume, developing countries must endeavor to put in place a knowledge management framework to guide its implementation in both public and private institutions. This is expected to include three main phases: initiation, adoption, and implementation. Since the dynamic capabilities approach follows a sequential path, the implementation of knowledge activities cannot take place before adopting organizational and technological infrastructures.

In the initiation phase of KM as core activity within an organization, it must have a high-level champion and sponsor. This must be an enthusiastic individual who is committed to the initiative and is willing to find the capital and human resources necessary for the implementation of the project. Knowledge-specific objectives must be aligned with the organizational or sectoral objectives. Examples of these KM objectives are (1) creating knowledge repositories, (2) improving knowledge access, (3) enhancing the knowledge environment, and (4) managing knowledge as an asset (Davenport et al., 1998). Once these objectives are set, they need to be communicated to all employees in the company. This lays the foundation for a clear beginning of a KM initiative. The final step in the initiation is assessing the current organizational and technological infrastructure (current position) to see how far they are from the target (future position), and what processes need to be adopted throughout the path to reach it (Mullin, 1996).

During the adoption phase, an organization's structure and processes are modified in order to create a positive orientation towards KM, which is an important prerequisite for the successful application of knowledge activities. It is not enough to assume that once knowledge is created, converted, transmitted, and applied, people would immediately start using it or participating in its activities. Therefore, the motivational component of KM adoption and implementation should be a top priority. Employees need to understand what KM is about, and what benefits they would gain from applying it.

Once the infrastructures for implementing KM are in place, knowledge activities can be executed. An organization embarking on the path to KM implementation first creates knowledge or captures it, then converts it into usable forms, transfers it, and finally uses and protects it (Soliman & Spooner, 2000). Along this path, the organizational and technological infrastructures established in the previous stages are utilized extensively and continuously updated to enhance the speed and effectiveness of these knowledge activities.

Knowledge management is a highly effective tool for organizations and sectors to building and sustaining a competitive advantage. The adoption and implementation of this concept requires changes to almost every aspect of the organization and/or the sector. However, these changes take time to materialize. Once the infrastructure is ready, KM activities need to be incorporated into the already existing set of processes. Though complex and time consuming, KM implementation yields numerous benefits to the company including enhancement of its economic performance and competitive position.

As intimated in the various chapters in the volume, the importance of continued research in knowledge management for development as an essential aspect to improve management processes and central to the organizational infrastructure in developing countries cannot be overemphasized. Local universities in developing countries, national think tanks and public and private institutions can play a vital role in facilitating the adoption and implementation of KM. Readers will find in this volume perspectives on "lessons learnt" in various domains and implementation details relevant for developing countries.

This volume provides readers with clear and useful guidelines for the implementation of certain technologies to facilitate achieving of KM goals. It is gathered from the chapters in this volume that internally, public and private organizations should also develop knowledge maps, since they are knowledge buyers. In a complex and global knowledge market, knowledge maps are essential to locate just in time key knowledge sources. Once knowledge is located, organizations and sectors need to have the capabilities necessary to acquire, absorb, and use it productively. This requires a significant amount of process and cultural change, as well as highly integrated information systems.

In this important volume, we have a worthy foundation for the next generation of work on knowledge management and development in developing countries.

Serrekunda, Gambia Muhammadou M.O. Kah

References

Alavi, M., & Leidner, D. E. (2001). Review: Knowledge management and knowledge management systems: Conceptual foundations and research issues. *MIS Quarterly, 25*(1), 107–135.

Birkinshaw, J. (2001). Making sense of knowledge management. *Ivey Business Journal, 65*(4), 32–37.

Cohen, W. M., & Levinthal, D. A. (1990). Absorptive capacity: A new perspective on learning and innovation, administrative. *Science Quarterly, 35*(1), 128–152.

Davenport, T. H., De Long, D. W., & Beers, M. C. (1998, Winter). Successful knowledge management projects. *Sloan Management Review*, 43–57.

Davenport, T. H., Jarvenpaa, S. L, & Beers M. C. (1996, Summer). Improving knowledge work processes. *Sloan Management Review*, 53–65.

Davenport, T. H., & Prusak, L. (1998). *Working knowledge: How organizations manage what they know*. Boston: HBS Press.

Gold, A. H., Malhotra, A., & Segar, A. H. (2001). Knowledge management: An organizational capabilities perspective. *Journal of Management Information Systems, 18*(1), 185–214.

Grant, R. M. (1996). Toward a knowledge-based theory of the firm. *Strategic Management Journal, 17*, 109–122.

Gupta, A., & McDaniel, J. (2002). Creating competitive advantage by effectively managing knowledge: A framework for knowledge management. *Journal of Knowledge Management Practice, 3*(2), 40–49.

Hariharan, A. (2002). Knowledge management: A strategic tool. *Journal of Knowledge Management Practice*. Retrieved September, 2010, from http://www.tlainc.com/articl46.htm

LaMonica, L. (2001, May). The case for knowledge management at DPA: Is what we don't know hurting us? *Journal of Knowledge Management Practice.*

Lane, P. J., & Lubatkin, M. (1998) Relative absorptive capacity and interorganizational learning. *Strategic Management Journal, 19*, 461–477.

Leonard-Barton, D. (1995). *Wellsprings of knowledge: Building and sustaining the sources of innovation.* Boston: Harvard Business School Press.

Leonard, D., & Sensipar, S. (1998). The role of tacit knowledge in group innovation. *California Management Review, 40*(3), 112–132.

Mullin, R. (1996). Knowledge management: A cultural revolution. *Journal of Business Strategy, 17*(5), 56–60.

Nonaka, I. (1994). A dynamic theory of organizational knowledge creation. *Organizational Science, 5*(1), 14–37.

Nonaka, I., & Takeuchi, H. (1995). *The knowledge creating company: How Japanese companies create the dynamics of innovation.* Oxford, England: Oxford University Press

O'Dell, C., & Grayson, C. J. (1998). If only we knew what we knew: Identification and Transfer of Internal Best Practices. *California Management Review, 40*(3), 154–174.

Sbarcea, K. (1998). Know what, know how, know why: Implementing a knowledge management system: The Phillips Fox experience. *Australian Law Librarian, 6*(1), 4–8.

Soliman, F., & Spooner, K. (2000). Strategies for implementing knowledge management: Role of human resources management. *Journal of Knowledge Management, 4*(4), 337–345.

Teece, D. J., Pisano, G., & Shuen, A. (1887). Dynamic capabilities and strategic management. *Strategic Management Journal, 18*(7), 509–533.

Tuomi, I. (1999). *Implications of the reversed hierarchy for knowledge management and organizational memory.* Paper presented at the 32nd Hawaii international conference on system sciences, Maui, HI.

Preface

This book presents a developing countries' perspective on knowledge management (KM). It includes chapters from several regions including Asia, Africa, Latin America and the Caribbean. A number of developing countries, particularly small island states, have common problems that have affected their development and growth. If these issues can be addressed it would lead to significant improvement in economic development and growth. Knowledge management initiatives can be used to address some of these issues and so these developing countries need to understand what knowledge management initiatives are possible, how they can improve economic conditions, and what is needed to get them implemented so that the benefits they offer can be realized.

Developing countries often believe that only developed countries can provide high quality technological solutions. This intellectual colonization has restricted certain regions in seeking and using knowledge from countries other than those considered to be developed. For information and knowledge management the research has primarily focused on the developed world; however, the decision makers in these countries may not consider the local context and the societal norms; additionally, the proposed solutions may be costly. Many developing countries have access to technologies that can be used to assist in knowledge management. Therefore, effective knowledge management solutions must consider the context and technologies of developing countries. Relevant and low cost KM initiatives need to be considered in improving the existing KM processes in developing countries.

There is a need to identify KM strategies and technologies which can be applied to those areas that are critical to the growth of these developing countries such as after that sectors critical to the growth of developing countries include health care, agriculture, disaster recovery management, and small and medium size enterprise development. This book will highlight the opportunities in these sectors and provide advice as to how these countries should go about understanding, building, and adopting the relevant KM strategies and technologies.

This book is intended to serve diverse groups including academics, practitioners, and software developers in the field of knowledge management and the broader information systems community. For academics this book serves as teaching resource as it provides literature and case studies to assist lecturers teaching courses at both the undergraduate and graduate levels to clarify important concepts and issues related to knowledge management. The book also provides direction for future research by identifying sectors and technologies that can be further explored in different contexts both by academics and doctoral students. This book is also useful for practitioners as it highlights mechanisms of managing knowledge in various domains. Practitioners are often faced with an abundance of theoretical concepts and have a difficult time in explicating what could be applicable in a given situation. The studies presented in this book can provide them with guidance on how certain strategies and technologies could be applied. Some of the chapters have provided architectures and technologies which can be used to develop systems which can facilitate knowledge management. The software developers can use these in designing domain-specific knowledge management systems (KMS).

The contributed chapters are from various developing countries from across the continents; Mexico, Jamaica, other English-speaking Caribbean islands, Sub-Saharan African nations, South Africa, India, and Indonesia. The chapters include case studies and provide much needed insights on strategies and technologies in various domains which are of vital importance for development. The domains that the book focuses on are agriculture, education, disaster management, health care, and culture. Chapter 1 provides a brief overview of KM and KMS foundational concepts. Chapters 2, 3, and 4 focus on implementation of KM technologies in disaster management and agriculture in Mexico, Jamaica, and Sub-Saharan African countries. Chapters 5, 6, and 7 present studies which focus on mechanisms to improve existing KM capability in organizations, domains, and small developing countries by focusing either on technology or on knowledge sharing at a macro level. Chapters 8 and 9 focus on the need for and development of ontologies which are a vital component in the development and use of KMS. Case studies on knowledge sharing which is essential for KM initiatives in organizations and domains are presented in Chaps. 10, 11, and 12. These chapters discuss issues with knowledge sharing in developing countries across the globe, such as Jamaica, India, and Indonesia. Chapters 13 and 14 focus on community-focused initiatives which are essential for development and the importance of community leaders and community projects is highlighted. The chapters present a "lessons learnt" perspective in various domains and implementation details presented in them can easily be duplicated by similar sectors in other developing countries. Chapters 5, 6, 8, 9, and 13 can provide guidance in assisting knowledge management consultants in the developing countries to implement certain technologies to achieve their KM goals.

Richmond, VA
Mona Campus, Jamaica

Kweku-Muata Osei-Bryson
Gunjan Mansingh
Lila Rao

Book Layout

Chapter 1 (Osei-Bryson, Mansingh, and Rao), *Understanding and Applying Knowledge Management and Knowledge Management Systems in Developing Countries: Some Conceptual Foundations*, provides an overview on KM and KMS. The authors present foundational concepts that are relevant to the other chapters in this book and aim to provide guidance to researchers and practitioners who wish to address KM in developing countries.

Chapter 2 (Osatuyi and Andoh-Baidoo), *Towards a Community-Centered Knowledge Management Architecture for Disaster Management in Sub-Saharan Africa*, describes a KMS architecture for disaster management in Sub-Saharan African nations. The architecture facilitates the creation, storage/retrieval, transfer, and application of knowledge on disaster response and management especially for ordinary citizens. The authors also address issues related to building information technology expertise on disaster response in developing nations and argue that information systems can be designed to facilitate collaboration and coordination across disaster response and management agencies.

Chapter 3 (Mansingh, Reichgelt, and Osei-Bryson), *Managing Expert Knowledge to Assist in the Management of Coffee Pests and Diseases in Jamaica*, discusses the importance of KM in agriculture and presents an expert system CPEST. The chapter identifies the knowledge items required to build such a system which exist in multiple experts and data sources, i.e., the know-with, the know-how, know-when, and know-about to assist with the decision making process. The various components of the CPEST's architecture are discussed in the chapter and system is evaluated for its accuracy, ease of use, and the effectiveness of its recommendations in the promotion of practices less damaging to the environment.

Chapter 4 (Lopez-Morales and Ouzrout), *Implementation of a Multi-agent Supervisory System for an Agricultural Products Sourcing Network*, describes a distributed knowledge management system (DKMS) for health control in a hydroponic agricultural framework that could improve production and subsequently be integrated into a sourcing network. The authors propose incorporating a forecasted production into an electronic auction and thus allowing for faster negotiations, with transparency in a previously agreed trading structure. In the chapter a multi-agent architecture for collaborative knowledge management in agricultural production in Mexico is discussed.

Chapter 5 (Lutu), *Progressive Usage of Business and Spatial Intelligence for Decision Support in the Delivery of Educational Services in Developing Countries*, provides a discussion of knowledge discovery technologies and systems that can be implemented to support the gathering, storage, and analysis of data for purposes of supporting decision making activities in the public sector in general and the public education sector in particular. The technologies discussed are business intelligence (BI), geographical information systems (GIS), and free/libre/open source software (FLOSS). The chapter provides a case study of an education department which makes effective use of BI and GIS technologies for decision support.

Chapter 6 (Anderson and Mansingh), *Migrating MIS to KMS: A Case of Social Welfare Systems*, describes a process model for evolving an existing information systems environment in social welfare into a KMS. The model provides guidance on the phases and the supporting activities. The authors use the model to guide the process of converting the management information system in social welfare system in Jamaica to a knowledge integrated system. They discuss each phase including knowledge integration process and a reference architecture.

Chapter 7 (Rossel-Cambier), *Addressing a Knowledge Externality Schism in Public Policy in the English Speaking Caribbean*, proposes an innovative framework to knowledge management from a public policy perspective. The author identifies possible adverse externalities when management of knowledge is incomplete in public policy making. This chapter gives special consideration to lessons learned of Caribbean governments in dealing with public policy development.

Chapter 8 (Rao, Reichgelt, and Osei-Bryson), *A Methodology for Developing High Quality Ontologies for Knowledge Management*, describes an approach to the development, representation, and evaluation of formal ontologies with the explicit aim of developing a set of techniques that will improve the coverage of the ontology, and thus its overall quality and the quality of the KMS in which the ontology is embedded. In the chapter, the proposed approach is illustrated by applying it to the development and evaluation of an ontology that can be used as a component of a KMS for the information technology (IT) infrastructure at a university campus.

Chapter 9 (Mansingh and Rao), *The Role of Ontologies in Developing Knowledge Technologies*, argues that knowledge management has been dependent largely on technologies that are used to manage data and information even though there is a distinction between knowledge and data and information. The authors propose the use of ontologies in development of knowledge technologies as an essential component. They describe three ontology-driven knowledge technologies and discusses how they can be beneficial in harnessing knowledge in varied sources.

Chapter 10 (Bandi and Mehra), *Knowledge Sharing in Repository-Based KM Systems: A Study in the IT Services Enterprises in India*, identifies the need for KMSs in IT services enterprises in India which employ over 150,000 professionals working in different parts of world in globally distributed teams. The chapter documents the lessons learned from the research on knowledge sharing strategies, in particular the factors encouraging or inhibiting the knowledge seeking and knowledge contributing behaviors. The chapter enumerates the practices employed by Indian enterprises to manage the organizational knowledge creation, dissemination, sharing, utilization, and deployment.

Chapter 11 (Firdaus, Suryadi, Govindaraju, and Samadhi), *Ability to Share Knowledge of Doctors in Teaching Hospitals in Indonesia*, discusses why tacit knowledge held by most physicians is rarely converted into explicit knowledge. In Indonesia, the main challenge for the doctors at teaching hospitals continues to be a high level of dependence on one doctor who has the knowledge. The chapter presents the results of a survey carried out to try to better understand the factors that can affect a physician's ability to share knowledge with his peers.

Chapter 12 (Mansingh, Osei-Bryson, and Reichgelt), *Knowledge Sharing in the Health Sector in Jamaica: The Barriers and the Enablers*, explores different scenarios in the healthcare sector in Jamaica to identify the factors which either facilitate or impede the knowledge flows while sharing knowledge. Multiple scenarios in health sector are analyzed to identify barriers and enablers of knowledge sharing. The results of the study helped identify patterns of accessibility of a knowledge item in a knowledge sharing forum which affects perceived usability and perceived usefulness, and relevance of a knowledge item.

Chapter 13 (McNulty), *The Ulwazi Programme: A Case Study in Community-Focused Indigenous Knowledge Management*, presents an indigenous knowledge preservation and dissemination system. The system was developed in a form of localized Wiki that contains archives of local knowledge and histories collected from the community by volunteers. The chapter describes the structure and the implementation details of the Ulwazi Programme in South Africa, an initiative that has been set up by the eThekwini Municipality Libraries and Heritage Department to preserve and disseminate indigenous knowledge of local communities in the greater Durban area.

Chapter 14 (Conger), *Knowledge Management for Programs on Information and Communications Technologies for Development (ICT4D) in South Africa*, describes the knowledge management characteristics of ICT4D type of development projects by analyzing multiple projects. The chapter develops best practices for ICT4D projects and emphasizes the knowledge management components in these projects. In the chapter the Siyakhula Living Lab, a part of Living Labs in South Africa (LLiSA), is evaluated with attention to the extent to which knowledge management best practices are applied and recommendations for knowledge management in ICT4D projects and more specifically the LLiSA projects are developed.

Acknowledgements

We would like to acknowledge the contributions of the international and the regional scholars who provided the chapters for this book and the reviewers for their invaluable contributions of time and expertise. Special thanks to Mrs. Judy Rao for her commitment to the preparation of the manuscript. We would also like to thank Professor Muhammadou Kah, Vice Chancellor and Professor of Information Technology and Communication, The University of the Gambia, for endorsing our efforts by graciously agreeing to contribute the Foreword for this book. As a distinguished researcher in this area we view his endorsement as a validation of the quality of the contribution this book makes.

Contents

Contributors

Ricardo Anderson Department of Computing, The University of the West Indies, Mona-Western Jamaica Campus, Montego Bay, Jamaica

Francis Kofi Andoh-Baidoo Department of Computer Information Systems & Quantitative Methods, College of Business Administration, University of Texas—Pan American, Edinburg, TX, USA

Rajendra K. Bandi Indian Institute of Management, Bengaluru, India

Sue Conger University of Dallas, Irving, TX, USA

Rhodes University, Grahamstown, Eastern Cape, South Africa

UNISA, Johannesburg, Gauteng, South Africa

Oktri Mohammad Firdaus Department of Industrial Engineering, Widyatama University, Bandung, Indonesia

Department of Industrial Engineering, Bandung Institute of Technology, Bandung, Indonesia

Rajesri Govindaraju Department of Industrial Engineering, Bandung Institute of Technology, Bandung, Indonesia

Virgilio Lopez-Morales Universidad Autonoma del Estado de Hidalgo, Pachuca, Hidalgo, Mexico

Patricia E. Nalwoga Lutu Department of Computer Science, University of Pretoria, Pretoria, South Africa

Gunjan Mansingh Department of Computing, The University of the West Indies, Mona Campus, Jamaica

Niall McNulty McNulty Consulting, Cape Town, South Africa

Vikas Mehra Researcher & Consultant, Information Systems, Bengaluru, India

Babajide Osatuyi Department of Computer Information Systems & Quantitative Methods, College of Business Administration, University of Texas—Pan American, Edinburg, TX, USA

Kweku-Muata Osei-Bryson Department of Information Systems, Virginia Commonwealth University, Richmond, VA, USA

Yacine Ouzrout DISP Laboratory, University Lumiere, Lyon, France

Lila Rao Mona School of Business and Management, The University of the West Indies, Mona Campus, Jamaica

Han Reichgelt School of Computing and Software Engineering, Southern Polytechnic State University, Marietta, GA, USA

Koen Rossel-Cambier Center for European Research on Microfinance (CERMi) - University of Mons (UMONS)/University of Brussels (ULB), Belgium

T.M.A. Ari Samadhi Department of Industrial Engineering, Bandung Institute of Technology, Bandung, Indonesia

Kadarsah Suryadi Department of Industrial Engineering, Bandung Institute of Technology, Bandung, Indonesia

Chapter 1
Understanding and Applying Knowledge Management and Knowledge Management Systems in Developing Countries: Some Conceptual Foundations

Kweku-Muata Osei-Bryson, Gunjan Mansingh, and Lila Rao

Abstract In this chapter we provide an overview on knowledge management (KM) and knowledge management systems. Foundational concepts that are relevant to the other chapters are discussed. This chapter along with the other chapters aims to provide guidance to researchers and practitioners who are looking to address KM in developing countries.

Keywords Knowledge management • Knowledge management systems

1.1 Introduction

Developing countries are prone to potentially adverse economic, social, and environmental factors that threaten their development. It has been posited that information and communications technologies (ICTs) provide an opportunity for economic and social progress in many of these countries. Furthermore, some of these countries have obtained high rankings in global indices related to their ICT

K.-M. Osei-Bryson
Department of Information Systems, Virginia Commonwealth University, Richmond, VA, USA
e-mail: kmosei@vcu.edu

G. Mansingh (✉)
Department of Computing, The University of the West Indies, Mona Campus, Jamaica
e-mail: gunjan.mansingh@uwimona.edu.jm

L. Rao
Mona School of Business and Management, The University of the West Indies, Mona Campus, Jamaica
e-mail: lila.rao@uwimona.edu.jm

K.-M. Osei-Bryson et al. (eds.), *Knowledge Management for Development*, Integrated Series in Information Systems 35, DOI 10.1007/978-1-4899-7392-4_1,

infrastructure, yet have not used ICTs effectively to realize the benefits that they can provide in terms of advancing national priorities and enabling developmental goals. In these developing countries certain sectors are considered to be critical for transformation. While there is general agreement that ICT is one of the significant factors in this transformation, there is a lack of knowledge of its role and impact in addressing specific issues in particular sectors. To maximize the benefits from the ICT infrastructure, there is a need to focus on the development of relevant applications, techniques, and systems in critical sectors. One important area that needs more focus is knowledge management (KM) and knowledge management systems (KMS) as they have immense potential for improved decision making and performance and providing cost-effective applications and processes.

Knowledge is an important organizational resource and accessing, creating, applying, and managing it significantly enhance the decision-making capability of an organization (Wickramasinghe & Davison, 2004). Knowledge, both tacit and explicit, is dispersed and embedded in several locations within an organization, in the form of memories, documents, databases, and other knowledge retainers. In recent years, the value of knowledge in enabling informed decision making when properly managed has been recognized in sectors such as healthcare and agriculture. However, there is still a need for further research in developing tools and techniques that can harness this knowledge so that it can be used to enhance the performance of an organization.

In order to realize the full potential of existing knowledge, organizations should strive to provide access to embedded knowledge, find mechanisms to retrieve it, and to share it through KMS (Alavi & Leidner, 2001; Zhuge, 2006). KMS are information systems which typically involve creating/generating, storing/representing, accessing/using/re-using, and disseminating/transferring knowledge (Alavi & Leidner, 2001; Davenport & Prusak, 1998). KMS provide an information and communication technology platform to enable knowledge-sharing by providing a range of services (Chua, 2004; Maier & Hadrich, 2006). The objective of these services is to harness knowledge that exists in disparate sources within organizations. This chapter will focus on foundational concepts of KM and KMS.

1.2 Foundational Concepts

In recent years, organizations have realized that their knowledge assets are an important capability. Organizations are considered to be knowledge systems and knowledge is considered to be the competitive resource. Controlled implementation of creation, storage, distribution, and utilization of knowledge has become part of the organizational strategy and vision (Shin, Holden, & Schmidt, 2001). In order to develop technologies to manage knowledge, it is important to first understand "what knowledge is." There are manifold perspectives and views of knowledge. Shin et al. (2001) present several definitions and conclude that the common factor in all the definitions is that knowledge is located at the top of a hierarchical structure above data and information.

Since there is no single definition of knowledge, Alavi and Leidner (2001), in their review of the knowledge management (KM) literature, present several perspectives of knowledge. These different perspectives advocate different implications for managing knowledge and implementing KMS. All these implications suggest that there exists a need to systematically and actively manage knowledge which resides in the different sources of an organization.

KMS are seen as enabling technologies for effective and efficient KM. They have been defined as a class of information systems which are applied to managing knowledge (Alavi & Leidner, 2001). The primary goal of these systems is to increase organizational effectiveness by using knowledge from the past to bear on present activities (Stein & Zwass, 1995). Organizations can have several KM initiatives, therefore the focus of a KMS should be on providing an integrated technology environment (Maier & Hadrich, 2006). Maier and Hadrich (2006) redefine KMS as ICTs platforms which enable collaboration and knowledge sharing by providing a range of knowledge services to its users.

The main components of a KMS are the knowledge items, the knowledge sources (or retainers), and the ontology. The knowledge items are the individual components of knowledge (e.g., a particular piece of knowledge that an employee may have about a process within the organization). The knowledge retainers (Nevo & Wand, 2005) are the repositories of knowledge items of the domain. These repositories can be both codified knowledge retainers (i.e., knowledge bases) as well as personalized knowledge retainers (i.e., the human knowledge resource of the organization). Ontologies have been defined in a number of ways; however, for the purpose of this paper, the ontology will be viewed as representing the schema of the organization (Nevo & Wand, 2005; Staab, Schnurr, Studer, & Sure, 2001). The ontology will consist of nodes and links. The nodes of the ontology represent the concepts of the organization while the links represent the relationships. The nodes at the lowest level, point to the knowledge retainers. The ontology can be searched or queried by end users in order for them to get a clear understanding of the domain in question i.e., the ontology can be traversed by end users. The ontology will also be used by the KMS to determine, based on queries posed by users, which knowledge retainers need to be accessed to process a query. Therefore, the ontology can be used either by the end user or the query processor component of the KMS. Once the relevant retainer has been identified, either the knowledge can be retrieved automatically (i.e., when the knowledge is stored in a knowledge base) or manually (i.e., if the knowledge belongs to a human then he/she will be consulted). In order to improve the retrieval of appropriate knowledge items through the ontology, the knowledge items will be associated with the concepts or relationships to which they are most relevant.

When managing the knowledge, it becomes necessary to identify the knowledge that exists in the organization (i.e., in various retainers), the environment within which it exists, and a perspective for managing it. Therefore, while developing a KMS it is important to determine the different types of knowledge that exist in the environment, identify the focus of the knowledge service, and then identify the relevant knowledge technologies to manage this knowledge. Each knowledge type will require a different focus. For example, if the knowledge is a capability which exists in experts then the focus should be on capturing this knowledge; if the knowledge is an object, the focus should be on gathering, storing, and transferring knowledge; and if the knowledge is embedded in the processes, the objective of the KMS is to improve knowledge flows. Therefore, different knowledge technologies would be needed to fulfill the objectives of the KMS.

The structure of the organization and the decision styles of both the organization and its individuals are important considerations in understanding how KM activities are carried out in the organization and the KMS design that would best suit them. It is important to identify the knowledge resources in which the organizational knowledge exists and the knowledge activities that need to be carried out on these resources. Knowledge can exist in people or within groups of people, or in other codified knowledge retainers, and can be visually represented using techniques such as knowledge mapping. After the retainers are identified, the knowledge activities such as the knowledge creation spiral and knowledge sharing can be performed to improve the knowledge flows within the organization. Finally, it also becomes important to assess the maturity of the KM efforts in the organization and determine the relevant quality dimensions for a KMS. The following sections describe some of the commonly used terms that will be mentioned throughout this book.

1.2.1 Knowledge Organizations

A knowledge organization has emerged as the dominant structure of both public and private organizations as we transition from an industrial to a knowledge society. Knowledge is an important resource available to organizations, and therefore the primary driver of an organization's value (Grant, 1996). Grant (1996) emphasized that strategic knowledge is valuable, unique, rare, non-transferable, combinable, and exploitable. Performance differences can be explained by variance in the strategic knowledge of firms. Knowledge differs from other organizational resources in that the application of knowledge has the potential to generate new knowledge. Tacit knowledge resides within the individuals in a firm; in the employees who create, recognize, archive, access, and apply knowledge in their everyday work activities. As a consequence, how knowledge is shared in the organization is heavily dependent on the knowledge-sharing behaviors of employees.

Knowledge organizations are very different from bureaucratic organizations in terms of organization and leadership (Davenport & Holsapple, 2006). The former organizations emphasize the use of ideas and capabilities of employees to improve decision making and organizational effectiveness, while in contrast, bureaucracies are run with autocratic decision making by senior leadership with unquestioned execution by employees. Knowledge organizations are therefore flexible and customer-centric, while bureaucracies are focused on stability and the accuracy of repetitive internal processes. The autocratic leader flourishes in a bureaucracy while charismatic and transformational leadership is important to the knowledge organization's effectiveness, and motivating employees towards a collective goal set, mission, or vision.

Table 1.1 Organizational decision styles

	Leibniz	Locke	Kant	Hegel	Singer
Organizational decision-making style	• Formal • Analytical • Bureaucratic	• Open • Communicative • Consensual	• Open • Analytical	• Conflictual	• Teleological • Cooperative • Ethical
Knowledge perspective	• Functional	• Interpretive	• Functional	• Critical	• Interpretive/critical

A learning organization is a knowledge organization that changes as a result of its experiences, leading to performance improvements (Garvin, Edmondson, & Gino, 2008). Organizational intelligence is the ability to perceive, interpret, and respond to the environment in a way that meets the organization's goals and that satisfies multiple stakeholders. Creativity and innovation are of critical importance as knowledge is used in unique ways through processes that allow for creativity and tasks directed toward creative solutions.

1.2.2 Decision Styles and KM

To analyze knowledge within an organization, it is important to understand decision-making styles.

1.2.2.1 Organizational Decision Styles

Organizations tend to have different decision-making styles (Courtney, 2001). Courtney (2001) classified learning organizations into five types: Leibnizian, Lockean, Kantian, Hegelian, and Singerian (Table 1.1). The type determines the way decisions are made within an organization and how individuals interact to share knowledge. For example, in Liebnizian organizations the decision-making structure is very formal and the objective is to determine the best solution that is based on the presumption that for each problem there is one best answer. In these organizations tacit knowledge is given no importance. The Lockean style of decision making, on the other hand, tends to be group-oriented and open where interaction between actors is encouraged. The Hegelian decision style tends to be based on conflicts but again in organizations with this style, interactions between actors are considered important. In the Kantian style of decision making, the emphasis is on creating knowledge by applying models to data and not necessarily through interaction between actors. In the Singerian style, the problem and the knowledge are highly intertwined and there is high connectivity between the actors. In the decision-making environment there is emphasis on improving the interactions between different actors in the organization since the actors are more oriented towards consensus than conflict. The decision-making styles of an organization determine if there are interactions between actors within an organization as they work towards organizational goals. Even though knowledge is created at the individual level, it is the

Table 1.2 Individual decision styles

Style	Description
Analytical	Achievement oriented without the need for external rewards; make decisions slowly because orientated to examine a situation thoroughly and consider many alternatives systematically
Behavioral	Strong people orientation, driven primarily by a need for affiliation; typically receptive to suggestions, willing to compromise, and prefer loose controls
Conceptual	Achievement and people oriented with the need for external rewards; make decisions slowly because orientated to examine the situation thoroughly and consider many alternatives systematically
Directive	Results and power oriented but have a low tolerance for ambiguity and cognitive complexity. They prefer to consider a small number of alternatives based on limited information

interactions with other individuals and the external world that convert it to organizational knowledge (Nonaka, 1994).

1.2.2.2 Individual Decision Styles

Researchers have identified four major categories of individual decision styles (see Table 1.2) (Rowe & Boulgarides, 1994). Martinsons and Davison (2007) observed that in different cultures, different individual decision styles are dominant, and that these differences determine the types of decision support system that are most appropriate. For example, they noted that in several non-Western societies, decision-makers "focus on collective interests, emphasize relationships and intuition (at the expense of factual analysis), and discourage conflicting views that would threaten group harmony or the face of the individual," with some having "greater acceptance of tacit knowledge management" (Martinsons & Davison, 2007). To paraphrase Martinsons and Davison (2007), for such non-Western societies, KMSs that support interpersonal communications and encourage tacit knowledge sharing and individual discretion would be more helpful than KMSs that mainly involve codified knowledge.

1.2.3 Knowledge Resources

Several dependent and independent knowledge resources also exist in the organization (Grant, 1996; Holsapple & Joshi, 2001). Holsapple and Joshi (2001) describe a taxonomy for classifying organization's knowledge resources. They distinguish between resources that are schematic and those that are content-based. The schematic resources are dependent resources that rely on the organization's existence; examples of these resources are culture, strategy, infrastructure, and the purpose of the organization. The content knowledge resources are the participant's knowledge and the knowledge artifacts used in an organization. These resources in an organization are distinct but highly intertwined, and knowledge manipulation activities operate on them to create value for the organization.

1.2.4 Knowledge in Groups, Roles, and Actors

A human actor in an organizational setting can be considered to possess three different types of knowledge: namely *Role Knowledge*, *Instance Knowledge*, and *Transactive Knowledge* (Nevo & Wand, 2005). *Role Knowledge* is the knowledge that an actor must possess to be assigned a particular role. This knowledge is therefore useful in identifying who-does-what in an organization. *Instance Knowledge* is the knowledge that is not required by the formal definition of the actor's role. It is not required knowledge, but it is based on the experiential knowledge of an actor. *Transactive Memory* is the directory that an actor has about his/her group members. This knowledge is useful in identifying who-knows-what based either on their role or instance knowledge. This memory develops in task-performing groups (Brandon & Hollingshead, 2004). By building task-expertise-person mappings within the groups, this memory can be developed.

In our conceptualization of an organization, we take the view that organizations are made up of groups, roles, and actors. This differentiation is important as different types of knowledge are embedded in these concepts. Groups possess *transactive memory* and identifying groups within an organization becomes imperative. Group members act as directories of the location of knowledge and the subject of knowledge (Nevo & Wand, 2005). Therefore, the group members serve as a reference to the role knowledge and the instance knowledge that exists in the group. Identifying roles that are needed to fulfill a set of tasks enables recognition of the knowledge that is required in a process. The actors possess the instance knowledge that is based not only in their role, but also in their interactions within and between groups.

1.2.5 Knowledge Retainers and Items

Knowledge Retainers refer to the stores of knowledge within the KMS, while the knowledge items refer to the specific units of knowledge in the retainers (Staab et al., 2001). Each store will consist of a number of knowledge items that are extracted from one or more of sources. *Codified Knowledge* refers to knowledge that is stored in explicit form, while personalized knowledge is the knowledge of the people within the organization. Personalization seeks to link people to each other to foster "person-to-person" sharing of knowledge rather than storing it. In the case of personalized knowledge, the aim of the KMS is to provide the link between people and foster the sharing of knowledge. For example, knowledge-sharing forums are examples of personalized knowledge, whereas the organizational processes, and its structures are examples of codified knowledge.

When a user queries the KMS to retrieve specific knowledge, in the case of personalized knowledge, the system will aid in identifying the relevant retainer and then the user is responsible for retrieving the knowledge. In the case of codified knowledge, the system could locate the relevant knowledge retainer and, in some cases, automatically retrieve the actual knowledge. In the case of personalized knowledge the KMS will assist in identifying the relevant knowledge retainer, whereas in codified knowledge the KMS will identify both the retainers and the knowledge itself.

1.2.6 Knowledge Spiral

Individual and organizational knowledge are considered to be distinct yet interdependent (Bhatt, 1998). Bhatt (1998) defines individual knowledge as personal creativity and self-expression and organizational knowledge as being reflected in the products and services of an organization. Organizational knowledge is created when individuals collaborate and share knowledge. Thus, for individual knowledge to become organizational knowledge, it has to be combined and shared.

From the perspective of (Nonaka, 1994), new knowledge is created within the individual and is transferred using one of the following four modes: *Socialization* (tacit-to-tacit), *Externalization* (tacit-to-explicit), *Combination* (explicit-to-explicit), *Internalization* (explicit-to-tacit). In organizations triggers are required that induce a shift between these modes. Nonaka (1994) explains that the process of organizational knowledge creation is initiated by the enlargement of an individual's knowledge within an organization. The knowledge that is created needs to be crystallized into a concrete form and the process of crystallization occurs at the organizational level. Though organizational knowledge creation occurs continuously, it needs to converge to accelerate sharing beyond the boundary of the organization and further create knowledge.

Organizations are not concerned about the epistemological differences in knowledge, rather they wish to identify how knowledge works in their systems, i.e., knowing what to do (Swart & Powell, 2006). Swart and Powell (2006) build on the previous work on knowing and classify knowing as *Knowing-What*, *Knowing-How*, *Knowing-Why,* and *Knowing-Who*. Knowing-what is the knowledge about the facts in the domain and also the knowledge of what to do. Knowing-how is the knowledge that is inherent in the chains of causality between processes. Knowing-why is the holistic knowledge about the domain and is related to how goals interact with each other. Knowing-who is the knowledge about who knows what and is embedded in the interactions and social networks. It is important to combine these different types of knowledge to build a holistic picture that will help organizations identify the relevant knowledge for a given objective. Mansingh et al. (2009) propose a knowledge mapping method to combine and represent different types of knowing within an organization to facilitate knowledge sharing.

1.2.7 Knowledge Sharing and Knowledge Flows

Knowledge sharing is a critical activity for managing knowledge in organizations, as it improves the knowledge asset by adding to the organizational knowledge, since individuals' knowledge becomes part of organizational knowledge. Knowledge sharing can occur among individuals, among groups, among organizational units, and among organizations (King, 2006). Knowledge sharing in organizations occurs in two channels, one inside the organization and the other between the organization and its environment (Reychav & Weisberg, 2006). Knowledge-sharing forums are examples of knowledge sharing inside the organization. These sharing forums provide an environment where both explicit and sticky tacit knowledge can be shared. Sharing does not mean that one person's knowledge is transferred to another, but rather it provides an environment where different actors contribute within a context and, based on the absorptive capacity of the recipients, a flow of knowledge occurs. The knowledge distance between actors becomes important as they may have syntactic, semantic, and pragmatic boundaries (Carlile, 2004). Carlile (2004) found that the challenges to overcome sharing vary at these different boundaries. Hence, depending on where the actors come from, the boundaries should be ascertained, as the barriers and enablers may be different in each of these settings. Research has identified the importance of context in studying knowledge sharing, as the context changes the barriers can change too (Lindsey, 2006). Understanding the factors involved in knowledge sharing is considered the first step in understanding how to manage the knowledge-sharing process (Jacobson, 2006).

Knowledge flows enable knowledge sharing; however, these flows do not occur freely in organizations (Shin, 2004). For efficient knowledge sharing to occur, the costs associated with the knowledge flows should be identified and minimized. Shin (2004) emphasizes that doing this will assist in realizing greater benefits from knowledge sharing in organizations. Especially in scenarios where sharing occurs, mechanisms should be in place to access and reuse the knowledge that is created and shared. Transaction cost is the cost incurred in making economic exchange. In transaction cost theory, transaction cost, which is the same as coordination cost is defined as the costs of all information processing necessary to coordinate the work of people and machines that perform the primary processes (Williamson, 1981). Researchers have focused on the external transactions costs in organizations, e.g., decisions to outsource (Aubert, Rivard, & Patry, 2004); however, the transactions internal to the organizations can also have costs associated with them. The internal transaction costs for knowledge sharing from the perspective of KM are associated with searching, storing, distributing, and applying knowledge. To find mechanisms for efficient knowledge sharing, it is important to identify these costs and determine how the knowledge flows are affected by them.

In organizations sharing does not only happen between personalized knowledge sources; organizational memories can also be shared. These organizational memories include episodic and semantic memories (Stein & Zwass, 1995). Episodic memories are context-specific and situated knowledge as they contain contextually

Table 1.3 Knowledge maps and their objective

Type	Directories	Purpose
Knowledge source	Experts	Organizational knowledge assets: how to locate knowledge?
Knowledge assets	Core competencies	Organizational knowledge assets: how many x consultants are there in the company?
Knowledge structure	Skill domains	What skills/roles are needed and how do they relate to each other?
Knowledge application	Specific context	How to locate more specific problem-solving knowledge?
Knowledge development	Learning path	Learning maps

situated decisions and their outcomes, whereas semantic memories contain general, explicit, articulated knowledge. Both these memories are evident in the processes of an organization. Therefore, mechanisms to share these memories are important as they contain chunks of organizational knowledge. However, methods to extract these memories of the organization have not been discussed in literature. An objective for KMS states (Kwan & Balasubramanian, 2003),

> A knowledge management system should organize knowledge around organizational processes, each process being the scope of an application. Each application should contain process knowledge, case knowledge as well as knowledge resources.

1.2.8 Knowledge Maps

A knowledge map has been defined as a visual display of captured information and relationships (Eppler, 2001; Vail, 1999). These maps enable efficient and effective communication of knowledge at multiple levels of detail, by observers with differing backgrounds. A knowledge map is a knowledge representation technique that reveals the underlying relationships of the knowledge retainer using a map metaphor for visualization (Ong, Chen, Sung, & Zhu, 2005). Knowledge maps can be used in organizations in numerous ways. For example, knowledge maps have been used to represent participants' views and their interrelationships to other views and to represent the learning dependencies (Edwards, Hall, & Shaw, 2005; Gordon, 2000).

Eppler (2001) categorized different types of knowledge maps and emphasized that the process of building the maps is difficult compared to using a technology to implement them. The five knowledge maps are knowledge source maps, knowledge asset maps, knowledge structure maps, knowledge application maps, and knowledge development maps (see Table 1.3). According to Eppler (2001), *Knowledge Source Maps* structure the experts' knowledge based on their domain of expertise in an organization and are able to answer questions such as "Where can I find somebody who knows how to do a particular task?" or "Do we have people who have run large projects of a particular type?" *Knowledge Asset Maps* display the individuals,

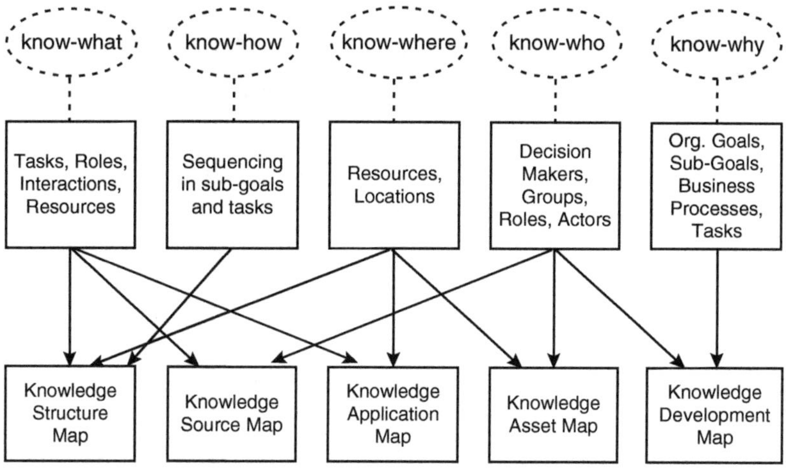

Fig. 1.1 Relationships between knowledge categories and knowledge maps

the groups, or a whole organization's stock of knowledge in terms of "How many experts in a particular domain exist?" or "How many projects of a particular type have we completed successfully?" *Knowledge Structure Maps* outline the global architecture of the domain. They answer questions like "What skills/roles are needed to do a particular project and how do they relate to one another?" *Knowledge Application Maps* show the knowledge that has to be applied in a particular process and they also provide pointers to locate the knowledge (e.g., documents, specialists, etc.). Lastly, the *knowledge development maps* depict the necessary stages to develop a certain competence or skill. They are developmental roadmaps which provide a corporate vision for organizational learning. All of these maps can be combined to form other types of maps. The knowledge maps provide a view to different types of knowing (see Fig. 1.1). For example, in knowledge structure maps, by defining the different roles that come together to perform a set of tasks, we can identify the knowledge items *know-what* and *know-why*.

1.2.9 KM Capability

A capability maturity model to measure the knowledge management capability has been proposed (Kulkarni & Freeze, 2006). It is based on the capability maturity model of the Software Engineering Institute and was adapted to the KM context (see Table 1.4). The goals that are related to the importance of managing the knowledge sources, and accessing and sharing knowledge have been highlighted in Table 1.4. They are as follows: the meaning of knowledge assets is understood, the value of knowledge assets is recognized, knowledge assets are stored/tracked in some fashion, sharing of knowledge assets is practiced, systems/tools to enable KM

Table 1.4 KM capability maturity (Kulkarni & Freeze, 2006)

Capability level	General goals
Level-1: Possible	Knowledge sharing is not discouraged
	There is a general willingness to share
	People who understand the value of sharing do it
	Meaning of knowledge assets is understood
Level-2: Encouraged	Culture encourages sharing of knowledge assets
	Value of knowledge assets is recognized
	Knowledge assets are stored/tracked in some fashion
Level-3: Enabled/practiced	Sharing of knowledge assets is practiced
	Systems/tools to enable KM activities exist
	Rewards/incentives promote knowledge sharing
Level-4: Managed	Employees expect to locate knowledge
	Training is available
	KM-related activities are part of workflow
	Systems/tools for supporting KM activities are easy to use
	KM capabilities and benefits are assessed
	Leadership exhibits commitment to KM
	Leadership provides KM strategy
Level-5: Continuous improvement	KM systems/tools are widely accepted, monitored/updated
	KM processes are reviewed/improved
	KM assessment generates realistic improvement

activities exist, employees expect to locate knowledge and systems/tools for supporting KM activities are easy to use. Knowledge assets are those knowledge sources of an organization which are going to be managed as an asset. Understanding the knowledge sources and the importance of sharing knowledge is seen in level 1. From examining the goals of levels 2, 3, and 4, it is evident that there is a need to harvest the knowledge sources of an organization in order to move to these levels of maturity.

1.2.10 Knowledge Managements Systems Quality

It is almost axiomatic that the usefulness of KMS and successful application derive from the quality of its various components. These components include the individual knowledge items, the knowledge sources (or retainers)—either knowledge repositories or personalized retainers, and the ontology (Nevo & Wand, 2005; Staab et al., 2001). Knowledge can be viewed from a number of different perspectives (Alavi & Leidner, 2001) and, depending on the perspective chosen, the dimensions that are applicable may vary. Therefore, the dimensions can be grouped based on the different perspectives of knowledge. Some of these groups, for example, ontology quality, knowledge quality, and knowledge usage quality (Jarke, Jeusfeld, Quix, & Vassiliadis, 1999), are also applicable to other systems such as data warehouses and databases, while some will be unique to KMS. Since the quality of the ontology, knowledge item, or knowledge retainer can be considered from several quality dimensions, rather than having a single value of quality, it is more appropriate to have a vector of quality measures for KMS (Rao & Osei-Bryson, 2007).

This vector of quality dimensions can then provide a number of benefits including: (1) Providing a set of criteria that can be used as a benchmark to measure the quality of the knowledge in a knowledge system and to compare the quality of similar knowledge in different systems. (2) Describing the quality of the knowledge in the system, in much the same way that metadata describes the data in data warehouses (Mallach, 2000). This will assist in ensuring that low-quality knowledge is not disseminated through the use of the KMS. (3) Supporting knowledge creators and knowledge engineers in structuring and maintaining the knowledge base (Nemati, Steiger, Iyer, & Herschel, 2002; Wen, Wang, & Wang, 2005).

1.3 Conclusion

The management of knowledge has always existed in human societies with various approaches being used including story telling, passing on of rituals, apprenticeships, initiation into trade guilds and societies of secrets, However, for modern societies, particularly those attempting to rapidly advance in the various dimensions of human development in the context of resource constraints and increasing competitiveness, the importance of knowledge management is even more significant. The focus of this book is on knowledge management for development. In this chapter we have presented some of the foundational concepts that are relevant to understanding the material in the succeeding chapters. We do not claim that all KM foundational concepts have been covered as this would be impossible to do in a single chapter. Our hope is that the material in this chapter will be beneficial to the reader, and that together with the succeeding chapters will spark the interest of the reader and motivate interest to do research and/or practice with regard to KM for development.

References

Alavi, M., & Leidner, D. E. (2001). Review: Knowledge management and knowledge management systems—Conceptual foundations and research issues. *MIS Quarterly, 25*(1), 107–135.

Aubert, B. A., Rivard, S., & Patry, M. (2004). A transaction cost model of IT outsourcing. *Information & Management, 41*, 921–932.

Bhatt, G. (1998). Strategies for individual and organizational knowledge. *Journal of Knowledge Management, 6*(1), 31–39.

Brandon, D. P., & Hollingshead, A. B. (2004). Transactive memory systems in organizations: Matching, tasks, expertise, and people. *Organization Science, 15*(6), 633–644.

Carlile, P. R. (2004). Transferring, translating, and transforming: An integrative framework for managing knowledge across boundaries. *Organization Science, 15*(5), 555–568.

Chua, A. (2004). Knowledge management system architecture: A bridge between KM consultants and technologists. *International Journal of Information Management, 24*, 87–98.

Courtney, J. F. (2001). Decision making and knowledge management in inquiring organizations. *Decision Support Systems, 31*, 17–38.
Davenport, D. L., & Holsapple, C. (Eds.). (2006). *Knowledge organizations (encyclopedia of knowledge management)*. Hershey: IDEA Group.
Davenport, T. H., & Prusak, L. (1998). *Working knowledge: How organizations manage what they know*. Boston: HBS Press.
Edwards, J. S., Hall, M. J., & Shaw, D. (2005). Proposing a systems vision of knowledge management in emergency care. *Journal of the Operational Research Society, 56*, 180–192.
Eppler, M. J. (2001). Making knowledge visible through knowledge maps: Concepts, elements, cases. In C. W. Holsapple (Ed.), *Handbook on knowledge management* (Vol. 1, pp. 189–205). Berlin: Springer.
Garvin, D. A., Edmondson, A. C., & Gino, F. (2008). Is yours a learning organization? *Harvard Business Review, 86*(3), 109–116.
Gordon, J. L. (2000). Creating knowledge maps by exploiting dependent relationships. *Knowledge Based Systems, 13*, 71–79.
Grant, R. M. (1996, Winter). Toward a knowledge-based theory of the firm. *Strategic Management Journal, 17*, 109–122.
Holsapple, C. W., & Joshi, K. D. (2001). Organizational knowledge resources. *Decision Support Systems, 31*, 39–54.
Jacobson, C. M. (2006). Knowledge sharing between individuals. In D. G. Schwartz (Ed.), *Encyclopedia of knowledge management* (pp. 507–514). Hershey: Idea Group.
Jarke, M., Jeusfeld, M., Quix, C., & Vassiliadis, P. (1999). Architecture and quality in data warehouses: An extended repository approach. *Information Systems, 24*(3), 229–253.
King, W. R. (2006). Knowledge sharing. In D. G. Schwartz (Ed.), *Encyclopedia of knowledge management* (pp. 493–498). Hershey: Idea Group.
Kulkarni, U. R., & Freeze, R. (2006). Measuring knowledge management capabilities. In D. G. Schwartz (Ed.), *Encyclopedia of knowledge management* (pp. 605–613). Hershey: Idea Group.
Kwan, M., & Balasubramanian, P. (2003). KnowledgeScope: Managing knowledge in context. *Decision Support Systems, 35*, 467–486.
Lindsey, K. L. (2006). Knowledge sharing barriers. In D. G. Schwartz (Ed.), *Encyclopedia of knowledge management* (pp. 499–506). Hershey: Idea Group.
Maier, R., & Hadrich, T. (2006). Knowledge management systems. In D. G. Schwartz (Ed.), *Encyclopedia of knowledge management* (pp. 442–450). Hershey: Idea Group.
Mallach, E. G. (2000). *Decision support and data warehouse systems*. Boston: McGraw Hill.
Mansingh, G., Osei-Bryson, K.-M., & Reichgelt, H. (2009). Building ontology-based knowledge maps to assist knowledge process outsourcing decisions. *Knowledge Management Research & Practice, 7*, 37–51.
Martinsons, M., & Davison, R. (2007). Strategic decision making and support systems: Comparing American, Japanese and Chinese management. *Decision Support Systems, 43*, 284–300.
Nemati, H. R., Steiger, D. M., Iyer, L. S., & Herschel, R. T. (2002). Knowledge warehouse: An architectural integration of knowledge management, decision support, artificial intelligence and data warehousing. *Decision Support Systems, 33*, 143–161.
Nevo, D., & Wand, Y. (2005). Organizational memory information systems: A transactive memory approach. *Decision Support Systems, 39*, 549–562.
Nonaka, I. (1994). A dynamic theory of organizational knowledge creation. *Organization Science: A Journal of the Institute of Management Sciences, 5*(1), 14–37.
Ong, T.-H., Chen, H., Sung, W.-k., & Zhu, B. (2005). Newsmap: A knowledge map for online news. *Decision Support Systems, 39*, 583–597.
Rao, L., & Osei-Bryson, K.-M. (2007). Towards defining dimensions of knowledge systems quality. *Expert Systems with Applications, 33*(2), 368–378.
Reychav, I., & Weisberg, J. (2006). Human capital in knowledge creation, management and utilization. In D. G. Schwartz (Ed.), *Encyclopedia of knowledge management* (pp. 221–229). Hershey: Idea Group.

Rowe, A. J., & Boulgarides, J. D. (1994). *Managerial decision making*. Englewood Cliffs, NJ: Prentice-Hall.
Shin, M., Holden, T., & Schmidt, R. A. (2001). From knowledge theory to management practice: towards an integrated approach. *Information Processing and Management, 37*, 335–355.
Shin, M. (2004). A framework for evaluating economics of knowledge management systems. *Information & Management, 42*(1), 179–196.
Staab, S., Schnurr, H.-P., Studer, R., & Sure, Y. (2001). Knowledge processes and ontologies. *IEEE Intelligent Systems, 16*(1), 26–34.
Stein, E. W., & Zwass, V. (1995). Actualizing organizational memory with information systems. *Information Systems Research, 6*(2), 85–117.
Swart, J., & Powell, J. H. (2006). Men and measures: Capturing knowledge requirements in firms through qualitative system modelling. *Journal of Operational Research Society, 57*, 10–21.
Vail, E. F. (1999). Knowledge mapping: Getting started with knowledge management. *Information Systems Management, 16*(1), 16–23.
Wen, W., Wang, W. K., & Wang, C. H. (2005). A knowledge-based intelligent decision support system for national defense budget planning. *Expert Systems with Applications, 28*, 55–66.
Wickramasinghe, N., & Davison, G. (2004). Making explicit the implicit knowledge assets in healthcare: The case of multidisciplinary teams in care and cure environments. *Health Care Management Science, 7*, 185–195.
Williamson, O. E. (1981). The economics of organization: The transaction cost approach. *American Journal of Sociology, 87*(3), 548–577.
Zhuge, H. (2006). Knowledge flow network planning and simulation. *Decision Support Systems, 42*(2), 571–592.

Chapter 2
Towards a Community-Centered Knowledge Management Architecture for Disaster Management in Sub-Saharan Africa

Babajide Osatuyi and Francis Kofi Andoh-Baidoo

Abstract Disasters in developing nations are typically caused by frequent and intense climate changes, which contribute to the socio-economic vulnerabilities of such nations. It is important to be strategic in the management of disasters in such regions in order to minimize their impact on thriving communities. There is therefore the need for effective disaster response that allows for access, analysis, and integration of information from varied sources. This Chapter presents architecture for managing knowledge on disaster in Sub-Saharan African nations. This architecture captures the critical contextual variables using process view of knowledge management to assist citizens who are less knowledgeable about disaster management to understand the various forms of knowledge on disaster response while developing extensive knowledge and building capability necessary to address disaster response and management. It also addresses issues with building IT expertise on disaster response in developing nations. More importantly, the architecture facilitates the creation, storage/retrieval, transfer, and application of knowledge on disaster response and management especially for ordinary citizens. The architecture also helps overcome issues with lack of collaboration and coordination across disaster response and management agencies.

Keywords Disaster management • Disaster response • Knowledge management • Sub-Saharan Africa • Awareness • Architecture • Enforcement

---

B. Osatuyi (✉) • F.K. Andoh-Baidoo
Department of Computer Information Systems & Quantitative Methods, College of Business Administration, University of Texas—Pan American, Edinburg, TX, USA
e-mail: osatuyib@utpa.edu; andohbaidoof@utpa.edu

K.-M. Osei-Bryson et al. (eds.), *Knowledge Management for Development*,
Integrated Series in Information Systems 35, DOI 10.1007/978-1-4899-7392-4_2,

2.1 Introduction

The conventional approach to sharing information on disasters with the public typically emphasizes response to unexpected disaster that has adverse devastation of infrastructure, lives, and property. This information-sharing approach has created the notion that disasters are abnormal situations that occur rarely. This notion is catastrophic as it promotes negligence for effective plan development for potential hazards that may result from the location of settlements, infrastructure, and commerce. This approach is particularly problematic for the developing nations, especially the Sub-Saharan African (SSA) nations, where culture and other contextual factors may prevent individuals and communities from developing effective mechanisms because of the belief that there is little that they can do. In the context of developing nations, the predominant sources of disasters are those from natural causes such as climate change. Climate change potentially causes damage to vulnerable communities as a result of frequent extreme weather events such as flooding, earthquakes, and tsunamis. Damages from such extreme events contribute to recession in development of the disadvantaged populations. An incumbent problem that is associated with disasters is the availability of information from multiple sources, which lends itself to multiple interpretations and consequently to inaccurate information about the impact, source, and progression of the disaster. It is therefore imperative to create awareness about threat likelihoods, accurate estimates of the extent of threats, and potential project implementation decisions as well as policy implications that may enable vulnerable communities like those in SSA to prepare for and better manage rather than merely respond to disasters, whether man-made or natural.

Since the early 1990s, various perspectives that have been employed in the exploration of the potential association between development and disasters report that the impact of disasters is largely dependent on the current and historical developmental activities in the region under investigation (Allen, 2006; Baker, Sciglimpaglia, & Saghaffi, 2010; Drabek & Key, 1976; Paton & Johnson, 2001; Tobin, 1999; Wisner, Blaikie, Cannon, & Davis, 2003). Social science researchers who have explored developed economies suggest that the impact of extreme natural events could have been mitigated if systems were in place to warn people, if settlement patterns were regulated, and if building codes were strategically established and enforced with the knowledge of their future hazardous vulnerabilities (see for example (Hewitt, 1983; Quarantelli, 1989)). Similarly, in the context of developing nations, researchers reported that disaster relief agencies struggle with disasters that reoccurred with increasing complexity. Particularly, the disaster relief efforts stifled rather than encouraged development initiatives as they failed to properly assess and incorporate potential vulnerabilities that the interventions may induce (Christoplos, Mitchell, & Liljelund, 2001; Hay, 1986; Ross, Maxwell, & Buchanan-Smith, 1994; Siddiqui, 2008). The lack of structured knowledge base in most SSA countries makes it difficult to assess the impact of previous catastrophic events in order to manage the response to future threats.

It has been reported that about 92 % of deaths resulting from natural disasters occurred in countries that are within the low and medium development indices (IFRC, 2009). For instance, although about 37 % of all the natural disasters that occurred in 2007 affected the Asia Pacific region of the world, the actual impact on the reported victims was about 90 % and the economic damage was estimated at about 50 % (UNESCAP, 2008). Such varying impacts are suggestive of the vulnerabilities arising from factors such as insufficient infrastructure, increasingly high population densities, environmental degradation, and poverty that are typical of developing nations (Quarantelli, 1998). It is often the case that possible preventive lessons are learnt after the occurrence of a disaster event. The authors argue that a proactive approach to disaster management is needed to guide how preventive measures are implemented at the individual, regional, national, and international level. More specifically we believe any architecture or framework focused on managing knowledge on disaster in SSA should include contextual factors. For instance the culture indices of the SSA region (Hofstede, 1980) suggest that citizens and communities in SSA may find it difficult to believe that they can deal with natural disaster. Hence, encouraging citizens and providing the necessary information that will empower them to overcome their cultural tendencies and believe that they can plan against natural disaster will be as important if not more important as the technical knowledge management systems (KMS) that have proved effective in other developed regions.

The erratic inevitable changes in the climate continue to challenge historic weather patterns, which potentially make affected regions vulnerable. Disaster preparedness, prevention, and response measures need to be integrated into a broader development strategy that addresses the root causes of vulnerability.

In the event of a catastrophic event such as a disaster, information becomes one of the most important assets. Disaster-related information can occur in several forms, which may include information about the progression of the disaster, information about available resources, and information about available relief agencies with capabilities to provide support or help at a given time. Developing nations have been characterized as having high usage of information and communication technologies (ICTs), which then becomes an avenue for sharing information with the understanding that access to the right kind of information that may be utilized at the right time may save lives, infrastructure, and resources (Coyle & Meier, 2009; Denning, 2006). The role of ICTs in community and national adaptation strategies to the long-term impacts of climate change has been reviewed in several recent publications (Apikul, 2010; Kalas & Finlay, 2009; Ospina & Heeks, 2010). This chapter focuses on the utility of ICTs in contributing knowledge to and sharing knowledge from a knowledge management system to minimize and manage the impacts from acute climate-related events.

To begin to promote awareness and information sharing, effective disaster awareness and management demands seamless access to reliable and accurate data with the ability to analyze and integrate information from multiple sources. This chapter describes architecture for managing knowledge on disasters in SSA nations with the acknowledgment of the role of governments, non-governmental organizations (NGOs), donors, epistemic communities and businesses as stakeholders as well as the contextual factors that may influence the functionality of the knowledge management system. The use of wireless technologies in developing nations is rather prevalent. Hence the development of multi-stakeholder partnerships and the use of the proposed knowledge management system by individuals with information technology experience will enable the standardization and interoperability, data availability, greater reach at lower costs, and to some extent, transparency and accountability of disaster resource allocation and delivery.

We believe that our research makes several contributions. First, we examine the contextual factors that need to be considered when addressing disaster response and management in SSA region. The challenges of disaster response and management in SSA are different due to context, cultural, and other relevant factors. Understanding and sharing knowledge on disaster response and management can enable organizations and citizens in SSA nations to effectively address the disaster response and management challenges. Thus, we contend that contextual variables are critical when applying existing knowledge management framework in addressing a problem in SSA region. Second, the architecture that is proposed in this paper can facilitate the management of knowledge on disaster response and management such that stakeholders can participate in the creation, storage, retrieval, and sharing, as well as the use of knowledge on disaster response and management. Third, by enhancing the knowledge of stakeholders such as disaster response agencies, first responders, and fire services, expertise can be built up while minimizing the effect of disaster in SSA. Fourth, although our framework focuses on SSA region, it has implications at the global level. For instance, when there is a disaster in a developing nation such as the earthquake in Haiti in 2010, all citizens are called into duty. By preparing the citizens in SSA to deal effectively with disaster will limit the need for other nations to provide assistance. International relief agencies can use the available resources to build the necessary capacity to help citizens deal with disasters in SSA and other nations. Finally, the architecture, if implemented, can help citizens use their mobile and other communication systems effectively in a safer environment, thus increasing customer satisfaction. Eventually this could be beneficial to telecommunication service providers who could use the knowledge management system as an incentive to enhance customers' Internet experience.

The rest of this chapter is organized as follows: Sect. 2.2 presents a review of relevant work on disaster response and management in SSA. It is followed by the framework that serves as a foundation for the architecture of a knowledge management system that can be used to acquire, store, and share information on disaster response and management. Section 2.4 presents the main contextual variables of the SSA environment that may influence the management of knowledge on disaster response and management. We then present the architecture in Sect. 2.5. Section 2.6 discusses the implications of the study and Sect. 2.7 concludes the chapter with potential future research directions.

2.2 Relevant Literature on Disaster Management in Sub-Saharan Africa

A review of disaster management approaches studied by several researchers revealed five different problem areas associated with the responding organizations; they include intra- and inter-organizational interactions between organizations, within systems of organizations, from organizations to the public, and from public to organizations (Quarantelli, 1998). Communication process, the exercise of authority, and a systematic coordination process among responding agencies and with the affected communities have also been reported as problematic to effectively responding to disasters. In the context of SSA nations, the focus of disaster management should be geared towards enabling citizens as well as response organizations to be more prepared in order to better adapt when disasters occur.

The extent to which SSA nations can adapt to catastrophic changes is based on existing preparedness and response strategies. A robust adaptive capacity to manage catastrophic events holds the potential to minimize the degree of social, human damage, and consequently, infrastructural and economic investments in terms of relief aid to recover from the disaster (Mirza, 2003).

It is often the case that responding agencies are created after the occurrence of a disaster, with efforts devoted to training volunteers and setting up a chain of command at the expense of responding to victims and the community under distress. Researchers have warned lending agencies and international humanitarian organizations to reevaluate their investments to focus on building capacity rather than recovery activities. Upon the establishment of the vulnerabilities that developing nations face in the event of a disaster, disaster management and adaptation must be part of long-term sustainable development planning in developing countries (Mirza, 2003).

2.3 Framework

Our proposed architecture is built on three main models. The importance of a community-centered knowledge sharing model to disaster management is argued followed by a presentation of the knowledge management framework (Alavi & Leidner, 2001) and application of awareness and enforcement framework (Kritzinger & von Solms, 2010). The goal of the framework is to provide *home users* (HUs) with information on disaster response and management while ensuring that they protect their systems against cyber attack. All the frameworks are described in this section. We explain how they form the foundation of the architecture presented in a later section.

2.3.1 The Community-Centered Disaster Management Model

Disasters are known cataclysmic events that bring the affected community together to share the grief of the devastation as well as the loss as a result of the event. For instance, the earthquake that struck Haiti in 2010 created a united front across the globe to respond to the event by providing aid as necessary regardless of the responders' race, country of origin, or political allegiances. The tendency to stimulate a sense of community among the disaster-affected population suggests that the impact is localized and should be treated as such. This means decisions about relief efforts need to be made in consultation with the local community members in order for a successful intervention to be implemented. In reference to an old African proverb which states that "the new broom sweeps well, but the old broom knows the corners," the International Red Cross and Red Crescent Movements as well as NGOs remind aid agencies during disaster relief to involve the community inhabitants in the relief planning and implementation. Effective disaster response will ultimately depend on community capacities to reduce their medium and long-term risks as well as the ability to cope with the impacts of acute climate-related events.

The focus of disaster management organizations in SSA nations tends to be national instead of local. In addition, vulnerability in developing nations is often defined in socio-economic terms leaving natural disasters as lower ranking issues compared with other political issues. The authors argue that the focus of disaster management organizations needs to be oriented towards the individual citizen. Risk factors that are germane to individuals during responses to disasters are influenced by the safety of their family members, their possessions, and their source of livelihood. Ordinary citizens in local communities therefore need to make policy decisions as it concerns the risk assessments of disasters in the planning, preparation, execution, and response phases. The involvement of the community in the disaster management will ensure that interventions are implemented with a consideration for the language that is familiar to the locals, which will make it easier for them to adopt and effectively utilize the interventions.

There are strong parallels between the security and disaster domains. In both there is a potential attack, which is unpredictable. Awareness helps in addressing the impact of the attack. Also, in both domains the problems are not just technical, but also cultural and political and require multi-level analysis at the individual, group, organization, communities, regional, and global levels. Like security, a lack of technical knowledge and awareness about disaster management may contribute to ineffective response and management of disaster in SSA. For instance, in the case of cyber security, some researchers have suggested that the lack of technical know-how about cyber crime in enforcement agencies, and among legal practitioners and individual home users contributes to the cyber crime problem in Africa (Boateng, 2009; Danquah & Longe, 2011; Moses-Òkè, 2012).

Kritzinger and von Solms (2010) identified two groups of Internet users, non-home users (NHUs) and home users (HUs). NHUs are "those users accessing the Internet from their corporate workstations within their work environments—such users will come from the Industry area, Government areas, Academic areas etc." (Kritzinger & von Solms, 2010, p. 841). A home user is "a citizen with varying age and technical knowledge who uses ICTs for personal use anywhere outside their work environments" (European Network & Information Security Agency, 2006). In this chapter, a home user is defined as a citizen of varying age, technical knowledge, and mode of access who uses ICTs from anywhere outside of formal work environments (industry, government, academia), where modes of access include cybercafés, mobile phones, and personal computers. In other words, a home user could be a local farmer, an uneducated citizen in a rural community on a personal (or borrowed) cell phone or computer. Unlike NHUs who have a responsibility to gain and apply knowledge on cyber security and threats, HUs is under no such obligation. However, the HUs still manage cyber security risks on their home computers, networks, and systems. Thus, if HUs are not aware of proper information security knowledge, they will also lack the awareness of cyber risks while managing the responsibility to secure their cyber environment (Furnell, Valleria, & Phippen, 2008; Kumar, Park, & Subramaniam, 2008). The lack of information security awareness by HUs is attributed to the lack of enforcement by a third party to ensure that HUs are secured while using the Internet or that their information security awareness is up to date (Kritzinger & von Solms, 2010).

In the same way, we believe the problems with cyber security may not be different from those with disaster management. In fact, knowledge of disaster management may be problematic, especially for HUs as compared to NHUs, since NHUs may be trained about the disaster management plan of their organization and how to respond in the case of disaster, whereas HUs may not have such training and responsibilities. Besides, federal, state, regional, and district level disaster management organizations in SSA nations have no effective mechanisms to train and/or prepare citizens to respond to natural disasters as is done in other developed nations. In fact mobile systems would be an effective medium through which potential victims can be trained and prepared to deal with natural disasters.

Drawing from Kritzinger and von Solms (2010) definition, we refer to NHUs as individuals who work in areas such as the public, government, and non-governmental agencies and have access to information on disaster response and management because they are trained to protect the organization's assets and their own safety during disasters. Home users are those who do not work in formal organizations and therefore have no training and knowledge on disaster management and/or response strategies. Based on the above description of HUs and NHUs we assert that because of the knowledge available to the NHUs and the specific expectations of the NHUs to protect themselves against corporate systems, NHUs are more knowledgeable about disaster management. Thus, they are more likely to use this knowledge to protect their organizations, families and their own self-interests, whereas HUs might not be capable to do so. Given the challenge with disaster management in Africa in general and SSA in particular, the focus of this paper is on managing knowledge on disaster in SSA. In this paper, we expand the notion proposed by (Kritzinger & von Solms, 2010). We propose an incentive-based enforcement approach where governments and telecommunication organizations will provide incentives for citizens that comply with disaster management awareness programs. More specifically, the current work presents architecture for sharing knowledge on disaster management in SSA region. This architecture which is based on Alavi and Leidner's (2001) framework supports the exchange of both tacit and explicit knowledge. The architecture also considers contextual factors including economic, cultural, social, technical, governmental, and legal and diverse knowledge management perspectives. We believe that HUs can benefit from the knowledge that NHUs have. One of the challenges with disaster response and management is awareness. Hence, we present an incentive-based approach to push information on disaster response and management to citizens, especially HUs. In this architecture, we identify *knowledge users* that may include HUs who may use the knowledge base in the architecture to enhance their knowledge and improve their awareness on disaster management to better protect themselves against disaster. We also describe *knowledge contributors* who are those who contribute knowledge to the architecture. These include NHUs, disaster management experts from governmental, non-governmental institutions, well-meaning individuals with knowledge on disaster response and management, and HUs who develop expertise even as they learn from others through the proposed architectural solution presented in this paper.

2.3.2 Knowledge Management

Tacit and Explicit are two forms of knowledge that have been identified in the knowledge management literature. Tacit knowledge comprises the beliefs, perspectives, and mental models ingrained in a person's mind. This is knowledge that has been acquired by the individuals as they gain experience through repeated tasks and activities. This knowledge is difficult to codify, share, or verbalize because it cannot be broken down into specific rules. Several authors assert that this type of knowledge can be articulated, captured, and represented (Goldman, 1990; Grant & Gregory, 1997; Howells, 1995; Nonaka, Takeuchi, & Umemoto, 1996; Pylyshyn, 1981). In the knowledge management literature, two types of tacit knowledge have been classified (Alavi & Leidner, 2001). One type is cognitive (mental model) and the other is technical (know-how applicable to a specific task). Both types of knowledge will be relevant in the disaster response and management environment and need to be captured, stored, and shared.

Knowledge management (KM) is defined as "a systemic and organizationally specified process for acquiring, organizing, and communicating both tacit and explicit knowledge of employees so that other employees may make use of it to be more effective and productive in their work" (Alavi & Leidner, 1999, p. 6). While this definition focuses on organizations, others have defined knowledge management in a broader sense as the formal management for facilitating the creation, access, and reuse of knowledge, typically using advanced technology (O'Leary, 1998). In this paper, we use the broader definition. KM systems are "a class of information systems applied to managing organizational knowledge. That is, they are

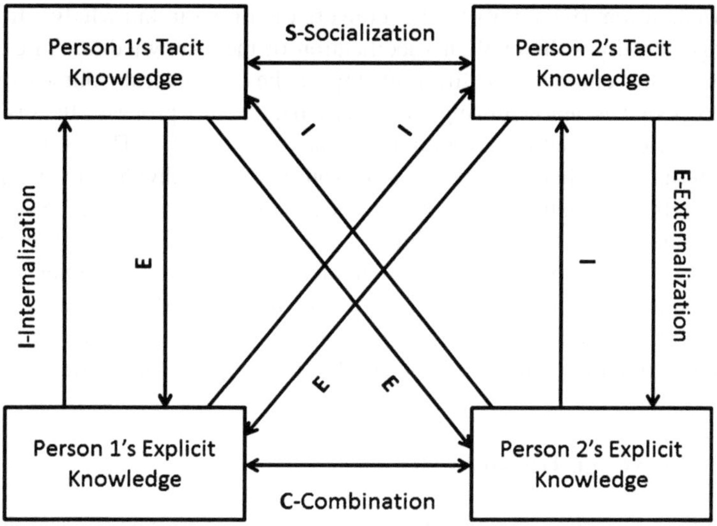

Fig. 2.1 Knowledge creation modes (adapted from Alavi & Leidner, 2001)

IT-based systems developed to support and enhance the organizational processes of knowledge creation, storage/retrieval, transfer, and application" (Alavi & Leidner, 2001, p. 114). HUs and NHUs can gain knowledge about disaster response and management, lesson learnt as well as response and readiness strategies as they share their experiences.

Alavi and Leidner (2001) present the various perspectives of knowledge and their implications for knowledge management. In this paper, we take the process view perspective. Managing knowledge from this perspective emphasizes the process of the flow, and the creation, sharing, and distribution of knowledge. Alavi and Leidner (2001) describe the different knowledge types. Effective knowledge management requires that various forms of knowledge are acquired, stored, and shared. Based on the extant literature, Alavi and Leidner (2001, p. 124) argue that the "four knowledge processes of creation, storage/retrieval, transfer, and application are essential to effective organizational knowledge management." They also present various information technologies that enable the four knowledge management processes. A brief description of each knowledge process is presented below.

2.3.2.1 Knowledge Creation

As shown in Fig. 2.1, knowledge creation involves externalization, internalization, socialization, and combination. The figure shows that externalization and internalization can occur between an individual or between two or more individuals, whereas socialization and combination only occur between two or more individuals and not within a single individual.

Externalization (E) involves the conversion of tacit knowledge to explicit knowledge. It allows the explicit specification of tacit knowledge. An example is when an expert enumerates different approaches to several courses of action. New knowledge is learnt during the Internalization (I) process. In this process, explicit knowledge is converted to implicit (tacit) knowledge. This is when an individual internalizes what they have learnt from another individual over a period of time and gets new insights, which becomes their tacit knowledge. Socialization (S) is the sharing of tacit knowledge, e.g., during a response event, experienced emergency response officers share their tacit knowledge with other responders and less experienced responders or citizens of the affected community learn new techniques by watching the experts. Combination (C) is the knowledge conversion step where explicit knowledge is converted to new explicit knowledge.

2.3.2.2 Knowledge Transfer

Figure 2.1 depicts the transfer of knowledge among individuals and groups. Once person 1 shares (transfers) some knowledge with person 2, this may trigger person 2's knowledge processes. For example, the transfer of knowledge from person 1 may lead to the creation of knowledge in person 2. Person 2 may choose to apply the knowledge, consult with other members, or record the knowledge. Hence, knowledge flows between individuals and a major challenge of knowledge management is to facilitate these flows so that the maximum amount of transfer occurs (assuming that the knowledge individuals create has value and can improve performance).

2.3.2.3 Storage and Retrieval

The storage, organization, and retrieval of organizational knowledge, also referred to as organizational memory (Stein & Zwass, 1995; Walsh & Ungson, 1991), constitute an important aspect of effective organizational knowledge management. Organizational memory includes knowledge residing in various component forms, including written documentation, structured information stored in electronic databases, codified human knowledge stored in expert systems, documented organizational procedures and processes, and tacit knowledge acquired by individuals and networks of individuals (Tan, Teo, Tan, & Wei, 1998). Organizational memory is defined as "the means by which knowledge from the past, experience, and events influence present organizational activities" (Stein & Zwass, 1995, p. 85). Organizational memory extends beyond an individual's memory to include other components such as organizational culture, transformations (production processes and work procedures), structure (formal organizational roles), ecology (physical work setting), and information archives (both internal and external to the organization) (Walsh & Ungson, 1991). Emergency responders and volunteers can benefit from stored knowledge in order to address issues they may encounter during the response process.

Stored knowledge repository is useful when it is easily available. Advanced information systems storage technology and sophisticated retrieval techniques, such as query languages, multimedia databases, and database management systems, have been effective tools in enhancing the utilization of stored knowledge. The effective appropriation of the technology for retrieving knowledge can encourage volunteers and citizens to leverage knowledge stored in knowledge systems that is available to responders at different levels.

2.3.2.4 Knowledge Application

Organizations can only gain a competitive advantage from the knowledge they create when that knowledge is used (Alavi & Leidner, 2001). Three mechanisms can be used to create organizational capability from knowledge integration (Grant, 1996). These are directives, routines, and self-contained task teams. Directives include sets of rules, standards, procedures, and instructions that are developed by specialists. The specialists convert their tacit knowledge to explicit knowledge which can be integrated and efficiently communicated to non-specialists. Routines refer to the developed task performance and coordination patterns, interaction protocols, and process specifications that allow individuals to apply and integrate their specialized knowledge without the need to articulate and communicate what they know to others. The knowledge integration mechanism is the creation of self-contained task teams. In situations in which task uncertainty and complexity prevent the specification of directives and routines, teams of individuals with prerequisite knowledge and specialization are typically formed for problem solving (Alavi & Leidner, 2001, p. 122). However, in the context of SSA, where responding agencies are short of experienced emergency response officers, a repository of stored knowledge on how similar events have been responded to becomes invaluable as a starting point.

2.3.3 Disaster Management Awareness and Enforcement

Kritzinger and von Solms (2010) present an awareness and enforcement framework that we use in this study. According to them (2010), HUs typically would take the preferred route of going directly to the Web with little or no consideration for the security consequences. They propose an approach that would force HUs to use a route where they would be guided by policies, procedures, guidelines, best practices, and awareness courses before they access the Internet. In the case of disaster, we argue that since HUs may lack knowledge on disaster management and response mechanisms, making them aware of and providing them with knowledge on disaster and response strategies can help them be proactive in dealing with disasters.

2.4 Relevant Contextual Variables

The disaster response and management solutions proposed in the literature are typically based on developed nations' context. However, Muriithi and Crawford (2003) argue that the prescriptions should be made with consideration being given to how cultural, economic, and other variables may influence the validity of the orthodox approaches in SSA region. Organizational theorists argue that western-oriented management techniques may not be valid in non-western contexts. Therefore, factors such as culture and economics have been shown to play a potent role in determining the shared norms, values, attitudes, and beliefs about work organizations, among both managers and employees. Thus, what works in one context may not necessarily work in another (Muriithi & Crawford, 2003). Hence, while the architecture that we propose uses the Alavi and Leidner (2001) and Kritzinger and von Solms (2010) frameworks, we address the SSA contextual factors as well. Specifically, we discuss the economic, cultural, technical, social, governmental, and legal frameworks. These variables have been found to be relevant when dealing with ICT in SSA nations (Akuta, Ong'oa, & Jones, 2011; Andoh-Baidoo & Osatuyi, 2009; Atsu, Andoh-Baidoo, Osatuyi, & Amoako-Gyampah, 2010; Boateng, 2009; Foster, Goodman, Osiakwan, & Bernstein, 2004; Ngwenyama, Andoh-Baidoo, Bollou, & Morawczynski, 2006; Roztocki & Weistroffer, 2011). Table 2.1 highlights the main conditional variables and the conditions in SSA. We argue that these conditions, which are peculiar to the SSA environment, would influence any specific KMS that is built to enhance the knowledge of HUs on disaster response and management. We will discuss the specific effects of these conditions and their implications in later sections.

Table 2.1 Contextual variables affecting disaster management solutions

Factor	Conditions	References
Economic	Low GDP, low income, call for using scarce resources for healthcare and education	Ngwenyama et al. (2006), Roztocki and Weistroffer (2011)
Cultural	High power distance (PD), high collectivist-individualist (CID) society, high uncertainty avoidance (UA)	Atsu et al. (2010)
Technical	Lack of technical expertise, high usage of mobile devices especially cell phones, lack of national data on citizens, poor infrastructure	Akuta et al. (2011), Andoh-Baidoo and Osatuyi (2009), Foster et al. (2004)
Social	Low computer literacy, resistance to change, digital divide, higher usage of cyber café	Andoh-Baidoo and Osatuyi (2009), Boateng (2009), Foster et al. (2004)
Governmental	Generally weak democracy, relatively lack of continuity of projects	Akuta et al. (2011), Atsu et al. (2010), Roztocki and Weistroffer (2011)
Legal	Lack of legal frameworks, weak laws, weak enforcement	Akuta et al. (2011), Atsu et al. (2010), Boateng, Olumide, Isabalija, and Budu (2011), Moses-Òkè (2012), Roztocki and Weistroffer (2011)

Table 2.2 Cultural dimensions and definitions

Dimension	Definition
Power distance	This is the extent to which a society accepts the fact that power in institutions and organizations is distributed unequally (Hofstede, 1980, p. 45)
Uncertainty avoidance	This is the extent to which a society feels threatened by uncertain and ambiguous situations (Hofstede, 1980, p. 45)
Collectivism individualism	Individualism implies a loosely knit social framework in which people are supposed to take care of themselves and their immediate families only, while collectivism is characterized by a tight social framework in which people distinguish between in-groups and out-groups to look after them and in exchange for that they feel they owe absolute loyalty to it (Hofstede, 1980)
Masculinity vs. femininity	This expresses the extent to which the dominant values in society are masculine, i.e., assertiveness, the acquisition of money and things and not caring for others, the quality of life or people (Hofstede, 1980). In feminine societies men can assume nurturing roles, quality of life is important to both men and women and there is equality among the sexes (Hofstede, 1980)
Long-term vs. short-term orientation	Long-term orientation can be said to deal with virtue regardless of truth. Values associated with Long-term orientation are thrift and perseverance; Values associated with Short-term orientation are respect for tradition, fulfilling social obligations, and protecting one's "face" (Hofstede, 1983)

Hofstede (1980) defines culture as "a collective mental programming of the people in an environment" (1980, p. 43). Therefore, the culture of the actors or institutions influences the structures that may be enacted which may facilitate or impede effective management of knowledge on disaster. Table 2.2 provides brief descriptions of the dimensions of culture as defined by Hofstede (1980, 1983).

With respect to the cultural dimensions studied by Hofstede (1980), individuals in SSA are generally very different from those in developed nations. One of the key differences is the orientation towards individualism or collectivism: the people in SSA usually have a more collectivist outlook compared to those in developed nations. People in SSA nations exhibit especially strong ties to extended families, clans, and ethnic groups and make clear distinctions between those who belong to these in-groups and others who they consider outsiders (Muriithi & Crawford, 2003). Additionally, people in SSA nations feel a substantial responsibility to share scant resources among those within the in-group (Blunt & Jones, 1997). Although urban areas of SSA tend to have a more individualist orientation, the strong influence of African collectivism is still prevalent in these regions (Beugré, 2002).

Another pertinent difference between people in SSA and the developed nations is uncertainty avoidance. People in SSA typically have low tolerance for uncertainty. They are also generally more risk-averse and likely to resist change. Further, people would generally desire to implement rules to reduce or avoid uncertainty (Dinev, Goo, Hu, & Nam, 2009; Hofstede, 1993). As heavily ritualistic countries, individuals in SSA adhere to numerous unwritten rules that have been passed on as tradition, contributing to generally high uncertainty avoidance (Hofstede, 1984).

Conversely, people in developed nations are generally low in uncertainty avoidance (Hofstede, 1980).

A third cultural difference that generally exists between individuals in the developed nations and SSA is related to power distance. People in SSA are more likely to regard people in authority highly compared to people in developed nations. Most SSA nations exhibit a high degree of power distance, as authority is typically allocated based on age and experience (Muriithi & Crawford, 2003). Higher power distance societies find it difficult to challenge authority. In contrast, individuals in developed nations usually espouse a much lower degree of power distance and seek to achieve power equality in both organizations and government (Hofstede, 1980). Hence, people in SSA are more likely to respond to instructions from superiors without questioning and obey authority even when they disagree with the superior's position. Individuals in developed nations tend to exhibit more masculine traits, while people in SSA usually possess more traditionally feminine qualities. People in SSA are more short-term oriented as opposed to the long term orientation of people in South Asia and other developed nations. Hence, individuals in SSA may be more interested in addressing issues that are short term and be less concerned about acquiring knowledge that is needed to meet challenges that are not predicted to occur in the very short term but may happen in the future such as disasters.

The architecture for the knowledge management proposed in this study would provide a platform for sharing knowledge while building capacity against disaster among the stakeholders, particularly the HUs in the SSA region. Given the differences in the adoption and appropriation of information systems between developed and developing nations (Roztocki & Weistroffer, 2011), the proposed architecture for managing knowledge will incorporate customized, contextual interactions. In SSA, where the adoption and use of the Internet is still in its nascence, HUs are completely oblivious to disaster response and management implications. The proposed comprehensive framework prescribes context-based strategies to create avenues for HUs to acquire the awareness they need in order to be informed about disaster response and management so as to prepare them for potential disaster.

In the disaster response and management environment both tacit and explicit knowledge are relevant. NHUs and experts in disaster management can assess a situation in a disaster response and management awareness training session and deliver information to the HU in an effective way because of their individual experiences. The way a specific question or situation is addressed may depend on the type and level of the threat. The NHUs or expert use their mental models to effectively lead HUs thus using their cognitive tacit knowledge (Alavi & Leidner, 2001). Since the process is carried out intuitively, the experts may not be able to explain exactly how they adapt to a situation. However, this process can be stored in a knowledge system for others to access, retrieve, and use to solve or address similar problems or situations.

As noted in an earlier section, the perspective that we have taken is the process view for managing knowledge, therefore it is essential to improve the knowledge flows. We believe that to address disaster response and management problems in SSA, knowledge that exists on disaster response and management needs to be shared among the citizens, the majority of whom are HUs who are in the environment where there is little enforcement in ensuring that they protect themselves and their properties against disaster. We argue that IT can be deployed to link existing sources of knowledge to HUs who need such information. While the focus of the proposed solution is on process perspectives, it is important that other perspectives are considered to ensure the effectiveness of the solution. For instance, the object perspective will ensure that the knowledge gathering, storage, and transfer activities are efficient and effective. If the access perspective is not considered, the solution is endangered because HUs may not be able to search and retrieve specific relevant knowledge that is needed in a particular situation and/or time. The capability perspective is relevant in our solution because in SSA there is a lack of expertise in IT in general and disaster response and management and knowledge management in particular. Hence, even as the solution seeks to encourage awareness and enforcement of disaster response and management, it is very important that stakeholders build the necessary capabilities in various areas such as fire fighting, first responders agencies, and technical IT experts in SSA nations to ensure that the proposed solution can be maintained and expanded to keep abreast of new threats and new approaches in response to the dynamics of the disaster phenomenon.

Here, we argue that addressing the various perspectives of knowledge management in the design of a knowledge management system for disaster response and management in SSA will enable the IT personnel to employ the various tools necessary to support all the different requirements in the domain. More importantly, the different perspectives will enable HUs to appreciate the distinction between various knowledge forms through the contribution of knowledge acquisition, storage, and sharing all the way to building capability in SSA. Hence, the different knowledge perspectives prescribed by Alavi and Leidner (2001) should be considered in developing a knowledge management system. First, there is the need for HUs to understand the differences between data, information, and knowledge. In the information age, where the presence and advancement in social network technologies and infrastructure facilitate the sharing of the various types of knowledge, the inability of HUs to distinguish valid information from rumors may prevent them from treating disaster response and management information seriously. The proposed architecture should facilitate the validation of information on disaster response and management so that stakeholders would be able to differentiate between information and rumor and thereby respond appropriately to disaster response and management.

Alavi and Leidner (2001) present the various knowledge types. The proposed architecture seeks to capture both tacit and explicit knowledge. In addition, an effective knowledge management system should capture the declarative (know-about), procedural (know-how), causal (know-why), conditional (know-when), relational (know-with), and pragmatic (useful knowledge) knowledge types (Alavi & Leidner, 2001).

2.5 Architecture

The architecture that we present in this paper will serve as a portal that home users can access to learn about disaster response and management and apply this knowledge to address situations before, during, and after disasters. Specifically the architecture has the following components: domain ontology, knowledge-base, and user interface (knowledge contributor and knowledge consumer). The domain ontology includes the metadata that defines a consistent description of the data types coming from the different data sources. It provides comprehensive information such as the data sources, definitions of the data warehouse schema, dimensional hierarchies, and user profiles. A metadata repository is used to manage and store all of the metadata associated with the knowledge base. The ontology also defines the relationships between the various data types in the knowledge base.

The benefits of adopting an ontology include: communication, interoperability, reusability, reliability, specification, and distinction (Nogueira & De Vasconcelos, 2007; Uschold & Gruninger, 1996). First, the ontology enhances communication between stakeholders with different needs and viewpoints arising from their differing contexts. Second, the ontology allows information sharing among different computational systems by facilitating translation between different modeling methods, paradigms, languages, and software tools. Third, the shared understanding is the basis for the formal encoding of entities/concepts and their relationships in the domain of interest. This formal representation may be a reusable component in information systems. Fourth, an ontology-based information representation makes possible a consistent and more trustworthy implementation. Fifth, the shared understanding can assist in the process of identifying requirements and design specification for an IS. This is especially true when the requirements involve different groups using different terminologies in the same domain, or multiple domains. Sixth, an ontology allows the domain knowledge to be separated from the operational knowledge.

The knowledge base contains all the information on disaster response and management and awareness information. Specifically, knowledge on disaster, severity, likelihood of disaster, effects and mechanisms, documentation of disaster scenarios, prevention mechanisms, prevention strategies, best practices, origins of disasters, etc. would be captured in the knowledge base.

Finally the user interface has two components: (1) knowledge contributor: where knowledge contributors such as NHUs contribute knowledge on disaster response and management, and (2) knowledge users where HUs can access knowledge on disaster response and management and awareness information. Also, the knowledge base allows the sharing of metadata among tools and processes for capturing new knowledge.

In the next section, we describe in more detail how the framework presented in Sect. 2.3 is used to support knowledge sharing on disaster management including how awareness and enforcement programs can be implemented for HUs.

2.5.1 Application of Research Framework to Proposed Architecture

The proposed architecture is comprised of three main components as shown in Fig. 2.2 below. The first component is the access interface which allows actors to

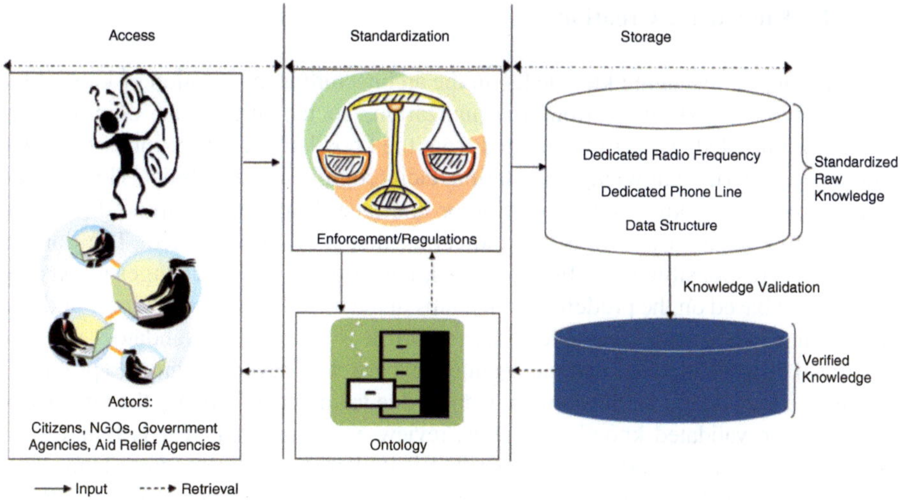

Fig. 2.2 Ontology-based knowledge architecture for disaster management

interact with the knowledge management system. Interaction can only be in the form of information input or retrieval from the knowledge management system. The second component is the standardization module that includes enforcement policies, regulations, and ontologies used to standardize information in the knowledge management system. The third component is the knowledge base that is used to store information in various formats such as audio, video, and documents. Particularly in developing nations, a dedicated radio frequency for the purpose of creating awareness during disasters should also be considered as another format for sharing information from the knowledge base.

The proposed architecture has actors: knowledge contributors such as citizens, knowledge validators, NGOs, governmental agencies, aid agencies, and law enforcement representatives. Actors will interact with the architecture through the multiple ICTs available to them. A dedicated radio frequency will be generated and maintained that allows citizens to tune in to the knowledge base of the knowledge management system to relay information in the form of updates that are relevant to the disaster event. A dedicated phone line will be maintained to allow citizens to contribute information to the knowledge base. Three roles are defined to represent the privileges of the three types of actors. Knowledge consumers can only read from the knowledge base. Knowledge contributors can both contribute knowledge to and retrieve information from the knowledge base; thus, as knowledge contributors they can create new knowledge. They can also modify and delete the knowledge that they create before it is validated. A knowledge contributor can also make a request for information from the knowledge base where they have read-write-only privileges. A knowledge consumer, on the other hand, has read-only privileges. A knowledge validator can modify, delete, assess the usefulness, and validate any non-validated knowledge in their subject areas.

2.5.1.1 Knowledge Creation

The first step in managing knowledge in the architecture is the creation of knowledge which involves externalization, internalization, socialization, and combination. First new knowledge has to be elicited from the knowledge contributor (knowledge elicitation). During knowledge elicitation, tacit (cognitive and technical) knowledge is captured via the knowledge contributor interface. Knowledge captured is stored in the knowledge base with a flag indicating that it is not validated. The domain ontology is responsible for validating new knowledge as well as changes to existing knowledge based on the predefined attributes in the metadata schema. Non-validated knowledge is not made available to users until it is released by validators who are respected disaster response and management experts who have been granted privileges to validate knowledge in this domain. Knowledge validators will query the knowledge base for non-validated knowledge items, review each item and, if it is found to be appropriate, validate and release it so that it is then available for use. Thus, only validated knowledge is returned from the knowledge base as a response to user queries. During knowledge capture and validation, each knowledge item can be categorized (e.g., level of severity, recency, relevance, and likelihood of incident or information) so that during knowledge retrieval, the user is presented with the most relevant information. The domain ontology ensures that these categories are consistent.

2.5.1.2 Externalization

Externalization involves the tacit to explicit knowledge conversion. The architecture allows knowledge workers to respond to a series of hypothetical events ultimately resulting in a scenario. A scenario is a customized, goal-oriented narration or description of a situation, with mention of actors, events, outputs, and environmental parameters (Cheah & Abidi, 1999). Similarly, a scenario can be considered an ordered set of interactions between partners, usually between a system and a set of actors external to the system for generating some output. Domain experts (who are the knowledge contributors with knowledge of disasters) can be prompted to provide or suggest informational values to the attributes of a scenario in the electronic form. In order to facilitate an assortment of knowledge acquisition activities, scenarios are distinguished as: Solved scenarios, which are scenarios of actual circumstances and problems encountered and solved by knowledge workers. Scenario bases typically start out as having only solved scenarios. Solved scenarios may be modified to form challenge scenarios. Challenge scenarios represent hypothetical situations and are presented to domain experts to challenge their expertise. Domain experts respond to such challenges and explicate their tacit knowledge to address or solve the posed problem.

Internalization converts explicit knowledge to tacit knowledge. New knowledge is learnt during the internalization stage. Explicit knowledge is converted to implicit knowledge. Explicit to implicit knowledge conversion occurs with the modification of the knowledge worker's or a knowledge consumer's mental model and can occur after discovering new relationships. As knowledge workers gain a better understanding of how they can improve their activities through the shared knowledge from the architecture, they gain new tacit knowledge by performing as the architecture suggests. The architecture becomes a support system as the knowledge workers validate the new knowledge that has been created.

2.5.1.3 Socialization

Socialization allows tacit to tacit knowledge conversion. The ontology facilitates the creation of common vocabulary for communication among the knowledge consumers and knowledge workers, who include knowledge contributors and knowledge validators. This vocabulary then serves as the basis for expressing knowledge contents and for sharing and managing knowledge on disaster response and management. Kritzinger and von Solms (2010) observe that there can be an overlap between HUs and NHUs. However, there is no such requirement with respect to their personal mobile and home computers and networks. With the experience from their workplaces, these individuals are more likely than the HUs to practice good disaster response and management behaviors with their personal and home systems. In so doing, they build tacit knowledge on disaster response, management, threats, likelihood, strategies, and mechanisms for addressing disaster. Such tacit knowledge can be shared with HUs through socialization.

Interestingly, several HUs in the SSA have a presence on social network sites. Hence, knowledge workers may be able to interact with HUs using social networks instead of by face-to-face interaction. The knowledge management literature suggests that the sharing of tacit knowledge through socialization is effective in small groups. Hence, Google Hangouts for instance, a service that allows individuals to organize meetings for small groups, may be useful. Knowledge workers may invite HUs into their meetings where the tacit knowledge they have acquired on disaster response and management can be shared in these informal settings.

Story telling is a mechanism that has been practiced all over the world, but especially in SSA, for centuries to teach children about culture, morals, and ethics. In Ghana for instance, Kwaku Ananse is used to represent a wise individual who seems to have answers to all the world's problems. Hence, typically children will group under a tree in the evening where an older woman will tell a story depicting a problem that Kwaku Ananse solved. In information systems design, storytelling has been used effectively to capture system requirements from users. We believe that story telling can also be used effectively as a mechanism for knowledge workers to share knowledge on disasters to HUs in SSA. For instance, a story on recent disaster can be told to HUs where the specific characteristics of the disaster and its effects can be shared. An imaginary figure such as Kwaku Ananse can be employed to explain to HUs planning for future disasters how, where, when, and why an attack happened; the tools to address problems; and how to detect, prepare and respond to such disasters to assist them. This, according to Alavi and Leidner (2001), helps to capture the various knowledge types. This type of socialization can take place in various ways including face-to-face environment, as a push of relevant information to HUs mobile phones or in a social network setting.

Combination is the explicit to explicit knowledge conversion. The ontology reconfigures the explicit knowledge in the architecture. Through daily interaction with the architecture, knowledge workers explicate knowledge that has been captured from diverse knowledge and data sources (e.g., archival data, books, experts on disaster, relief agencies, HUs, and NHUs). Knowledge consumers can also use the explicit knowledge in the architecture in the process of settling a cognitive conflict. A cognitive conflict is regarded as one's awareness of contradiction between the cognitive structure (prior knowledge) and the external information.

2.5.1.4 Knowledge Transfer

When knowledge workers share or transfer knowledge on disaster response and management with HUs, it may trigger the HUs' knowledge processes. Once HUs acquire such knowledge, they may apply the knowledge to address problems they have or they may learn new knowledge. Hence, in some situations, HUs can become knowledge workers since they may be motivated to contribute to the knowledge storage because of the benefits the system provides. Hence, knowledge transfer can be expanded between a knowledge worker and a knowledge consumer, a knowledge worker and another knowledge worker, or between two knowledge consumers and also from a knowledge consumer to a knowledge worker. This will ensure that the maximum amount of transfer occurs (after the knowledge has been validated to ensure that it has value).

2.5.1.5 Storage and Retrieval

The storage, organization, and retrieval of organizational knowledge also referred to as organizational memory (Stein & Zwass, 1995; Walsh & Ungson, 1991) constitute an important aspect of effective organizational knowledge management which is the purpose of the domain ontology and the knowledge base. The domain ontology metadata specifies validated set of vocabulary that is consistent among the diverse sources and maintained by the knowledge workers more specifically the knowledge validators. New vocabulary from new knowledge is used to modify the systems and is communicated among the knowledge workers. Each piece of data, information, or knowledge has its own data source. As all these sources are captured into the integrated system, inconsistencies may occur. The ontology-based metadata therefore represents a common global metadata that manages all the other metadata associated with the diverse data, information, and knowledge sources and also provides explicit semantics. It therefore presents a source–independence vocabulary for the domain that the architecture supports. The ontology-based metadata also facilitates the sharing of metadata among the diverse tools that would be used for knowledge elicitation and sharing. It has been recognized that ontology-based metadata enhances users' accessibility to domain knowledge. The ontology forces the explicit specification of this conceptualization and ensures that information is stored consistently in the knowledge base. Given that schema definitions are based on ontology definitions, and vice versa, a symbiotic relationship is constructed between the domain ontology and knowledge base. Knowledge consumers can retrieve knowledge from the knowledge base through the knowledge consumer user interface.

2.5.1.6 Knowledge Application

This is where awareness and enforcement become relevant. We advocate that governments and private institutions will come together to encourage the use of the system once it is implemented. Telecommunications organizations particularly would be key to the success of the knowledge application. As the majority of people use mobile phones, one way of encouraging use of the knowledge is by prompting users, through push mechanisms, to visit the portal where the knowledge resides to improve their awareness of disaster response and management knowledge.

2.6 Implications

We have presented an architecture that allows knowledge contributors and knowledge users to share knowledge on disaster response and management in SSA. We anticipate that a prototype of this architecture can be implemented to test the validity of the claims made in this paper. When such a system becomes operational, it can be made freely available to all users but it would be managed by a non-profit organization to ensure that access policies are adhered to. We have also noted that there are contextual variables that would impact the success of such a system, if implemented. In this section, we discuss the implications of the contextual variables on the management of knowledge on disaster response and management using the proposed system. First, as noted in an earlier section, HUs are more vulnerable to disaster and knowledge gained from an information technology infrastructure on disaster response and management awareness and mechanisms to address catastrophic events as well as enforcement mechanisms to ensure that HUs are protected against disaster are critical issues that need to be addressed. Kritzinger and von Solms (2010) attribute the lack of information security awareness by HUs to the lack of enforcement by a third party to ensure that HUs are secured while using the Internet or that their information security awareness is up to date. In this paper, we propose that governments and telecommunication organizations that provide Internet services will encourage the use of the system. Most citizens in SSA purchase modems with limited units that allow them to connect to the Internet. Few citizens buy unlimited packages. Hence, citizens (including HUs and NHUs) who cannot afford to buy unlimited units and are likely to use the proposed system to enhance their knowledge on disaster response and management and also use tools that could be made available through the system to protect themselves against disaster may be given incentives such as free units for Internet access. Similarly, those who contribute to the knowledge base can also be granted similar incentives. Governments can also offer tax breaks to telecommunications organizations that provide free units and other offerings to enhance citizen's knowledge on disaster management. Telecommunication organizations and the government can benefit from this practice because increasing safety and preparedness of individuals against disasters will encourage the use of the Internet for electronic commerce and electronic government.

Although SSA typically with has challenges with infrastructure, mobile technology has made it possible for those with mobile phones to have access to a wide range of online services. Hence, organizations and governments need to expand wireless networks. In addition, social network infrastructure has become widely acceptable to people in SSA. Therefore, knowledge contributors can point users to the system or knowledge from the systems can be disseminated to social networks such as Facebook, Twitter, and MySpace.

Making people aware of disaster response and management and solutions alone will not be enough to get HUs to protect themselves and their systems against disaster. Awareness should be accompanied by training. Most awareness studies have addressed training issues (D'arcy, Hovav, & Galletta, 2009).

The legal systems as well as response agencies should be encouraged to use knowledge from the proposed systems so that they can effectively help. The use of the system can also enable effective communication and coordination between the various agencies so that common knowledge can be sent to individuals in the affected communities to alleviate confusion that often results from diverse conflicting information from different disaster response agencies during crisis. Governments should provide training for the legal and enforcement agencies to equip themselves with the knowledge and tools needed to effectively deal with disaster.

2.7 Conclusion

In this paper, we have presented an architecture for managing knowledge on disaster response and management in SSA. This architecture captures the critical contextual variables and the various perspectives of knowledge management to ensure that home users, who are less knowledgeable, understand the various forms of knowledge on disaster response and management while developing extensive knowledge bases and building the capability necessary to plan and respond to disaster. The architecture also addresses issues with building IT expertise on disaster management and response strategies in the SSA region. More importantly, the architecture facilitates the creation, storage/retrieval, transfer, and application of knowledge on disaster response and management especially for HUs. Finally, the architecture provides awareness and enforcement mechanisms to help home users protect themselves against disasters. We have identified various actors who would contribute to the creation and sharing of knowledge and those who can use the proposed systems. We have discussed the implication of an implemented system from the proposed architecture.

There are limitations. For instance, we have not implemented the architecture. Future research can implement the architecture to evaluate the validity of the claims proposed in this paper. Here, we have discussed in detail how story telling can be used to support knowledge sharing in SSA. We believe that several such tools may be useful in the managing of knowledge in SSA that future research can include.

Paramount to the design of disaster management systems is the need for interoperability among stakeholders who will interface with the system. For data integrity, the commitment to standardizing disaster data collection and processing is imperative and may be enforced on NGOs as well as the community members. The proposed system allows for ubiquitous usage since it can be accessed via simple cell phones and with limited functional requirements.

References

Akuta, E. A.-M., Ong'oa, I. M., & Jones, C. R. (2011). Combating cyber crime in Sub-Sahara Africa; a discourse on law, policy and practice. *Journal of Peace, Gender and Development Studies, 1*(4), 129–137.

Alavi, M., & Leidner, D. (1999). Knowledge management systems: Emerging views and practices from the field. *Communications of the AIS, 1*(5), 1–37.

Alavi, M., & Leidner, D. E. (2001). Review: Knowledge management and knowledge management systems: Conceptual foundations and research issues. *MIS Quarterly, 25*(1), 107–136.

Allen, K. (2006). Community-based disaster preparedness and climate change adaptation: Local capacity building in the Philippines. *Disasters, 30*(1), 81–101.

Andoh-Baidoo, F. K., & Osatuyi, B. (2009). Examining online banking initiatives in Nigeria: A value network approach. *Electronic Journal of Information Systems in Developing Countries, 1*(38), 1–14.

Apikul, C. (2010). *Overview. ICT for disaster risk reduction* (pp. 9–50). Incheon City, Republic of Korea: APCICT.

Atsu, Y. M., Andoh-Baidoo, F. K., Osatuyi, B., & Amoako-Gyampah, K. (2010). An exploratory study of the contextual factors that influence success of ICT projects in developing nations: A case study of a telecommunications company in Ghana. *Journal of Information Technology Case and Application Research, 3*(12), 56–81.

Baker, W. E., Sciglimpaglia, D., & Saghaffi, M. (2010). Branding of post-purchase ancillary products and services: An application in the mobile communications industry. *European Journal of Marketing, 44*(5), 547–566.

Beugré, C. D. (2002). Understanding organizational justice and its impact on managing employees: An African perspective. *The International Journal of Human Resource Management, 13*(7), 1091–1104.

Blunt, P., & Jones, M. L. (1997). Exploring the limits of Western leadership theory in East Asia and Africa. *Personnel Review, 26*(1/2), 6–23.

Boateng, V. (2009). Electronic/mobile government in Africa: Building capacity in knowledge management through partnership. In U. N. P. A. Network (Ed.), *UN public administration programme*. Addis Ababa, Ethiopia: United Nations Public Administration Network.

Boateng, R., Olumide, L., Isabalija, R. S., & Budu, J. (2011). Sakawa—Cybercrime and criminality in Ghana. *Journal of Information Technology Impact, 11*(2), 85–100.

Cheah, Y. N., & Abidi, S. S. R. (1999). *Tacit knowledge creation in a knowledge management context*. In Fourteenth International Symposium on Computer and Information Sciences, Kusadasi, Turkey.

Christoplos, I., Mitchell, J., & Liljelund, A. (2001). The changing context of disaster mitigation and preparedness. *Disaster, 25*(3), 185–198.

Coyle, D., & Meier, P. (2009). *New technologies in emergencies and conflict. The role of information and social networks*. Washington, DC: UN Foundation-Vodafone Foundation Partnership.

D'arcy, J., Hovav, A., & Galletta, D. (2009). User awareness of security countermeasures and its impact on information systems misuse: A deterrence approach. *Information Systems Research, 20*(1), 79–98.

Danquah, P., & Longe, O. B. (2011). An empirical test of the space transition theory of cyber criminality: Investigating cybercrime causation factors in Ghana. *African Journal of Computing & ICT, 2*(1), 37–48.

Denning, P. J. (2006). Hastily formed networks. *Communications of the ACM, 49*(4), 15–20.

Dinev, T., Goo, J., Hu, Q., & Nam, K. (2009). User behaviour towards protective information technologies: The role of national cultural differences. *Information Systems Journal, 19*(4), 391–412.

Drabek, T. E., & Key, W. H. (1976). *The Impact of Disasters on Primary Groups Mass Emergencies, 1*, 89–105.

European Network and Information Security Agency. (2006). *A users' guide: How to raise information security awareness. e ENISA*. Retrieved from http://www.enisa.europa.eu/act/ar/deliverables/2006/ar-guide/en

Foster, W., Goodman, S., Osiakwan, E., & Bernstein, A. (2004). Global diffusion of the internet IV: The internet in Ghana. *Communications of the AIS, 13*, 47.

Furnell, S., Valleria, T., & Phippen, D. (2008). Security beliefs and barriers for novice internet users. *Computers & Security, 27*, 235–240.

Goldman, G. (1990). The tacit dimension of clinical judgment. *The Yale Journal of Biology and Medicine, 63*(1), 47–61.

Grant, R. M. (1996). Toward a knowledge-based theory of the firm. *Strategic Management Journal, 17*, 109–122.

Grant, E., & Gregory, M. (1997). Tacit knowledge, the life cycle and international manufacturing transfer. *Technology Analysis & Strategic Management, 9*(2), 149–161.

Hay, R. (1986). Food aid and relief-development strategies. *Disasters: Relief-Development Strategies of Africa, 10*(4), 273–287.

Hewitt, K. (1983). The idea of calamity in a technocratic age. In K. Hewitt (Ed.), *Interpretations of calamity* (pp. 3–32). London, England: Unwin-Hyman.

Hofstede, G. (1980). *Culture's consequences: International differences in work related values*. London, England: Sage Publishing.

Hofstede, G. (1983). The cultural relativity of organizational practices and theories. *Journal of International Business Studies, 14*, 75–89.

Hofstede, G. (1984). The cultural relativity of the quality of life concept. *The Academy of Management Review, 9*(3), 389–398.

Hofstede, G. (1993). Cultural constraints in management theories. *The Executive, 7*(1), 81–94.

Howells, J. (1995). *Tacit knowledge and technology transfer*. Cambridge, England: University of Cambridge.

IFRC. (2009). *World disasters report. Focus on early warning, early action*. Geneva, Switzerland: IFRC.

Kalas, P., & Finlay, A. (Eds.). (2009). *Planting the knowledge seed. Adapting to climate change using ICTs*. Geneva, Switzerland: BCO.

Kritzinger, E., & von Solms, S. H. (2010). Cyber security for home users: A new way of protection through awareness enforcement. *Computers & Security, 29*, 840–847.

Kumar, R. M. L., Park, S., & Subramaniam, C. (2008). Understanding the value of countermeasure portfolios in information systems security. *Journal of Management Information Systems, 25*(2), 241–280.

Mirza, M. Q. (2003). Climate change and extreme weather events: Can developing countries adapt? *Climate Policy, 3*(3).

Moses-Òkè, R. O. (2012). Cyber capacity without cyber security: A case study of Nigeria's national policy for information technology (NPFIT). *The Journal of Philosophy, Science & Law, 12*, 1–14.

Muriithi, N., & Crawford, L. (2003). Approaches to project management in Africa: Implications for international development projects. *International Journal of Project Management, 21*(5), 309–319.

Ngwenyama, O., Andoh-Baidoo, F. K., Bollou, R., & Morawczynski, O. (2006). Is there a relationship between ICT, health, education and development? An empirical analysis of five West African countries from 1997-2003. *The Electronic Journal on Information Systems in Developing Countries, 26*(5), 1–11.

Nogueira, J. H. M., & De Vasconcelos, W. W. P. (2007). *Ontology for complex mission scenarios in forensic computing*. In 2nd International Conference of Forensic Computer Science, Guarujá, Brazil.

Nonaka, I., Takeuchi, H., & Umemoto, K. (1996). A theory of organizational knowledge creation. *International Journal of Technology Management, 11*(7–8), 833–845.

O'Leary, D. E. (1998). Using AI in knowledge management: Knowledge bases and ontologies. *IEEE Intelligent Systems and their Applications, 13*(3), 34–39.

Ospina, A. V., & Heeks, R. (2010). *Unveiling the links between ICTs and climate change in developing countries: A scoping study*. Centre for Development Informatics, Institute for Development Policy and Management, SED. Retrieved from http://www.manchester.ac.uk/cdi

Paton, D., & Johnson, D. (2001). Disasters and communities: Vulnerability, resilience and preparedness. *Disaster Prevention and Management, 10*(4), 270–277.

Pylyshyn, Z. W. (1981). The imagery debate—Analog media versus tacit knowledge. *Psychological Review, 88*(1), 16–45.

Quarantelli, E. L. (1989). Conceptualizing disasters from a sociological perspective. *International Journal of Mass Emergencies and Disasters, 7*(3), 243–251.

Quarantelli, E. L. (1998). *Major criteria for judging disaster planning and managing and their applicability in developing countries.* Paper presented at the International Seminar on the Quality of Life and Environmental Risks, 10–11 October, Rio de Janeiro, Brazil.

Ross, J., Maxwell, S., & Buchanan-Smith, M. (1994). *Linking relief and development. Discussion paper*. Sussex, England: Institute of Development Studies.

Roztocki, N., & Weistroffer, H. R. (2011). Information technology success factors and models in developing and emerging economies. *Information Technology for Development, 17*(3), 163–167.

Siddiqui, S. (2008). *Post disaster rehabilitation of livelihoods in the upper Siran valley of Pakistan after the earthquake*. Guelph, Ontario, Canada: MSc University of Guelph.

Stein, E. W., & Zwass, V. (1995). Actualizing organizational memory with information systems. *Information Systems Research, 6*(2), 85–117.

Tan, S. S., Teo, H. H., Tan, B. C., & Wei, K. K. (1998). Developing a preliminary framework for knowledge management in organizations. In E. Hoadley, & I. Benbasat (Eds.), *Fourth Americas Conference on Information Systems* (pp. 629–631), Baltimore, MD.

Tobin, G. A. (1999). Sustainability and community resilience: The holy grail of hazards planning? *Environmental Hazards, 1*, 13–25.

UNESCAP. (2008). *Information and communication technology-enabled disaster risk reduction in Asia and the Pacific*. Bangkok, Thailand: UNESCAP.

Uschold, M., & Gruninger, M. (1996). Ontologies: Principles, methods and applications. *Knowledge Engineering Review, 11*, 96–137.

Walsh, J. P., & Ungson, G. R. (1991). Organization memory. *Academy of Management Review, 16*(1), 57–91.

Wisner, B., Blaikie, P., Cannon, T., & Davis, I. (2003). *At risk. Natural hazards, people's vulnerability and disasters*. London, England: Routledge.

Chapter 3
Managing Expert Knowledge to Assist in the Management of Coffee Pests and Diseases in Jamaica

Gunjan Mansingh, Han Reichgelt, and Kweku-Muata Osei-Bryson

Abstract The recent focus on knowledge-based economies brings to the forefront the importance of knowledge in developing nations. The capability to harness and manage knowledge has become essential and the Knowledge Management community has been developing technologies and applications to aid this process. Sustainable agriculture and environmental concerns have led to the emergence of the Integrated Management of Pest and Pesticides as a new way to deal with pests and pesticides in agriculture. In this chapter we present the architecture of an expert system CPEST and identify the knowledge types that are necessary to build such systems. CPEST incorporates different types of knowledge, i.e. the know-with, the know-how, know-when, know-about which exists in multiple experts and data sources to assist with the decision making process. The system is evaluated for its accuracy, ease of use, and effectiveness of its recommendations in the promotion of practices less damaging to the environment.

Keywords Expert systems • Knowledge base systems • Knowledge types • Coffee pests • Coffee diseases • Developing countries • Agriculture

---

G. Mansingh (✉)
Department of Computing, The University of the West Indies, Mona Campus, Jamaica
e-mail: gunjan.mansingh@uwimona.edu.jm

H. Reichgelt
School of Computing and Software Engineering, Southern Polytechnic State University, Marietta, GA, USA
e-mail: hreichge@spsu.edu

K.-M. Osei-Bryson
Department of Information Systems, Virginia Commonwealth University, Richmond, VA, USA
e-mail: kmosei@vcu.edu

K.-M. Osei-Bryson et al. (eds.), *Knowledge Management for Development*, Integrated Series in Information Systems 35, DOI 10.1007/978-1-4899-7392-4_3,

3.1 Introduction

Knowledge systems in organizations consist of four sets of knowledge processes; creation, storage/retrieval, transfer, and application (Alavi & Leidner, 1999). In organizations, the source of competitive advantage lies not in knowledge but in the application of knowledge. The knowledge application systems facilitate the transfer of knowledge between various communities of practice. In agricultural domain to ensure sustainable practices are followed, agricultural extension officers and farmers need to have access to knowledge of experts from different fields. Integrated Management of Pest and Pesticide (IMPP) requires knowledge of the crop itself, the different kinds of pests that affect the crop and their biological cycles, the different types of disease that attack the crop, and the types of pesticide and other chemicals that may affect these pests and diseases, as well as their environmental impact.

This reliance on the knowledge of many experts makes IMPP difficult to implement in practice. Typically, the knowledge of different diseases, their diagnosis, and controls resides with a small and select group of experts or experienced farmers. The decision making process of the farmers and different stakeholders requires access to different knowledge items in the domain such as "know-how", "know-what", and "know-when". At times it may be difficult for a common farmer to consult an expert and access all the different knowledge items. This affects their decision making and their capability to manage the crops effectively and efficiently.

This chapter describes an expert system CPEST which advises farmers how to effectively manage coffee pests and diseases. This system enables the transfer of knowledge between different communities of practice (e.g. researchers, agricultural officers, small farmers) involved in the agricultural domain. These domains are not traditional organizations involved in products or services, but can benefit from the collaborations between different researchers and small farmers or agricultural officers to maintain their competitiveness.

3.2 Literature Review

Knowledge management literature has identified four dynamic and inter-related processes of creation, storage/retrieval, transfer, and application (Alavi & Leidner, 2001). The process of knowledge creation focuses on creating new content or refreshing and updating existing content. Once knowledge is created, it needs to be stored and retrieved. Organizational memories need to be stored so that they can be transferred and shared with others. According to the knowledge-based view, knowledge has unique characteristics as it grows when it is used and depreciates when it is not used (Grant, 1996). Therefore, ensuring that the existing knowledge is applied is critical in the management of knowledge. Information technology plays an integral role in all processes and in knowledge application it ensures that the existing knowledge can be duplicated and applied efficiently to assist decision making.

Expert systems are computer systems which capture the knowledge of human experts within a domain to assist in decision making. These systems try to emulate human experts by capturing and codifying their knowledge and also the knowledge in the domain.

Knowledge has been broadly classified as tacit and explicit (Nonaka, 1994). This classification originates with Polanyi's research into tacit knowledge in which he expressed the opinion that we will always know more than we can tell as there will always be a part of knowledge which cannot be expressed. Tacit knowledge is known to be difficult to articulate and is possessed by individuals and explicit knowledge is the knowledge that can be captured and codified as procedures and rules and is easy to disseminate. According to Nonaka (1994) the key to understanding knowledge creation lies in the ability to make tacit knowledge explicit. The objective of an expert system is to capture both tacit and explicit knowledge within a specific domain to assist is decision making (Mansingh, Reichgelt, & Osei-Bryson, 2007). Besides the tacit and explicit distinction, knowledge can also be classified as know-how, know-about, know-why, know-when, and know-with (Alavi & Leidner, 2001). Know-how is the procedural knowledge, know-about is the declarative knowledge, know-why is the causal knowledge, know-when is the conditional knowledge, and know-with is the relational knowledge. Delong (2004) argued that the tacit-explicit dimension is too general and can pose a problem in deciding which knowledge transfer techniques can be applied in a situation. He defines four states of tacit knowledge (Delong, 2004); they are:

- Implicit rule-based knowledge—knowledge that can be explicated and codified by agents doing a particular task.
- Implicit know-how—knowledge that can be communicated easily but is not codified because of contextual complexity.
- Tacit know-how—knowledge difficult to verbalize.
- Deep Tacit—the collectively shared beliefs, mental models, and values that determine what individuals view as important and even what they define as relevant knowledge.

Knowledge elicitation techniques are used to acquire the knowledge of experts which can later be converted into a format where it is used in the reasoning process to assist in decision making. The objective of knowledge elicitation is to extract the knowledge which human experts' posses. Some knowledge the experts can articulate easily; for some, experts have to apply knowledge elicitation techniques to extract and some knowledge cannot be elicited (Reichgelt & Shadbolt, 1992). Based on Delong's (2004) definition of tacit knowledge, the implicit knowledge can be seen as a component of tacit knowledge that can be explicated by employing some knowledge elicitation techniques.

Therefore, the construction of knowledge-based systems requires that the knowledge engineer is aware of the different knowledge types that can exist as this will guide the selection of an appropriate knowledge elicitation technique. Knowledge elicitation techniques can be divided into natural and artificial; examples of natural techniques are unstructured/structured interviews and case studies and examples of artificial techniques are laddering, card sort, and repertory grid (Reichgelt & Shadbolt, 1992). Each of these techniques is useful in extracting implicit knowledge from the human experts.

3.3 Expert System: CPEST

3.3.1 Components of CPEST

The development of expert systems in the field of agriculture is not new (López-Morales, López-Ortega, Ramos-Fernández, & Muñoz, 2008; Prasad & Babu, 2006); they have been used for decades for different types of crops. Different architectures from stand-alone applications, to web-based and now mobile applications have been developed to assist the farmers and other stakeholders. These systems capture various types of knowledge within a domain to provide recommendations that mimic the decision making of human experts. In this study we identify the knowledge types used in the design of an expert system CPEST which gives expert advice on the management of a coffee farm (see Table 3.1). This system incorporates qualitative domain-specific information about the farm into the Integrated Management of Pests and Pesticides (IMPP) process. The architecture of the system is shown in Fig. 3.1 and Table 3.2 provides a description of each of the components.

3.3.2 Elicitation of Rule-Set from Experts

CPEST's knowledge base was built with the help of experts from different fields. Table 3.3 provides background information about the experts. One of these experts played the role of "knowledge czar", an overall expert who guided the whole knowledge acquisition exercise. Knowledge acquisition, though critical, has always been a bottleneck in developing expert systems (Gaines, 1987). This knowledge acquisition process tends to be very long and time-consuming (Liebowitz & Baek, 1996). IMPP requires knowledge from many different fields. Our knowledge acquisition

Table 3.1 Knowledge types in CPEST

Knowledge types	CPEST's knowledge
Know-with Know-when Know-about Implicit	Knowledge on how to identify pests and diseases, knowledge on what to do when, knowledge on what pesticides can be combined, knowledge on when to do certain actions, knowledge on what pesticides to use for a pest or a disease
Explicit	Knowledge of pesticides and their properties
Know-how	Knowledge on how a recommendation was reached
Tacit know-how	Graphical images to share mental models

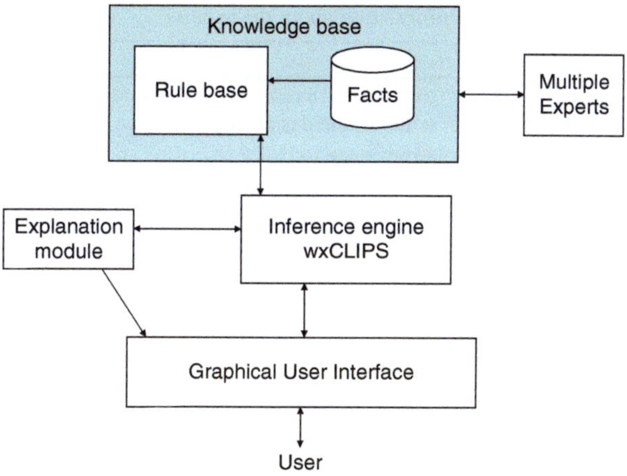

Fig. 3.1 Architecture of CPEST

Table 3.2 Description of the components

Component	Description
Rule base	Contains around 150 production rules as standard IF-THEN rules. These rules are forward chaining where the system reasons "forward" from the information entered by the user
Facts	Information about the pesticides and their properties are stored as default facts
Explanation module	The explanation module provides a simple trace of the rules fired so far and screens have a recommendation buttons which can be invoked at any time (see Fig. 3.5)
Inference engine	The inference engine provides the matching mechanism. The facts are compared with the left hand side of the rules. The inference structure of CPEST is known as heuristic classification and is similar to other expert systems which perform tasks like diagnosis and data interpretation (Clancy, 1995)
Graphical user interface	The system has about 40 screens, including data entry, pictures, and simple text screens

techniques included unstructured and structured interviews, decision trees, and laddering (Durkin, 1994). Although on some occasions using multiple experts during the knowledge acquisition stage can be problematic, we did not encounter any problems during the elicitation of the rule-set.

Our knowledge elicitation process resulted in a consistent rule-set of 150 production rules. Table 3.4 gives an example of the types of rules that are encoded in the expert system.

3.3.3 Reasoning in CPEST

We used forward chaining, rather than backward chaining, as our reasoning mechanism. In other words, rather than setting out to try to determine which of a set of

Table 3.3 Basic information about the experts

Experts	Experience
Expert 1	50 years experience in research and development in entomology, integrated management of pest and pesticides and eco-toxicity. Studying coffee pests for over 25 years
Expert 2	18 years experience in IMPP of coffee and vegetable pests (particularly organic cultivation) and eco-toxicity
Expert 3	15 years experience in IMPP for coffee leaf miner, biological control of coffee berry borer, and IMPP of vegetable pests

Table 3.4 Type of rules

Rule type	Role	Example of English rules
General input	General information about the farm, such as size, soil type, colour of leaves	**If** there is *leaf fall* on the plot **Then** Select the colour of leaves on that plot
Disease	Used to determine what diseases, if any, the coffee on the farm is suffering from and to make some initial recommendations about the treatment	**If** one in every 10 leaves have rust and *leaf fall* is heavy and *climate* is dry and cool **Then** Recommend fertilization if not done in the last 3 months and limit the movement of people coming in contact with infected leaves on the plot
Leaf miner	Used to diagnose and make provisional recommendations for the treatment of leaf	**If** *percentage of infested leaves on a tree* are between 16 and 20 % and *percentage area damage on a leaf* is between 11 and 15 % **Then** Find out about the shade on the farm, the weeds on the farm, and the rainfall frequency and intensity
Coffee berry borer	Used to diagnose and make provisional recommendations for the treatment of coffee berry borer	**If** the coffee plants have pimento size berries or green berries and plot has more than 6 % infestation and the abdomen of the borer is exposed **Then** The plot needs chemical treatment
Chemical	Information about different chemicals	**If** the *soil types* is sandy or sandy loam and the *slope* is gentle and the *climate* is wet and cool or wet and hot **Then** Use a pesticide with persistence low
Housekeeping	The user interface of wxCLIPS added some additional facts. These rules compare the time stamp of similar facts and delete the earlier facts	**If** *borer-stage* 1 time1 and *borer-stage* 2 time2 and time2>?time1 **Then** Delete the fact *borer-stage* 1

given hypotheses is likely to hold, as one would do in a backward reasoning system, CPEST starts out by getting some initial information from the user and storing this in a component called "working memory". The information in working memory is used to guide the entire problem solving process. During the problem solving process, CPEST may add further information to working memory, either because of intermediate conclusions it has been able to draw or because the user has been prompted to answer additional questions.

Our choice of a forward chaining reasoning mechanism was based on two factors. First, the task seemed to naturally lend itself to a data-driven reasoning strategy and such reasoning strategies are simply more straightforwardly modelled in a forward chaining system. Second, a farm can suffer from more than one problem. Since CPEST is knowledgeable about four diseases and two pests, CPEST would therefore have to consider all possible combinations of these problems in turn. In other words, if we had used a simple goal-driven reasoning strategy, CPEST would have to examine 64 possible hypotheses, which we did not consider to be a feasible option for farmers and agricultural officers.

3.3.4 Problem Resolution with CPEST

CPEST goes through three different phases when solving a problem, namely:

1. General data-gathering phase
2. Diagnosis and possible treatments
3. Integration of treatments

During the general data-gathering phase, CPEST asked the user for general information about the farm and the state of coffee plants on the farm. Initial information requested includes the size of the farm, its slope, and its soil type. CPEST then continues to ask the user for information about the plants, such as bearing stage of the plants, their leaf density, and the intensity of any leaf fall.

During the diagnosis phase, CPEST invokes, where appropriate, the disease module, the leaf miner module, and/or the coffee berry borer module. The decision which module to invoke depends, to a large extent, on the data gathered in the first phase. For example, if the plants have been determined to be in the flowering stage, then the coffee berry borer module will not be invoked as this pest will only affect plants that have berries. On the other hand, if the leaves have been determined to have brown patches, the leaf miner module will be invoked as this particular pest may cause brown patches.

Invoking a module during this phase typically involves three sub-tasks. CPEST will first determine whether the disease or pest is indeed present. If it is, the system will try to determine the level of infestation. Finally, each module will recommend a provisional treatment.

Typically, trying to determine whether a disease or pest is indeed present leads to the system asking for further information from the user. For example, if the leaf miner module has been invoked because of the presence of brown patches on the leaves, CPEST will ask for further information about the nature of the patches, such as whether the top part of the leaf peels off, or whether there are orange spores at the back of the leaf.

Having established the possible presence of any diseases and/or pests, and having determined the extent of the infection or infestation, CPEST will decide on the type of treatment required, including cultural practices, biological practices, and if such practices cannot control the disease of pest, chemical treatment. Again, this often requires CPEST to obtain additional information from the user about the prevailing weather conditions, such as wind speed and the frequency and intensity of rainfall.

After the different modules have submitted their individual treatments, CPEST integrates the recommended treatments. In this integration effort, it relies on a fourth module, namely the chemical module. Factors that are of relevance here are the chemicals, if any, whose use has been suggested, and environmental factors such as soil type, slope of the land, and rainfall and wind conditions. For example, it is pointless to spray pesticides during the heavy rainy season as most of the pesticide applied would simply run off. Also, special care has to be taken on very steep sloping lands, as run off is very high in such cases. The type of soil determines which additional sticking agents have to be added to ensure that spraying is fully effective. Finally, the system takes into account the desired ecological balance. For example, spraying for coffee berry borer can result in killing off other flying insects which are natural enemies of leaf miner, thus making the plot more susceptible to leaf miner. Special rules also determine which chemicals can be mixed together, and how the spraying should be planned, as in some cases different pesticides may have to be used.

3.3.5 CPEST'S User Interface

As stated, one of the most important design considerations behind CPEST was that the resulting system should be as user-friendly as possible. The target users were farmers and it would be unrealistic to expect them to be intimately familiar with either the use of the computer or the terminology used by agricultural experts. We therefore incorporated a relatively sophisticated graphical user interface into CPEST. Also, in order to increase the chances of user acceptance of the recommendations made by CPEST, we felt that it was important to build an explanation facility into CPEST.

CPEST's graphical user interface consists of about 40 screens. About 60 % of these screens are data input screens, with the remainder being simple text display screens. As one would expect, the data entry screens help the user in entering the data and thus make the system easier to use. Figure 3.2 shows an input screen.

Although the use of data entry screen makes the use of the system more straightforward for a user who is less familiar with the computer, it obviously does not solve the problem of the user's unfamiliarity with the terminology used by agricultural experts. We solved this problem by incorporating pictures, for example, in Fig. 3.3, a data entry screen allows users to determine the pest or disease by looking at the images seen in Fig. 3.4.

The final aspect of the user interface that we want to highlight is the system's ability to give a rudimentary explanation of its recommendations. For example, after the system has displayed the recommendation given in Fig. 3.5, a user can ask for a further explanation by clicking the "explanation" button.

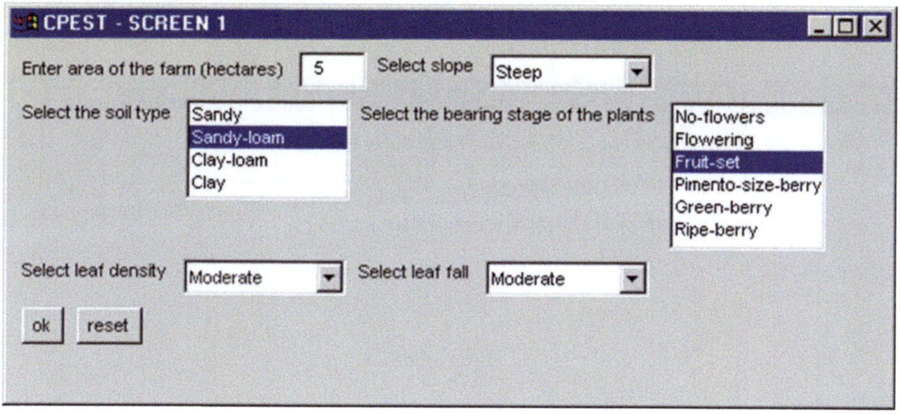

Fig. 3.2 The CPEST start-up screen

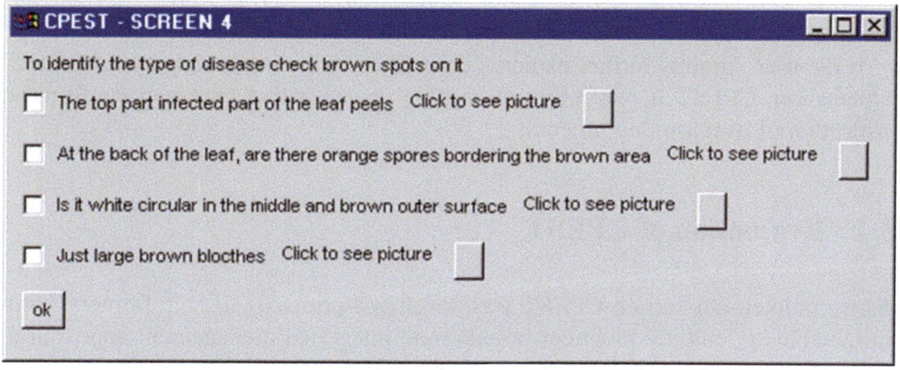

Fig. 3.3 A CPEST data entry screen

Fig. 3.4 Pictorial help

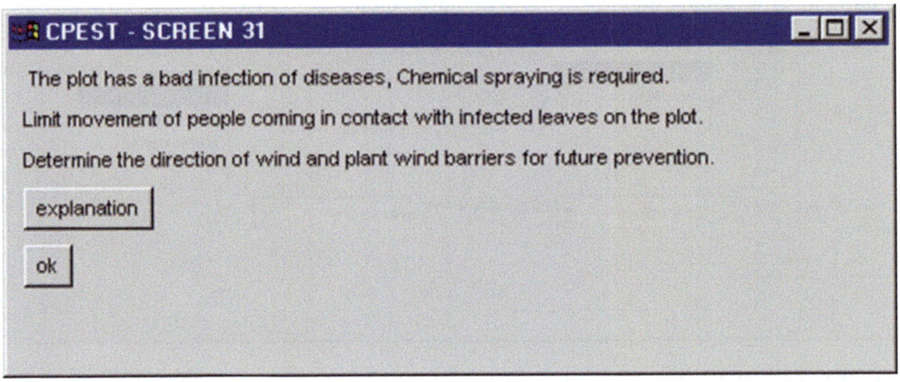

Fig. 3.5 A CPEST recommendation screen

If the user requires further explanation, CPEST will simply display a "canned" explanation. CPEST is currently not capable of generating explanations from an inspection of its reasoning process.

3.4 Evaluation of CPEST

As we pointed out earlier, CPEST was developed primarily to help farmers adopt sustainable agricultural practices based on an integrated management approach to pests and pesticides. CPEST can only achieve this goal if (1) the advice it gives is correct, (2) it can be used by farmers, and (3) its advice, if followed, would lead to a lower incidence of chemical treatments of pests and diseases, while still enabling a farmer to minimize economic losses due to the pest or disease. To validate CPEST, we subjected it to three evaluations.

3.4.1 Validation of CPEST

Our first evaluation primarily addressed the issue of CPEST's advice being correct. To this end, we submitted a set of three scenarios to CPEST. The scenarios reflected the different size farms that one finds in Jamaica, as well as different climatic and slope conditions. We also asked three human experts to solve the cases (see Table 3.5). The first expert was one of the domain experts who had participated in the development process. The other two were independent in that they had not been involved in the construction of CPEST.

In two of the three scenarios, all three experts were in full agreement with the recommendations put forward by CPEST. In the third scenario, two experts agreed fully with CPEST, while the third agreed in essence, except for a minor detail, namely whether to apply a sticking agent to a chemical selected for application.

Table 3.5 Scenarios for validation

	Description	CPEST's recommendations	Experts recommendation
Scenario 1	A plot of 3 ha with moderate slope, clay soil type, plant bearing stage is fruit-set, leaf density is moderate, and leaf fall on the farm is also moderate. The leaves are green in colour and have brown coloured spots and blotches. The top part of these brown blotches can peel. On the plot the percentage of damaged leaves on a tree is between 16 and 20 % and the percentage area damaged on the leaf itself is between 1 and 10 %. There are heavy weeds on the plot and plot has moderate shade. It rains about once a week with low intensity	The farm has leaf miner infestation. The level is not near any danger levels and therefore does not need any chemical treatment. But the leaf miner population should be monitored next month. CPEST also recommended bushing the weeds on the farm as weed presence is heavy and the leaf miner pest can pupate on the weeds. Also the weeds rob the plant of nutrients which the plant needs to withstand the effect of the pest damage	All three experts agreed with CPEST's recommendations
Scenario 2	A plot of 0.5 ha on a gentle slope. There are no rivers near the farm (approx. further than 1,000 m). The soil type is clay-loam and the plant bearing stage is pimento size berries. The leaf density is sparse and a moderate number of leaves are falling from the coffee trees. The colour of leaves is yellow and leaves have both brown and yellow spots on them. In the brown spots the top part of some of the leaf peels. Also, on the back of some spots there are orange spores bordering the patch while some have just brown patches. For both, the infection is seen in 1 in 10 leaves. The weather is dry and cool. On the plot the percentage of leaves on a tree for which the brown patches peels is between 16 and 20 % and the percentage area damaged on the leaf itself is between 11 and 15 %. There are few weeds on the plot and plot has moderate shade. It rains about once a week with low intensity. About 15 % of the coffee berries have holes in them. On checking the berries it was seen that the coffee borer pest was boring the berries and the abdomen of the pest is exposed	The plot has evidence of leaf rust and anthracnose diseases. The level of infection does not need any chemical spraying, but it needs monitoring. Also, the movement of people coming in contact with the infected leaves has to be limited. Leaf miner is also present on the plot. The rainfall conditions on the farm are not good and this pest could reach danger levels. Do not spray at this stage but monitor the population again next week. If the population increases then check the system again for chemical requirements. The following practices must be done to control leaf miner on the farm. Keep the drip circle clean and fertilize the farm if this has not been done in the past 3 months. The system also detected the presence of coffee berry borer. Chemical spraying for the coffee berry borer pest has been recommended. The pesticide endosulfan was selected from the pesticide list. Looking at the rainfall conditions no sticker (a sticking compound) needs to be added to the pesticide	All three experts agreed with CPEST's recommendation
Scenario 3	A plot of 50 ha on a gentle slope. The weather is hot and dry. There is a river near the farm. The soil type is clay and the plant bearing stage is green berries. The leaf density is dense and moderate numbers of leaves are falling from the coffee trees. The colour of leaves is green and they have brown spots on them. The top infected part of the brown spots can peel. The percentage of leaves on a tree for which the brown patches peels is greater than 20 % and the percentage area damaged on the leaf itself is greater than 15 %. On inspecting the leaves it was found that the pest is in its larvae stage. About 7 % of the coffee berries have holes in them. On checking the berries it was seen that the coffee borer pest was boring the berries and on opening some berries it was seen that the borer was inside the berry	Leaf miner pest is present on the plot. The pest has reached danger levels. Chemical treatment is recommended for the pest. Because the pest is in its larvae stage a pesticide that is foliar systemic should be used. Weed and shade management should be done and foliar fertilizing should also be done on the plot. The system also detected the presence of coffee berry borer. As the borer is already inside the green berries and has damaged it, there is no point in spraying for this pest at this stage. The cost of spraying will just result in more economic losses. Looking at the rainfall conditions no sticker needs to be added to the pesticide which is selected for the leaf miner pest	All three experts agreed with CPEST's recommendations*

*There was a minor disagreement from one expert with regard to adding sticker to the pesticide formulation

However, the dissenting expert, when further quizzed on this case, agreed with CPEST's recommendations not to apply a sticking agent. Based on the admittedly small sample of three scenarios, we tentatively conclude that CPEST's recommendations are correct. Although we are aware that a sample of three scenarios is hardly sufficient, small samples have been used in numerous studies (Yap, Ngwenyama, & Osei-Bryson, 2003).

3.4.2 Acceptance of CPEST

The second question that we wanted to answer concerned the effectiveness of CPEST's user interface. We therefore gave six randomly selected farmers access to CPEST, and after a brief introduction, asked them to evaluate it. They were asked to evaluate CPEST on cases they had actually encountered on their farms.

We observed the farmers while they were using CPEST and also solicited their comments afterwards. Both from our own observations and from the comments made by the farmers afterwards, it was apparent that the farmers had very little difficulty in navigating through the different screens, or answering the questions posed by CPEST. In general, they were more than satisfied with the interface that CPEST provided. We conclude that CPEST does indeed meet the stated objective that it be useable by actual farmers.

3.4.3 Effectiveness of CPEST

The third criterion that we wanted to evaluate was whether the adoption of its recommendations would indeed lead to agricultural practices less damaging to the environment. We therefore ran 12 real life scenarios on the system and compared CPEST's recommendations with the actual actions that had been taken on the farm (see Table 3.4). These scenarios were obtained from interviews with farmers and experts and came from a cross-section of conditions on coffee farming in Jamaica. The major criteria used in selecting scenarios were altitude, the prevailing climatic conditions at the time (dry or wet), and the type of farm (low input versus high input).

There was agreement between CPEST's recommendations and the actual actions performed by coffee farmers in only 2 of the 12 scenarios. According to CPEST, only three farms needed chemical application, whereas in fact 11 farms had been sprayed (see Fig. 3.6). In the two scenarios where there was full agreement between CPEST's recommendations and the actual actions, CPEST's recommendations included spraying pesticides. If farmers were to follow CPEST's advice, they would rely more on cultural practices to control pests, rather than chemicals and hence adopt environmentally less damaging practices. It is evident that by following CPEST's recommendation, the farmers would have been able to save on spraying costs and also cause less pollution in the environment.

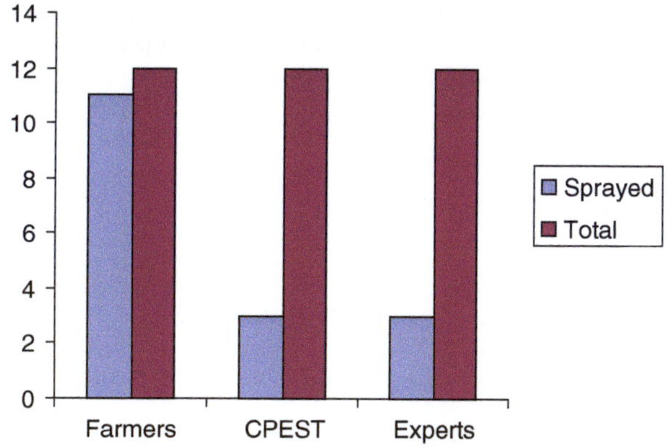

Fig. 3.6 Graphical representation of effectiveness

However, the fact that CPEST recommended chemical treatments in significantly fewer scenarios is in a sense neither here nor there. We also need to make sure that the treatment recommended by CPEST would indeed have controlled the pest or disease that was affecting the farm. We therefore also consulted experts about the appropriateness of CPEST's recommendations. All agreed that CPEST's recommendations would indeed have led to a satisfactory solution to the problem the farm was facing, thus providing further evidence of the correctness of CPEST's advice.

Based on the above, we conclude that CPEST's recommendations are indeed correct, that farmers would have no difficulty in using CPEST, and that an adoption of CPEST's recommendations would indeed lead to agricultural management practices that result in less environmental stress.

3.5 Conclusion

There is little doubt that many current agricultural practices, and especially the almost exclusive reliance on chemicals to combat diseases and pests, are not sustainable in the long run, and agriculture has therefore seen the emergence first of Integrated Pest Management and later the Integrated Management of Pests and Pesticides. Unfortunately, both require access to the knowledge of experts in different fields and such access is often simply not available for small farmers, especially in developing countries. The system described in this paper, CPEST, is an illustration of how information technology in general, and expert systems in particular can help overcome some of these problems. Our preliminary evaluation suggests that this system gives correct, credible recommendations that small farmers would find valuable as it can result in significant savings. Further, our results suggest that they are likely to find this system to be easy to use. We believe that the use of CPEST, and systems like it, could go a long way towards making agriculture in developing countries both economically more viable and environmentally friendlier.

Acknowledgment Material in this chapter has appeared in "CPEST—An Expert System for Management of Pests and Diseases in the Jamaican Coffee Industry", Expert Systems with Applications, Vol. 32, 2007.

References

Alavi, M., & Leidner, D. E. (1999). Knowledge management systems: Issues, challenges, and benefits. *Communications of AIS, 1*, Article 7.

Alavi, M., & Leidner, D. E. (2001). Review: Knowledge management and knowledge management systems: Conceptual foundations and research issues. [Theoretical]. *MIS Quarterly, 25*(1), 107–135.

Clancy, W. J. (1995). Heuristic classification. *Artificial Intelligence, 27*, 289–350.

Delong, D. W. (2004). *Lost knowledge: Confronting the threat of an ageing workforce*. New York: Oxford University Press.

Durkin, J. (1994). *Expert systems: Design and development*. Englewood Cliffs, NJ: Prentice-Hall.

Gaines, B. R. (1987). An overview of knowledge acquisition and transfer. *International Journal of Man-Machine Studies, 26*(4), 453–472.

Grant, R. M. (1996). Toward a knowledge-based theory of the firm. *Strategic Management Journal, 17*(Winter), 109–122.

Liebowitz, J., & Baek, S. I. (1996). The protocol multimedia expert system. *The New Review of Applied Expert Systems, 1*, 3–17.

López-Morales, V., López-Ortega, O., Ramos-Fernández, J., & Muñoz, L. B. (2008). JAPIEST: An integral intelligent system for the diagnosis and control of tomatoes diseases and pests in hydroponic greenhouses. *Expert Systems with Applications, 35*, 1506–1512.

Mansingh, G., Reichgelt, H., & Osei-Bryson, K. M. (2007). CPEST—An expert system for management of pests and diseases in the Jamaican coffee industry. *Expert Systems with Applications, 32*, 184–192.

Nonaka, I. (1994). A dynamic theory of organizational knowledge creation. [Article]. *Organization Science, 5*(1), 14–37.

Prasad, G. N. R., & Babu, A. V. (2006). A study on various expert systems in agriculture. *Computer Science and Telecommunications, 4*(11), 81–86.

Reichgelt, H., & Shadbolt, N. (1992). ProtoKEW: A knowledge-based systems for knowledge acquisition. In D. S. O. Bernsen (Ed.), *Research advances in cognitive science: Artificial intelligence* (Vol. 5, pp. 171–200). Mahwah, NJ: Lawrence Erlbaum.

Yap, A., Ngwenyama, O., & Osei-Bryson, K.-M. (2003). Leveraging knowledge representation, usage, and interpretation to help reengineer the product development life cycle: Visual computing and the tacit dimensions of product development. *Computers in Industry, 51*, 89–110.

Chapter 4
Implementation of a Multi-agent Supervisory System for an Agricultural Products Sourcing Network

Virgilio Lopez-Morales and Yacine Ouzrout

Abstract A Distributed Knowledge Management System (DKMS) for health control in hydroponic agricultural framework could improve production and subsequently be integrated into a sourcing network. The forecasted production could also be integrated into an electronic auction and thus allow for faster negotiations, with transparency in a previously agreed trading structure. Such a DKMS can address a variety of regulations (e.g., production control, package, labeling) and environmental concerns (Integrated Pest Management). In this supervisory intelligent network scenario, a high degree of collaboration and transparency promote the solution to such technical critical aspects. In this chapter, a multi-agent architecture for collaborative knowledge management in agricultural production in Mexico is introduced. Since diagnosis and control of diseases and pests, regulations, and environmental issues can be involved in the whole process, from the production control up to the marketing and distribution stages, agricultural sustainability can be later analyzed.

Keywords Agricultural sustainability • Multi-agent system • Multi-expert system • Distributed decision making

4.1 Introduction

About 80 % of Mexico's total productive land has erratic rainy seasons and droughts (Servicio Meteorológico Nacional, 2012). Besides, 52.4 % of its surface is composed of poor soils, leptosol (formerly rendzinas), regosol, and calcisol,

---

V. Lopez-Morales (✉)
Universidad Autonoma del Estado de Hidalgo, Pachuca, Hidalgo, Mexico
e-mail: virgilio@uaeh.edu.mx

Y. Ouzrout
DISP Laboratory, University Lumiere, Lyon, France
e-mail: yacine.ouzrout@univ-lyon2.fr

K.-M. Osei-Bryson et al. (eds.), *Knowledge Management for Development*,
Integrated Series in Information Systems 35, DOI 10.1007/978-1-4899-7392-4_4,

with limited agricultural use. Soils with a higher fertility phaeozems (European Soil Portal, 2012), luvisols, and vertisols (Instituto Nacional de Ecología y Cambio Climático, 2012) cover 29.4 % of Mexico's surface. In the rest of the country, the soils are divided into 20 edaphic groups (Secretaría de Medio Ambiente y Recursos Naturales, 2008). These factors together with climate change and more stringent environmental regulations have made seasonal farming almost unsustainable.

Other problems faced by farmers are poor transportation and their inability to obtain a fair final price for their products. With a product quality degrading over the time, they might end up with a poor return on their investment. Furthermore, there is a well-established network of intermediaries, which prevents small suppliers, or associated producers, from being able to make contact with large wholesalers. Even when producers have access to supply networks, in a rapidly changing market they need clear, well-structured information, such as how to locate the nearest distribution points, how to make a successful bid, the rules of negotiation, competitive pricing, and so on.

The incorporation of technological innovations could improve this productive activity. Two important trends are converging to meet this aim. The first is a set of methods based on the well-known Integrated Pest Management (IPM), and the other, the emergence of Automated Hydroponics Greenhouses (AHG). While IPM tackles the correct handling of pesticides to comply with environmental regulations, AHG are a solution to the problems of poor soil and seasonal farming. Therefore, it is possible to develop more useful AHG with the integration of IPM techniques and providing them with features such as cooperation and autonomy. Such AHG could then share information and knowledge in order to better manage crop production cycles and to reduce the risk of pests or diseases.

A Distributed Knowledge Management System (DKMS), having features such as cooperation, autonomy, and ease of use, is a useful tool for health supervision and production control in AHG. It can subsequently be integrated with a sourcing network and the forecasted production could then be managed in an electronic auction resulting in faster negotiations with transparency in a previously agreed trading structure. Such a DKMS can address a variety of regulations (production control, packaging, labeling), environmental concerns (IPM), and negotiations (Multiagent Trading System). In this supervisory intelligent network scenario, a high degree of collaboration and transparency promotes the solutions to such critical technical aspects.

In this paper, a multi-agent architecture for collaborative knowledge management in agricultural production is introduced. Since the diagnosis and control of diseases and pests, regulations, and environmental issues can be involved in the whole process, from the production control up to the marketing and distribution stages, the agricultural sustainability of this kind of specialized production can be determined later.

Our main objective is to describe and illustrate how our proposed DKMS architecture, based on some freely available JAVA tools (JAVA RULE, JADE, and a database engine), can overcome the problems referred to above. For the sake of clarity, the main issues addressed by our DKMS and the modules required to do so are as follows:

- Online information and data acquisition from the AHG about the current state of the production and IPM which could be provided by a system such as JAPIEST (López-Morales, López-Ortega, Ramos-Fernández, & Muñoz, 2008).
- Based on the information and data from the former module, a good estimation of the crop size and date of maturity can be scheduled in an electronic auction with some previously agreed negotiation, pricing, and transaction rules. To achieve this task, a Production Order System (Lopez-Ortega, Lopez-Morales, & Villar-Medina, 2008), with some heuristic-based capabilities to obtain a scheduled production orders, is necessary.
- High value farm products complying with regulations (internal and environmental), forecasted distribution points (transport logistics), and fair transaction rules should lead to a higher return on investment. This Environmental and Production Module (EPM) should be constantly interchanging information with the POS module to make necessary decisions to be implemented in the lifecycle of the product. These decisions will affect the logistics of labeling, packaging, quality control, distribution, and transportation which should be managed by a Product Lifecycle Management Module (e.g., @UDROS suite PLM).

To describe the conception and construction of our proposed architecture, the paper is organized as follows. In Sect. 4.2, we state the main methodology and context of the problem. Section 4.3 describes the architecture of the proposed system. Section 4.4 gives some insight into the implementation of the system. Finally, in Sect. 4.5 we state the conclusions and propose future work.

4.2 Multi-agent Systems and Network Marketing

In addition to the industrial standards and governmental legislations, the use of the right underlying information systems is another key enabler to implement successful marketing. As Reid and Plank (2004) state, the use of expert systems in business marketing could be fruitful and provide more guidance for managers, by suggesting the need for exploring the following research questions (p. 74):

- How can a firm incorporate field experimental segmentation research into their new product/service introductions?
- How should value be defined for purposes of segmenting business markets?
- How should relationships be defined for purposes of segmenting markets?
- How useful is the concept of switching costs for purposes of defining and segmenting markets?

However, the sparse scientific contributions in the areas of computer usage in business marketing, the development of management science models, and decision support systems have been of descriptive and normative work in the area of expert

Table 4.1 Classes used in RULE

Rule		
AboutDialog	FuzzyDefs	RuleFrame
BooleanRuleBase	FuzzyOperator	RuleVarDialog
BooleanRuleBaseVariablesDialog	FuzzyRule	RuleVariable
Clause	FuzzyRuleBase	Sensor
Condition	FuzzyRuleBaseVariablesDialog	SensorClause
ContinuousFuzzyRuleVariable	FuzzyRuleVariable	SholuderFuzzySet
Effector	FuzzySet	TrapezoidFuzzySet
EffectorClause	Rule	TriangleFuzzySet
Fact	RuleApp	Variable
FuzzyClause	RuleBase	WorkingFuzzySet

systems and work dealing with the use of information—how to get it and how to use it. For more details please refer to Turban (1988).

An expert system is a computer program that has a wide base of knowledge in a restricted domain; it uses complex inferential reasoning to perform tasks which a human expert could do. Basically it consists of three essential components: the knowledge base, the inference engine, and the user interface. The knowledge base has facts and heuristics (e.g., experiences, opinions, judgments, predictions, algorithms), needed to solve a specific problem. This knowledge is synthesized from the experts in the relevant domain and can be represented using a variety of representation techniques (e.g., semantic nets, frames, predicate logic), but the most commonly used technique is "If-Then" rules, also known as production rules. In this case, the expert system is coded in JAVA-RULE,[1] which provides two reasoning methods, forward and backward chaining. See "Annexure" (Table 4.1) for the classes' structure, the JAVA classes inheritance, and the 30 classes conforming RULE.

Multi-agent systems (MAS) evolved from methods which appeared in distributed artificial intelligence (Bond & Gasser, 1988) and contributions focusing on logic extensions to rational behavior to capture the expertise in narrow domains to create reusable and sharable knowledge repositories. A consequence of this work was to consider multiple cognitive entities acting in communities (Doyle & Dean, 1996), and with the evolution of network-based computing technology, the Internet, mobile computing, ubiquitous computing as well as novel, human-oriented software engineering methodologies, how the agent paradigm of computing might be developed (Luck, McBurney, Shehory, & Willmott, 2012; Monostori, Váncza, & Kumara, 2006). Since the globalization of project and manufacturing marketing, a system with central management capabilities, possessing the ability of central task decomposition/allocation, coordination, and monitoring, is paramount. This is the essence of a MAS framework which can facilitate the development of a collaborative platform with the ability to allocate resources and tasks efficiently. For more details refer to Bigus and Bigus (2001).

[1] Classes and inference engine are provided by Bigus and Bigus (2001).

In the context of a MAS, the addition of some capabilities to emulate intelligence in agents can be achieved via an Expert System or a Feed Forward Artificial Neural Network. For more details on expert systems' main features and a systematic methodology for their development, see Metaxiotis, Askounis, and Psarras (2005) who review the use of expert systems in the area of production planning and scheduling.

Rand and Rust (2011) opined that marketing phenomena are often complex because they are the result of many individual agents (e.g., consumers, sellers, distributors) whose motivations and actions combine so that even simple behavioral rules can result in surprising patterns issuing from multiple interactions. Moreover, these aggregate patterns feed back to affect individual choices. Agent-based modeling is a tool that can help researchers understand and analyze these complex patterns.

Based on soft computing techniques, such as MASs, fuzzy logic, approximate reasoning, and neural nets, many contributions address the synthesis of marketing models in order to react to the needs of markets, based on consumer lifestyles or behaviors (Kito, Fujita, Takenaka, & Ueda, 2008; Martínez-López & Casillas, 2009). Purvis and Long (2011) provide an interesting discussion on the use of multi-agent systems for business marketing practice.

In this chapter, we focus on the DKMS architecture and the main interactions among agents, therefore the methodologies of the synthesis of marketing models and consequently their negotiation rules and implemented strategies have not been addressed.

The system introduced here uses a MAS to provide a collaborative platform where each agent has a specific task to perform. The following section presents the architecture of DKMS which is based on the JAVA-JADE (Java Agent Development Environment) open source software platform and is compliant with Foundation for Intelligent Physical Agents (FIPA) specifications.

4.3 The Knowledge Management Architecture

In this section a knowledge management system using multi-agent architecture to enable the communication and cooperation among the agents is proposed. The architecture is composed of several agents. In Fig. 4.1 the conceptual model of the system architecture is described.

The MAS is connected to a database in PLM where the production orders information is stored. It is also connected to the databases in the EPM. These environmental and production knowledge databases are shared by the agents in each stage of the PLM process. Each agent has its own knowledge base which contains the knowledge related to environmental impacts and performance. In the following section, we describe this MAS.

Once the production orders are completed (scheduled) with all the information needed during the negotiation execution (i.e., agricultural product type, weight, forecasted or current production/materials, etc.), the information can be sent to the database and the P agent can drive it to the EPM module.

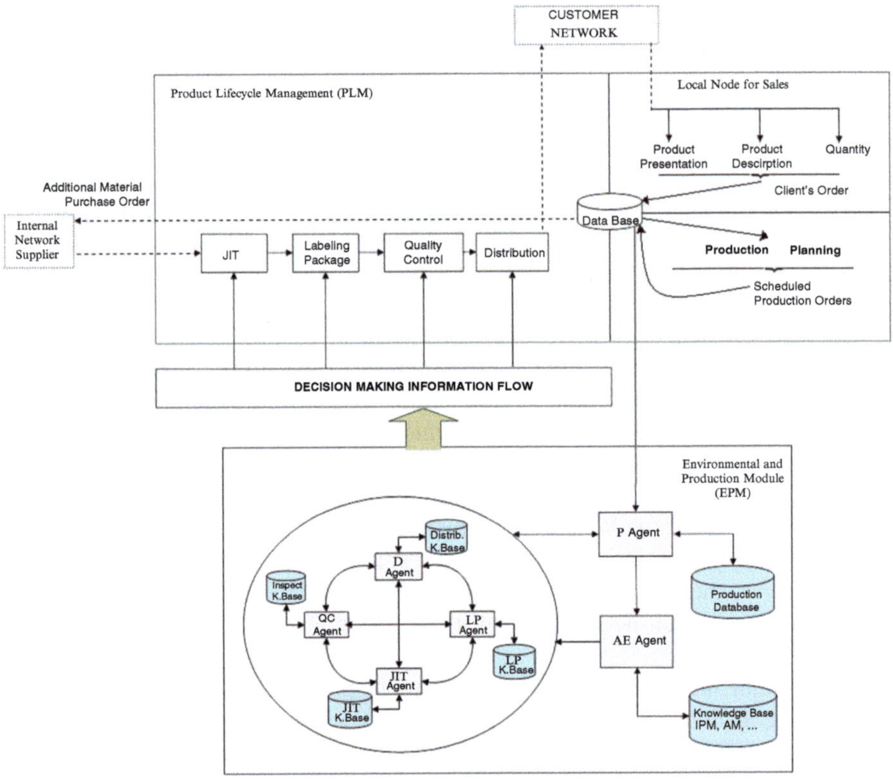

Fig. 4.1 Distributed knowledge management system architecture

In our case, all the systems' modules are coded in JAVA. For instance,

- The knowledge base for Expert Systems is coded in RULE. The rule base defines the set of possible combinations based on the requirements (Product order) from the user characterizing the future input to be presented to a classification algorithm.
- The classification algorithm helps to choose the right components by entering the combinations and taking the current solutions which can be used to comply with the requirements.
- The MAS coordinates and maintains data consistency along with the process (JADE, 2011).

4.3.1 The EPM Multi-agent System

The EPM multi-agent system here proposed includes six agents: JIT agent, LP agent, QC Agent, D agent, P agent, and AE Agent (see Fig. 4.1). Each agent is autonomous and works independently of the others. However, they communicate

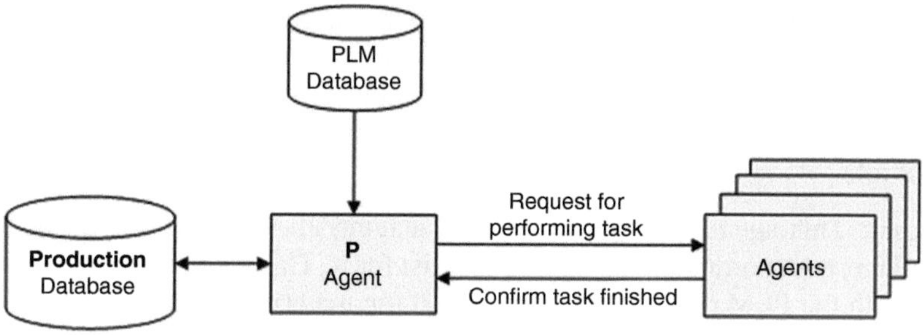

Fig. 4.2 The interaction between P Agent, the other Agents, and the PLM database

Fig. 4.3 The structure of the rule-based system of the AE agent

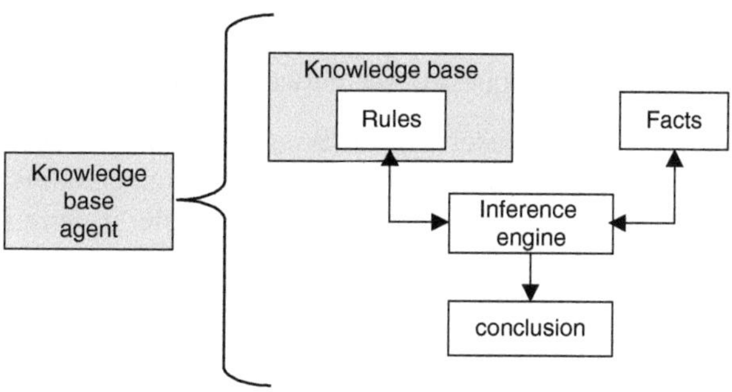

and interact to share knowledge and information through Agent Communication Language (ACL) which complies with the FIPA specifications (Foundation for Intelligent Physical Agents, 2012). ACL is a standard language that provides agents with a means of exchanging information and knowledge and it defines the types of messages. The role and the reasoning process of each agent are as follows:

P agent: This agent handles tasks concerning the interface with the PLM system. It receives requests from the involved agents and provides them with the requested information extracted from the Production technical database of the PLM module (see Fig. 4.2).

AE agent: It receives the request messages from the P agent. Its knowledge base contains facts and rules related to agricultural methods (AM), the environmental regulations (IPM), owner directives, etc. After running its inference engine, the AE agent sends information back directly to the agents who made the initial request through the P agent. Figure 4.3 shows the structure of rule-based system in AE agent.

The knowledge base of the AE agent contains the domain knowledge useful for problem solving. In our rule-based system, the knowledge is represented as condition action rules (i.e., If-Then). Each rule specifies a relation, a recommendation, or a solution. When the condition parts of a rule are satisfied, the rule is fired and the action part is executed. A set of facts matched against the IF (conditions) part of rules is stored in the knowledge base. The inference engine carries out the reasoning to reach a solution; it matches the facts with the rules given in the knowledge base. Other agents' knowledge bases use the same architecture (rule-base structure and inference engine), but the knowledge domains differ depending on each agent's role.

JIT agent: This agent is responsible for managing all the materials needed for a particular product order and having a checklist for it. This agent is in full communication with the PLM database to oversee that the materials are sent by the production order module for all steps. Its knowledge base contains information to manage all of the existing materials and materials sent by internal network suppliers. This agent will help the organization to reduce the use of resources, energy, and time by reusing materials and by sending early alerts about lack of materials. For instance, in the case of a lack of some components, it can update the PLM database to send a request to the network suppliers for new materials.

LP agent: After receiving a message from the JIT agent about the Product order, the LP agent searches its knowledge base which contains rules related to the particular problem sent by the JIT agent. For example, if there is a need for a new container, or there is lack of some material, then the request to fulfill these orders should be performed in an environmental friendly way; the producers of the containers should be informed that the use of organic solvents and toxic compounds should be avoided.

QC agent: It receives requests from the system to apply some Quality Control to the product characteristics. Naturally, this agent performs tasks with human help (QC Dept.) and, based on the results and on the parameters of the problem, it rechecks if there are similar problems in its knowledge base by using the Case-Bases Reasoning approach. Then the QC agent either allows the product to continue or proposes to the PLM system some rules and solutions to manage the product. Since the quality control process is of utmost importance to ensure the product's quality (whether to be re-managed or it is OK), to complete its task the QC agent needs supporting information from the LP agent and the JIT agent. The expertise of the different agents and the fact that they share their information and knowledge allow the system to find the proper decision for each Product order. If the QC agent, after analyzing the information, finds that the Fulfilled Product order needs to be refurbished, it can send all this information to be managed again by the JIT agent and the cycle restarts. When the Fulfilled Product Order is considered OK, it is communicated to the D Agent.

D agent: The Fulfilled Product Order proposed by the QC agent is sent with special instructions for Delivery to the D agent. This agent has a knowledge base which helps to schedule trucks for almost the same routes and also maximize the carriage capacity of the trucks. The routes can be carefully planned such that trucks can be dispatched to different suppliers to gather partial shipments so that the transportation costs are reduced among suppliers, intermediaries, and firms (Schneider & Leatherman, 1992).

4.3.2 Knowledge Representation and the Reasoning Process

Multi-agent systems have several collaborative subsystems which are autonomous and distributed. These subsystems cover areas from elaboration of a production order, scheduling of these production orders, integration of available products and materials, process planning, up to delivery and each possesses specific goals and functionalities. To achieve this superior autonomous state, it is necessary to construct the subsystems so that they behave as absolutely cooperative systems. This is the reason why agent-based systems are gaining importance in the creation of autonomous, intelligent applications aimed at improving the performance of such subsystems. For instance, Lopez-Morales and Lopez-Ortega (2005) presented a methodology to model a semantic network for a collaborative system, in order to support and to define an associate intelligent cooperative system. The same method is applied here to extract a basis of entities from the application domain, and then a family of sets is synthesized that forms a network of elementary and complex concepts linked in a decision tree. We use ontologies to formalize the knowledge of the product end-of-life. By defining each object and its relationship in the domain of recycling which related to environmental performance, this knowledge can be presented in the form of statements which can be converted to If-Then rules.

4.4 The MAS/KMS Implementation

Following previous work (cf. Miladi, Krichen, Jmaiel, & Drira, 2010), we used a Use Case Diagram to specify our agents and to define the tasks and behaviors of these agents as shown in Fig. 4.4. Functional requirements were modeled using use-cases during the analysis phase.

The class diagram helped to model the behaviors, attributes, and relations for product order in the negotiation process which begins from the P agent to the AE agent where the AE solution may come from the JIT and QC agents' knowledge base and the AE knowledge base.

Figure 4.5 illustrates the various activities of the D agent including the communication with the other agents. After the D agent receives the information needed, it analyzes the fulfilled product order. To find a solution to distribute a satisfactory product order (fulfilled product order), it sends the message requesting information to support other agents. Then it applies the facts of product information to rules and current regulations in the knowledge base. The agent D tries to find the appropriate solution by adding various components. In order to reduce the environmental impacts, some recycling and disposal rules are applied. Finally, the D agent sends a message to the P agent to confirm that the task has been completed.

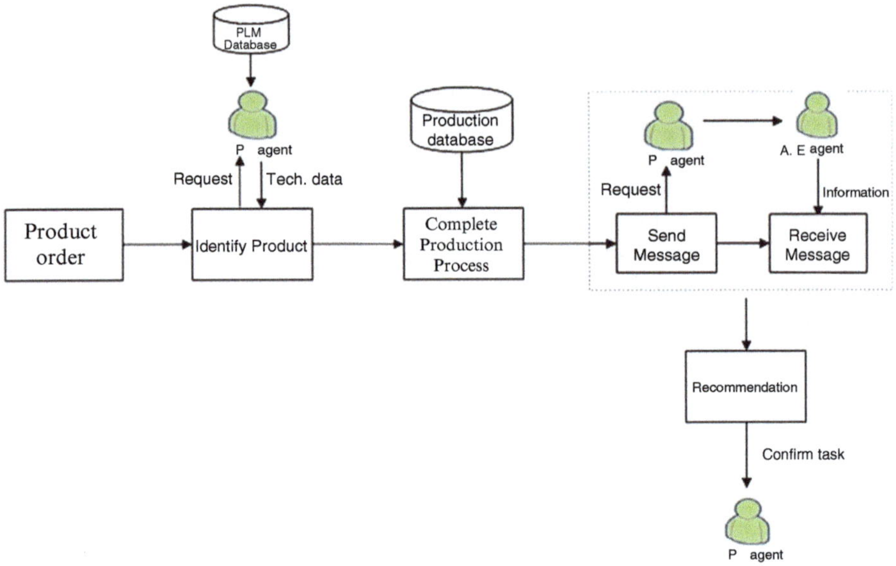

Fig. 4.4 Example of interactions between agents during the negotiation of the complete production process

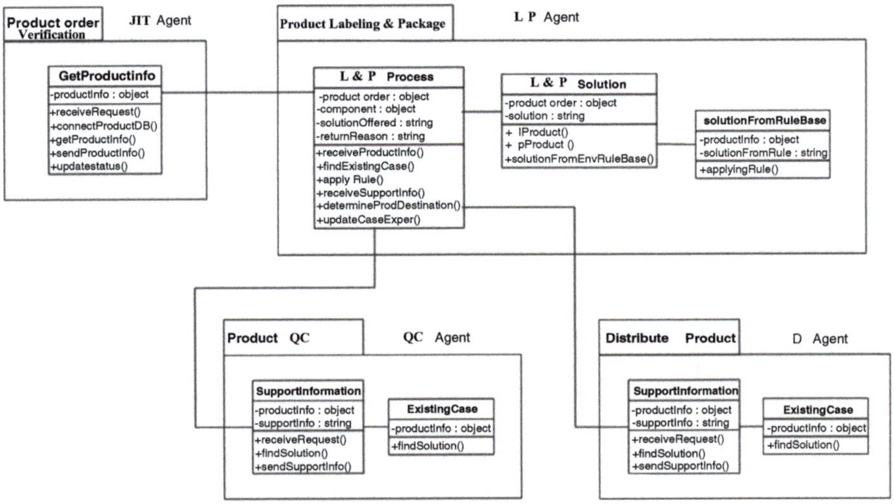

Fig. 4.5 UML class diagram: information sharing during the completion of the product order process

4.5 Conclusions and Future Work

For sustainable performance agricultural organizations need to improve their negotiation processes in terms of time, cost, and quality. In this paper, a Collaborative and Intelligent Knowledge Management System for agricultural products having a network of producers and customers, and based on multi-agent systems, has been proposed. The aim of this system is to obtain a fulfilled product order, and taking it through various steps culminating in an electronic negotiation with a high degree of collaboration and transparency.

Using the knowledge-based theory and the multi-agent system as a foundation, this study examines how particular IT tools could be used to help the producers and customers in the different phases of the product lifecycle and the complete logistic up to the distribution process.

In this first stage we have developed a complete system. The architecture proposed here is a first step towards the integration of a production network from the clients' orders up to the distribution process in order to comply with sustainable and more environmentally friendly products. Future works concern the implementation of this system to different real cases.

Annexure

Finally and in order to codify an expert system, the classes structure and the JAVA classes inheritance conforming RULE is shown.

```
class java.lang.Object
    ⇒ class rule.BooleanRuleBase
    ⇒ class rule.Clause
            ▸ class rule.EffectorClause
            ▸ class rule.SensorClause
    ⇒ class java.awt.Component
            ▸ class java.awt.Container
                    > class java.awt.Window
                            → class java.awt.Dialog
                                    › class javax.swing.JDialog
                                            • class rule.AboutDialog
                                            • class rule.BooleanRuleBaseVariablesDialog
                                            • class rule.FuzzyRuleBaseVariablesDialog
                                            • class rule.RuleVarDialog
                            → class java.awt.Frame
                                    › class javax.swing.JFrame
                                            • class rule.RuleFrame
    ⇒ class rule.Condition
    ⇒ class rule.Fact
    ⇒ class rule.FuzzyClause
    ⇒ class rule.FuzzyDefs
    ⇒ class rule.FuzzyOperator
    ⇒ class rule.FuzzyRule
    ⇒ class rule.FuzzyRuleBase
    ⇒ class rule.FuzzyRuleVariable
            ▸ class rule.ContinuousFuzzyRuleVariable
    ⇒ class rule.FuzzySet
            ▸ class rule.ShoulderFuzzySet
            ▸ class rule.TrapezoidFuzzySet
            ▸ class rule.TriangleFuzzySet
            ▸ class rule.WorkingFuzzySet
    ⇒ class rule.Rule
    ⇒ class rule.RuleApp
    ⇒ class rule.SensorEffectorTest
    ⇒ class rule.Variable
            ▸ class rule.RuleVariable
```

References

Bigus, J. P., & Bigus, J. (2001). *Constructing intelligent agents using Java* (2nd ed.). New York: Wiley.

Bond, A. H., & Gasser, L. (Eds.). (1988). *Readings in distributed artificial intelligence*. San Mateo, CA: Morgan-Kaufmann.

Doyle, J., & Dean, T. (1996). Strategic directions in artificial intelligence. *ACM Computing Surveys, 28*(4), 653–670.

European Soil Portal. (2012). *Phaeozems*. Retrieved from http://eusoils.jrc.ec.europa.eu/awareness/Documents/calendar2012/April2012.pdf

Foundation for Intelligent Physical Agents. (2012). *FIPA ACL message structure specification.* Retrieved from http://www.fipa.org/specs/fipa00061/SC00061G.pdf

Instituto Nacional de Ecología y Cambio Climático. (2012). *Contexto nacional.* Retrieved from http://www2.ine.gob.mx/publicaciones/libros/615/contexto.pdf

Java Agent Development Environment. (2011). *Java Agent Development framework.* Retrieved July 2013, from http://jade.tilab.com/

Kito, T., Fujita, K., Takenaka, T., & Ueda, K. (2008). Multi-agent market modeling based on analysis of consumer lifestyles. In M. Mitsuishi, K. Ueda, & F. Kimura (Eds.), *Manufacturing systems and technologies for the new frontier: The 41st CIRP conference on manufacturing systems May 26–28, 2008, Tokyo, Japan* (pp. 507–510). London: Springer.

Lopez-Morales, V., & Lopez-Ortega, O. (2005). A distributed semantic network model for a collaborative intelligent system. *International Journal of Intelligent Manufacturing, 16*, 515–525.

López-Morales, V., López-Ortega, O., Ramos-Fernández, J., & Muñoz, L. B. (2008). JAPIEST: An integral intelligent system for the diagnosis and control of tomatoes diseases and pests in hydroponic greenhouses. *Expert Systems with Applications, 35*, 1506–1512.

Lopez-Ortega, O., Lopez-Morales, V., & Villar-Medina, I. (2008). Intelligent and collaborative multi-agent system to generate and schedule production orders. *Journal of Intelligent Manufacturing, 19*, 677–687. doi:10.1007/s10845-008-0119-z.

Luck, M., McBurney, P., Shehory, O., & Willmott, S. (2012). *Agent technology: Computing as interaction: A roadmap for agent-based computing.* Retrieved from http://www.agentlink.org/roadmap/al3rm.pdf

Martínez-López, F. J., & Casillas, J. (2009). Marketing intelligent systems for consumer behaviour modelling by a descriptive induction approach based on genetic fuzzy systems. *Industrial Marketing Management, 38*, 714–731.

Metaxiotis, K., Askounis, D., & Psarras, J. (2005). Expert systems technology in production planning and scheduling. *Intelligent Knowledge-Based Systems, 3*(2), 797–817.

Miladi, M. N., Krichen, F., Jmaiel, M., & Drira, K. (2010). A UML based deployment and management modeling for cooperative and distributed applications. In R. Lee, O. Omandjieva, A. Abran, & C. Constantinides (Eds.), *Software engineering research management and applications* (pp. 87–101). Berlin: Springer. doi: 10.1007/978-3-642-13273-5_6.

Monostori, L., Váncza, J., & Kumara, S. R. T. (2006). Agent-based systems for manufacturing. *Annals of the CIRP, 55*(2), 697–720.

Purvis, M. K., & Long, A. L. S. (2011). Affinities between multi-agent systems and service-dominant logic: Interactionist implications for business marketing practice. *Industrial Marketing Management, 40*(2), 248–254.

Rand, W. M., & Rust, R. T. (2011). Agent-based modeling in marketing: Guidelines for rigor. *International Journal of Research in Marketing, 28*(3), 181–193.

Reid, D., & Plank, R. (2004). *Fundamentals of business marketing research.* Binghamton, NY: Haworth Press.

Schneider, J. D., & Leatherman, M. A. (1992). Integrated just-in-time: A total business approach. *Production and Inventory Management Journal, 33*(1), 78–82.

Secretaría de Medio Ambiente y Recursos Naturales. (2008). [Report of the state of the environment in Mexico. Compendium of Environment Statistics in Spanish]. Mexico, D.F.: Author.

Servicio Meteorológico Nacional. (2012). *Monitor de sequía para Norteamérica, 2012.* Retrieved from http://smn.conagua.gob.mx/index.php?option=com_content&view=article&id=236:monitor-dde-sequia&catid=1:general&Itemid=23

Turban, E. (1988). Review of expert systems technology. *IEEE Transactions on Engineering Management, 35*, 71–81.

Chapter 5
Progressive Usage of Business and Spatial Intelligence for Decision Support in the Delivery of Educational Services in Developing Countries

Patricia E. Nalwoga Lutu

Abstract Managers and administrators in public sector organisations have the responsibility to make various decisions concerning service delivery to the citizens of the country. The provision of education to the children of the country is one fundamental type of service. Decision makers often work within many constraints, some of which are budgetary, political, geographical, and lack of relevant and timely information to support decision making. A well-educated population is a necessity for the economic development and well-being of a population. The provision of effective educational services is therefore crucial for every economy. The purpose of this chapter is to provide a discussion of knowledge discovery technologies and systems that can be implemented to support the gathering, storage, and analysis of data for purposes of supporting decision-making activities in the public sector in general and the public education sector in particular. The technologies discussed are business intelligence (BI), geographical information systems (GIS), and free/libre/open source software. It is argued in this chapter that the combination of these technologies can and should provide operationally effective and cost-effective solutions to the problem of gathering, storage, and analysis of data to support decision makers' information needs. A case study of an education department which makes use of BI and GIS technologies in their management activities is provided as an example of effective usage of BI and GIS technologies for decision support.

Keywords Business intelligence • Spatial intelligence • Geographic information system, GIS • Open source software • FLOSS • Decision support • Service delivery • Educational services • Developing countries

---

P.E.N. Lutu (✉)
Department of Computer Science, University of Pretoria, Pretoria, South Africa
e-mail: Patricia.Lutu@up.ac.za

K.-M. Osei-Bryson et al. (eds.), *Knowledge Management for Development*, Integrated Series in Information Systems 35, DOI 10.1007/978-1-4899-7392-4_5,

5.1 Introduction

One of the primary responsibilities of managers and administrators in public sector organisations is to make various decisions concerning service delivery to the citizens of the country. One fundamental type of service is the provision of education to the children of the country. It is often the case that the decision makers work within many constraints, some of which are budgetary, political, geographical, and the lack of relevant and timely information to support decision making (Information Builders, 2005; Present, 2005). Budgetary constraints are concerned with having limited funds to spend on service provision as well as appropriate information systems that can be used to gather, store, and analyse data for purposes of decision support. Political constraints involve the fact that these decision makers are (or should be) accountable to the public and to higher level decision makers. Geographical constraints are concerned with the fact that if the required infrastructure (e.g. roads, bridges) is not in place in some parts of the country, the services in questions (i.e. schools) cannot be provided in a conventional manner using clearly identifiable physical school structures (Information Builders, 2005; Present, 2005).

It goes without saying that a well-educated population is necessary for the economic development and well-being of a population. The provision of effective educational services is therefore crucial for every economy. The purpose of this chapter is to provide a discussion of knowledge discovery technologies and systems that can be implemented to support the gathering, storage, and analysis of data for purposes of supporting decision-making activities in the public sector in general and the public education sector in particular. The technologies discussed are business intelligence (Gartner, 2013; Ponniah, 2001; Posthumus, 2008; Turban, Sharda, & Delen, 2011), geographical information systems (Environmental Systems Research Institute [ESRI], 2006), and free/libre/open source software (Free Software Foundation, 2013). It is argued in this chapter that the combination of these technologies can and should provide operationally effective and cost-effective solutions to the problem of gathering, storage, and analysis of data to support decision makers' information needs. A case study of an education department which makes use of business intelligence (BI) and geographic information system (GIS) technologies in their management activities is also provided (Information Builders, 2005; Present, 2005).

The rest of the chapter is organised as follows: Sect. 5.2 provides a discussion of the types of data and analysis required to answer the types of questions with which provincial and district managers in the public school sector are commonly faced. Section 5.3 provides a discussion of BI technology in terms of the utility of BI, the database technologies that support BI, the types of analysis used for BI, and the common challenges for BI implementations. Section 5.4 discusses GIS and spatial analysis. The databases used for GIS, types of data analysis for GIS, and challenges for GIS implementation are discussed. Strategies for combining BI and GIS technology are presented in Sect. 5.5. The approaches to combining spatial and traditional online analytical processing (OLAP) analysis, BI architectures and GIS integration, and challenges in BI and GIS integration are discussed. Free/libre open source software (FLOSS) for spatial databases and GIS are discussed in Sect. 5.6. The case study for BI and GI adoption and usage by the education department of a South African provincial government is presented in Sects. 5.7–5.9, respectively, and provide a discussion and conclusions for the chapter.

5.2 Decision Making for Public School Education Management and Administration

Decision makers in the public school education sector are faced with many questions which require different types of information to answer. Three typical questions are discussed in this section in order to provide background for the discussion in the sections that follow. These questions have been proposed by Present (2005), but are by no means exhaustive. One fundamental question that managers need to answer is: How should teaching posts be allocated for each public school? In order for decision makers to answer this question, information about student numbers, type of school (pre-school, primary, secondary, high school), current staff-to-student ratios, etc. for each school must be available.

The second question that needs to be answered is: How much funding should be allocated to each school for the development of school infrastructure, e.g. new classrooms, sports facilities? In order to answer this question, information on the expected increase in the numbers of school-going children in the feeder areas and whether there is space (land) available for the infrastructure expansion for each school must be available The third question is: Which schools require special intervention, e.g. due to high drop-out rates, high failure rates at the school exit level, and what are the reasons for this? In order to answer this question, information should be available on the drop-out and failure statistics as well as the nature of the feeder areas for the schools.

The example questions discussed above indicate that typically, a wide variety of information is required to support the decision-making activities and enable managers and administrators to acquire knowledge of the service delivery domain within which they work. It has been said that knowledge is power. So, an empowered manager or administrator is in a much better position to make decisions that have a positive impact on the population of a country. All three questions point to the need for the school administrators (school principals) to be able to supply data to the district/government administrators in a timely manner. The second and third questions point to the fact that geographic, demographic, and economic (e.g. income levels) data need to be made available to decision makers and need to be easily relatable to the schools about which decisions must be made. In order for this to happen, appropriate technologies need to be combined/integrated into information systems for gathering, storing, and analysing numeric, textual, and geospatial data to provide actionable information to decision makers (Present, 2005).

5.3 Traditional Approach to Business Intelligence

Business intelligence (BI) is commonly used by business and public sector organisations to support decision making. This section provides a discussion of BI technology in terms of the utility of BI, the database technologies that support it, the types of analysis used for it, and the common challenges faced in its implementation.

5.3.1 What Is Business Intelligence?

Business intelligence may be defined as a collection of technologies and applications that enable business organisations to collect, integrate, and analyse data about business operations in order to obtain information that is useful for decision making (Gartner, 2013; Ponniah, 2001; Posthumus, 2008; Turban et al., 2011). Data warehousing technology, OLAP analysis, statistical tools for data mining, and timely information delivery via web technology form the core of BI (Hobbs, Hillson, Lawande, & Smith, 2005; Inmon, Imhoff, & Sousa, 2001; Kimball, Ross, Thornwaite, Mundy, & Becker, 2008; Ponniah, 2001; Turban et al., 2011). BI enables businesses to turn data into information and then knowledge. The knowledge may be about business performance, customer behaviour, the competition, conditions in the industry, and general economic, technological, and cultural trends. Golferelli, Rizzi, and Cella (2004) have pointed out that since the mid 1990s businesses have come to understand the importance of enforcing the achievement of business goals, as defined by the business strategy, through metrics-driven management. Managers are therefore required to ensure that all business processes are effective by continually measuring their performance through key performance indicators (KPIs) and balanced score cards (Kaplan & Norton, 1992).

In the public sector, many organisations have come to realise the benefits of BI and metrics-driven management. Examples of the benefits have been seen in healthcare (Cognos, 2007), education (Information Builders, 2005; Present, 2005), and social services for housing (Cognos, 2003). Managers in public sector organisations need to monitor the organisation's activities and formulate strategies that will result in the best service delivery possible for the target sector of the population. In developing countries in particular, such organisations work within many constraints including budgetary and geographical constraints.

5.3.2 Databases That Support Business Intelligence

Modern (business) organisations use operational database systems to support the recording and processing of business transactions as they occur. Operational database systems are also known as transactional database systems or online transaction processing (OLTP) systems. The design and implementation of operational databases are optimised to support fast insert, delete, and update operations. To this end, the relational database consisting of normalised relations (tables) is commonly used. Business intelligence based on database queries is most effectively supported using OLAP analysis. Fast OLAP analysis requires de-normalised tables that store data for the business (organisational) dimensions which form the basis for the analysis of business (organisational) performance. Additionally, business intelligence requires integrated data from various operational systems used by the organisation. For this reason, operational data is typically extracted from the operational databases, loaded into a data warehouse, and then prepared for OLAP and other types of analysis (Connolly & Begg, 2010; Ponniah, 2001).

Traditionally, a data warehouse forms the basis for data analysis which provides business intelligence. A data warehouse has been defined as a subject-oriented, integrated, non-volatile, and time-variant collection of data in support of management decisions (Inmon et al., 2001). There are two approaches to data warehousing. The first approach is the Inmon approach (Inmon et al., 2001). This approach prescribes that through extraction transformation and loading (ETL) data is extracted from operational systems into a staging area where all necessary transformations are done, and then loaded into an enterprise data warehouse (EDW) (Inmon et al., 2001). From the EDW data, business subject-specific data marts are then created to support the data analysis needs of various business users. The second approach is the Kimball approach (Kimball et al., 2008). For this approach, the informational needs of the business are identified and recorded first, including a specification of the (conformed) dimension tables to be used by all data marts in the organisation. Data marts are then created one by one for each business subject as the need arises. Again the ETL process is used to load data into the data marts. The collection of all the data marts is then called the data warehouse.

While the EDW has a relational database structure representing entities and relationships, the data marts are multi-dimensional databases. The star schema is commonly used to design and implement a data mart. It consists of dimension tables and a fact table linked by foreign keys. The fact table stores numeric values that reflect organisational performance and are related to the KPIs discussed in Sect. 5.2. The dimension tables contain descriptive data (for the facts) which are used in OLAP analysis. The attributes in a dimension table are typically organised into levels that form a hierarchy. When used in the SQL queries for OLAP, the highest level in the hierarchy provides the highest level of summarisation of fact table data, while the lowest level in the hierarchy provides the highest level of detail (i.e. no summarisation) for the dimension.

5.3.3 *Data Analysis and Reporting for Business Intelligence*

The two types of analysis for the traditional data warehouse are OLAP analysis and data mining. OLAP analysis involves the summarisation of data values stored in the fact table of a data mart, based on the dimensions represented in the dimension tables. For the provincial school management and administration domain discussed in Sect. 5.2, some possible dimensions might be SCHOOL, CLASS, TEACHER, SUBJECT, and TIME. One dimension table would be used to store the data for a dimension. The TIME dimension is always present in a data mart. One possible management subject would be academic performance and a performance key indicator could be the pass rates for each year. A fact table for this subject could be called PERFORMANCE with each record storing the following facts: *number-of student-enrolled*, *number-who-dropped-out*, *number-who-passed*, for each class, school, subject, teacher, and year. A provincial administrator/manager could conduct analysis by district, school, subject, and year to view the academic performance at different levels of detail, e.g., pass rate for all schools, pass rate per school, pass rate for all schools for each subject, and pass rate for each school for each subject.

OLAP supports this type of dimensional analysis by providing an easy way of performing roll-up and drill-down operations based on the hierarchies defined for each dimension. BI tools, for example, Oracle Discoverer (Hobbs et al., 2005) and WebFOCUS (Information Builders, 2004), make it easy for analysts to create web-based reports with parameterised SQL queries for OLAP analysis. Users can use data entry controls to specify values for the SQL queries and click different links on a web page to execute SQL queries that provide the results for drill-down and roll-up operations. More sophisticated BI reporting tools such as digital dashboards and score cards are also available to business managers. A digital dashboard provides a comprehensive graphic view of KPIs, trends, and exceptions. Information is integrated for multiple business areas in order to present an at-a-glance view of business performance (Turban et al., 2011). Scorecards, on the other hand, are used by organisations to align business activities to the vision and strategy of the organisation, improve internal and external communications, and monitor organisation performance against strategic goals (Turban et al., 2011).

5.3.4 Challenges in Business Intelligence System Implementation

Two major problems in data warehouse implementation are poor quality of data in operational (transactional) systems and incompatibility of data formats in different systems. These result in the need to invest large amounts of resources (time and effort) on the ETL process, leading to projects that go way beyond budget. A third problem arises from the fact that in most organisations, business units tend to work in silos, which makes it very difficult to obtain operational data for integration in the data warehouse (Connolly & Begg, 2010; Ponniah, 2001). It should be noted that in recent years, service-oriented architecture (SOA) has begun to supplant or augment data warehousing and BI implementations (ESRI, 2007; Wu, Barash, & Bartolini, 2007). One advantage of this is that reporting and decision making are based on a 'single version of the truth'.

5.4 Geographical Information Systems and Spatial Analysis

Geographical information systems (GIS) have traditionally been used for conducting analysis in specialist domains by highly skilled personnel. More recently, GIS has become more accessible to business organisations who strive to use this technology to enhance BI data analysis. This section discusses GIS and spatial analysis. The databases used for GIS, types of data analysis for GIS, and challenges for GIS implementation are presented.

5.4.1 Geographical Information Systems

GIS is a mature technology that originated in university computer science departments in the 1960s (ESRI, 2006). A GIS is an application that supports operations that are needed for the collection, editing, updating, and analysis of spatial data. Spatial data, also known as geospatial data, is data that can be manipulated and analysed based on a spatial representation of locations on or near the earth's surface (Yeung & Hall, 2007, p. 94). The spatial representation is typically provided in the form of sets of coordinate pairs that allow the positions and shapes of spatial features to be measured and represented graphically. Examples of spatial features are physical features such as roads, rivers, forests, and conceptual features such as political boundaries and service areas (ESRI, 2006). Spatial data is referenced to a geographic space. A geographic space is an accepted geographic coordinate system covering some area of the Earth's surface. A variety of geographic scales are available for a geographic space (Yeung & Hall, 2007).

5.4.2 Databases That Support Spatial Analysis for GIS

According to Yeung and Hall (2007), government and commercial organisations have been actively distributing spatial data since the mid 1990s. The data has been distributed via the Internet through spatial data depots, digital geolibraries, and spatial data warehouses. This has made geospatial data easily available to organisations and individuals and has resulted in increased interest in browsing of this data and incorporation of this data into the data analysis activities of many organisations. The spatial database has played a major role in making spatial data easily accessible for spatial analysis. Guting (1994) (cited in Yeung & Hall, 2007, p. 109) has defined a spatial database system as a database system that offers spatial data types in its data model and query language. The spatial database system also provides database management functions including spatial indexing and efficient algorithms for spatial join operations. This definition points to the fact that a spatial database system can provide all standard relational database functionality, that is, storage and processing of numeric and textual data, indexing, transaction management, and at the same time can store and process geographically referenced data.

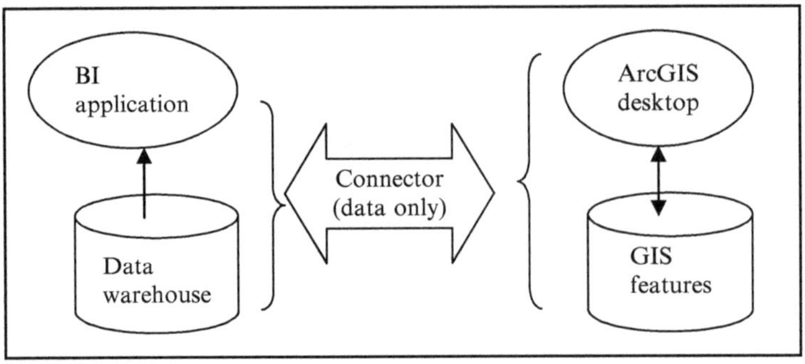

Fig. 5.1 Three-layer architecture for GIS technology

A GIS can be built as a front-end to a spatial database system, so that the GIS accesses spatial data through the spatial database in order to perform the required spatial analysis. An object-relational database management system (ORDBMS) provides the platform to support the spatial database. When the spatial database uses the ORDBMS as the underlying DBMS engine, spatial data is queried using the SQL language. The relationship between the GIS, spatial database system, and object-relational database system is depicted in Fig. 5.1 in the Appendix. Currently, all major database vendors (e.g. Oracle, IBM, Microsoft) offer spatial data processing capabilities in their products. A typical spatial database system today is an ordinary commercial database with additional capabilities and functions that include spatial data types, spatial operators, spatial indexing, and spatial data management functionality which includes data loading and transaction control.

In the spatial database and GIS environment, data is commonly grouped according to the function it serves in spatial analysis. Four typical layers are: (1) base map layers, (2) framework data layers, (3) application layers, and (4) business solutions layers. The base map data layers provide the geodetic (survey) control network and topographic base data. The framework data layers are three-related layers for the geographical referencing of human activity on land. The facilities layer forms the basis for facilities management in public utilities and resource management. The application data layers are comprised of various spatial datasets collected for different database applications in land and resource management. The business solutions layers consist of collections of spatial data layers including framework and application data layers plus related spatial and non-spatial data. The data is assembled to support operations and decision-making functions of the business units in an organisation (Yeung & Hall, 2007). A detailed discussion of these layers is provided in the appendix and the grouping for the layers is depicted in Fig. 5.2 of the appendix. The spatial data for the base map data layers, framework data layers, and application data layers can be purchased or obtained freely from public and private sector organisations. The spatial data for the business solutions layers needs to be generated specifically for the organisation based on the required spatial analysis of the organisation's activities.

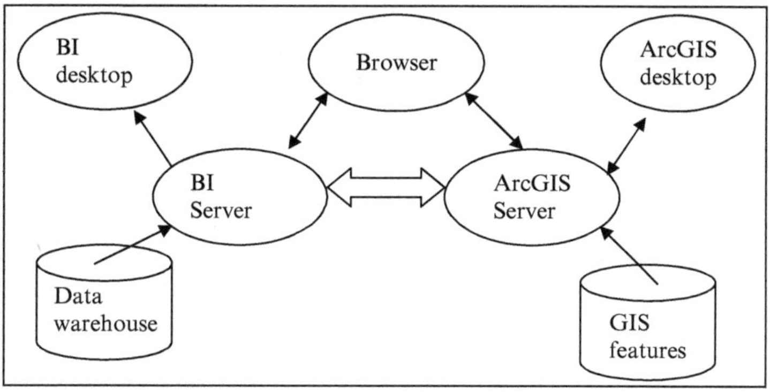

Fig. 5.2 Classification of spatial data as layers. *Source*: Yeung and Hall (2007)

5.4.3 *Types of GIS Analysis*

Traditionally, GIS applications have been used in the business and public sectors by professionals with expertise in these systems. Examples of applications in the public sector include land and resource management, environmental monitoring, facilities and utilities management, and public and community safety (ESRI, 2006; Yeung & Hall, 2007). ESRI (2006) has noted that GIS has also been used for a long time for predictive analytics. For example, urban planners have been using GIS for decades to predict population growth and migration patterns in order to plan infrastructure projects. Examples of GIS applications in the business sector include transportation and logistics, and network planning. Banks, for example, use the spatial analysis information provided by GIS to conduct network planning optimisation for the placement of new branches and auto-teller machines (ATMs) (Posthumus, 2008).

5.4.4 *Challenges in GIS*

As stated above, GIS applications have traditionally been used in the business and public sectors by professionals with expertise in these systems. Four main reasons for the exclusive usage of GIS by professionals have been (1) the perceived high cost of GIS technology, (2) the complexity of GIS and shortage of individuals with skills in GIS usage, (3) the lack of spatial data and data standards, and (4) the lack of system interoperability (ESRI, 2006). In the past, several issues concerning GIS data created obstacles to wider adoption of GIS in business and public sector organisations. GIS data providers and GIS application providers (e.g. ESRI) have traditionally provided packages of data tailored to the users needs. However, the users would need an understanding of GIS in order to load the data into the GIS. Secondly, the cost of purchased data could be prohibitive, especially when large geographic areas are to be analysed at a detailed level. Thirdly, high-resolution image data for large areas requires a very large amount of storage capacity (ESRI, 2006).

To address the issue of high data costs, many organisations now provide free geospatial data via the Internet. Examples of organisations that provide free geospatial data in South Africa are Free GIS (FREE, 2013) and Planet GIS (Planet, 2013). Both organisations provide spatial data for many different map layers for African countries including base map layers, road networks layers, districts, and municipality boundaries layers. Another recent development in affordable GIS data provision comes from the GIS providers. Currently, GIS providers (e.g. ESRI) provide GIS-ready data either free or as a service on the web (e.g. ArcWeb Services) on a subscription basis. Available data includes data that is commonly used for BI applications, such as demographics, streets, and aerial images (ESRI, 2006).

5.5 Combining BI and GIS Applications

Sections 5.4 and 5.5 have presented the BI and GIS applications and have highlighted the types of data analysis that can be conducted using these applications. The benefits of combining these technologies and the combination strategies are presented in this section. The challenges that arise when these technologies are combined are also discussed.

5.5.1 Why Is It Useful to Combine BI and GIS Applications?

It was pointed out in Sect. 5.4.2 that, due to the ease of access to geospatial data and the emergence of standards to govern geospatial data, many organisations are beginning to incorporate this data into their internal databases for the purpose of supporting day-to-day business operations and for generating information for decision support. Posthumus (2008) has discussed various types of South African business organisations that have adopted GIS in recent years. These include financial services and insurance companies. The motivation for adopting GIS has been to better understand the complex and dynamic business environment which is typical of developing countries. Some of the dynamics that take place in developing countries are: changing political and economic landscapes, changing incomes and lifestyles in the population, and urban migration. ESRI (2006) and Posthumus (2008) have noted that even though geographic location data is a crucial component in organisational activities, traditional BI systems do not incorporate the location element in data analysis activities. GIS can process the location component of data with the geographic features maintained in the GIS. Information Builders (2005), ESRI (2006), and Posthumus (2008) have highlighted the fact that new versions of BI systems now provide compatibility with GIS technology, such as ESRI's ArcGIS. This enables the traditional BI system to make use of spatial analysis via GIS tools.

When traditional numeric and textual database data are associated with spatial features, BI users are able to organise the data based on the geographic location of each record in the database (ESRI, 2006). This type of association has many advantages. The main advantage is that the internal organisational environment for which BI was originally designed can be directly related to the external environment for which GIS was designed. While OLAP analysis for BI answers 'what', 'who', and 'when' types of questions, spatial analysis provides answers to 'where' types of questions in graphic form. When database data is organised geographically and presented on a map, it becomes much easier to answer all the above types of question (what, who, when, where). Secondly, when numeric and textual data are organised and displayed on a map, it becomes easier to deduce spatial relationships and influences on organisational activities. A second advantage, according to Posthumus (2008), is that when divisions within an organisation work in silos, each with different databases and data marts, the GIS can provide a common point of reference for relating the information in the BI reports obtained from the silo databases and data marts.

5.5.2 *Approaches to Combining Spatial Data and Traditional Data in Spatial Analysis*

Yeung and Hall (2007) have discussed advances in spatial data warehousing technology. They have observed that many applications of spatial data analysis have motivated the need for spatial data warehouses. These include healthcare planning, crime analysis, and homeland security. Yeung and Hall (2007) have observed that such applications require the use of data from multiple disparate sources, resulting in the need for data warehouses where data is integrated. Spatial data warehouses are designed for such applications to support data sharing between organisations. Spatial data marts are created to support OLAP analysis and decision making. The most basic spatial data mart consists of the traditional BI dimension tables such as time and customer or service recipient, as well as a geography dimension with spatial data (Yeung & Hall, 2007).

5.5.3 *Architectures for Integration*

In recent years, standards for system interoperability have emerged in the IT sector. BI providers (e.g. SAS, Fijutsu, Cognos) have created connectors for common file formats used in organisations. GIS providers (e.g. ESRI) have created connections and transformations for geographic/spatial feature formats used worldwide, as well as standards for interoperability of GIS data. The ArcGIS family of products (ESRI, 2006) enjoys widespread usage in business and public sector organisations. ESRI (2006) has discussed two approaches to the integration of GIS with BI technologies. The first option is called desktop integration which is depicted in Fig. 5.3.

Desktop integration involves the use of a desktop GIS application (e.g. ArcView) which accesses spatial features from a GIS features database. Access to the data warehouse data is done through a special connector application. The GIS application combines the GIS features and data warehouse data for analysis and writes the

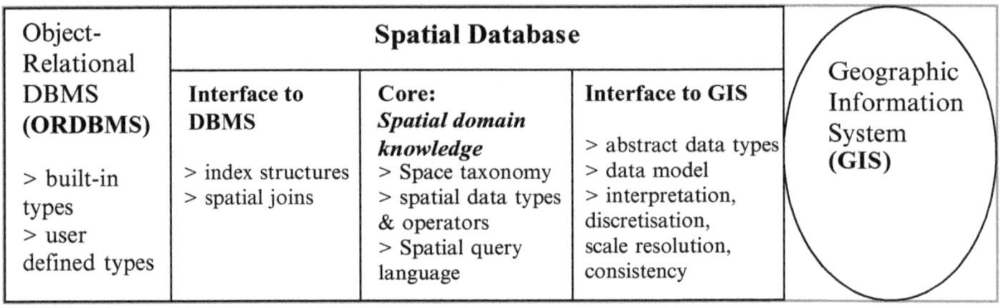

Fig. 5.3 BI and GIS desktop integration. *Source*: ESRI (2006)

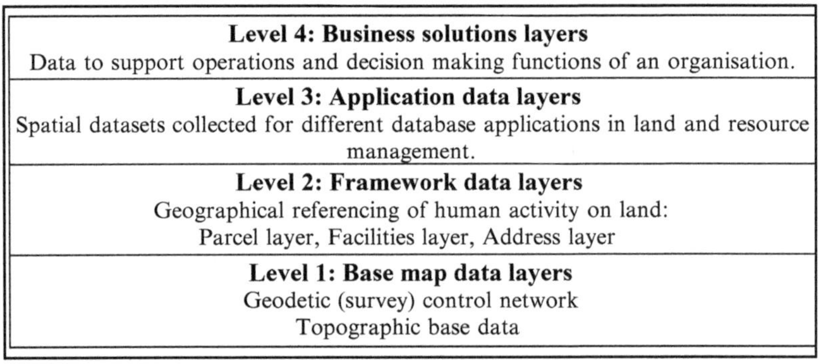

Fig. 5.4 BI and GIS server integration. *Source*: ESRI (2006)

analysis results back into the BI environment where BI tools can incorporate the results into BI reports. One advantage of this approach is its simplicity which makes it easy for proof of concept projects. The disadvantage is that no actual maps are created in the BI environment. The maps for presenting the analysis results are created in the GIS environment. The second option for BI and GIS integration is called server integration. Server integration supports a centralised approach to GIS management. Server integration provides a bi-directional interaction between GIS and BI data and enables users/analysts to utilise the BI reporting environment to distribute GIS-generated maps (ESRI 2006). ESRI (2006) has discussed three different architectures for the implementation of this option. One of these architectures is shown in Fig. 5.4.

5.5.4 Challenges for Ordinary Users When BI and GIS Are Integrated

GIS provides many types of sophisticated analyses (e.g. predictive analytics) which require high levels of expertise acquired through technical training on the GIS product (ESRI, 2006). This complexity creates limitations on who can conduct sophisticated analysis using GIS. To overcome this limitation, GIS providers (e.g. ESRI) and BI providers can work closely with users to define a set of persistent analytic requirements that can be initiated with very little effort from the user. In other words, the end-user runs a pre-configured model that does the heavy business and geographic analytics on the BI and GIS servers and returns the analysis results to the user in the form of a web report.

5.6 Open Source Software for Spatial Databases and GIS

Spatial databases and GIS applications were presented in Sects. 5.4 and 5.5. Practical examples of GIS usage were given for proprietary software such as ESRI's ArcGIS. Typically, proprietary software licences are not cheap, especially for highly specialised applications such as GIS. The open source software licence provides a low cost option for organisations. Open source software for spatial databases and GIS are discussed in this section.

5.6.1 Open Source Software

Free/open source software (FOSS), also known as free/libre/open source software (FLOSS), is software that is licensed to grant users the right to use, copy, study, change, and improve its design through the availability of its source code. 'Free' refers to the freedom to copy and re-use the software, rather than to the price of the software (Free Software Foundation, 2013). FLOSS development relies on the peer-to-peer development model. The FLOSS licence specifies four levels of freedom. Freedom-0 is the freedom to run the program for any purpose. Freedom-1 is the freedom to study how the program works and change it to make it do what you wish. Freedom-2 is the freedom to re-distribute copies so that you can help your neighbour. Freedom-3 is the freedom to distribute copies of your modified versions (including source code) to others. By doing this, the developer gives the whole community the chance to benefit from the changes. Well-known FLOSS projects include Apache web server, GNU Linux, FreeBSD, MySQL, OpenOffice.org, and Mozilla.

FLOSS offers a number of benefits for organisations. These include reduced software costs, vendor independence, open standards, and the ability to customise software based on the organisational requirements. For developing countries specifically, FLOSS supports local skills development, localisation and customisation, and participation in global projects. FLOSS also eliminates the high costs of dollar-based software licences, since FLOSS licences are much cheaper and are not specific to a machine (freedom-0). There are a number of recognised challenges associated with FLOSS usage. One is the fact that skills are scarce and therefore

Table 5.1 Strengths of PostreSQL

Functionality	Description
Transaction management	Proven reliability and transactional integrity by default (ACID)
Support for SQL	Full support for SQL92 standard
Extensible	Pluggable type extension and function extension
	Easy to add custom functions
Support for large data objects	No limit on column sizes. This enables storage of big GIS objects

more expensive. A second challenge is that there is no accountability or possible recourse to legal claims should there be a major problem with the software. A third challenge is the lack of a 24/7 help-desk. These challenges indicate that an organisation must weigh the pros and cons of FLOSS before deciding to adopt it.

5.6.2 Open Source Databases

PostreSQL is a powerful ORDBMS (PostgreSQL Global Development Group, 2013). It is free and open source software (FLOSS) which is distributed under a FreeBSD type of licence and has a global community of developers and companies involved in its development. PostGIS (Open Source Foundation, 2013) from the Open GIS Consortium (OGC) is a geospatial database front-end that easily integrates with the PostgreSQL database. The provision of data type extension is one of the strengths of PostgreSQL. This is the ability to add new data types, functions, and access methods. This has made it possible for the PostGIS development team to extend PostgreSQL in order to provide a seamless integration between PostgreSQL and PostGIS. Some of the strengths of PostgreSQL are described in Table 5.1.

PostGIS turns the PostgreSQL DBMS into a spatial database by adding support for the three features: spatial types, indexes, and functions. Due to the fact that it is built on PostgreSQL, PostGIS automatically inherits important functionality as well as open standards for implementation, which make it suitable for use in organisations. Spatial types and indexes were discussed in Sect. 5.4. The full list of spatial types and functions provided by PostGIS is available in the PostGIS documentation provided by OpenGEO (OPENGEO, 2013). It should be noted that the functions are typically invoked through SQL queries which make them very easy to use. OPENGEO (2013) have noted that many organisations currently use PostGIS. One such organisation is the national mapping agency of France, *Institut Geographique National* (IGN). IGN use PostGIS to store the high-resolution topographic map of the country. OPENGEO (2013) have also noted that currently there are many GIS applications, both open source and proprietary, that support or can use PostGIS. Some examples are uDig (open source desktop and Internet GIS), MapServer (open source GIS), and ESRI ArcGIS desktop and server (proprietary GIS).

5.6.3 Open Source GIS Applications

There are a number of desktop GIS applications available under the open source licencing model. Examples of these applications are OpenJUMP (Open Jump, 2013), UDig (UDig, 2013), and Quantum GIS (QGIS) (Quantum, 2013). The QGIS) project started in 2002 and to date the QGIS application appears to have reached a high level of maturity. QGIS provides six categories of GIS functionality as follows: (1) viewing data, (2) exploring data and composing maps, (3) creating, editing, and exporting spatial data, (4) analysing spatial data, (5) publishing maps on the web, and (6) extending QGIS functionality through the use of plug-ins. For data analysis, QGIS can be used to access data stored in a PostgreSQL/PostGIS spatial database (Quantum, 2013). The QGIS extensible plug-in architecture enables users to create new application plug-in software in order to meet any special needs for spatial analysis.

5.7 Case Study of the Western Cape Department of Education

There are many areas in which public sector institutions can employ business intelligence tools. According to Cognos (2003) areas such as defence, public safety and law enforcement, justice, education, healthcare, labour, and human resources have successfully adopted business intelligence. In this section, a case study is reported on the adoption and usage of BI and GIS for decision support in public sector management in one province of South Africa. The case study has been chosen as a good exemplar of the typical challenges continually faced by planners and decision makers in developing countries.

5.7.1 Education Department of the Provincial Government of Western Cape Province

In 2005, the Western Cape Province of South Africa had a population of four million people. The education department for the province (WCED) had a budget of approximately five billion rand (about US$650 million) (Information Builders, 2005; Present, 2005). The department supported a staff of approximately 29,000 educators and 8,000 support staff responsible for the schools throughout the province. There were more than one million students at more than 1,500 schools in the eight districts of the province. The department also coordinated and monitored adult education programs, early childhood development centres, and further education and training colleges. The main challenge faced by the department of education was how to prioritise the needs of the students and schools given its limited budget (Present, 2005). The department needed to balance its role as an agent for social change with its limited financial resources.

5.7.2 Data Analysis Requirements for the Education Department

Some of the questions the WCED managers needed to answer and required management information about were (Present, 2005):

1. How many and which schools do not have basic services such as sanitation, water, and electricity?
2. How long will it take, and how easy/difficult is it, to provide these basic services?
3. How should teaching posts be allocated annually for each school in the province?
4. Which schools have unacceptably high student/teacher ratios?
5. The department is spending in excess of R100 million annually on learner transport. Is this spending effective?
6. Which schools and grades have unacceptably high dropout rates?

The district managers typically needed a system that supports self-service reporting functionality so that they could quickly view and analyse information for each educational institution. The information needs of the Western Cape Education Department were (and are still) managed by EMIS (Educational Management Information Systems) section, which is a subsection of the research division of the department. EMIS acquired a suite of BI tools from two leading vendors, one for data warehousing and one for BI analysis and reporting. On an annual basis a variety of surveys were (and are still) conducted. The data is captured and stored in an Oracle data warehouse/data mart. WebFOCUS BI tools are used for OLAP analysis, report generation, and deployment to their intranet. As a result of the BI implementation managers and other users with limited IT skills are able to conduct analysis, produce reports, and deploy them to other members of the department via the web. This has resulted in improved communication and co-operation between various sections of the department and the creation of a common understanding of the problems faced by the department.

5.7.3 The Use of BI and GI to Support Planning for the Future

The department also recently acquired GIS technology that is linked to the BI tools. This technology consists of ESRI GIS server and desktop applications and WebFOCUS ESRI adapters which connect the GIS tools to the WebFOCUS BI tools. The system is designed for infrastructure planning. This system, which is available in all district offices, enables mapping and spatial analysis which enables decision makers to identify factors (e.g. infrastructure, rivers, mountains, population growth) that affect the provision of education in diverse geographical areas of the province. One major activity that the WCED has embarked on recently is planning the expansion of school infrastructure in terms of new schools, additional class rooms for existing schools, and provision of mobile classrooms (Grant, 2012).

The combined BI and GIS system has enabled the planners to conduct spatial analysis in order to establish the gaps between supply and demand for educational facilities, where in the province these gaps exist and why these gaps exist. The analysis was conducted by combining geospatial data from various map layers and school specific data. The school specific data includes enrolment levels and trends, required size of school facilities, ownership of school premises (leased or government owned), and the nature of school structures (permanent or temporary) (Grant, 2012).

Arising from the above analysis, the WCED was able to compile a 3-year infrastructure development plan which they embarked on in 2010. The plan included the building of 25 new schools, 20 replacement schools, additional classrooms, and mobile units. The plan also included the closure of 17 schools (Grant, 2013). It was expected that the plan implementation would be completed in 2013 (Grant, 2012). Furthermore, arising from the above analysis, the district and provincial managers of WCED have come to realise the dynamic nature of the environment within which they have to plan, and the need to constantly and spatially monitor the environment so that they can react effectively to changes. In recognition of this, the WCED have already developed the next infrastructure development plan to be implemented from 2013 to 2015 (Grant, 2012). It should, however, be noted that some residents of the Western Cape Province obtained a court interdict which prevented the closure of the 17 schools mentioned above (Grant, 2013).

5.8 Discussion

An important knowledge management initiative for developing countries is the use of appropriate technologies to gather and analyse data in order to support decision making for (1) planning and allocation of limited resources, (2) monitoring the use of these limited resources, and (3) planning future infrastructure development projects. The discussion in this chapter has addressed the problem domain of delivery of educational services in the public sector and the technologies that can be used by decision makers for knowledge acquisition and management in this problem domain. A discussion of BI and GIS technologies was provided in Sects. 5.3–5.5. The combination of these technologies enables the integration of external geospatial data with internal numeric and textual organisational data for purposes of spatial analysis. This analysis can provide answers to ‘what’, ‘who’, ‘when’, and ‘where’ types of questions. The answers to these questions provide useful information for solving current problems and making plans to solve future problems and enable decision makers to acquire knowledge of the evolving environment and problem domain within which they work.

The discussion in Sects. 5.3–5.5 also highlighted the technical and operational challenges in implementing GIS and BI systems. Several organisations have a silo culture which has impeded many efforts in the organisation-wide adoption of BI systems. The point was made in Sect. 5.5 that GIS reports that provide maps can be used as a common reference for relating and understanding the information in the

BI reports from different sections of the organisation. The point was made in Sects. 5.4 and 5.5 that using a GIS typically requires high technical expertise. However, GIS and BI technology providers have started working with end users in order to create pre-configured models and reporting templates which make it much easier for ordinary users to quickly conduct spatial analysis and predictive analytics. In the past, geospatial data was an expensive commodity. In recent years, this data has become easily accessible and freely available from many public organisations and GIS providers.

Proprietary GIS is perceived to be expensive. When considering knowledge management initiatives for developing countries, it is important to identify low cost solutions for the necessary technologies. Open source (FLOSS) databases and GIS applications were discussed in Sect. 5.6. Open source databases (e.g. PostGreSQL and PostGIS) and open source GIS applications (e.g. QGIS) are mature technologies and enjoy widespread acceptance in organisations, so they should be reliable low-cost alternatives to proprietary spatial databases and GIS, for the implementation of integrated BI and GIS systems. Another aspect in support of open source databases is their extensibility, that is, the ability to easily add new functionality to the database through programmer-defined data types. This property directly supports the objective of being able to tailor the knowledge management technologies to the local context for developing countries. Finally, the use of open source software supports the long-term objectives of human capital development in IT skills and the creation of job opportunities in developing countries.

A case study on the usage of BI and GIS in public sector education planning and monitoring in a developing country was given in Sect. 5.7. This case study demonstrates that BI and GIS technologies can be effectively combined and successfully used in a developing country to support decision making for service provision.

5.9 Conclusions

This chapter has presented a discussion of business intelligence (BI), geographical information systems (GIS), and free/libre/open source software (FLOSS) as appropriate technologies and systems for use in knowledge management initiatives in developing countries. The technologies for BI and GIS that are currently available have been discussed in detail. Low-cost spatial databases and GIS applications available as open source software have been proposed as an affordable alternative for knowledge management initiatives. It has been argued that the combination of these technologies can and should provide operationally effective and cost-effective solutions to the problem of gathering, storage, and analysis of data to support the information needs of decision makers. A case study on BI and GIS usage in public sector education management has been presented as an example of how these technologies can be effectively combined to provide information for decision support. The point has also been made that the use of FLOSS can lead to human capital development in IT skills and the creation of job opportunities in developing countries.

Appendix

Technical details on databases that support spatial analysis for GIS are provided in this appendix. Figure 5.1 shows the relationship between the GIS, spatial database system, and object-relational database system. As depicted in Fig. 5.1, a GIS can be used as a front-end to a spatial database system, so that the GIS accesses spatial data through the spatial database in order to perform the required spatial analysis. An ORDBMS provides the platform to support the spatial database. When the spatial database uses the ORDBMS as the underlying DBMS engine, spatial data is queried using the SQL language. ORDBMSs provide constructs that have been specified in the SQL:2008 standard (Connolly & Begg, 2010). These constructs include built-in data types such as row types and collection types as well as programmer-defined types which are object-oriented programming (OOP) constructs in the form of classes and class hierarchies, objects, methods, and operators. A row type is an aggregate data type with fields of various atomic types, e.g. numeric, date, and character strings. Collection types include arrays, sets, and lists (Connolly & Begg, 2010). The SQL:2008 constructs described above make it easy to implement the necessary computational data structures for spatial data. As a result, the specification provided by the OGC for incorporating two-dimensional geospatial abstract data types (ADTs) into SQL can be easily implemented. These ADTS are based on the computational object model and include operations for specifying *topological* and *spatial analysis* operations.

A typical spatial database system today is an ordinary database with additional capabilities and functions that include spatial data types, spatial operators, spatial indexing, and spatial data management functionality which includes data loading and transaction control. Spatial data types are stored as simple features as defined by the Open Geospatial Consortium (OGC, 2013) or as binary large objects (BLOBs). A simple feature is a graphic representation of a physical spatial feature (e.g. road) or conceptual spatial feature (e.g. service area). OGC simple features are defined inside the spatial database and can therefore be processed by the database. The SQL:2008 standard specifies user-defined types (similar to classes in OOP) which can be used to define data types and operations (methods) on these data types. On the other hand, the processing of BLOBs requires additional software components. Spatial operators are functions for performing spatial joins of tables, performing calculations on table data, retrieving data from tables, etc. These functions are invoked through SQL queries. Spatial indexing differs from transactional database indexing since spatial data is typically represented as coordinate pairs in two-dimensional or three-dimensional space.

In the spatial database and GIS environment, data is commonly grouped according to the function it serves in spatial analysis. These groupings were discussed in Sect. 5.4.2. The relationships between the layers are shown in Fig. 5.4. The base map data layers provide the geodetic (survey) control network and topographic base data. Geodetic (survey) control network provides the spatial reference framework for all database data. Topographic base data provides geographical referencing required for collections, analysis, and the display of data in higher layers (application and business). The framework data layers are three related layers for the geographical referencing of human activity on land. The parcel layer provides the framework for land development and administration applications. The facilities layer forms the basis for facilities management in public utilities and resource management. The address layer supports various land and resource applications that require postal addresses. The application data layers comprise of various spatial datasets collected for different database applications in land and resource management. Application datasets use the base map and framework data layers for geographical referencing. The business solutions layers consist of collections of spatial data layers including framework and application data layers plus related spatial and non-spatial data. The data is assembled to support operations and decision making functions of the business units in an organisation (Yeung & Hall, 2007).

References

Cognos. (2003). *Business intelligence for the public sector*. Retrieved from ftp://ftp.software.ibm.com/software/data/sw-library/cognos/pdfs/whitepapers/wp_bi_for_the_public_sector_drilling_down.pdf

Cognos. (2007). *Intermountain Healthcare selects Cognos as business intelligence standard*. Retrieved June 25, 2013, from http://www.prweb.com/releases/cpgnos/healthcare/prweb554113.htm

Connolly, T. M., & Begg, C. (2010). *Database systems: A practical guide to design, implementation and management* (5th ed.). Boston, MA: Addison Wesley.

Environmental Systems Research Institute. (2006). *GIS and business intelligence: The geographic advantage* (ESRI White Paper). Redlands, CA: Author.

Environmental Systems Research Institute. (2007). *Geospatial service-oriented architecture (SOA)* (ESRI White Paper). Redlands, CA: Author.

FREE GIS. (2013). Retrieved from http://freegis.org

Free Software Foundation. (2013). Retrieved from http://www.fsf.org

Gartner. (2013). *IT glossary—business intelligence*. Retrieved from http://www.gartner.com/it-glossary/business-intelligence-bi

Golferelli, M., Rizzi, S., & Cella, I. (2004). Beyond data warehousing: What's next in business intelligence? In *Proceedings of the seventh ACM international workshop on data warehousing and OLAP (DOLAP'04)* (pp. 1–6). New York: ACM.

Grant, D. (2012, September 4). Minister Grant releases details on the WCED's infrastructure plan. *Media release, Minister of Education, Western Cape Province*. Retrieved June 11, 2013, from http://wced.pgwc.gov.za/documents/LearnerPlacementPlans/

Grant, D. (2013, March 26). Minister Grant approaches the constitutional court on school closures. *Media release, Minister of Education, Western Cape Province*. Retrieved June 11, 2013, from http://wced.pgwc.gov.za/documents/LearnerPlacementPlans/

Guting, R. H. (1994). An introduction to spatial database systems. *The VLDB Journal, 3*(4), 357–399.

Hobbs, L., Hillson, S., Lawande, S., & Smith, P. (2005). *Oracle database 10g data warehousing*. New York: Elsevier Digital Press.

Information Builders. (2004). *Business intelligence goes operational on the front lines making a bottom-line difference*. Retrieved June 25, 2013, from http://www.informationbuilders.com/about_us/whitepapers/pdf/WP_BIGoesOperational_WF_2005.pdf

Information Builders. (2005). *South Africa's Western Cape Education Department shares and manages information using WebFocus*. Retrieved June 25, 2013, from https://www.informationbuilders.com/new/magazine/v15-2/pdf/38_PAWC.w05.pdf

Inmon, W. H., Imhoff, C., & Sousa, R. (2001). *Corporate information factory* (2nd ed.). New York: Wiley.

Kaplan, R. S., & Norton, D. P. (1992). The balanced scorecard: Measures that drive performance. *Harvard Business Review, 70*(1), 71–79.

Kimball, R., Ross, M., Thornwaite, W., Mundy, T., & Becker, B. (2008). *The data warehouse lifecycle toolkit* (2nd ed.). Indianapolis, IN: Wiley.

Open Geospatial Consortium. (2013). Retrieved from http://www.opengeospatial.org

Open Jump. (2013). Retrieved from http://www.openjump.org

Open Source Foundation. (2013). Retrieved from http://www.opensorce.org

OPENGEO. (2013). Retrieved from http://www.opengeo.org

Planet GIS. (2013). *Maps*. Retrieved from http://www.planetgis.co.za/maps.php

Ponniah, P. (2001). *Data warehousing fundamentals: A comprehensive guide for IT professionals*. New York: Wiley.

PostgreSQL Global Development Group. (2013). *PostgreSQL [Computer software]*. Retrieved from http://postgreSQL.org

Posthumus, R. (2008). GIS as a tool in business intelligence. *PositionIT*, (May/June), 71–74.

Present, P. (2005) Innovation in education: Western Cape, South Africa education department shares and manages information with WebFOCUS. *Information Builders Magazine*, pp. 38–40. Retrieved from http://www.informationbuilders.com/magazine. (Cited June 25, 2013).

Quantum GIS. (2013). Retrieved from http://www.qgis.co.za

Turban, E., Sharda, R., & Delen, D. (2011). *Decision support and business intelligence systems* (9th ed.). New York: Addison-Wesley.

UDig. (2013). Retrieved from http://udig.refractions.net/

Wu, L., Barash, G., & Bartolini, C. (2007). A service oriented architecture for business intelligence. In *IEEE international conference on service-oriented computing and applications (SOCA'07)* (pp. 279–285). Newport Beach, CA. doi:10.1109/SOCA.2007.6.

Yeung, A. K. W., & Hall, G. B. (2007). *Spatial database systems: Design, implementation and project management*. Dordrecht, The Netherlands: Springer.

Chapter 6
Migrating MIS to KMS: A Case of Social Welfare Systems

Ricardo Anderson and Gunjan Mansingh

Abstract Knowledge management and knowledge-based systems can be critical to organizations and their success. The integration of knowledge resources into existing information systems can help improve decision making and possibly drive efficiency gains in business processes. In this chapter we propose a process model for evolving an existing information system into a knowledge management system. Our model provides guidance on the phases and supporting activities needed in this evolution. We discuss each phase and a reference architecture for a conditional cash transfer system for the social welfare domain in Jamaica.

Keywords Process model • Knowledge management systems • Social welfare system

6.1 Introduction

Social welfare exists in various forms across the world. Over the period 1995–2008 a new type of social welfare programme called Conditional Cash Transfers (CCTs) was introduced in Latin America and the Caribbean (LAC) and has become popular as a new paradigm in social protection. These programmes, currently existing in Jamaica (Programme for Advancement Through Health and Education, PATH), Brazil (Bolsa Familia), among other countries, require persons who qualify based

R. Anderson (✉)
Department of Computing, The University of the West Indies,
Mona-Western Jamaica Campus, Montego Bay, Jamaica
e-mail: ricardo.anderson02@uwimona.edu.jm

G. Mansingh
Department of Computing, The University of the West Indies,
Mona Campus, Jamaica
e-mail: gunjan.mansingh@uwimona.edu.jm

K.-M. Osei-Bryson et al. (eds.), *Knowledge Management for Development*,
Integrated Series in Information Systems 35, DOI 10.1007/978-1-4899-7392-4_6,

on their economic/social status to maintain conditionalities related to healthcare and education. Generally, the poor can apply for benefits and provide economic data to support their claim. The agency will assess the application and determine if the applicant meets the threshold of poverty set by the programme. Once approved, cash and non-cash benefits are disbursed to households provided they continue to maintain their educational and healthcare obligations.

The information systems environment in LAC-based CCTs consist mainly of computer-based management information systems (MIS) which manage large quantities of data collected by these programmes during the application, approval, and subsequent monitoring phases of the assistance cycle, which can last for several years. Predominantly, these MIS primarily provide programme support through data management and simple reporting.

Several processes involved in the application through to approval and monitoring phases are characterized by data-driven decision making directly related to the managed data. Integrated knowledge support does not currently exist in this environment. This can be addressed by transitioning the current information system into knowledge management systems (KMS).

We posit that CCT-based MIS systems can be migrated to a system that meets key requirements for classification as a KMS (Alavi & Leidner, 2001). The migrated system will provide for the creation of knowledge from data, a means for storing and retrieving this knowledge, and applying the knowledge to support decision making and process improvement.

The new environment will allow for the use of knowledge to improve decision making, more efficient use of resources, and improvements in the administrative capacity of the programme agencies. These improvements will allow the agencies to better meet the programme objectives while satisfying the requirements set by multinational donors and governments. Further, we posit that integrated knowledge can assist in long-term programme improvement.

This study presents a methodology for evolving MIS in CCTs into knowledge KMSs. The resulting system integrates knowledge services into the current information system environment. In the rest of this chapter we review relevant existing research, introduce the methodology and the knowledge integration architecture. Section 6.2 reviews literature relevant to knowledge management and CCT programmes. Section 6.3 gives an overview of information systems in LAC CCT programmes followed by a discussion of the process model for converting MIS to KMS. The application of the model is discussed in relation to the PATH CCT followed by conclusion and future work.

6.2 Background

Organizations today are driven by the need to record and manage data that is used by different levels of staff to carry out their duties. Modern information systems include hardware, software, communication devices and infrastructure, people, and procedures (Oz, 2006). These components generally allow the storage and processing of data. Data is often translated for different levels of workers and stakeholders. One important group of stakeholders is the decision makers—usually managers. There are several classifications of information systems qualified by different metrics; one system may fall into different categories based on the support that each component may provide to different organizational functionaries.

Today, most computer-based systems support recording basic business events. Systems that allow for the recording of business events or transactions are classified as transaction processing systems (TPS). These have capability to provide summarizations of these transactions to other systems in the organization. Decision Support Systems are most often applied to solving unstructured problems with unclear requirements or objectives. They have been proposed for and implemented in many different ways across several domains including healthcare, strategic management, human resource management, and education, accounting (Eom & Kim, 2005; Eom, Lee, Kim, & Somarajan, 1998; Wen, Wang, & Wang, 2005). Knowledge-driven DSS is one category of decisions support systems that is used in many domains (Power, 2001).

6.2.1 *Knowledge Management Systems*

Knowledge has been defined in different ways throughout the literature; for the purpose this study knowledge is a "fluid mix of framed experience, values, contextual information and expert insight that provide a framework for evaluation and incorporating new experiences and information" (Davenport & Prusak, 1998, p. 5). This differs significantly from information and data which are lower according to the Data-Information-Knowledge (DIK) hierarchy (Rowley, 2007). Data is a collection of facts and figures, while information is organized data that provides meaning. Context, experiences, and expert insights can then be added to information to produce knowledge. The concept of knowledge has long been discussed with early researchers focusing on definitions and setting frameworks for understanding knowledge construct and taxonomy.

Polanyi (1966) specified two types of knowledge; tacit and explicit. Tacit knowledge is said to reside in one's subconscious and is not easily codified, while explicit knowledge is easily codified and can be stored on machines. This has given rise to an explosion in research on how to create and manage knowledge within organizational contexts. Nonaka (1994) adds to this discussion and further proposes four modes of knowledge creation: Socialization, Externalization, Combination, and Internalization. This provides a framework for understanding the important types of knowledge, how they can be created in different contexts, and how best to develop the knowledge architecture of an organization.

Given the significant work done on knowledge creation in recent years, studies on how to manage knowledge gained much traction. Knowledge management has become very important in most modern societies. Researchers have also focused on the creation of organizational knowledge structures and developing a culture of knowledge sharing in organizations. Several researchers have underscored the importance of knowledge management in today's firms to the extent that it is seen as a possible source of significant competitive advantage (Jennex, Smolnik, & Croasdell, 2009; Ryan, Harden, Ibragimova, & Windsor, 2012). Several researchers have focused on categorizing different types of knowledge and enlisting frameworks for organizing and establishing knowledge organizations. Studies have been done to assess best practices and tangible outcomes from utilizing knowledge and how this improves decision making and process improvement in firms. Further, Bowman argues that knowledge can be critical to an organization's success as it can improve their capability (Bowman, 2002). Today, with the proliferation of computer-based information systems, consideration must be given to how these technologies can help and facilitate the knowledge management initiatives in the firm.

Knowledge-based systems (KBS) have been explored from many directions in the literature ranging from frameworks that cover knowledge creation (Nonaka, Umemoto, & Senoo, 1996), methods and techniques (Wiig, Hoog, & Spex, 1997), organizational impact, and innovation (Hendricks & Vriens, 1999; Johannessen, Olsen, & Olaisen, 1999). The literature explores KBS implemented and assessed in various industries and applications including the petroleum industry (Cauvin, 1996), human resource management (Martinsons, 1997), manufacturing (Kang, Lee, Shin, Yu, & Park, 1998) the military (Liao, 2000, 2001), agriculture (Fleurat-Lessard, 2002; Kim, Nute, Rauscher, & Lofits, 2000), microbiology (McMeekin & Ross, 2002), tourism (Cooper, 2006; Hallin & Marnburg, 2008), and project management (Tian, Ma, & Liu, 2002). KBS often are implemented as stand-alone applications within the context of a domain or organizations and have become synonymous with expert systems. The critical component is the application of knowledge to assist in solving some problem. The nature of KBS as defined in the literature reviewed suggests that they fall short of being classified as knowledge management systems.

KMS are primarily designed to provide supporting knowledge to decision makers. KMS extend beyond traditional information systems and KBS as they provide a context within which information is coded and presented for use (Gallupe, 2000). KMS within this context must therefore be comprised of a toolset that facilitates proper organization of resources with emphasis on information technologies that will drive the knowledge processes in the organization. KMS must provide components that will support the acquisition, modeling, representation, and use of knowledge (Alavi & Leidner, 2001; Schreiber et al., 1999). This is essential as knowledge must be constantly updated, suitably modeled so that it integrates into the organization, and suitably represented for application. Alavi and Leidner (2001) contend that ICTs can actualize and strengthen the knowledge processes through scope enhancement, timing and overall strategy. The concern is also noted that knowledge can continued to be applied after it is outdated and its usefulness has passed as a result of changes in the organization or industry. There is, therefore, a need to constantly update knowledge so that it continues to be relevant.

Table 6.1 MIS functional areas in CCTs

Identification	Registration	Certification	Payment	Accountability
Targeting	Database development	Data collection	Eligibility	Complaints
Enrollment	Validation	Verification	Disbursement	Processes
Exit	Updating	Penalization	Reconciliation	Impact

Although the literature on KM is extensive and covers a wide range of applications throughout industries and organizations, research is lacking in some areas such as social welfare.

6.2.2 Social Welfare: Conditional Cash Transfers

Governments, voluntary organizations, and multinational agencies provide different types of aid to assist vulnerable peoples across the world. These programmes take many different forms and vary from immediate relief to long-term assistance especially for persons with special needs due to disabilities. CCT programmes are a special type of social protection funded through the cooperation of multinational agencies and governments worldwide. These programmes were first introduced in LAC in 1995 (Johannsen, Tejerina, & Glassman, 2009) and are also used in Africa as part of their suite of social welfare interventions. CCTs have been seen and credited as a new paradigm in social welfare as persons who benefit from these schemes are assessed initially and, once they are approved for the programme, they are required to maintain conditionalities related primarily to healthcare and education. This paradigm shift seeks to improve the economic and social status of beneficiaries and households by providing cash and non-cash benefits once they maintain the required conditionalities. The aim is to provide education, healthcare and, in some cases, cash to vulnerable people as an investment that will eventually allow them to become economically independent (Holzmann & Jorgensen, 1999). Thus, the investment up to the point of violation would have been lost and the objective of independence would not have been met.

Based on the structure of CCTs in the Caribbean, there are five key processes that should be supported by any MIS for CCTs (Baldeon & Arribas-Baños, 2008). Table 6.1 above identifies these key activities and gives a list of subtasks associated with them.

The groupings are based on functional areas which are refined and implemented by each programme. The identification process covers the means by which applicants can access the programme. This can be demand-driven or geographic. Once the person requests benefits, the data must be validated and verified before enrollment; this process converts an applicant into a beneficiary. The updating process covers the modification of data as a result of further data collection or verification. Once the eligibility requirements have been met, disbursement and monitoring begins. Depending on the maintenance of conditionilities, there may be penalties resulting in suspension or cancellation of the benefit.

6.3 Information Systems Environment in CCTs

Two recent studies have converged on proposed best practices for developing MIS for CCTs (Chirchir & Kidd, 2011; Villalobos, Blanco, & Bassett, 2010). In particular, Villalobo et al. (2010) indicate that the main objectives of any MIS system for CCTs in Latin America should be guided by the following objectives:

- Support and management of internal programme operations
  - Beneficiary selection, enrollment, management alerts, and performance reports.
- Management of programme and related services through the generation and distribution of information to participating agencies
  - Service provision tracking, programme service quality management.
- Integrated management of social protection systems through the provision of common information for inter-agency management
  - Common beneficiary registry, networking programmes under social protection portfolio, and a single entry point from which access to social protection programmes is provided.

Based on the outlined metric above, the 2010 report on MIS in Latin America identifies the stages reached by current information systems solutions in these programmes:

As shown in Table 6.2 below, while all the programmes studied currently have computer based information systems in place, they are at different stages of capability. The integrated management of social protection is set out as providing the best use of resources, preventing double access to social services and easing many issues related to targeting. All programmes studied currently collect and store vast amounts of data about applicants and, in some cases, behavior data linked to their adherence to the set conditionalities. Therefore, the basic resource for knowledge discovery is data, which is available in all programmes studied. Anderson and Mansingh (2012) in a study of the PATH programme demonstrated the use of knowledge discovery in data mining to extract rules which were used to create an expert system for decision support.

Table 6.2 CCTs MIS capability in LAC

MIS capability across CCTs in Latin America		
Stage 1: internal program and process management	Stage 2: program and related services management	Stage 3: integrated management of social protection systems
Bono Juan Azurduy—Bolivia	Programa Solidaridad—Dominican Republic	Bolsa Familia—Brazil, Chile
Familias en Accion—Colombia	Programa Oportunidades—Mexico	Solidario—Chile
Programa Juntos—Peru Red de	Mi Familia Progresa—Guatemala	
Oportunidades—Panama	PATH—Jamaica	

The knowledge management literature does not provide insight into knowledge management research in social services. Governments and institutions worldwide struggle to provide the key social services that are essential in order to break the cycle of poverty for many of their people. Knowledge management and supporting tools can be used to assist in more efficient use of resources and better decision making (Alavi & Leidner, 2001; Davenport & Prusak, 1998; Esper, Ellinger, Stank, Flint, & Moon, 2010) and can, therefore, provide insights into better management of CCT services. The management of each case to ensure that the potential of the household is realized through monitoring conditionalities towards outcomes can be enhanced by data-driven KBSs. One such example has been demonstrated in (Anderson & Mansingh, 2012) where a knowledge driven decision support system was implemented and evaluated within the context of the PATH social welfare programme in Jamaica.

6.4 MIS to KMS Process Model

Similar to many other domains, LAC-based CCTs use computers to manage relatively large data sets that support their operations. They also maintain archived notes from experts and reference documents published by the World Bank that help in their operations. This data accumulates rapidly as new beneficiaries and monitoring data are added for existing beneficiaries. These programmes do not currently have initiatives to acquire and utilize knowledge that may reside in this data and are therefore missing out on potential benefits such as improved programme administration, better resource allocation, cost reductions, and improved decision making.

Anderson and Mansingh (2012) have demonstrated that the data in CCTs programmes can be harnessed, integrated, and mined to acquire new knowledge that can be used to improve decision making and programme administration. In their study, a decision support system was developed to assist in the verification of applicants to the PATH CCT. The model used for decision making was the result of mining historical data from the electronic database of the programme using the Knowledge Discovery and Data Mining (KDDM) methodology. The work demonstrated that knowledge can be acquired from data and used to impact operations and decision making positively.

We seek to build on the success of this study (Anderson & Mansingh, 2012) by expanding the knowledge management capabilities of LAC-based CCTs. We propose a formal process model that will guide the mechanism of creating new knowledge and storing that knowledge for retrieval and use in the domain. This will have the effect of transforming the existing information systems environment to include knowledge management capabilities.

In evolving the information systems environment to include knowledge-integrated capabilities, this study identifies the critical business processes and examines the information system environment and builds the knowledge component by extending the current architecture. An inventory of the organization's processes is conducted and the information system, together with the level to which processes

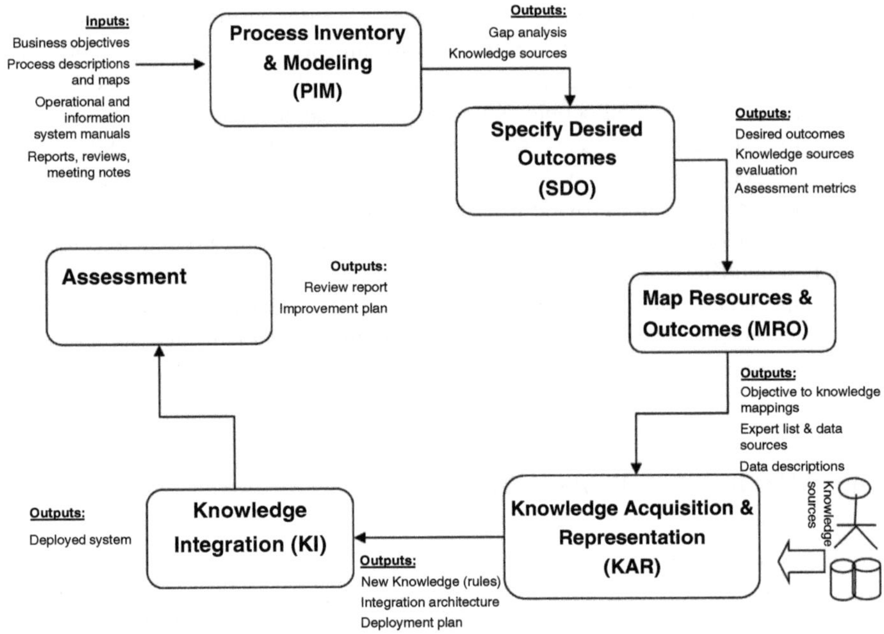

Fig. 6.1 CoMIS-KMS process model

are automated, is mapped. The data collection and management procedures are also examined. The data are reviewed to determine relevant subsets that are useful to the decision-making processes within the organization. Knowledge is extracted, then integrated into the information systems to provide integrated knowledge support to the organization. While other process models exist for building KBSs such as commonKADS (Schreiber et al., 1999; Schreiber, Wielinga, de Hoog, Akkermans, & Van de Velde, 1994), MIKE (Angele, Fensel, Landes, & Studer, 1998), we are proposing evolving a current information system to a KMS, which is not the focus of those models. Although there is significant emphasis on Knowledge Discovery and Data Mining, our model addresses the need to use knowledge acquired from other sources such as international funding agencies and domain experts. We therefore go beyond the activities suggested by data mining process models such as SEMMA and CRISP-DM (Azevedo, 2008; Kurgan & Musilek, 2006) and the integrated model proposed by Sharma and Osei-Bryson (2010).

We propose the CoMIS-KMS process model that guides the evolution of CCT MIS into KMSs which gather, store, and allow for the retrieval and use of knowledge. We further emphasize that our methodology and architecture assume an existing computer-based information systems which evolves to integrate knowledge into that environment. Figure 6.1 demonstrates the CoMIS-KMS process model.

Each phase of the model can be broken down into a set of activities. We explain a suggested set of activities that are to be completed in each phase. We also note that the model can be applied iteratively as operational processes and business objectives change; however, the nature of CCTs is that objectives do not change very rapidly as these are often set by external factors. The following gives a breakdown of each phase:

Process inventory and modeling (PIM):

- Review business processes; identify data that supports each business process and the level to which the data and computer-based information systems support the process from start to finish.
- Identify knowledge sources: people, processes, and data.
- Identify gaps in the data and information systems that could be useful to the achievement of greater efficiencies and improvements in processes.
- Map relationships between the processes, the data, and the interactions that are needed to achieve the organizational objectives. This can be done through developing a domain ontology.
- Validate Models.
  - Review mappings and interactions with stakeholders for validation. Use tools to instantiate ontology and check for consistency.

Specify desired outcomes (SDO):

- Identify and specify outcomes. Review the shortfalls in relation to programme objectives and current state of those indicators.
- Assess the suitability of data-driven analytics in assisting to meet those outcomes. This is premised on the MIS application providing useful indicators.

Map resources to outcomes (MRO):

- Link outcomes with knowledge sources (data, processes, and experts), to ascertain method for knowledge acquisition.
- Identify the data necessary to support identified outcomes.
- Identify domain expertise that may be necessary for integrating knowledge.

Knowledge acquisition and representation (KAR):

- Determine algorithms to apply based on outcome required and the selected supporting data.
- Identify and apply coding of domain expertise.
- Proceed with knowledge discovery, acquisition algorithms.

Knowledge integration

- Determine architecture for integrated knowledge support within the current information system environment.
- Combine expert knowledge with knowledge acquired from data.
- Deploy services based on architecture.

Assessment

- Implement review and knowledge update strategy.
- Monitor outcomes.

This model can be applied iteratively to impact different processes within the programme and may be done on the basis of the objectives which have not been met based on the programme indicators.

6.5 Case Study: PATH CCT and CoMIS-KMS

Currently the PATH programme in Jamaica is a CCT that serves over 300,000 beneficiaries who have been assessed to be vulnerable based on their poverty level. The programme provides cash and non-cash benefits to households provided they continue to meet the set conditionalities for school attendance and healthcare access.

6.5.1 PIM in PATH

PATH is mainly demand-driven as persons may contact the parish office or welfare representative and submit an application which details their economic and social conditions. This includes items owned, type of shelter, educational level, earnings (if any), dependents, health status, and general day-to-day survival information. This data is entered into the beneficiary management system which applies a proxy means test to determine if the household qualifies for benefits based on the data submitted. If the application falls above the threshold, the applicant pre-qualifies. A social worker is then dispatched to the household to verify the information submitted. Once verification is complete, the payment process is activated and the supporting service and government agencies are contacted to provide monitoring and supply data to the PATH office regarding conditionalities. This data includes visits to clinic by the sick, elderly, and any lactating mothers in the household, and school attendance for those within the school age. This information is used for monitoring to ensure the beneficiaries continue to comply with conditions for the transfer of cash and other benefits. Health and education benefits are provided free for beneficiaries as well as a cash transfer made periodically, usually monthly. The program requires periodic visits to households that have beneficiaries to collect data for evaluation to determine if the household is still below the poverty level to continue on the programme. Upon update, the household may continue to benefit or is deemed to have improved economically to be able to survive without the benefits provided under the programme. This is scheduled every 6 months for each household to make adjustments related to new economic data of the family or changes in the local economy and is called recertification. Table 6.3 below lists the processes critical to the administration of the PATH CCT and a description of the activities associated with each.

Table 6.3 CCT process descriptions

Process	Description
Targeting	Method by which potential beneficiaries can access the programme
Assessment	Review of application details submitted by households target group members. This includes the administration of a special economic assessment using a proxy-means test. If the application meets the set test threshold, they would pre-qualify for benefit and listed for the next phase which is verification
Verification	Social worker visit the address indicated as residence for applicant and reviews the information submitted with applicant and verifies details. If verification is successful, the applicant becomes a beneficiary and disbursements begin
Beneficiary management/ monitoring	Distribution of benefits, collection of data from support agencies related to conditionalities set for beneficiaries
Re-certification	Social worker will periodically visit current beneficiary to determine if data submitted still represents the current living conditions of beneficiary

6.5.2 *SDO in PATH*

The programme currently struggles with verification and subsequent recertification due to significant resource constraints. The number of social workers available is insufficient and hence a significant backlog of months is experienced between application and verification, thus the start of the benefit disbursement is delayed. Once disbursement begins, monitoring the beneficiaries' adherence to conditionalities is necessary. In the PATH programme, beneficiaries are eventually removed from the programme when they fail to meet the conditionalities. In these cases, the major objective of the programme—to break the vicious cycle of poverty—is not achieved and the investment would have been lost.

The application, verification, and recertification processes accumulate vast amounts of data about living conditions and the behaviors and progress of beneficiaries over the period that they remain on the programme. In many cases household beneficiaries remain on the programme for many years, especially children of school age. This accumulated data can be a significant source of knowledge providing insights into social behaviors, economic patterns, school and healthcare services access, and trends in agencies that provide these services. There are benefits to be derived, especially in the specific processes of *application verification* and *proactive monitoring* of "at-risk" households, such as continued support in meeting the conditionalities. Verification and proactive monitoring are identified as processes that need improvement and have significant supporting data that can be used for knowledge discovery.

6.5.3 MRO in PATH

If the knowledge extracted from the data can provide insights into why beneficiaries renege on the conditionalities, proactive intervention can be taken to keep persons compliant and thus better improve the impact of the programme. In addition, Anderson and Mansingh (2012) proposed a decision support system that has been shown to allow automatic verification of applicants with an accuracy exceeding 90 % using knowledge from historical data. This has implications for reducing the number of social workers required for verification and re-certification.

The vast amount of data collected and maintained on applicants and beneficiaries and the stakeholders involved in monitoring the conditionalities can be used to assist in decision making and improve efficiencies in the administration of the programme. This data resides mainly in the computer-based system used by PATH. To complete this phase, we identified subject matter experts in PATH who guided us in identifying and accessing relevant data sources which were then mapped to the outcomes from the SDO phase.

6.5.4 KAR in PATH

Based on the knowledge sources that are mapped to the processes that will be supported by knowledge, the relevant subsets of data are identified. To support the application verification processes, we examined the data that was collected during the application process. This includes the living conditions, the address and contact information, the biographic and income data for all household members, and a brief summary of general education and any chronic illnesses.

The data that is collected during the application and verification processes is then examined with the subject matter expert and the relevant fields are selected and new fields are created to ensure that the data is adequately prepared to meet the objectives. This resulted in 56 fields that were then formatted for input to our mining tool SAS eMiner for application of algorithms. We used decision trees (DT) as the objective was to use the results for predictive purposes. Thus, the English rules produced by DT modeling were most suitable. These rules were then used for our knowledge base.

6.5.5 KI in PATH

This stage depends on the knowledge produced from the KAR phase. The English rules were coded into production rules and were then used to implement an expert system (ES) using the Clips Engine. Given the existing information system architecture of the PATH MIS, this ES was integrated as a service which used the live

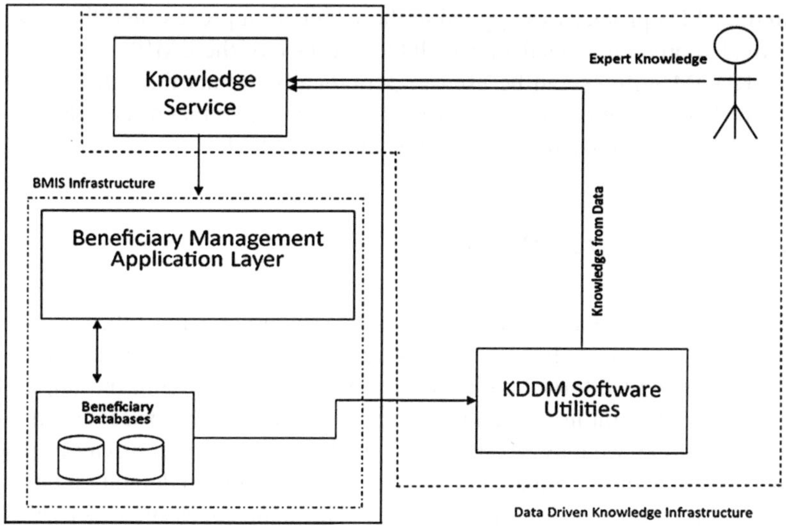

Fig. 6.2 Knowledge-integrated architecture

data available in the Beneficiary Management Information System (BMIS) data sources to evaluate and produce suggestions to the users. This architecture shows the revised information system environment with existing BMIS infrastructure and the knowledge service. The resulting system architecture demonstrates the use of the current information system environment, with integrated knowledge management. Figure 6.2 above illustrates the architecture of the deployment.

This diagram outlines the key components of the revised PATH system architecture. The knowledge service represents the expert system which depends on facts and new rules provided by domain experts and the KDDM utilities. In PATH project the purpose of the KDDM utilities is to extract relational tables and transform them according to the requirements of the knowledge acquisition tool. The process for selecting relevant fields and their derivatives that was done in the MRO phase was also implemented as an automated tool in the KDDM software utilities component.

The BMIS infrastructure is the current application used to manage applicants and beneficiaries in PATH. This application manages the interface and processing of data requests to the beneficiary databases and also provides reporting tools. We intend knowledge discovery to be an ongoing process where new knowledge is added to the knowledge service through a plugin architecture. This can be done in the KDDM software utilities.

The knowledge service provides a means for accepting the output of the KDDM utilities and expert knowledge and makes it available to the original BMIS infrastructure. The current implementation is through a shared database view that is accessible to both tools. The knowledge provided through the knowledge service within the PATH project was applied to the verification process and the expert system provided predictive results through the interface of the BMIS.

The KDDM utilities can be used to periodically extract the data to apply and update the knowledge passed to the knowledge service so that as new data is added to the BMIS, new knowledge can emerge and be applied.

6.5.6 Assessment in PATH

Indicators that showed a shortfall in the verification process must then be examined over time to determine the extent to which the knowledge service supports the objective. This will inform how to move forward by improving the implemented system and/or integrating more knowledge to support other processes and objectives. For example, we may be able to use knowledge to support *proactive intervention* where trends indicate that beneficiaries may be likely to default on obligations set out in the schedule of conditionalities. The main assessment activities were related to the quality of the knowledge provided. The knowledge service evaluated by comparing actual historical verification results with the results suggested through the knowledge service and a 94 % accuracy was recorded on a dataset of 296,000 assessed applicants. In addition, the programme managers evaluated the probable efficacy of the solution and indicated that they would utilize the knowledge service to verify all applicants to PATH, but would randomly select 20 % of those evaluated by the system for review and validation periodically.

6.6 Discussion

The CoMIS-KMS model guides the evolution of an existing information system to a KMS. In this study we identified that LAC-based CCTs are not actively engaged in harnessing and using the knowledge that is potentially resident in their data, processes, and people. We established that this knowledge can be used in advantageous ways that can improve their program capacity.

Within the context of this study and the PATH CCT, knowledge was acquired primarily from data stored in relational databases in the current information system. The knowledge acquired was then integrated into the existing information system environment using a revised system architecture which facilitates access to knowledge through the existing infrastructure. We used the defined phases in the CoMIS-KMS model to guide the identification of key processes, the supporting data sets, knowledge resources, and the critical decisions supported by information systems in this environment. Our work included the application of algorithms to extract knowledge from current data which was represented as production rules and implemented as a DSS for integration based on the proposed architecture.

Assessment of the DSS had 94 % accuracy when compared to the original processes. The evolved system provides knowledge that assists in automated verification of applicants to the PATH CCT. Further automated verification of applicants reduces the need for manual applicant verification by social workers, thus programme managers for PATH may re-organize resources for greater efficiency. We restricted our work to the verification of applications which the domain experts indicated was in need of improvement.

Our study therefore demonstrates the use of the CoMIS-KMS process model to guide the evolution of the information system environment in the PATH programme into KMS. The architecture used for integration can also improve the usage of the knowledge by decision makers as it forms a part of the current operational software and is not a stand-alone system.

6.7 Conclusions and Future Work

The CoMIS-KMS model proposed in this study provides a comprehensive process model that guides the evolution of a MIS environment into a KMS. The model specifies six phases which require some inputs and produce defined outputs which are fed into the subsequent phase. The phases provide guidance on the inputs required, the tasks to be completed, and the outputs produced at the end of each phase. We developed an integration architecture that modifies the existing environment to integrate the new knowledge for application in the domain. Once integration occurs, our model requires an assessment of the deployed knowledge. This assessment may suggest further improvements which may require another iteration through the model.

Through our application of the CoMIS-KMS in the PATH CCT, we have demonstrated that the model is useful and applicable in guiding the evolution of MIS to KMS. We have outlined the significant value of knowledge to organizations in our literature review and conclude, given our work thus far, that there are significant cost savings and process improvement implications for CCTs in LAC.

The CoMIS-KMS contributes to knowledge management literature and the relatively small amount of research on information systems in CCTs and provides a novel process model that has been tested in this domain.

In the future we intend to conduct an assessment of the impact of the integrated knowledge within the current information systems environment to determine its effect on the administration of the PATH programme and to propose improvements if necessary. Its usefulness as a model for similar programs across LAC region as well as the possibility that it can be generalized for other environments will be examined.

References

Alavi, M., & Leidner, D. E. (2001). Review: Knowledge management and knowledge management systems: Conceptual foundations and research issues. *MIS Quarterly, 25*(1), 107–136.

Anderson, R., & Mansingh, G. (2012). An intelligence based knowledge-driven decision support system for Social Protection programmes. In *SIG DSS proceedings of the third BI congress, pre-ICIS 2012*, Orlando, FL.

Angele, J., Fensel, D., Landes, D., & Studer, R. (1998). Developing knowledge-based systems with MIKE. *Automated Software Engineering, 5*(4), 389–418.

Azevedo, A. I. R. L. (2008). KDD, SEMMA and CRISP-DM: A parallel overview. In Ajith A (Ed.), *Proceedings of the IADIS european conference on data mining* (pp. 182–185), Amsterdam, The Netherlands.

Baldeon, C., & Arribas-Baños, M. D. (2008). *Management information systems in social safety net programs: a look at accountability and control mechanisms*. SP Discussion Paper no. 0819, Social Protection and Labor, The World Bank, August 2008.

Bowman, B. J. (2002). Building knowledge management systems. *Information Systems Management, 19*(3), 32–40.

Cauvin, S. (1996). Dynamic application of action plans in the Alexip knowledge-based system. *Control Engineering Practice, 4*(1), 99–104.

Chirchir R., & Kidd, S. (2011). *Good practice in the development of management information systems for social protection* (Briefing No. 5). London: HelpAge International. Retrieved from http://www.pension-watch.net/about-social-pensions/about-social-pensions/pension-watch-briefing-series/

Cooper, C. (2006). Knowledge management and tourism. *Annals of Tourism Research, 33*(1), 47–64.

Davenport, T. H., & Prusak, L. (1998). *Working knowledge: How organizations manage what they know*. Cambridge, MA: Harvard Business School Press.

Eom, S., & Kim, E. (2005). A survey of decision support system applications (1995-2001). *Journal of the Operational Research Society, 57*, 1264–1278.

Eom, S. B., Lee, S. M., Kim, E. B., & Somarajan, C. (1998). A survey of decision support system applications (1988-1994). *Journal of the Operational Research Society, 49*, 109–120.

Esper, T. L., Ellinger, A. E., Stank, T. P., Flint, D. J., & Moon, M. (2010). Demand and supply integration: A conceptual framework of value creation through knowledge management. *Journal of the Academy of Marketing Science, 38*(1), 5–18.

Fleurat-Lessard, F. (2002). Qualitative reasoning and integrated management of the quality of stored grain: A promising new approach. *Journal of Stored Product Research, 38*, 191–218.

Gallupe, R. B. (2000). *Knowledge management systems: Surveying the landscape* (Queens's School of Business Framework Paper 00-04). Kingston, ON: Queens University. Retrieved from http://citeseerx.ist.psu.edu/viewdoc/download?doi=10.1.1.104.7777&rep=rep1&type=pdf

Hallin, C. A., & Marnburg, E. (2008). Knowledge management in the hospitality industry: A review of empirical research. *Tourism Management, 29*, 366–381.

Hendricks, P. H. J., & Vriens, D. J. (1999). Knowledge based systems and knowledge management: Friends or foes? *Information and Management, 35*, 113–125.

Holzmann, R., & Jorgensen, S. (1999). *Social protection as social risk management: Conceptual underpinnings for the social protection sector strategy paper* (Social Protection Discussion Paper No. 9904) Washington, DC: World Bank, Social Protection Unit. Retrieved from http://citeseerx.ist.psu.edu/viewdoc/download?doi=10.1.1.200.9746&rep=rep1&type=pdf

Jennex, M. E., Smolnik, S., & Croasdell, D. T. (2009). Towards a consensus knowledge management success definition. *VINE, 39*(2), 174–188.

Johannessen, J.-A., Olsen, B., & Olaisen, J. (1999). Aspects of innovation theory based on knowledge-management. *International Journal of Information Management, 19*, 121–139.

Johannsen, J., Tejerina, L., & Glassman, A. (2009). *Conditional cash transfers in Latin America: Problems and opportunities (IDB Publication 9316)*. Washington, DC: Inter-American Development Bank.
Kang, B. S., Lee, J. H., Shin, C. K., Yu, S. J., & Park, S. C. (1998). Hybrid machine learning system for integrated yield management in semi-conductor manufacturing. *Expert Systems with Applications, 15*, 123–132.
Kim, G., Nute, D., Rauscher, H. M., & Lofits, D. L. (2000). AppBulider for DSSTools: An application development environment for developing decision support systems in Prolog. *Computers and Electronics in Agriculture, 27*, 107–125.
Kurgan, L. A., & Musilek, P. (2006). A survey of knowledge discovery and data mining process models. *Knowledge Engineering Review, 21*(1), 1–24.
Liao, S. H. (2000). Case-based decision support system: Architecture for simulating military command and control. *European Journal of Operational Research, 123*(3), 558–567.
Liao, S. H. (2001). A knowledge-based architecture for implementing military geographical intelligence system on Intranet. *Expert Systems with Applications, 20*, 313–324.
Martinsons, M. G. (1997). Human resource management applications of knowledge based systems. *International Journal of Information Management, 17*(1), 35–53.
McMeekin, T. A., & Ross, T. (2002). Predictive microbiology: Providing a knowledge-based framework for change management. *International Journal of Food Microbiology, 78*, 133–153.
Nonaka, I. (1994). A dynamic theory of organization knowledge creation. *Organization Science, 5*(1), 14–37.
Nonaka, I., Umemoto, K., & Senoo, D. (1996). From information processing to knowledge creation: A paradigm shift in business management. *Technology in Society, 18*(2), 203–218.
Oz, E. (2006). *Management information systems*. Boston: Thomson Course Technology.
Polanyi, M. (1966). *The tacit dimension* (p. 1966). London: Routledge and Kegan Paul.
Power, D. J. (2001). Supporting decision-makers: An expanded framework. In *Proceedings of informing science conference*, Cracow, Poland. Retrieved from http://www.academia.edu/1179619/Supporting_decision-makers_An_expanded_framework
Rowley, J. (2007). The wisdom hierarchy: Representations of the DIKW hierarchy. *Journal of Information Science, 33*(2), 163–180.
Ryan, S., Harden, G., Ibragimova, B., & Windsor, J. (2012). The business value of knowledge management. In *Proceedings of the eighteenth Americas conference on information systems*, Seattle, Washington. Retrieved from http://aisel.aisnet.org/amcis2012/proceedings/DecisionSupport/6
Schreiber, G., Akkermans, H., Anjewierden, A., de Hoog, R., Shadbolt, N., Van de Velde, W., et al. (1999). *Knowledge engineering and management: The CommonKADS methodology*. Cambridge, MA: MIT Press.
Schreiber, G., Wielinga, B., de Hoog, R., Akkermans, H., & Van de Velde, W. (1994). CommonKADS: A comprehensive methodology for KBS development. *IEEE Expert, 9*(6), 28–37.
Sharma, S., & Osei-Bryson, K.-M. (2010). Toward an integrated knowledge discovery and data mining process model. *The Knowledge Engineering Review, 25*(1), 49–67.
Tian, Q., Ma, J., & Liu, O. (2002). A hybrid knowledge and model system for R&D project selection. *Expert Systems with Applications, 23*, 265–271.
Villalobos, V. S., Blanco, G., & Bassett, L. (2010). *Management information systems for conditional cash transfers and social protection systems in Latin America: A tool for improved program management and evidence-based decision-making*. World Bank, Social Protection Unit, Latin America and the Caribbean Region. Retrieved from http://siteresources.worldbank.org/SAFETYNETSANDTRANSFERS/Resources/mis_ctt_english_full_report.pdf
Wen, W., Wang, W. K., & Wang, C. H. (2005). A knowledge-based intelligent decision support system for national defense budget planning. *Expert Systems with Applications, 28*, 55–66.
Wiig, K. M., Hoog, R., & Spex, R. (1997). Supporting knowledge management: A selection of methods and techniques. *Expert Systems with Applications, 13*, 15–27.

Chapter 7
Addressing a Knowledge Externality Schism in Public Policy in the English Speaking Caribbean

Koen Rossel-Cambier

Abstract This chapter proposes an innovative framework to knowledge management from a public policy perspective. It identifies possible adverse externalities when management of knowledge is incomplete in public policy making. For public policies to be effective, four knowledge functions—policy planning, legislation, budgeting, and implementation—must be maximised and linked. Should these respective functions fail to connect with one another, overall policy effectiveness may decrease. This chapter gives special consideration to lessons learned of Caribbean governments dealing with public policy development. Taking into account the specific context of small island development states, numerous opportunities exist for knowledge-based innovations.

Keywords Knowledge management • Public policy • Caribbean small island states

7.1 Introduction

Over the last 2 decades knowledge management has received increased interest from both private and public sector stakeholders. In the public sector, the concept of evidence-based policy making has gained importance and has progressively inspired research to link knowledge management tools with public policy making (Alavi & Leidner, 2001).

Knowledge management has become a buzz word for a wide array of information, management, and technology-related interventions (UNECLAC, 2010). Various interpretations of the concept exist and it is important to frame these into their context in order to develop common understanding. Knowledge management

K. Rossel-Cambier (✉)
Center for European Research on Microfinance (CERMi) - University of Mons (UMONS) / University of Brussels (ULB), Belgium
e-mail: koenrc@yahoo.com

K.-M. Osei-Bryson et al. (eds.), *Knowledge Management for Development*, Integrated Series in Information Systems 35, DOI 10.1007/978-1-4899-7392-4_7,

initiatives aim at enhancing the efficiency of public services by connecting information. It involves the development of new knowledge, but can also consolidate evidence from outdated systems. Knowledge management can improve overall performance and capitalise on a broader and more integrated knowledge base (Riege & Lindsay, 2006). It often improves accountability and mitigates risks by encouraging informed decisions. Knowledge management should allow for better and more cost-effective constituent services, such as enhancing partnerships with and responsiveness to the public. Therefore, knowledge management focuses on the sharing of knowledge, often through the distribution of good practices and lessons learned.

Knowledge management should be key to public policy making, but the way policies are planned, budgeted, implemented, or legislated in knowledge isolation may generate unintended effects—or externalities—on the planned outcomes.

This chapter aims to conceptualise a comprehensive knowledge management framework for public policy making. Paying special attention to experiences in the Caribbean region, it explores the following research question: How can knowledge management support public policies in the most effective way?

Referring to literature, policy plans, and qualitative evidence from the Eastern Caribbean, the second section of this chapter describes possible adverse externalities linked to ineffective knowledge-based policy making. The following sections suggest ways to reverse this schism between policy making and successful implementation and propose a conceptual integrated knowledge function framework which can be the basis for future public policy making and ongoing research.

7.2 Adverse Externalities in Knowledge-Based Policy Making

Knowledge management deals primarily with the organisation, integration, sharing, and delivery of knowledge. A knowledge management function can be described as a cycle linking the generation, access, use, monitoring, and evaluation of information. In the context of public policy decision making, a comprehensive knowledge function needs to ensure that all its elements are taken into account. While these knowledge cycles may exist in the Caribbean region in practice, there remain challenges in ensuring the use of knowledge for effective policy making (Rossel-Cambier, Olsen, & Pourzand, 2007). These challenges often relate to the disconnection between policy, legal, financial, or implementation planning efforts.

Many Caribbean countries have endorsed well-informed and knowledge-driven sectoral and development plans, but these tend not to link to rigid budgeting processes (Feeny & McGillivray, 2010). Most of the poverty reduction plans developed during the period 2008–2012, for instance, were based on a well-prepared knowledge-gathering function. Most refer to country-specific qualitative and quantitative analyses from earlier poverty assessments and propose more advanced knowledge-driven approaches for poverty monitoring. In practice, however, the poverty plans lack effectiveness and relevance as they often do not relate to the existing national budgeting processes. Innovations which would need additional resources are often not included in the capital budget lines and can be referred as "wish lists" without clear perspective on the source of funding.

In many cases, public policy plans do not take adequately into account the national legal context. Evidence-based policy innovations often need to be enforced through adapted knowledge-driven legislation. Enacting policy decisions can allow long-term political commitment. Legalisation of policy decisions can also ensure that rights and responsibilities are enforced, promoting universality and transparency. Many Caribbean governments have challenges in ensuring an up-to-date legal framework. Commitments made through the ratification of international human rights or the signing of trade treaties find slow adjustment and enactment in national legislation. Many ministries of justice in the Caribbean are coping with long waiting lists of legislation to be drafted. In many cases these problems are related to the limited financial, institutional, and human resources capacity the Caribbean countries have, which can be linked to their small size.

Evidence-based policy plans refer to objectives or results and are accompanied by a monitoring framework. In practice, however, in many Caribbean countries national statistical and administrative systems are not equipped to generate and monitor the proposed indicators in a timely manner. National budget audits are often not timely enough to allow for adequate assessment of the budgeting exercise. There is often a detachment between national statistical functions and the monitoring of policy plans. These elements can challenge knowledge-based policy monitoring.

The presence of knowledge functions working in "silos" or separate dimensions of public policy such as planning, budgeting, legislation, and statistics generation can lead to adverse efficiency externalities. Externalities occur when activities have an unintended knock-on effect on other factors (Karlsson & Gråsjö, 2012). When policy planning is driven too unilaterally by specific elements of a knowledge cycle, other important elements may be overlooked. Knowledge-sensitive adverse externalities may lead to an unintended knock-on effect on the overall effectiveness of policy interventions. Policy makers, for example, can be much focused on well-documented budgeting issues, but overlook important aspects relating to strategic policy decisions or implementation needs. Syndromes of these externalities can also be non-implemented policy plans; inaccurate regulatory frameworks; inadequate legal enforcement mechanisms; missed opportunities for innovative investments in national budgets; or inadequate policy implementation and monitoring mechanisms.

7.3 A Four Pillar Knowledge Function for Public Policy Making

Knowledge-based policy planning can embrace different knowledge cycles by ensuring that policy, legal, financial, and programming aspects are integrated in a joint framework. This framework would need to, as is the case for a knowledge function, start with a needs assessment which would look beyond problem statements, but also look into the availability of financial, legal, and knowledge mechanisms to respond to the problems.

This chapter argues that the success of public policies by governments is heavily dependent on a number of knowledge functions. It proposes a model which can provide an appropriate environment for effective public policies. For the model to succeed, a number of key factors need to be enhanced during the process from creation to execution: the planning, legal, budget, and implementation functions (PF_i, LF_i, BF_i, IF_i). These four factors should work together in order to ensure effective delivery and desired outcome of policy interventions.

This question can be expressed by comparing the expected public policy outcomes, expressed by $E[\mathrm{PP}|W]$ where $E[\mathrm{PP}|W]$ is the expected (average) policy effectiveness of a public policy (PP) measured by the same indicator—given (or conditional on) the situation set W.

In order to estimate possible effects, one can specify the following relation for the PP_i:

$$PP_i = \beta_0 + \beta_1.PF_i + \beta_2.LF_i + \beta_3.BF_i + \beta_4.IF_i + \mathrm{w}_{ik}\mathrm{b}_k + \mathrm{u}_i. \tag{7.1}$$

In the proposed model (7.1), PP_i is the effectiveness indicator of public policy i (PP_i); PF_i is a variable expressing the effectiveness of the planning function. In this way, the associated coefficient β_1 estimates the impact of this indicator. Similarly LF_i, BF_i, and LF_i are explaining variables of interest for the effectiveness of, respectively, the legal, budget, and implementation function. Their respective associated coefficients are presented as well. The equation also includes w_{ik} which is a vector of k independent control variables explaining PP_i effectiveness; b_k is the vector of the k associated coefficients measuring the effect of each control variable and u_i is the error term associated to PP_i effectiveness.

Each public policy function can be stimulated with knowledge management tools which can contribute to the overall public policy effectiveness.

7.3.1 The Planning Function

Knowledge-based public policy necessitates both understanding and planning, acting in unison. Policy making is the process by which governments translate their political vision into programmes and actions to deliver "outcomes", in other words, the desired changes in the real world (CIVICUS 2013). Policy making is above all making decisions and setting priorities. Governments formulate desired results with mission statements, objectives, or projected outcomes. Policy initiatives must derive from a core, well-managed, and collated data set. In order to successfully understand and plan for the implementation of policies, data must be acquired, collated, presented, and organised in a coherent and structured manner. This allows policy planners to analyse and use knowledge. The quality of the knowledge-based planning function can strongly influence the overall effectiveness of a public policy.

7.3.2 The Legislative Function

A knowledge-driven policy planning function is fundamental to public policy making. However, this function does not exist in isolation. While public policy planning projects objectives and results to be met, legal work is designed to make certain that public policies are ensured in a universal way. The legislative function should build on findings from research and knowledge management. While producing a robust legal framework is in itself a process of negotiation and compromise, qualitative and quantitative data management can ensure that the key issues are being tackled by law makers. Many bills can fail to become Acts, falling at the legislative hurdle due to a lack of political consensus. Legal initiatives can be developmental, promoting social and economic rights. They can also be protective to ensure that the needs and rights of vulnerable groups are taken into account. Legislation creates government accountability in the long run. Law enforcement initiatives can aim at ensuring that all citizens benefit or respect public policy options (Arora, 2011). Therefore, in many cases, the legal function provides an essential support structure on which a public policy can exist and its quality can be detrimental to the effectiveness and relevance of the overall public policy.

7.3.3 The Budget Function

A plan or a law without a budget is simply rhetoric (Hollister, 2007). A knowledge-based budgeting process is as essential to public policy as the legislative framework. A well-planned policy framework is ineffective without a solid evidence-based financial plan behind it. Knowledge-driven public finance management can ensure that transparency and accountability are at the heart of the budgeting function. Tools such as public finance assessments (PFA) and action plans, results-based budgeting, and mid-term budget planning can promote a more structured, predictable, and comprehensive approach to budgeting. Often public policy plans count on recurrent expenditure to implement plans and oversee the need for capital investment to ensure change dynamics. Acts of Parliament are more powerful if they are accompanied by a realistic approved budget. Without such a budget, policy objectives become symbolic laws rather than achievable goals. Therefore, a knowledge-driven budget function is a key component for the achievement of effective public policy making.

7.3.4 The Implementation Function

Public policy implementation represents the stage at which governments are accountable for the execution of their adopted policy. "Formal" responsibility is created as implementation occurs post-legislation adoption, namely the bill is now an Act of Parliament (Theodoulou & Kofinis, 2004). It is at this implementation stage that the ultimate results of the public policy are realised, often through the collective work of numerous actors. At the implementation stage it is important to allow policy makers to ensure not only that necessary inputs (financial, material, and human resources) are being procured, but also that planned change activities lead to the intended outputs, outcomes, and impacts. A knowledge-based implementation function is therefore more than a procurement apparatus; it should also allow knowledge-driven monitoring and evaluation of planned results. The recording of baselines and periodic measurement of indicators can ensure that progress can be measured. Statistical offices need to ensure that economic and social changes are timely measured. A knowledge-driven implementation function is key to ensuring public policy effectiveness.

7.4 How to Address the Schism: Opportunities for Caribbean Governments

Many sources in the literature describe the different challenges faced when implementing and monitoring policy interventions in the Caribbean. One of the main reasons cited for these challenges is the small size and insular context of the island state countries, as human, financial, and material resources are limited (Amuedo-Dorantes, Pozo, & Vargas-Silva, 2010; Easter, 1999; Strachan & Vigilance, 2008). This reasoning can be applied to the "externality schism" dynamics presented above, as many Caribbean countries have only limited capacity to develop policies, or to ensure a comprehensive budgeting function or the timely provision of corresponding legislation. Many countries are also grappling with the need to innovate their statistical departments, lacking adequate human resources and using outdated data collection mechanisms. Also national procurement mechanisms are slow, inadequate, and lack the ability to respond to evidence-based policy decisions.

The inclusion of the four knowledge functions in policy making can prevent the occurrence of adverse externalities on overall policy outcomes. The various model parameters can be enhanced with adapted instruments, which promote the use of knowledge to make each of the four policy domains more effective.

A common catalyst for improved knowledge management in the four functions is information technology. Each of the respective policy functions can be strongly enhanced with support of knowledge-driven software which allows for the collecting and summarising of key facts. However, in practice, different public software programmes do not allow easy compatibility or communication for data sharing. Therefore, efforts should be undertaken to design interconnected knowledge management systems, where policy decisions can be made, monitored, and evaluated in a more knowledge transparent and comprehensive manner. Planning should be fully integrated with budgeting, as it does not make much sense to plan for activities if no budgets are available. Through the legislation process, not only are problems to be addressed identified and the objectives to be perused stipulated, but in a number of ways in certain cases, the Act can help structure the implementation process

(Sabatier & Mazmanian, 1980). Knowledge-driven procurement and monitoring systems should be drivers for decision making impacting on new cycles of budgeting, planning, and legislation.

This chapter proposes that political will—with the support of technology—can help to address the schism and enhance favourable external spillovers between different public policy functions. This would not only need adapted management information systems, but also adequate human resources training to ensure that the information is adequately collected, analysed, and used.

Many Caribbean societies have achieved quasi-universal literacy and can use this as an asset to promote not only the supply of but also demand for public policy knowledge. Riege and Lindsay (2006) highlight the importance of stakeholders in policy making. Often the entire community is affected by public policy, thus it is important to ensure that governments have sufficient knowledge to ensure that they achieve the projected outcomes for all stakeholders. Budget allocations and ruling laws are key elements of knowledge allowing better appreciation of problems affecting societies (Feeny & Rogers, 2010). In this regard, simple and clear channels of communication are key to ensure understanding and use of this information.

In summary, knowledge management in policy making encourages decision makers to plan, implement, monitor, and enforce policies in an informed way. The aggregate combination of the respective knowledge functions can lead to more favourable results on public policy making than the sum of their individual contributions. In this context, it is important to ensure that the effectiveness of the respective knowledge functions are not measured in isolation, but also a part of a knowledge-driven interrelated results chain.

7.5 Conclusion

This chapter, referring to public policy challenges in the Eastern Caribbean, highlights generic challenges to coherent knowledge-based policy making. It suggests that while at the national level knowledge functions in related sectors may coexist in silos, they do not always connect with each other. This can lead to negative externalities to overall public policy effectiveness.

A conceptual model, involving four related knowledge functions, provides a framework which can give insights into how to address this knowledge externality schism. The current chapter proposes a model which allows a comprehensive design of public policies enhancing knowledge-based policy planning, budgeting, legislating, and implementation.

Often Caribbean small island states (SIDS) are associated with vulnerable states, lacking the capacity to ensure basic knowledge-driven governing function. However, this chapter argues that numerous opportunities exist for knowledge-based innovations taking into account the specific context of SIDS. Reviewing governance through a more integrated knowledge lens may allow innovations in governance and can promote policy outputs with relation to transparency, simplification, efficiency, and coherence. These may ultimately give the smaller countries an added value in comparison to larger states, as they are more capable of quickly adjusting and adapting to new policy opportunities and challenges.

Regional integration can also enhance efficient knowledge-based innovation, taking into account the peculiarities of SIDS. The backlog of legal drafting, for example, which currently exists, can be tackled by pooling regional resources available, rather than a system of duplication between states. Further, their cultural, historical, and religious backgrounds and overall political landscapes have many similarities, enhancing the argument for improved integration.

Many Caribbean states have made important achievements in terms of literacy and their educated human resources can become a solid basis for both knowledge supply and demand stimulation.

Education enhances innovation which can become the engine of growth. Positive externalities from existing knowledge can be considered as the "renewable" fuel for this engine (Peri, 2002). A major opportunity is the use of advanced information technology, which allows the collection, structuring, and connection of strategic knowledge. This can guide policy makers to make more evidence-based policy decisions, taking into account intended outcomes. The availability of a well-monitored IT-driven board table can allow policy makers to have a more objective feedback on the effectiveness of its policy options.

Advanced education can also enhance public participation in public policy making. An educated population can stimulate aggregate demand for transparent, accountable, timely, and user-friendly knowledge dissemination systems. The appropriate use of information technology and media can bring policy decision making and monitoring closer to the households.

The current chapter is limited to the conceptualization of a four-pronged knowledge-based public policy model. Future research can build on the proposed model to develop quantitative measurements of these respective knowledge functions to allow monitoring of the effectiveness of evolving public policies over time. Future public policy economic models may disaggregate the quality and effectiveness of the respective knowledge functions and estimate the effects of possible proposed solutions or changes on them.

Acknowledgment The author thanks Jill St. George for her valuable contributions.

References

Alavi, M., & Leidner, D. E. (2001). Review: Knowledge management and knowledge management systems: Conceptual foundations and research issues. *MIS Quarterly, 25*(1), 107–136.

Amuedo-Dorantes, C., Pozo, S., & Vargas-Silva, C. (2010). Remittances in small island developing states. *The Journal of Development Studies, 46*(5), 941–960.

Arora E. (2011). Knowledge management in public sector. *Journal of Arts, Science and Commerce, II*(1), 165–171.

CIVICUS. (2013). *PG exchange tool*. Retrieved from http://pgexchange.org

Easter, C. (1999). Small states development: A Commonwealth vulnerability index, The Round Table. *The Commonwealth Journal of International Affairs, 88*(351), 403–422.

Feeny, S., & McGillivray, M. (2010). Aid and growth in small island developing states. *Journal of Development Studies, 46*(5), 897–917.

Feeny, S., & Rogers, M. (2010). Policy arena: Public sector efficiency, foreign aid and small island developing states. *Journal of International Development, 20*(4), 526–546.

Hollister, D. (2007). *A public policy primer: How to get off the sidelines and into the game.* Institute of Educational Leadership. Retrieved from http://www.iel.org/pubs/publicpolicy.pdf

Karlsson, C., & Gråsjö, U. (2012). *Knowledge flows, knowledge externalities and regional economic development* (CSIR Electronic Working Paper No. 2012/5). Retrieved from http://www.bth.se/mam/forskning.nsf/attachments/WP5_1_pdf/$file/WP5_1.pdf

Peri, G. (2002). *Knowledge flows and knowledge externalities.* CESIFO working paper no. 765. Retrieved from http://www.cesifo-group.de/portal/pls/portal/docs/1/1190108.PDF

Riege, A., & Lindsay, N. (2006). Knowledge management in the public sector: Stakeholder partnerships in the public policy development. *Journal of Knowledge Management, 10*(3), 24–39.

Rossel-Cambier, K., Olsen, T., & Pourzand, N. (2007). Investing in knowledge for evidence-based social policies for children: Two case studies of knowledge dissemination initiatives in the Eastern Caribbean. *Knowledge Management for Development Journal, 3*(2–3), 74–84.

Sabatier, P., & Mazmanian, D. (1980). The implementation of public policy: A framework of analysis. *Policy Studies Journal, 8*(4), 538–560. doi: 10.1111/j.1541-0072.1980.tb01266.x.

Strachan, J., & Vigilance, C. (2008). *Sustainable development in small island developing states: Issues and challenges.* London: Commonwealth Secretariat.

Theodoulou, S. Z., & Kofinis, C. (2004). *The art of the game: Understanding American public policy making.* Belmont, CA: Wadsworth.

UN Economic Commission for Latin America and the Caribbean. Subregional Headquarters for the Caribbean. (2010). *Knowledge management for development: Towards a practical approach for the Caribbean.* (n.p.): Author.

Chapter 8
A Methodology for Developing High Quality Ontologies for Knowledge Management

Lila Rao, Han Reichgelt, and Kweku-Muata Osei-Bryson

Abstract Ontologies have been identified as important components of Knowledge Management Systems (KMS), and the quality of such systems is therefore likely to be heavily dependent on the quality of the embedded ontology. This chapter describes an approach to the development, representation, and evaluation of formal ontologies with the explicit aim being to develop a set of techniques that will improve the coverage of the ontology, and thus its overall quality. This will ensure that when the ontology is integrated into the KMS it will not jeopardize the quality of the system as a whole. The proposed approach will be illustrated by applying it to the development and evaluation of an ontology that can be used as a component of a KMS for the information technology (IT) infrastructure at a university campus.

Keywords Ontology • Knowledge management systems • Knowledge acquisition

L. Rao (✉)
Mona School of Business and Management, The University of the West Indies, Mona Campus, Jamaica
e-mail: lila.rao@uwimona.edu.jm

H. Reichgelt
School of Computing and Software Engineering, Southern Polytechnic State University, Marietta, GA, USA
e-mail: hreichge@spsu.edu

K.-M. Osei-Bryson
Department of Information Systems, Virginia Commonwealth University, Richmond, VA, USA
e-mail: kmosei@vcu.edu

K.-M. Osei-Bryson et al. (eds.), *Knowledge Management for Development*, Integrated Series in Information Systems 35, DOI 10.1007/978-1-4899-7392-4_8,

8.1 Introduction

Although there is a growing recognition of the importance of ontologies for knowledge management and knowledge management systems (KMS), there are many different definitions of the term "ontology" and different proposals for what should be represented in the ontology. However, most agree that it is a formal description of a domain, which can be shared among different applications and expressed in a language that can be used for reasoning (Noy, 2004).

The term ontology refers to an engineering artifact, constructed in a specific vocabulary, used to describe a certain reality plus a set of explicit assertions regarding the intended meaning of the expressions in the vocabulary (i.e., concepts and relations). In the simplest case, an ontology describes a hierarchy of concepts related by subsumption relationships; in more sophisticated cases, suitable axioms are added in order to express other relationships between concepts and to constrain their intended interpretation. For this research, we interpret the term ontology to include both a concept hierarchy and a set of axioms (Fensel et al., 2001).

Ontologies have been identified as important components of a number of information systems (Guarino, 1998; Pinto & Martins, 2004) including KMS (Rao & Osei-Bryson, 2007; Sicilia, Lytras, Rodriguez, & Garcia-Barriocanal, 2006). As ontologies grow in size and complexity and as an increasing number of demands are being placed on them, ensuring their quality is an important consideration in the development of the systems of which they are a part.

Quality is a multidimensional concept (Wand & Wang, 1996; Wang, Storey, & Firth, 1995) and, in order to assess the quality of the ontology, a set of quality dimensions must be defined. These dimensions are important for deriving metrics that can then be used not only to assess the quality of the ontology, but also to determine whether proposed quality improvement techniques are actually effective. This chapter will focus on one such quality dimension, namely coverage/completeness (Jarke, Jeusfeld, Quix, & Vassiliadis, 1999), which has been defined as the extent to which the ontology covers the domain of interest (Rao & Osei-Bryson, 2007). Coverage/completeness can be measured as the difference between what is required of the ontology and what is available in the ontology. Techniques for ontology development should seek to ensure that the ontology has a high level of coverage. We propose an ontology development and assessment method that focuses primarily on the quality of the coverage.

Since the ontology is a formal description of the domain that must be expressed in a language that can be used for reasoning (Noy, 2004), the choice of an appropriate representation language is crucial. We will demonstrate that one suitable representation language is sorted logic and we describe how an informal ontology can be converted into this formal representation.

The proposed approach also considers the evaluation of the ontology. One of the most commonly used techniques to evaluate ontologies is competency questions (Staab, Schnurr, Studer, & Sure, 2001; Sure et al., 2002). Competency questions define the ontology's requirements in the form of questions that the ontology must be able to answer (Gangemi, 2005; Gruninger & Fox, 1994). These competency questions can be used for measuring the coverage of the ontology as coverage is the percentage of the total set of competency questions posed that can be answered by the ontology. However, in order for the measure to be accurate, we must ensure that the set of competency questions also has a high level of coverage. It would be misleading to measure the coverage of the ontology using a set of competency questions if it is unlikely that the set of questions has a high level of coverage. Thus, appropriate techniques are needed to identify a set of competency questions with a high level of coverage.

Knowledge elicitation involves the gathering of knowledge from experts (Shadbolt & Burton, 1989). There are a number of existing knowledge elicitation techniques (e.g., interviews, 20-questions, card sorts, repertory grids, and laddering) (Hickey & Davis, 2003). These techniques have been used extensively for various types of applications (e.g., expert systems) (Nakhimovsky, Schusteritsch, & Rodden, 2006; Reichgelt & Shadbolt, 1992). Since the competency questions are essentially the questions that end users would ask of the ontology and these would normally be answered by domain experts, it seems reasonable to approach experts to elicit competency questions. In order to perform this elicitation process effectively, applicable knowledge elicitation techniques must be identified. Additionally, each end user has a formally defined role and, based on the definitions of these roles, there are certain types of information that the ontology can provide. Therefore, additional competency questions can be derived from these definitions of formal roles.

Once the formal ontology and the corresponding set of competency questions have been developed, the competency questions will be posed to the ontology. Based on the results of this assessment, further development can be done to either the competency questions or the ontology, or both (if necessary).

We will demonstrate the applicability of our proposed approach by building an ontology and a set of corresponding competency questions for a university's information technology (IT) infrastructure domain. Knowledge about this domain is routinely used to solve a diverse set of problems, ranging from troubleshooting to network redesign, and decisions about software acquisition to server administration. Once developed, this ontology could then be used by other universities that require the same types of problem solving. Additionally, the proposed approach is applicable to any domain that can benefit from the development and use of an ontology. Ontologies are applicable in domains that require a number of different groups of stakeholders to come together to share information to solve common problems, for example, healthcare and disaster recovery planning (Joshi, Seker, Bayrak, & Connelly, 2007; Mansingh, Osei-Bryson, & Reichgelt, 2009).

The rest of this chapter is organized as follows. We first provide a review of the literature that is relevant to this research. We then describe the approach that we are proposing for the development and evaluation of formal disaster recovery plans (DRPs). The applicability of this approach is demonstrated by applying it to the university domain. Finally, we provide some concluding remarks and some directions for future research.

8.2 Literature Review

8.2.1 Ontology and Competency Questions

A number of approaches have been proposed for developing ontologies (Gruninger & Fox, 1995; Staab et al., 2001). Gruninger and Fox (1995) propose a number of steps to engineering ontologies which, slightly reformulated are listed below:

1. Identification of motivating scenarios (i.e., story problems or scenarios not adequately addressed by existing ontologies).
2. Defining an ontology's informal competency in the form of informal competency questions that an ontology must be able to answer.
3. Defining the terminology of the ontology, (e.g., concepts, relationships, objects, and their attributes and behaviors). This provides the vocabulary that will be used to express the definitions and the constraints required by the application.
4. Formalizing the informal competency questions in the vocabulary of the ontology.
5. Specification of a set of axioms describing the properties of the various entities in the domain of interest and the relationships between them.
6. Defining the conditions under which the solutions to the questions are complete.

An enterprise (organizational) model is a computational representation of the structure, activities, processes, information, resources, people, behavior, goals, and constraints of a business, government, or other enterprise (Fox, Barbuceanu, Gruninger, & Lin, 1998). These enterprise models are the core of the information infrastructure of the organization. A number of researchers have stressed that the representation for the enterprise model must have the ability to deduce what is implied by the model (i.e., must be able to reason) (Fox et al., 1998; Kim, Fox, & Sengupta, 2007). Thus, the formal ontology must have a set of formal axioms that provide the basis of an ontology's deductive capability. We will return to this point.

8.2.2 Knowledge Elicitation Techniques

There are several existing knowledge elicitation techniques such as interviews (e.g., structured, unstructured and semi-structured), case studies, prototyping, sorting (e.g., card sorting), triad analysis, 20-questions, laddering, and document analysis (Nakhimovsky et al., 2006; Shadbolt & Burton, 1989). The more structured knowledge elicitation techniques (e.g., laddering, card sort, 20-questions, and triad analysis) have proven to be useful in knowledge elicitation for expert systems (Curran, Rugg, & Corr, 2005; Shadbolt & Burton, 1989; Wagner & Zubey, 2005; Wang, Sure, Stevens, & Rector, 2006) and therefore we will explore their use in the elicitation of information for the development of the initial ontological structure and the competency questions.

The laddering, card sort, triad analysis, and 20-questions techniques assume that the knowledge engineer has some prior knowledge of the domain under consideration. This initial knowledge can be obtained through available documentation as well as by conducting unstructured interviews. The available documentation can be used to get a sense of the domain under consideration (i.e., some of the basic concepts and relationships within the domain). Once the knowledge engineer has some understanding of the domain, unstructured interviews can then be used to provide high level knowledge of the domain. Unstructured interviews suit the early stages of elicitation when the knowledge engineer is trying to learn about the domain but does not know enough to set up indirect or highly structured tasks (Cooke, 1999).

8.2.2.1 Laddering

Laddering is used to construct a graphical representation of the concepts and relations in a domain. It has been used as the elicitation technique for a number of applications. For example, Guenzi and Troilo (2006) use laddering in an exploratory effort to use the means end theory in explaining marketing-sales integration (Guenzi & Troilo, 2006). Chen, Khoo and Yan (2002) employ the laddering technique for customer requirements elicitation in a customer-oriented approach they propose and investigate. They claim that their approach provides a systematic strategy for soliciting customer requirements, and subsequently, for analyzing customer orientations quantitatively (Chen et al., 2002). Peffers and Gengler (2003) use laddering to extend critical success factors with concepts from marketing and research to create the critical success chain method for IS planning (Peffers & Gengler, 2003).

Using laddering, the elicitor makes use of prompts (based on her/his prior knowledge in the domain) to explore the expert's understanding of the domain. A graph, consisting of nodes representing concepts and labeled arcs representing relationships, is constructed in the presence of the expert. This technique involves three main steps. The first step involves asking the expert to identify a starting point called the seed item, which represents a concept that is important in the domain. The next step involves moving around the domain using various prompts (i.e., asking questions to move down, across, and up the expert's domain knowledge). The final step involves the elicitation of attributes for the various concepts (Reichgelt & Shadbolt, 1992).

8.2.2.2 Card Sort

Card sort utilizes a set of cards with the names of relevant concepts or descriptions of problems in the domain. Experts sort the cards into several piles according to whatever criteria they choose. This process is repeated until the expert has exhausted the ways to partition the elements (Shadbolt & Burton, 1989). Card sort is useful when the aim is to uncover the different ways that an expert sees the relationships between a set of concepts (Reichgelt & Shadbolt, 1992). This technique has been successful for a number of applications. For example, Nakhimovsky et al. (2006) adopted the card sort method to redesign the information architecture of the AdWords Help Centre (which assists advertisers on google.com) to enable users to find information faster and with fewer errors (Nakhimovsky et al., 2006).

Upchurch, Rugg, and Kitchenham (2001) identify Web page design quality attributes and explain how to measure them using card sorts (Upchurch et al., 2001). Hölscher and Strube (2000) use a specialized card sorting task to help investigate the types of knowledge that are relevant for Web-based information seeking, and the knowledge structures and strategies involved (Hölscher & Strube, 2000).

8.2.2.3 Triad Analysis

Triad analysis requires that the expert is given or asked to generate a set of elements representing the objects that are the focus of study (e.g., concepts) that he/she considers to be important in the domain. The interviewer randomly selects three of these examples and asks the expert to distinguish between them such that two of the examples in the triad have a common property not possessed by the third (Bhatia & Yao, 1993; Ryan & Bernard, 2000). This distinguishing property is known as the construct. The process continues with different triads of elements until no further discriminating constructs can be identified by the expert (Reichgelt & Shadbolt, 1992). This technique has been used for a variety of problems. Pike (2003) used triad analysis in a series of personal interviews to identify short break destination attributes in New Zealand (Pike, 2003). Hassenzahl and Trautmann (2001) used triad analysis, for construct elicitation, to analyze and evaluate the user-perceived "character" of Web site designs (Hassenzahl & Trautmann, 2001).

8.2.2.4 20-Questions

The 20-questions technique requires that the knowledge engineer selects an element from the domain or a problem. The domain expert is then required to determine what the element or problem is by asking questions to which the knowledge engineer can only answer either yes or no (Kemp, 1996). This allows the knowledge engineer to determine the heuristics that an expert uses in his/her problem-solving process. This technique was part of a Cognitive Task Analysis on intelligence analysts to capture data that provided input to support the development of a computational model of the analyst's processes and analytic strategies (Pirolli, 2006).

8.3 An Approach to the Development, Representation, and Evaluation of an Ontology

Our approach to the development, representation, and evaluation of the ontology refines the steps proposed by Gruninger and Fox (1995) and consists of:

1. The development of an initial ontological structure using a hybrid approach that combines the laddering technique with prior work on ontologies relevant to the domain of interest. This first step will help in defining the terminology of the ontology.
2. The translation of the initial ontological structure to the vocabulary of a sorted logic. This provides part of the language for the formal ontology.

3. The development of a set of informal competency questions that will be used to help create and evaluate the formal ontology. This step will identify appropriate knowledge elicitation techniques for the development of these competency questions.
4. The specification of a set of axioms describing the concepts and relationships between them. The competency questions will be used to help specify these axioms.
5. A method for assessing the competency questions and the ontology. Information regarding discrepancies between the ontology and the competency questions can be used to further refine the ontology and/or competency questions.

The steps will be discussed in more detail in the following sections.

8.3.1 Development of an Initial Ontological Structure

The initial ontological structure to identify the terminology of the ontology will be developed using a hybrid approach that combines the information from existing literature on organizational ontologies (Fox et al., 1998; Kwan & Balasubramanian, 2003; Sharma & Osei-Bryson, 2008; Zhang, Kishore, Sharman, & Ramesh, 2007) with the information obtained by using the laddering knowledge elicitation technique. Laddering has proven to be useful for identifying the relationships between concepts, subclasses, goals, and values (Wang et al., 2006), all of which are important in ontology development. The rationale for using this hybrid approach is that although the laddering is an accepted technique for ontology development, it is not always possible for end users to articulate all the concepts and relationships in the domain. Using a set of relevant, existing organizational ontologies will help to fill these gaps as these ontologies describe the concepts and relationships that are commonly found in most organizations. Thus, combining the concepts and relationships identified using both approaches will help improve the coverage of the ontology.

We identified a number of relevant organizational ontologies and considered the concepts and relationships in each of these (Fox et al., 1998; Sharma & Osei-Bryson, 2008). Fox et al. (1998) consider an organization to be a set of constraints on the activities performed by organizational agents. In particular, the *organization* consists of a set of *divisions* and *subdivisions*, a set of *organization-agents* (who are members of a division of the organization), a set of *roles* that the members play in the organization, and an *organization-goal* tree that specifies the goals (and their decomposition into subgoals) the members try to achieve. An agent *plays* one or more roles. Each role is defined with a set of *goals* that the role is created to fulfil and is allocated the *authority* at the level that will allow the role to achieve its goals. Agents *perform activities* in the organization; each activity may *consume resources* and may have a set of *constraints*. These agents can also belong to a *team* set up in response to a special task; they also have *skill* requirements, and a set of *communication-links* defining the protocol by which they communicate with other agents in the organization (Fox et al., 1998). Sharma and Osei-Bryson (2008) have extended the ontology proposed by Fox et al. (1998) to include additional concepts and relationships such as *business processes* and various types of *resources*.

Zhang et al. (2007) propose a conceptual modeling grammar (i.e., The Agile Integration Modelling Language (AIML)). This grammar is based on established ontological foundations for the MIBIS (multi-agent-based integrative business information systems) universe. The AIML universe consists of *agents* working together to accomplish *business goals*. These *agents* play *roles* which are abstractions for the *tasks* that are necessary to be performed and/or the *interactions* that need to occur to achieve individual agent's *goals*, the *information* that needs to be accessed or will be generated during the course of performance of those *tasks/interactions*, and the *knowledge* that is needed for the successful execution of *tasks* and *interactions* and achievement of the *goals*.

Kwan and Balasubramanian (2003) propose and implement a design for a KMS which organizes *knowledge* around the *organizational processes* in which the *knowledge* is created, captured, and used. Its knowledge structure is a process metamodel (i.e., the knowledge-in-context (KIC) model). The KIC model specifies the elements of a *process* and the *relationships* between them and organizes them into four perspectives.

8.3.2 Conversion of an Initial Ontological Structure to a Formal Representation

Once this informal representation of the ontology has been developed it will be translated to a formal representation. This formal representation will support automated reasoning (using the axioms) and will be able to automatically derive answers to competency questions (Fox et al., 1998).

Fox and Gruninger (1998) propose the use of first-order logic for defining the semantics of the terms and a set of Prolog axioms for implementing the semantics which allows the answers too many commonsense queries about the enterprise to be automatically deduced. While we agree with Fox and Gruninger (1998) on the use of logic as a formal representation language for an ontology, we propose a more expressive and sorted logic. First, rather than restricting ourselves to the Horn clause logic used in Prolog, we will use the full expressive power of first-order logic. Second, following Kim et al. (2007), we use sorted logic for the following reason:

1. Sorted logic supports structural knowledge representation (using partially ordered sorts), a common feature of an ontology, whereas the description of first-order logic is flat (Guarino, Carrara, & Giaretta, 1994; Kaneiwa & Mizoguchi, 2004).
2. Sorted first-order logics improve the efficiency of inferencing as they reduce the search space by restricting the domains of predicates and variables to subsets of the universe (Kaneiwa & Mizoguchi, 2004; Walther, 1988). Efficiency of access has been identified as a quality dimension for information systems (Alavi & Leidner, 2001); therefore, by using sorted logic to represent the ontology, it may be possible to improve the efficiency of searching the ontology and thus improve the quality of the system of which it is a component.

Fig. 8.1 Sort-Hierarchy

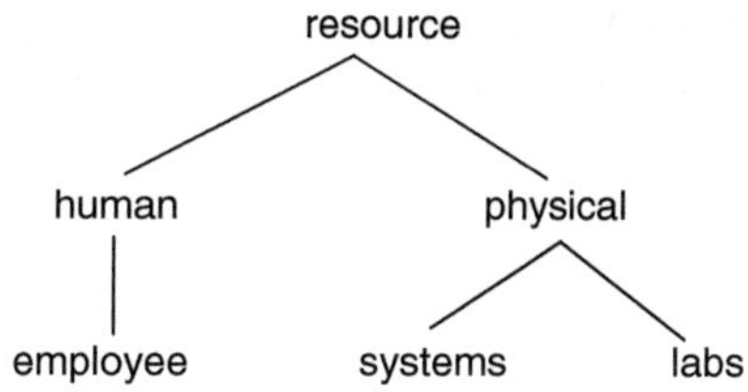

3. Sort errors can be detected which may have some implication for the *consistency* (quality dimension) of the ontology. *Consistency* has been defined as the conformity of the terms (i.e., concepts and relationships) used in the ontology (Burton-Jones, Storey, Sugumaran, & Ahluwalia, 2005; Jarke et al., 1999). Identifying techniques for addressing the consistency of the ontology will help to improve its quality.

Sorted logic is a refinement of standard first-order logic. The primary refinement consists of the use of sorts and a sort-hierarchy. A sort hierarchy is a pair $(S, \leq)$ of a set S of sorts and a sub-sort relation $\leq$ over S (Kaneiwa & Mizoguchi, 2004). For example, for the sort-hierarchy specified in Fig. 8.1, $S=\{$resource, human, employee, physical, systems, labs$\}$ with the sub-sort relations: human $\leq$ resource, physical $\leq$ resource, employee $\leq$ human, systems $\leq$ physical and labs $\leq$ physical. This can be compared to entities (i.e., sorts) and IS-A (i.e., sub-sort) relations in an entity-relationship (E-R) diagram or classes (i.e., sorts) and inheritance hierarchies (i.e., sub-sort) in an object-oriented model.

Each term in the language has a sort s in S associated with it. For example, let x be a variable, let A be a constant and let human and letter be sorts. We can then represent the sorted variable x:human and the sorted constant A:letter (Kaneiwa & Mizoguchi, 2004). For s, s' in S, if $s \leq s'$, then every term of sort s is also of sort s'. With each n-place predicate symbol P in the language, we associate a sortal signature $P(s_0,s_1,..,s_{n-1})$. A formula $P(x_0,x_1,..,x_{n-1})$ is well-formed if and only if x_0 is of sort s_0, x_1 is of sort s_1, .., and x_{n-1} is of sort s_{n-1}.

The initial ontological structure will be translated into the vocabulary of a sorted logic using the following two steps:

1. Each of the nodes (i.e., concepts) becomes a sort.
2. Each of the links (i.e., relationships) between the nodes is translated in one of the two ways:
   (a) If it is an IS-A link, then it is translated to a sub-sort relationship.
   (b) All other links are translated to 2-place predicates, whose name coincides with that of the link. The sortal signature of the predicate is determined by the sorts associated with the nodes it links. For example, assume that the relationship represented in Fig. 8.2 was part of an ontology. Then Works_in(Human, Department) would be a 2-place predicate. The sortal signature specifies that the first term of Works_in must be of sort Human and the second term must be of sort Department.

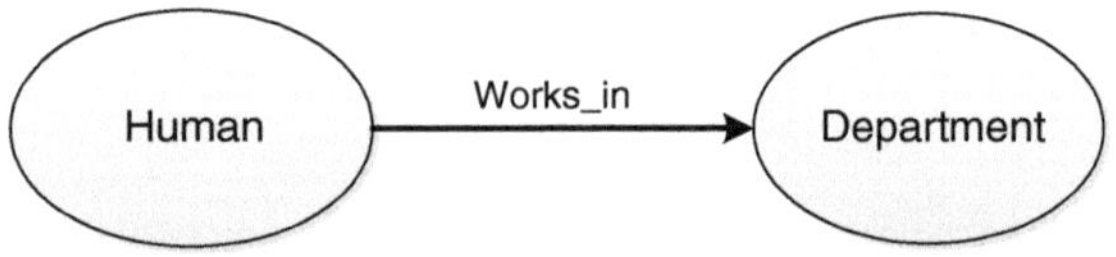

Fig. 8.2 Example of a relationship

This translation from the initial ontological structure will provide part of the vocabulary in that it determines the sorts and some of the major relationships between the sorts. Although this initial ontological structure may be able to answer an initial set of competency questions, it may be unable to answer others without the specification of additional axioms, which may in turn require the addition of predicates to the language. Thus, the development of the vocabulary is an iterative process (i.e., as competency questions arise that cannot be answered using the existing vocabulary, additional predicates may have to be specified in order to be able to handle these questions).

8.3.3 Developing and Using Competency Questions

Despite the importance of competency questions for ontology development and evaluation, there is limited work describing appropriate techniques for developing them (Gruninger & Fox, 1995; Noy & Hafner, 1997; Sure et al., 2002). Gruninger and Fox (1995) state that motivating scenarios should be used for generating informal competency questions. However they do not elaborate on how these motivating scenarios will be identified. Similarly, Sure et al. (2002) stress the importance of the domain expert as a valuable source of knowledge for structuring the domain, and argue that personal interviews are a viable method to elicit competency questions, but they do not elaborate on how to conduct these interviews. Noy and Hafner (1997) also point to the need for interaction between the knowledge engineer and domain expert for the development of competency questions but do not mention any techniques that can be used to facilitate this interaction.

Given the success that structured knowledge elicitation techniques have had in the construction of expert systems (Curran et al., 2005; Shadbolt & Burton, 1989; Wagner & Zubey, 2005; Wang et al., 2006), it is reasonable to expect that the use of appropriate knowledge elicitation techniques will increase the likelihood that competency questions will adequately reflect what is needed of the ontology. However, the applicability of these techniques to the development of competency questions has not been fully explored. We will, therefore, explore the applicability of three knowledge elicitation techniques, namely card sort, triad analysis, and 20-questions, to the development of competency questions. For our initial exploration, these three seem to lend themselves best to the development of competency questions.

For the 20-questions technique, the domain expert generates questions he/she considers important in that domain and which therefore should be answered by the ontology. Using card sort, the ontology engineer will be able to determine concepts that are important to the domain expert for grouping similar cases, and these concepts form the basis of the competency questions as the expert will expect the ontology to be able to answer queries about them. Similar considerations apply for triad analysis.

It is probable that a combination of techniques (Harper et al., 2003; Shadbolt & Burton, 1989) may actually be very effective for eliciting competency questions. As mentioned previously, each of the three techniques requires some knowledge of the domain which can be captured by reviewing available documentation and through unstructured interviews. To provide a more detailed description of the domain, the use of card sort, triad analysis, and 20-questions will be explored.

8.3.4 Assessing the Ontology and the Competency Questions

The competency questions will be posed on the ontology. There are a number of possible outcomes of this process, each of which may require some additional actions:

1. All the competency questions can be answered and all the concepts and/or relationships in the ontology are used in answering these questions. This would reflect that, based on the user groups, both the techniques for developing the ontology and those for developing the competency questions are viable. It would further indicate that the ontology is complete.
2. The ontology can answer all the competency questions but there are concepts and/or relationships in the ontology that the competency questions do not address. This can be interpreted in a number of ways:
   - There are concepts and/or relationships in the ontology that the end users are not interested in (i.e., the ontology is not minimal (Jarke et al., 1999; Rao & Osei-Bryson, 2007; Vassiliadis, Bouzeghoub, & Quix, 2000)). This would indicate that there is a problem in the way that the ontology has been developed and that the hybrid approach may not be suitable for ontology development.
   - There are concepts and/or relationships in the ontology that the end users have not initially identified as being useful. These concepts and relationships can be used to formulate additional competency questions. The end users could then ascertain whether or not these competency questions are actually useful. If so, it would suggest that these concepts and relationships should actually be in the ontology and would further enhance the process of developing the competency questions.
3. There are competency questions that the ontology is unable to answer.
   - These questions can be used to elicit further information. For example, if, after further investigation, it is established that some users find the answers to these competency questions useful, this would indicate that the ontology is not complete and additional concepts and/or relationships should be included.
4. If the competency questions cover concepts and/or relationships that are derived from both the laddering process and existing literature, this would indicate that the hybrid approach used to develop the initial ontological structure is a viable approach (i.e., neither the existing literature nor the laddering approach would be adequate).

8.4 Application

We will demonstrate the applicability of the proposed approach for the development and evaluation of ontologies by applying it to a particular domain, namely the IT infrastructure domain at the Jamaican campus of a multi-campus West Indian university. The IT infrastructure at the university is managed by a central body, the IT Services Department. A brief overview of this department is provided in the following section; this will be followed by a discussion of the benefits of a formal ontology for the IT infrastructure domain. We then describe how the IT infrastructure ontology was built and how the competency questions were developed and used. Finally, we provide an assessment of the proposed approach.

8.4.1 Information Technology Services Department

The IT Services Department's mission statement is to "Enable the use of Information and Communication Technology (ICT) in achieving institutional effectiveness, by strengthening the institutional capacity of the campus, to improve Teaching, Learning, Research and Administration and also to provide effective service to students, staff and the wider community."

In order to fulfil this mission, the following goals have been set:

- Increasing the awareness of management, executives, lecturers, and administrators of the power of ICT and its possibilities for the institution.
- Strengthening and preserving institutional memory.
- Providing an environment for constant learning in the use of ICT by the campus.
- Providing a secure and continuously available ICT infrastructure that is responsive to the institution's needs.
- Strengthening the capacity within each faculty and administrative department to manage the effective use of ICT for teaching, learning, research, and administration.
- Continuously improving the technical competencies and capabilities of the IT services department team.
- Responsiveness to students' needs for ICT in facilitation of their learning experience.
- Keeping the IT infrastructure up to date.
- Supporting linkages of the campus with the wider community including primary and tertiary institutions, the public and private sector and civic society.

The staff of the IT services department is organized into four areas, each of which has its own set of functions. The various managers of each functional area report to the Chief Information Officer (CIO) and University Director of Information Technology; those without a direct manager report directly to the CIO (see Table 8.1).

Table 8.1 Functional areas of the IT services department

Functional area	Head	Functions
Applications	Applications manager	• Deployment, maintenance, and support of enterprise operations (e.g., PeopleSoft, SCT Banner, TMA, Student Registration/Administration System) • Software delivery and management • Information delivery and management • Support and management of Web delivered services
Infrastructure	Infrastructure manager	• Operations—Web Servers, Email Servers, List Servers, FTP Servers, NT Servers, Internet Link, Backbone Network, Monitoring Modem pool • Networking design and installation, Campus fiber backbone, Faculty Networks, Departmental LANs • Configuration of machines—UNIX, Windows 2000, PCs This unit takes responsibility for computer hardware, campus data network infrastructure, communications wiring for data, and Internet services. In addition, it has recently become responsible for the provisioning, maintenance and support of all voice systems, including the supporting network infrastructure
Instruction support services		Responsible for technology to facilitate and enhance teaching and learning • Development, implementation, and management of multimedia enabled lecture theaters • Support academic staff in the use of multimedia systems to enhance teaching and learning • Ongoing support of academic staff in the utilization of courseware development tools • Preserving institutional memory by capturing and recording important aspects of university life in digital form • Maintenance of the university's learning management system (OurVLE)
User support services	Assistant manager	Keep the technology functioning and support efficient and effective usage by providing exemplary customer service, by promoting appropriate customer support options, by responsiveness to users • Offer immediate response to all calls for support • Offer service response within a 2-h time period • To provide a call to fix for PC problems of 4 h or less • To provide a guaranteed response to all service requests

An IT steering committee has been established to make decisions regarding IT on the campus. This committee comprises the Bursar (VP for Finance) who is the chair of the committee, three representatives from the IT Services Department, the deans of each of the faculties/colleges in the university, the Registrar (VP for Student Affairs), two representatives from the campus's maintenance department, and two other members.

8.4.2 Justification for an Ontology for the Campus's IT Infrastructure

Information about the university's IT infrastructure can be used to support various types of decision making (e.g., disaster recovery planning/business continuity planning, security and risk management, training and network design). Having a formal description of the entities, relationships, constraints, and behaviors in the domain facilitates the process of making all decisions with the same information (Gruninger & Fox, 1995). Additionally, decision makers belonging to various organizational units within the university may need to communicate in order to make decisions related to the IT infrastructure. Having an ontology as a reference can facilitate this communication as one of the main purposes of an ontology is to formally describe the domain of discourse so as to provide a common language for all decision makers to communicate, thus reducing the potential for ambiguity. A KMS for communication among decision makers should have as a component this formal ontology as a KMS requires access to the domain information and/or task information and/or organizational information all of which can be extracted from this ontology.

One of the domains requiring access to information about the IT infrastructure is disaster recovery planning. DRPs aim at ensuring that organizations can function effectively during and following the occurrence of a disaster (Osei-Bryson, Millar, Joseph, & Mobolurin, 2002). A DRP is a comprehensive statement of consistent actions to be taken before, during, and after a disaster. A well-organized DRP will directly affect the recovery capabilities of the organization. The contents of the plan should follow a logical sequence and be written in a standard and understandable format (Wold, 2002). For example, in the case of the university in Jamaica, there is an annual threat of hurricanes. Therefore, the DRP would require that certain tasks are performed in the event of a threat from a hurricane. These tasks require certain resources, but at the same time disasters can also affect these resources. Having this information readily available in a formal ontology and being able to reason with this information will make it possible to identify inconsistencies in these plans. If, for example, the DRP specifies that a task be performed that requires a resource and that resource is affected by the disaster, the plan would be inconsistent and would need to be modified.

Another potential benefit of the ontology is in the creation of deployment plans. One of the problems that the IT services department members of staff face is that they do not know the tasks that the various roles are required to perform and, therefore, they do not assign these roles the appropriate access levels, which obviously makes the execution of the tasks extremely inefficient. For example, the Dean's office may be required to print a list of students in a particular faculty by gender but does not have the access level to do this. In order to perform this task, the Dean's office will have to contact a representative in student records and wait for them to send the required list. The IT services department's staff could use the ontology to facilitate the development of more appropriate deployment plans. For example, the ontology can be used to ensure that each actor has the appropriate access level to use a system module that supports the tasks that the actor needs to perform. In other

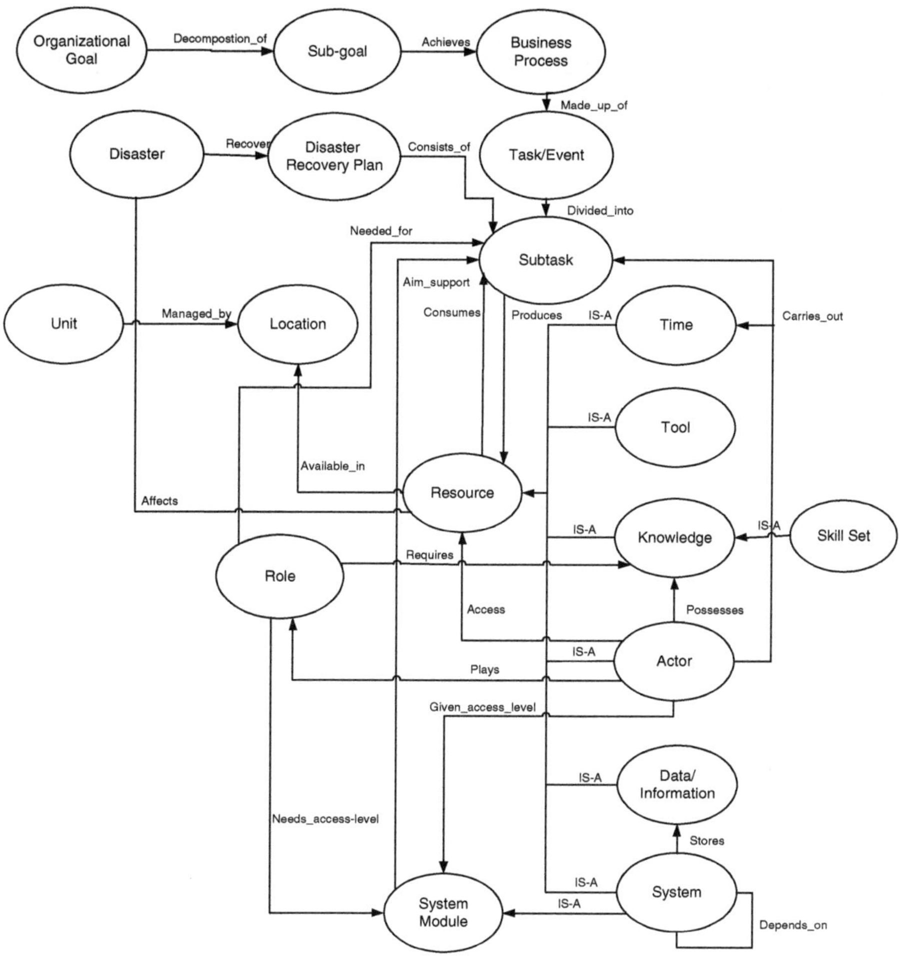

Fig. 8.3 Initial ontological structure for the IT infrastructure domain

words, the ontology could be used to infer whether the level of access assigned to an actor to a system is consistent with the access he/she needs to perform the tasks assigned to his/her role(s). In some cases an actor may play multiple roles and when deployment plans are established he/she may be given inconsistent access levels. The ontology can be used to identify such inconsistencies.

8.4.3 Building the IT Infrastructure Ontology

The initial ontological structure for the IT infrastructure at the university campus was developed using the hybrid approach proposed (see Fig. 8.3). Table 8.2 specifies how the concepts, relationships, and attributes used in this structure were derived.

Table 8.2 Source of concepts, relationships, and attributes

Term	Literature	Laddering	Term	Literature	Laddering
Organizational goal	✓		Needed_for	✓	✓
Subgoal	✓		Stores		✓
Business process	✓	✓	Plays	✓	✓
Task/event	✓	✓	Depends_on		✓
Subtask		✓	Divided_into		✓
Resource	✓	✓	Requires	✓	
Actor	✓	✓	Given_access_level		✓
Data/information	✓	✓	Affects	✓	
Tool	✓	✓	Aim_support	✓	✓
Knowledge		✓	Produces		✓
Time		✓	Managed_by		✓
System	✓	✓	Consumes	✓	
System module		✓	Available_in		✓
Location		✓	Achieves	✓	
Unit		✓	Made_up_of	✓	✓
Role	✓	✓	Consists_of	✓	✓
Skill set	✓		Possesses		✓
Disaster	✓	✓	Recover	✓	✓
Disaster recovery plan	✓	✓	Need_access_level		✓
Decomposition_of	✓				

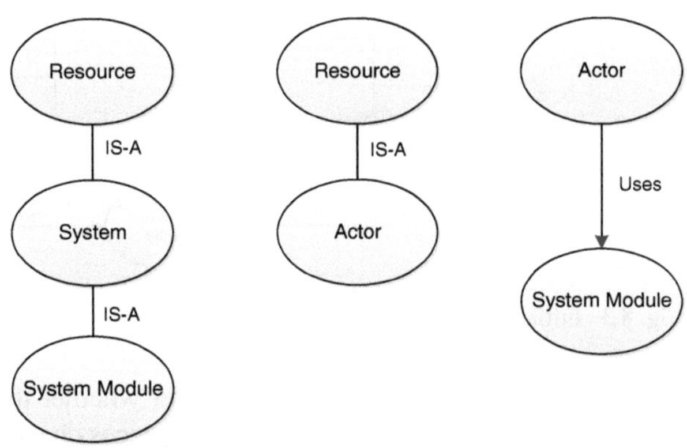

Fig. 8.4 Examples of nodes and links in the ontology

8.4.4 *Converting the Ontology to a Formal Representation*

The initial ontological structure will then be converted to first-order sorted logic. For example, the subgraph depicted in Fig. 8.4 will give rise to the sorts, sub-sort relations, and predicates listed in Table 8.3.

Once this translation has been completed, the axioms must be specified, using the vocabulary produced from the translation process. Competency questions could be used to elicit these axioms (Gruninger & Fox, 1995). For example, one of the competency questions might be "Which roles need training on a particular system

Table 8.3 Examples of sorts, sub-sort relations, and a predicate

Sorts	Sub-sort relations	Predicate
• Resource • System • System module • Actor	• System module $\leq$ system • System $\leq$ resource • Actor $\leq$ resource	• Uses (actor, system module)

module?" In order to be able to answer this competency question, we need to specify an applicable set of axioms. We may ascertain that for a role to use a system module, they must be trained in it. This will lead to the specification of the following axiom:

$$(\forall x : \text{ROLE})(\forall y : \text{SYSTEM MODULE})\left[\text{uses}(x,y) \rightarrow \text{train}(x,y)\right]$$

Some of these predicates will be derived from the ontology (e.g., uses) while others will be formulated when specifying the axioms (e.g., train), illustrating the iterative nature of the vocabulary elicitation process.

The laddering process also provided further information about the domain of interest as the experts were able to provide instantiations of the entities that had been identified. For example, using laddering, the experts articulated instances of the systems, roles, and tasks concepts (see Fig. 8.5), allowing us to introduce a set of constants into the language. Additionally, they provided instantiations for the tasks the systems support (i.e., instantiations of the *Aim-Support* relation) depicted in Fig. 8.3 and the roles that are needed to perform the tasks (i.e., instantiations of the *Needed-For*) relation depicted in Fig. 8.3. This information is represented in Fig. 8.6.

The instantiations of the initial ontological structure can be used to specify a set of constants and a set of facts that are needed for reasoning with axioms (see Table 8.4).

8.4.5 Developing and Using the Competency Questions

Both the formally defined and documented roles of the actors within the organization and appropriate knowledge elicitation techniques (i.e., an initial interview, followed by 20-questions) were used to develop the competency questions. A number of actors playing various roles were used in this exercise. Various actors provided information related to their roles, and using a variety of actors assigned to the various roles helped ensure that the competency questions had a high level of coverage. In order to compare the results of the elicitation processes for the development of the ontology and the development of the competency questions, we ensured that the same distribution of roles was used in both processes; however, we also ensured that the same actors were not used in both processes.

Based on the documented job descriptions of the roles, various benefits can be derived from the development of the ontology. In order to realize these benefits, the ontology must provide certain information, which can be formulated as a set of competency questions (see Table 8.5).

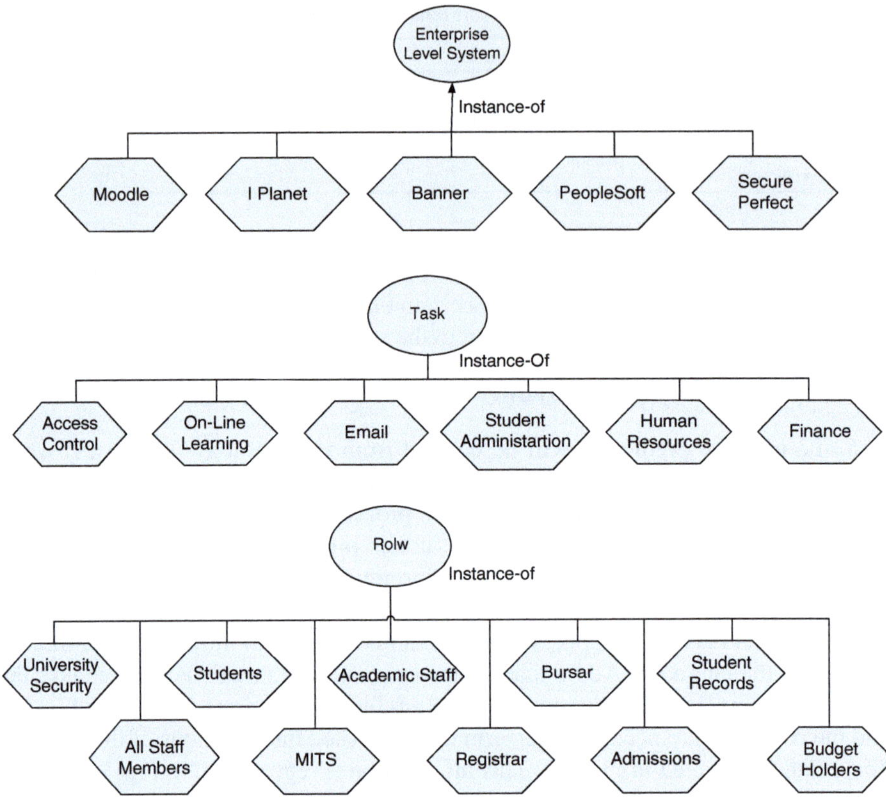

Fig. 8.5 Examples of instances of systems, tasks, and roles

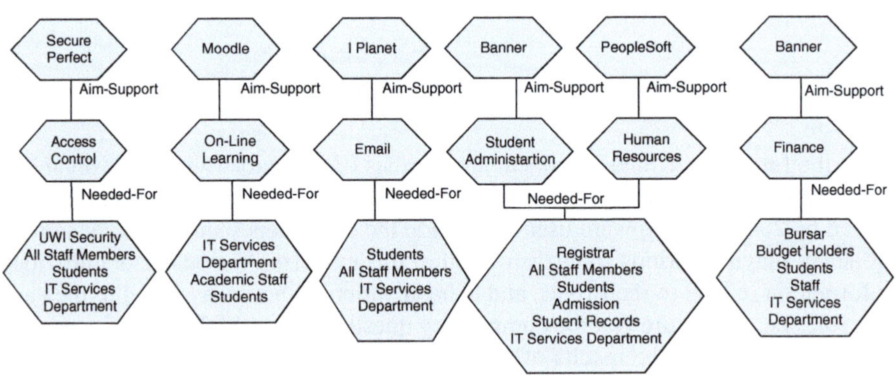

Fig. 8.6 Instances of the aim-support and needed-for relations

Table 8.4 Examples of constants and facts

Constants	Facts
• Bursar: role	• Aim_Support (Banner, Finance)
• Finance: task	• Needed_For (Bursar, Finance)
• Banner: system	

Table 8.5 Examples of competency questions derived based on the formal job descriptions of various roles

Roles	Job description	Potential benefits	Example competency questions
Application development staff	Deploy, maintain, and support enterprise systems	1. Representing the business processes of the organization and the system processes provided will help determine the fit between the two 2. Representing who needs access to what systems for what tasks will help to develop appropriate levels of security (i.e., security plans) 3. Representing what resources need to be protected in the event of disasters assist in the development of DRPs	1. What ERP process fits a particular business process? 2. What level of access to a system should a particular role have? 3. Which actors have which roles? 4. What resources should be protected in the event of a hurricane? 5. What DRP is needed to recover from a hurricane? 6. What tasks need to be performed for a DRP?
Bursar, Registrar	Identify the tasks the systems are performing	1. Knowing the tasks each system performs helps to determine the effect of a system being down	1. Which tasks are affected by the unavailability of a system?
Faculty/department lab manager; IT services department	Lab Managers are in charge of machines in the labs, acquiring the software for the lab (with IT services dept.)	1. Representing software and hardware that labs have will help sections considering acquiring these resources to determine whether they are already available on campus (can be used to negotiate contracts with vendors.) 2. Assists in DRP at the departmental and faculty level as it shows the location of the various resources and which resources will be affected	1. Do any labs have a particular software package? 2. Which units must protect which resources in the event of a hurricane?
The IT services department staff	Communicate with various end-users. Justify their proposed expenditure for the academic year	1. Representing which users are using which systems for what tasks helps identify who will be affected by maintenance 2. Knowing which systems are used for what tasks and what goals those tasks fulfil and the dependency of these systems helps with the justification of the expenditure	1. Which users will be affected by the maintenance of a particular system? 2. What tasks will be affected by the maintenance of a particular system? 3. What subgoals will be affected when certain tasks cannot be performed?
IT steering committee	Acquisition of systems	Looking at the subgoals and the fit of the system business processes with the tasks that need to be performed help with the cost-benefit analysis for systems	1. Which tasks are being performed to fulfil what subgoals? 2. Which subgoals achieve what goals? 3. Which system modules perform which tasks?

Table 8.6 Examples of competency question elicited from various roles

Role	Example competency questions
End users	1. Which tasks can a particular end user do (given certain access levels) with a particular system module? 2. What subsystem modules perform what tasks? 3. What skill set is needed to perform a role? 4. Where is a particular resource located?
IT services department staff	1. Which end users are affected by the unavailability of a particular resource? 2. Which system is dependent on other systems? 3. What tasks are various end users (roles) doing? 4. What access levels are needed to carry our certain tasks? 5. What are the roles the various actors playing? 6. Is there a contradiction in access levels assigned to an actor who is playing more than one role?
IT steering committee member	1. How well does a system module fit an organizational task? 2. What is the value of a system?

The various roles that were used for the elicitation of the competency questions are listed in Table 8.6. In some cases the same person played multiple roles.

8.4.6 Comparing the Competency Questions and the Ontology

Using the proposed approach we conclude:

1. Both the information gained from the organizational ontologies literature and the information gained from laddering were used to arrive at the competency questions. For example, from the organizational ontology literature it was not clear that the fit between the functionality of a system module and the task required to fulfil a business process was an important issue that an ontology could help resolve but the knowledge elicitation process made it clear that it was an issue. On the other hand, the end users did not readily articulate the need for information regarding the relationship between the tasks they are performing and the organizational goals, but this was identified as an important issue from the existing organizational ontology literature. This supports the claim that the hybrid approach is suitable for the initial ontological development.
2. There were concepts and relationships that were included in the ontology but were not covered by the competency questions. These concepts and relationships were used to formulate additional competency questions and end users helped to ascertain the importance of these questions. It was found that they were actually important concepts and relationships and so were left in the ontology and the questions were added to the set of competency questions.

8.5 Conclusion and Future Work

This research proposes an approach to the development, representation, and evaluation of formal ontologies using a quality framework. We have sought to improve on existing techniques proposed by researchers as well as provide new techniques for the process. The motivation behind this approach is that, if successful, it can lead to a higher quality ontology in terms of *coverage/completeness* and thus improve the quality of the systems (e.g., KMS, e-commerce systems, and DW) of which they are a component.

Although we have used the IT infrastructure domain at the university campus in Jamaica as an example, the proposed approach would be applicable to any domain that could benefit from the development and use of an ontology, that is, any domain in which different groups of stakeholders have to come together and share information to make decisions.

In the future, we will seek to extend the research in a number of ways:

1. We will use the proposed approach using sorted logic to fully develop, represent and evaluate the formal ontology for the example application above (i.e. the IT infrastructure domain at the university campus).
2. We will demonstrate the applicability of the proposed approach in other domains such as Disaster Recovery Planning.
3. We will evaluate the effect that the use of sorted logic has over first-order logic in terms of the *efficiency* of the usage of the system of which the ontology is a component and the *consistency* of the ontology.
4. We will explore further the applicability of various structured knowledge elicitation techniques for the development of competency questions.

Acknowledgement Portions of this chapter have appeared in "An Approach for Ontology Development and Assessment using a Quality Framework," Knowledge Management Research & Practice (2009) 7, 260–276.

References

Alavi, M., & Leidner, D. E. (2001). Review: Knowledge management and knowledge management systems: Conceptual foundations and research issues [Article]. *MIS Quarterly, 25*(1), 107.

Bhatia, S., & Yao, Q. (1993). A new approach to knowledge acquisition by repertory grids. Paper presented at the second international conference on information and knowledge management, Washington, DC.

Burton-Jones, A., Storey, V. C., Sugumaran, V., & Ahluwalia, P. (2005). A semiotic metrics suite for assessing the quality of ontologies. *Data & Knowledge Engineering, 55*, 84–102.

Chen, C.-H., Khoo, L. P., & Yan, W. (2002). A strategy for acquiring customer requirement patterns using laddering technique and ART2 neural network. *Advanced Engineering Informatics, 16*(3), 229–240.

Cooke, N. J. (1999). Knowledge elicitation. In F. T. Durso (Ed.), *Handbook of applied cognition* (pp. 479–509). Chichester: Wiley.

Curran, M., Rugg, G., & Corr, S. (2005). Attitudes to expert systems: A card sort study. *The Foot, 15*, 190–197.

Fensel, D., van Harmelen, F., Universiteit, V., Horrocks, I., McGuinness, D., & Patel-Schneider, P. (2001). OIL: An ontology infrastructure for the semantic web. *IEEE Intelligent Systems, 16*(2), 38–45.

Fox, M. S., Barbuceanu, M., Gruninger, M., & Lin, J. (1998). An organization ontology for enterprise modeling. In M. Prietula, K. Carley, & L. Gasser (Eds.), *Simulating organizations: Computational models of institutions and groups* (pp. 131–152). Menlo Park, CA: AAAI/MIT Press.

Fox, M. S., & Gruninger, M. (1998). Enterprise modelling. *AI Magazine, 19*(3), 109–121.

Gangemi, A. (2005). *Ontology design patterns for semantic web content.* Paper presented at the 4th international semantic web conference (ISWC 2005), Galway, Ireland.

Gruninger, M., & Fox, M. S. (1994). *The design and evaluation of ontologies for enterprise engineering.* Paper presented at the workshop on implemented ontologies, European conference on artificial intelligence (ECAI), Amsterdam, NL.

Gruninger, M., & Fox, M. S. (1995). *Methodology for the design and evaluation of ontologies.* Paper presented at the IJCAI '95, workshop on basic ontological issues in knowledge sharing, Montreal, QC, Canada.

Guarino, N. (1998). *Formal ontology and information systems.* Paper presented at the first internation conference on formal ontologies in information systems, Trento, Italy.

Guarino, N., Carrara, M., & Giaretta, P. (1994). *An ontology of meta-level categories.* Paper presented at the fourth international conference on principles of knowledge representation and reasoning (KR '94), Bonn, Germany.

Guenzi, P., & Troilo, G. (2006). Developing marketing capabilities for customer value creation through marketing–sales integration. *Industrial Marketing Management, 35*, 974–988.

Harper, M. E., Jentsch, F. G., Berry, D., Lau, H. C., Bowers, C., & Salas, E. (2003). TPL–KATS-card sort: A tool for assessing structural knowledge. *Behavior Research Methods, Instruments, & Computers, 35*(4), 577–584.

Hassenzahl, M., & Trautmann, T. (2001). *Analysis of web sites with the repertory grid technique.* Paper presented at the human factors in computing systems, Seattle, WA.

Hickey, A. M., & Davis, A. M. (2003). *Elicitation technique selection: How do experts do it?* Paper presented at the requirements engineering conference, Monterey Bay, CA.

Hölscher, C., & Strube, G. (2000). Web search behavior of internet experts and newbies. *Computer Networks, 33*(1–6), 337–346.

Jarke, M., Jeusfeld, M., Quix, C., & Vassiliadis, P. (1999). Architecture and quality in data warehouses: An extended repository approach. *Information Systems, 24*(3), 229–253.

Joshi, H., Seker, R., Bayrak, C. S. R., & Connelly, J. (2007). *Ontology for disaster mitigation and planning.* Paper presented at the summer computer simulation conference, San Diego, CA.

Kaneiwa, K., & Mizoguchi, R. (2004, June 2–5). *Ontological knowledge base reasoning with sort-hierarchy and rigidity.* Paper presented at the ninth international conference on the principles of knowledge representation and reasoning (KR2004), Whistler, BC, Canada.

Kemp, E. A. (1996). *The role of the individual project in teaching knowledge acquisition.* Paper presented at the international conference on software engineering: Education and practice (SE:EP '96), Dunedin, New Zealand.

Kim, H. M., Fox, M. S., & Sengupta, A. (2007). How to build enterprise data models to achieve compliance to standards or regulatory requirements (and share data). *Journal of the Association for Information Systems, 8*(2), 105–128.

Kwan, M., & Balasubramanian, P. (2003). KnowledgeScope: Managing knowledge in context. *Decision Support Systems, 35*(4), 467.

Mansingh, G., Osei-Bryson, K.-M., & Reichgelt, H. (2009). Building ontology-based knowledge maps to assist knowledge process outsourcing decisions. *Knowledge Management Research and Practice, 7*, 37–51.

Nakhimovsky, Y., Schusteritsch, R., & Rodden, K. (2006). *Scaling the card sort method to over 500 items: Restructuring the Google AdWords Help Center.* Paper presented at the conference on human factors in computing systems CHI '06 Montréal, QC, Canada.

Noy, N. (2004). Semantic integration: A survey of ontology based approaches. *SIGMOD Record, 33*(4), 65–69.

Noy, N., & Hafner, C. (1997). The state of the art in ontology design. *AI Magazine, 18*(3), 53–74.

Osei-Bryson, K.-M., Millar, H., Joseph, A., & Mobolurin, A. (2002). Using formal MS/OR modeling to support disaster recovery planning. *European Journal of Operational Research, 141*(3), 679–688.

Peffers, K., & Gengler, C. E. (2003). How to identify new high-payoff information systems for the organization. *Communications of the ACM, 46*(1), 83–88.

Pike, S. D. (2003). The use of repertory grid analysis to elicit salient short break holiday attributes. *Journal of Travel Research, 41*(3), 326–330.

Pinto, H. S., & Martins, J. P. (2004). Ontologies: How can they be built? *Knowledge and Information Systems, 6*(4), 441–464.

Pirolli, P. (2006). *Assisting people to become independent learners in the analysis of intelligence: Final technical report (CDRL A002)*. Arlington, CA: Palo Alto Research Center.

Rao, L., & Osei-Bryson, K.-M. (2007). Towards defining dimensions of knowledge systems quality. *Expert Systems with Applications, 33*(2), 368–378.

Reichgelt, H., & Shadbolt, N. (1992). ProtoKEW: A knowledge-based systems for knowledge acquisition. In D. Sleeman & O. Bernsen (Eds.), *Research advances in cognitive science: Artificial intelligence* (Vol. 5, pp. 171–200). Mahwah, NJ: Lawrence Erlbaum.

Ryan, G. W., & Bernard, H. R. (2000). Data management and analysis methods. In N. Denzin & Y. Lincoln (Eds.), *Handbook of qualitative research* (pp. 769–802). Thousand Oaks, CA: Sage.

Shadbolt, N., & Burton, A. M. (1989). The empirical study of knowledge elicitation techniques. *ACM SIGART Bulletin, 108*, 15–18.

Sharma, S., & Osei-Bryson, K.-M. (2008, January 7–10). *Organization-ontology based framework for implementing the business understanding phase of data mining projects*. Paper presented at the 41st annual hawaii international conference on system sciences, Big Island, Hawaii.

Sicilia, M.-A., Lytras, M., Rodriguez, E., & Garcia-Barriocanal, E. (2006). Integrating descriptions of knowledge management learning activities into large ontological structures: A case study. *Data & Knowledge Engineering, 57*(2), 111–121.

Staab, S., Schnurr, H.-P., Studer, R., & Sure, Y. (2001). Knowledge processes and ontologies. *IEEE Intelligent Systems, 16*(1), 26–34.

Sure, Y., Erdmann, M., Angele, J., Staab, S., Studer, R., & Wenke, D. (2002). *OntoEdit: Collaborative ontology development for the semantic web.* Paper presented at the first international semantic web conference (ISWC 2002), Sardinia, Italy.

Upchurch, L., Rugg, G., & Kitchenham, B. (2001). Using card sorts to elicit web page quality attributes. *IEEE Software, 18*(4), 84–89.

Vassiliadis, P., Bouzeghoub, M., & Quix, C. (2000). Towards quality-oriented data warehouse usage and evolution. *Informations Systems, 25*(2), 89–115.

Wagner, W. P., & Zubey, M. L. (2005). Knowledge acquisition for marketing expert systems based upon marketing problem domain characteristics. *Marketing Intelligence & Planning, 23*(4), 403–416.

Walther, C. (1988). Many-sorted unification. *Journal of the ACM, 35*(1), 1–17.

Wand, Y., & Wang, R. Y. (1996). Anchoring data quality dimensions in ontological foundations. *Communications of the ACM, 39*(11), 86–95.

Wang, R. Y., Storey, V. C., & Firth, C. P. (1995). A framework for analysis of data quality research. *IEEE Transactions on Knowledge and Data Engineering, 7*(4), 623–640.

Wang, Y., Sure, Y., Stevens, R., & Rector, A. (2006). *Knowledge elicitation plug-in for Protégé: Card sorting and laddering.* Paper presented at the Asian semantic web conference (ASWC '06), Beijing, China.

Wold, G. H. (2002). Disaster recover planning process. *Disaster Recovery Journal, 5*(1), 29–34.

Zhang, H., Kishore, R., Sharman, R., & Ramesh, R. (2007). Agile integration modeling language (AIML): A conceptual modeling grammar for agile integrative business information systems. *Decision Support Systems, 44*(1), 266–284.

Chapter 9
The Role of Ontologies in Developing Knowledge Technologies

Gunjan Mansingh and Lila Rao

Abstract Knowledge management has been dependent largely on technologies that are used to manage data and information. However, it is widely accepted that there is an important distinction between knowledge and data and information and until there is a focus on building strategies and technologies specific to knowledge management, the full potential of knowledge cannot be realized. Within an organization knowledge resides in numerous sources of different types such as human experts, processes, and data stores. Therefore the development of the specific technologies should focus on the management of this knowledge within these different sources. Many of these technologies need access to the knowledge of the domain which can be formally represented using an ontology. In this chapter we describe three ontology-driven knowledge technologies and discuss how they can be beneficial in harnessing knowledge in these varied sources.

Keywords Knowledge technologies • Ontologies • Knowledge management

9.1 Introduction

Technology plays an important role in supporting the processes of knowledge management (KM). Traditionally knowledge management systems (KMS) have relied on information management technologies; however, given that knowledge

G. Mansingh (✉)
Department of Computing, The University of the West Indies,
Mona Campus, Jamaica
e-mail: gunjan.mansingh@uwimona.edu.jm

L. Rao
Mona School of Business and Management, The University of the West Indies,
Mona Campus, Jamaica
e-mail: lila.rao@uwimona.edu.jm

K.-M. Osei-Bryson et al. (eds.), *Knowledge Management for Development*,
Integrated Series in Information Systems 35, DOI 10.1007/978-1-4899-7392-4_9,

and information are not one and the same (Malhotra, 2000; McDermott, 1999), it has been recognized that for organizations to realize the full potential of their knowledge these technologies need to be extended to accommodate the nuances of knowledge. Often the technologies being proposed to improve knowledge management are actually focusing on data and information processing, for example, improving communications, reducing the cost and time of information access, and facilitating document search (Garavelli, Gorgolione, & Scozzi, 2002). However, it is felt that there is a need for more of a focus on technologies that actually affect individuals' or an organization's knowledge. Thus there is a need to ensure that the existing technologies are improved and evolve to focus on the processes of knowledge management (Jurisica, Mylopoulos, & Yu, 2004).

The problem with this technical approach to KM is that it may overemphasize the role of technology in the whole knowledge management process. Garavelli et al. (2002) pose and address a number of interesting questions pertaining to knowledge management, these include: "Which are the main features of a KM technology that are really suitable to support KM?", "Does a specific organization or cognitive context actually affect KM?", and "Is it possible to define some criteria to guide the selection of a Knowledge Technology (KT) in different contexts?" (Garavelli et al., 2002). We agree that these are important questions that need to be addressed if the field of knowledge management is to be advanced. In this chapter we seek to add to the discussion surrounding these questions and present three ontology-driven knowledge technologies.

KMS have been defined as systems that provide an information and communication technology platform to enable knowledge sharing and knowledge reuse through a range of services (Chua, 2004; Maier & Hadrich, 2006). These services are designed to harness knowledge that exists within organizations in disparate sources such as human experts, data and information stores, and processes. Multiple technologies are needed to support these different knowledge retainers. Expert systems, data mining, and knowledge mapping are three important knowledge technologies. These technologies all require access to domain, organizational and/or task knowledge and therefore the choice of a suitable knowledge representation format is important. We demonstrate that the ontology is ideal for this purpose.

Ontologies are formal representations that provide a shared understanding of a specified domain. In this chapter we support the need for an ontology in the development of these technologies and describe how they can be beneficial in addressing the specific needs of knowledge management.

We describe a number of important knowledge technologies and how ontologies play an integral role in improving their capability and, by extension, have the ability to improve the development of a KMS. We conclude that ontologies should be a main feature of knowledge technologies since they have the capability to represent the different concepts, relationships, and constraints of a domain. This chapter is organized as follows: Sect. 2 provides an overview of ontologies then Sect. 3 goes on to discuss how these ontologies can improve three existing knowledge technologies, namely knowledge mapping, data mining, and expert systems. Final we provide some concluding remarks.

9.2 Ontology

An ontology refers to an engineering artifact, constructed in a specific vocabulary, used to describe a certain reality, plus a set of explicit assertions regarding the intended meaning of the expressions in the vocabulary. More specifically they have been defined as the shared understanding within some domain of interest, which can be conceived as a set of classes (concepts), relations, functions, axioms, and instances (Cannataro and Comito 2003; Noy & McGuiness, 2001). These ontologies provide a framework for facilitating effective and efficient knowledge sharing by formally modeling the domain of discourse. Ontologies have been identified as important components of a number of types of information systems (Pinto & Martin, 2004) including KMS (Rao & Osei-Bryson, 2007).

Guarino (1998) categorized ontologies as general or top-level, domain and task, or application ontologies.

- A general/top level ontology represents domain-independent concepts. Is so general (e.g., object, event, action) that it is applicable across domains and therefore is relevant to many groups of users.
- A domain ontology and a task ontology describe the vocabulary of a generic domain (e.g., medicine) or generic task (e.g., diagnosing). This is done by applying specialized terms to the top-level ontology.
- An application ontology describes the concepts that are relevant to a particular domain and task under consideration.

All these ontologies can be represented in several forms ranging from a general lexicon to a fully logical represented system (Jurisica et al., 2004; Koenderink, Top, & van Vliet, 2006). They can be as simple as describing a hierarchy of concepts related by subsumption relations or as sophisticated as using axioms to express other relationships between concepts and to constrain their intended interpretation (Guarino, 1998).

In the context of information systems, ontologies have a temporal dimension and a structural dimension (Guarino, 1998). The temporal dimension is concerned with whether an ontology is used at the development stage or at run time, while the structure dimension is concerned with how an ontology affects the various components of an information system. For example, if the ontology is being used by the user-interface, data stores, or application programs.

Ontologies provide a number of benefits including sharing a common understanding of the structure of the information among people or software agents, enabling the reuse of domain knowledge, separating domain knowledge from operational knowledge, making domain assumptions explicit, and analyzing domain knowledge (Noy & McGuiness, 2001). They are seen as a useful tool in facilitating information sharing and reuse (Fensel, 2004) and have the capability to become a main component in knowledge technologies for both the development and the use of the KMS.

9.3 Ontologies and Knowledge Technologies

KMS typically have three-tiers: the presentation services layer, the knowledge services layer, and the infrastructure services layer. Various knowledge technologies can be used in these layers. In the knowledge services layer, the technologies are used to facilitate the discovery, capture, and sharing of knowledge which ensures that knowledge reuse occurs. In this layer the technologies manipulate different knowledge retainers within the domain including human experts, processes, and data stores (e.g., databases, data warehouses).

Many of these technologies require information about the domain which the technology will support, which, if represented formally can improve the quality and the efficiency of the process. One way to create this formal representation is through the development of an ontology. For example, an *organizational* ontology provides a set of terms and constraints that describe the structure and behavior of the organization (Fox and Gruninger 1998; Zhang et al. 2007). We now present three important knowledge technologies and describe how they have been enhanced by the use of ontologies. These technologies are knowledge mapping, data mining, and expert systems.

9.3.1 Knowledge Mapping

A knowledge map is a knowledge representation technique that displays the underlying relationships between different knowledge items in a given domain. It is used by organizations to reveal different aspects of knowledge which are embedded in the processes of the organization. It has been demonstrated that an ontology can play a critical role in the process of knowledge mapping (Mansingh, Osei-Bryson, & Reichgelt, 2009). Mansingh et al. (2009) propose an ontology-driven knowledge mapping technique and demonstrate its applicability in the medical-care domain by developing an ontology and describing how different knowledge items can be extracted and displayed as a knowledge map (see Figs. 9.1 and 9.2). A knowledge map is a subset of the instantiated ontology that is developed for a particular purpose. For example, Fig. 9.3 displays part of a knowledge structure map for performing hip replacement surgery. The medical-care domain ontology was used to develop this knowledge map. All the relevant knowledge items which are associated with a particular process are extracted and represented in the knowledge structure map. Therefore, the know-what, know-where, and know-how of a process are represented in the knowledge structure map. The know-what identifies all the different roles, groups, and resources that are associated with the tasks; the know-how is represented in the sequencing between the tasks; and the know-where represents the locations of the resources. Using ontologies in the development of specific knowledge maps makes the process more efficient as the ontology already models the domain knowledge. An ontology-driven knowledge mapping technique can be used to develop a knowledge technology which models the knowledge embedded in organizational processes.

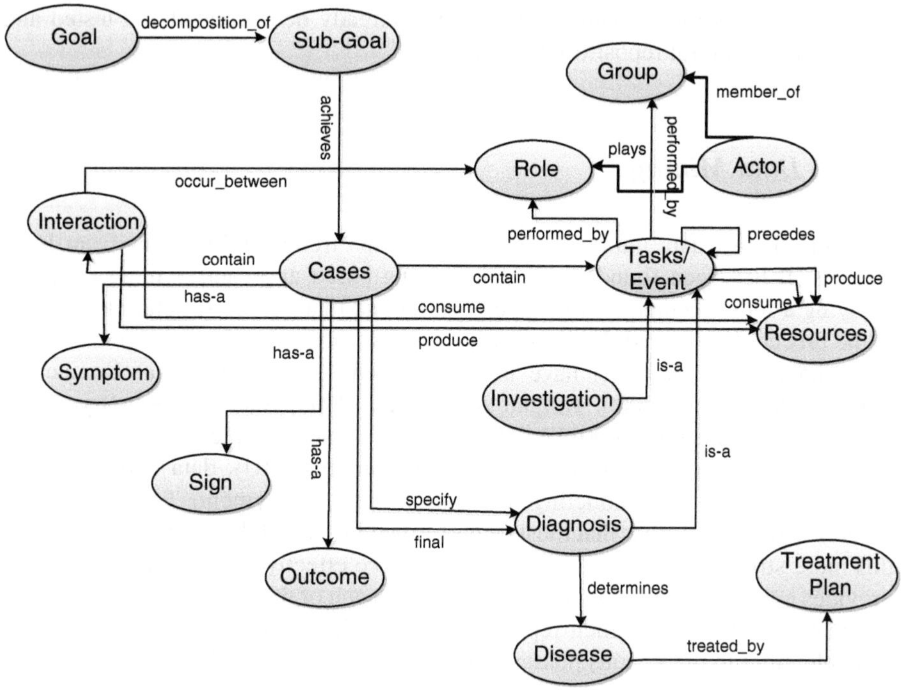

Fig. 9.1 Medical-care ontology

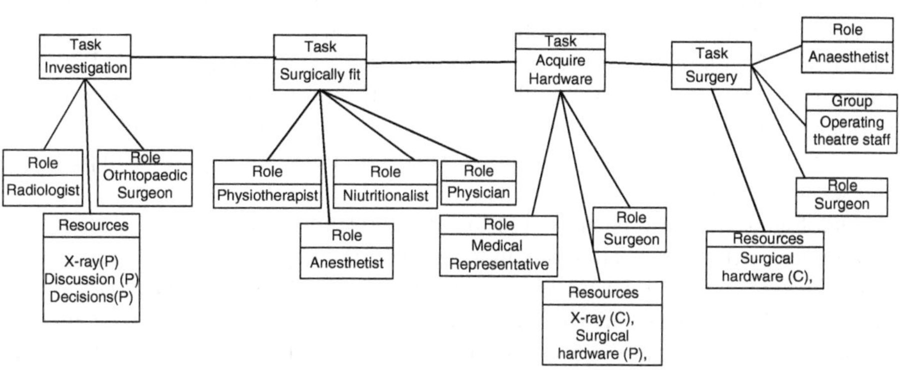

Fig. 9.2 Knowledge structure map for hip replacement

This ontology will be accessed in the development of a specific knowledge map and is used in the knowledge services layer to facilitate knowledge capture and sharing. When a user requests a knowledge map for a particular process, the request results in the extraction of a subset of the ontology (i.e., extracts the relevant knowledge items from the instantiated ontologies) which is then presented to the user for analysis. Using the ontology in the knowledge mapping process improves its reliability and efficiency as the domain knowledge has already been created and tested and resides in one central repository for reuse.

9.3.2 Data Mining

The objective of data mining is to extract hidden trends and patterns from large datasets. It has been found that a data mining-based approach is more than just applying a set of techniques to a given dataset and that a more structured approach to the process is required. Various formal process models for knowledge discovery and data mining (KDDM) have been proposed (Cios, Teresinska, Konieczna, Potocka, & Sharma, 2000; Kurgan & Musilek, 2006; Sharma, Osei-Bryson, & Kasper, 2012; Shearer, 2000). A KDDM process model typically consists of six phase: application domain or business understanding (BU), data understanding, data preparation, data modeling, evaluation, and deployment. The model also identifies all the activities that must be performed in each of these phases. Following this more structured approach will lead to a more effective discovery process as it provides guidance to the data mining analyst for each of the phases. The domain and application ontologies, which represent the domain and task knowledge, provide valuable input to the various phases of the KDDM process model.

An organizational domain ontology has been used in the BU phase of the KDDM process model. The organizational ontology models various concepts within an organization such as the organizational goals, sub-goals, activities, and resources which are linked by relationships and constraints. One of the objectives in the BU phase is to identify the business objectives of mining the data. These can be identified from the ontology by identifying the appropriate sub-goals (see Fig. 9.3) (Sharma & Osei-Bryson, 2008). The tools and techniques that can be used by the various activities in the BU phase can also be identified as they would have been categorized as resources in the ontology. Therefore the ontology assists in performing several activities in the BU phase.

Ontologies have also been used in the data modeling phase. Various data mining techniques, such as association rule induction (ARI) and predictive modeling can use ontologies to extract relevant knowledge from data (Mansingh, Osei-Bryson, & Reichgelt, 2010; Zhang, Silvescu, & Honavar, 2002). An issue with ARI is that the output generated typically consists of a large number of rules many of which may already be known and therefore the task of finding what was unknown is tedious. The prior knowledge represented in a medical ontology has been used to prune the number of association rules generated by ARI (see Fig. 9.4) (Mansingh et al., 2010). Mansingh et al. (2010) applied ARI to identify which disease codes in patients either co-occur or are associated-with each other (i.e., *p_co_occur* or *p_co_associated_with*). This lead to several association rules being generated and the ontology was used as a pruning mechanism to reduce the number of rules that the domain expert had to examine. This was done by matching the set of rules that exists in the instantiation of the domain ontology with those that were found by mining. The set difference of this

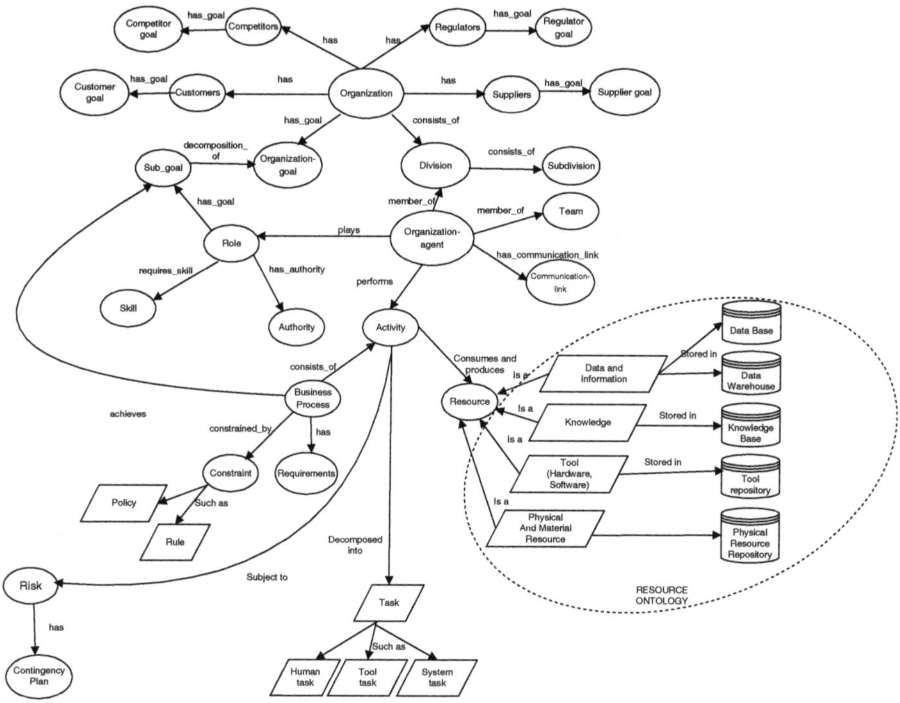

Fig. 9.3 Extended organizational ontology (Source: Sharma & Osei-Bryson, 2008)

(i.e., the difference between what was found by mining and what exists in the ontology) represents the new knowledge.

Often in data mining the number of variables available for analysis is large and techniques are needed to try to reduce this set without losing any value. Decision tree induction techniques have used domain ontologies to identify relationships between different values of variables or between different variables (Zhang et al., 2002). This helps to qualitatively select the appropriate variables required for predictive modeling. The integration of ontologies within the KDDM process has become essential in developing domain-specific data mining technologies in order to enable the extraction of more relevant patterns of knowledge from the data sources of an organization

The use of the KDDM process model to discover new knowledge is the core of knowledge discovery systems and ontologies play an essential role in all the phases especially BU, data preparation, and data modeling.

In data mining the ontologies are used during the development process (e.g., in the creation of rules) and in the knowledge discovery process which is a component of the knowledge services layer. Data mining consists of several phases and each phase could use a different ontology (e.g., domain or application ontology). The ontologies not only make knowledge explicit, but are also a useful resource for the data mining analyst as they provide a reference point for improving understanding

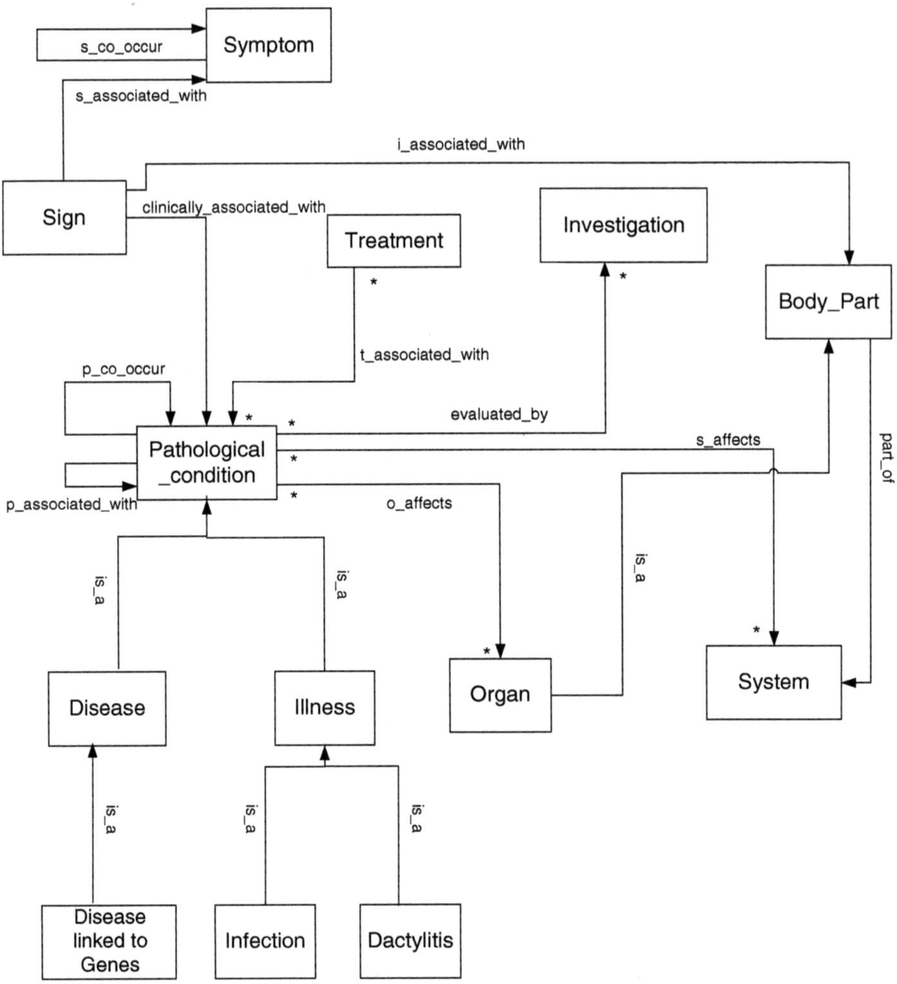

Fig. 9.4 Medical-domain application ontology (Source: Mansingh et al., 2010)

when the analyst is interpreting data, determining the business needs of the organization, and identifying the organizational resources available (Fig. 9.3).

9.3.3 Expert Systems

Expert systems capture the knowledge of human experts and represent it in an automated system to facilitate the reuse of this knowledge. Two important steps in the development of expert systems are knowledge acquisition and knowledge representation, both of which can be improved by the use of ontologies. The development of

Table 9.1 Ontology converted to CLIPS syntax

Class—disease	(defclass disease (is-a Pathological_Condition) (role abstract) (multislot cause (type SYMBOL)) (slot chronic (type SYMBOL)) (slot acute (type SYMBOL)) (slot severity (type SYMBOL)) ....)
SubClass—disease linked to genes	(defclass disease_linked_to_genes (is-a disease) (role concrete) (multislot genotype (type SYMBOL)) ....)
Instances of disease linked to genes	(definstances d_l_genes (SCD of disease_linked_to_genes (genotype SS SC SBo SB+) ....))
Instances of disease	(definstances Acute_Splenic_Sequestration (DCI7 of disease_spleen))
Facts in the knowledge base	p_co_occur (SCD, DCI7) p_associated_with (DCH4,DCK6)
Rules—Axioms	(defrule rule_af1 (signs (?x, DCH4)) (pathological_condition (DCH4)) (p_associated_with (DCH4,DCK6)) => (assert investigate(DCK6)))

expert systems requires access to domain and operational knowledge (Shue, Chen, & Shiue, 2009). The domain knowledge can be represented as an ontology while the operational knowledge as a set of production rules.

One of the bottlenecks in the development of expert systems is the process of acquiring knowledge. Domain and task ontologies have also been used to create knowledge acquisition tools (Studer, Benjamins, & Fensel, 1998). Studer et al. (1998) discuss a system which takes an application ontology as an input and generates a knowledge acquisition tool. The tool would allow the experts to provide instances of the application ontology (i.e., both the domain and task concepts).

In the knowledge representation stage, the ontology provides the domain concepts that need to be modeled in the expert system. The knowledge represented in the ontology can be integrated with production rules. CLIPS, a rule-based language, has the capability of integrating both rules and frames-based knowledge and thus represents objects and domain concepts in its object-oriented language COOL.

In an ontology, axioms represent how different concepts or roles are related, whereas assertions describe the domain by creating instances of concepts, and a collection of assertions describe the state of the world which is being modeled. Table 9.1 shows the different components of an ontology converted to COOL constructs. COOL provides an environment for representing classes, subclasses, instances, facts, rules, and also includes a reasoning mechanism. The *defclass* construct captures the concept hierarchy of an ontology where subclasses can also be defined using this construct. The properties of a concept can be represented as *Slots*. Instances of a concept can be created using the *definstances* construct. The axioms represent the rules which provide a basis for automated reasoning. For example, in Table 9.1 the rule reads, *if a patient presents with high blood pressure* (represented as DCH4 code) *then kidney function needs to be assessed since kidney failure causes an increase in blood pressure* (i.e., DCH4 is associated with DCK6). If the above facts are true, then we infer that *renal failure must be investigated* (investigate DCK6). The integration of ontologies with expert systems enables the integration of structural domain knowledge with the procedural knowledge embedded in the human experts.

An ontology can be used in expert systems during its developmental stage. These systems are used by the knowledge services layer to facilitate knowledge capture and knowledge application. The use of ontologies in expert systems facilitates reuse of domain knowledge and assists in analyzing the domain.

9.4 Conclusion

The technologies presented in this chapter focus on managing knowledge. This work seeks to address the need for technologies that are designed to support the specific needs of knowledge as there is general agreement that technologies designed for data and information are inadequate. Such technologies can be applied to diverse sources of knowledge and support the discovery, capture, sharing, and utilization of knowledge. In designing these technologies, it is evident that there is a need to have access to domain, task, and/or organizational knowledge.

This chapter supports an emerging body of research which emphasizes the need for the formal development of ontologies and recognizes their role in facilitating knowledge sharing in systems such as KMS. Domain, task, and application ontologies play an integral role in the development of the knowledge technologies which can be used in a KMS. We discuss three important knowledge technologies and describe the role an ontology can play in their development. These technologies along with an ontology will become essential in delivering the knowledge services required by a domain and will assist developers to design more domain and/or application-oriented knowledge services in the future.

Representing this knowledge in an ontology provides an accurate and efficient way for these technologies to access this knowledge. We have tried to address the first two questions posed by Garavelli et al. (2002). An ontology is one of the main features of a knowledge technology that is suitable to support KM. Additionally, we have shown in answer to their second question how the specific context of an organization or domain can be easily represented in an ontology;

therefore, context does affect KM. In the future we hope to address their third question and develop some criteria to guide the selection of knowledge technologies in different contexts.

References

Cannataro, M., & Comito, C. (2003). *A data mining ontology for grid programming*. Paper presented at the 1st International Workshop on Semantics in Peer-to-Peer and Grid Computing (SemPGrid2003), Budapest, Hungary, 113–134.

Chua, A. (2004). Knowledge management system architecture: A bridge between KM consultants and technologists. *International Journal of Information Management, 24*, 87–98.

Cios, K., Teresinska, A., Konieczna, S., Potocka, J., & Sharma, S. (2000). Diagnosing myocardial perfusion from PECT bull's-eye maps—A knowledge discovery approach. *IEEE Engineering in Medicine and Biology Magazine, 19*(4), 17–25.

Fensel, D. (2004). *Ontologies: A silver bullet for knowledge management and electronic commerce* (2nd ed.). Berlin, Germany: Springer.

Fox, M. S., & Gruninger, M. (1998). Enterprise modelling. *AI Magazine, 19*(3), 109–121.

Garavelli, A. C., Gorgolione, M., & Scozzi, B. (2002). Managing knowledge transfer by knowledge technologies. *Technovation, 22*, 269–279.

Guarino, N. (1998, 6–8th June). *Formal ontology and information systems*. Paper presented at the first international conference on formal ontologies in information systems, Trento, Italy.

Jurisica, I., Mylopoulos, J., & Yu, E. (2004). Ontology for knowledge management: An information systems perspective. *Knowledge and Information Systems, 6*, 380–401.

Koenderink, J. J. P., Top, J. L., & van Vliet, L. J. (2006). Supporting knowledge-intensive inspection tasks with application ontologies. *International Journal of Human Computer Studies, 64*, 974–983.

Kurgan, L. A., & Musilek, P. (2006). The survey of knowledge discovery and data mining process models. *Knowledge Engineering Review, 21*(1), 1–24.

Maier, R., & Hadrich, T. (2006). Knowledge management systems. In D. G. Schwartz (Ed.), *Encyclopedia of knowledge management* (pp. 442–450). London: Idea Group.

Malhotra, Y. (2000). From information management to knowledge management: Beyond the 'Hi-Tech Hidebound' systems. In K. Srikantaiah & M. E. D. Koenig (Eds.), *Knowledge management for the information professional* (pp. 37–61). Medford, NJ: Information Today.

Mansingh, G., Osei-Bryson, K.-M., & Reichgelt, H. (2009). Building ontology-based knowledge maps to assist knowledge process outsourcing decisions. *Knowledge Management Research and Practice, 7*, 37–51.

Mansingh, G., Osei-Bryson, K.-M., & Reichgelt, H. (2010). Using ontologies to facilitate post-processing of association rules by domain experts. *Information Sciences, 181*(3), 419–434.

McDermott, R. (1999). Why information technology inspired but cannot deliver knowledge management. *California Management Review, 41*(4), 103–117.

Noy, N., & McGuiness, D. L. (2001). *Ontology development 101: A guide to creating your first ontology*. Stanford: Stanford Medical Informatics, Stanford University.

Pinto, H. S., & Martin, J. P. (2004). Ontologies: How can they be built? *Knowledge and Information Systems, 6*, 441–464.

Rao, L., & Osei-Bryson, K. M. (2007). Towards defining dimensions of knowledge systems quality. *Expert Systems with Applications, 33*(2), 368–378.

Sharma, S., & Osei-Bryson, K. M. (2008). *Organization-ontology based framework for implementing the business understanding phase of data mining projects*. Paper presented at the 41st Hawaii international conference on systems sciences, Big Island, HI.

Sharma, S., Osei-Bryson, K.-M., & Kasper, G. M. (2012). Evaluation of an integrated knowledge discovery and data mining process model. *Expert Systems with Applications, 39*(13), 11335–11348.
Shearer, C. (2000). The CRISP-DM model: The new blueprint for data mining. *Journal of Data Warehousing, 5*(4), 13–22.
Shue, L.-Y., Chen, C.-W., & Shiue, W. (2009). The development of an ontology-based expert system for corporate financial rating. *Expert Systems with Applications, 36*(2), 2130–2142.
Studer, R., Benjamins, V. R., & Fensel, D. (1998). Knowledge engineering: Principles and methods. *Data & Knowledge Engineering, 25*, 161–197.
Zhang, H., Kishore, R., Sharman, R., & Ramesh, R. (2007). Agile Integration Modeling Language (AIML): A conceptual modeling grammar for agile integrative business information systems. *Decision Support Systems, 44*(1), 266–284.
Zhang, J., & Silvescu, A., & Honavar, V. (2002). Ontology-driven induction of decision trees at multiple levels of abstraction. In: S. Koenig & R. C. Holte (Eds.), *Paper presented at the symposium on abstraction, reformulation, and approximation: Vol. 2371. Lecture notes in artificial intelligence.* Berlin, Germany: Springer

Chapter 10
Knowledge Sharing in Repository-Based KM Systems: A Study in the IT Services Enterprises in India

Rajendra K. Bandi and Vikas Mehra

Abstract The rapid evolution of the Internet and global telecommunication infrastructure has provided organizations with a choice of service providers located anywhere in the world. Developing economies, like India, have emerged as the leading destination for outsourcing of eWork, both in Software Services as well as in IT Enabled Services (or Business Process Outsourcing). India has capitalized on its early mover advantage and Indian firms now develop software or provide IT Enabled Services for more than half of the Fortune 500 companies. Many have acknowledged the success of Indian organizations, by calling India the back office to the world.

Owing to their success, the Indian IT services organizations have grown very fast, and today some of these organizations employ more than 150,000 software professionals working in different corners of the world. Working in globally distributed teams is a norm in most of these organizations. Members of these distributed teams are separated not just by time and space but also by different social and organizational cultural experiences.

Many of the Indian IT services organizations have put in place formal knowledge management (KM) systems as part of the initiatives to manage the complexities arising from the rapid organizational growth and globally distributed teams.

In this chapter, we document the lessons learned from our research on Knowledge Sharing strategies, in particular, the factors encouraging or inhibiting the Knowledge Seeking and Knowledge Contribution behaviors in the context of repository-based KM systems in Indian Software and Services organizations.

R.K. Bandi (✉)
Indian Institute of Management, Bengaluru, India
e-mail: rbandi@iimb.ernet.in

V. Mehra
Researcher & Consultant, Information Systems, Bengaluru, India
e-mail: vikas.mehra@outlook.com

K.-M. Osei-Bryson et al. (eds.), *Knowledge Management for Development*, Integrated Series in Information Systems 35, DOI 10.1007/978-1-4899-7392-4_10,

There are important lessons to be learned from the experiences of Indian software and services organizations by similar knowledge-intensive organizations experiencing the forces of globalization.

This chapter is written in a descriptive format, enumerating the practices employed by Indian enterprises in repository-based KM systems to manage the organizational knowledge creation, dissemination, sharing, utilization, and deployment. This chapter also lists the lessons learned from successful and not so successful initiatives for managing knowledge.

Keywords India • Developing countries • Software • Services • Outsourcing • Knowledge management • Knowledge contribution • Knowledge seeking • Knowledge sharing

10.1 Indian IT Services and Business Process Outsourcing Industry

The worldwide spending on IT products and services was estimated to be USD 1.6 trillion in 2010 (NAASSCOM, 2011). India was the leading global outsourcing and offshoring destination with a 55 % share in the global IT and BPO market in 2010 (NAASSCOM, 2011). The Indian IT software and services sector was estimated to aggregate revenues worth USD 76.1 billion in the financial year 2011, and account for 6.4 % of the national GDP in the financial year 2011. The IT services industry was estimated to grow by 3.5 % in 2011 and 4.5 % in 2012.

Although today it is a force to be reckoned with, the Indian IT industry had humble beginnings. It started in the 1980s with an initial focus on what is notoriously known as "body shopping," where the primary task of the Indian IT firms was to provide their clients with onsite professionals who would be managed by the clients. By the late 1980s, almost 75 % of the workforce of these firms was working onsite in this model. While it was highly successful, it was not a sustainable model as it faced severe sociopolitical problems like immigration and was considered to be low-end and non-scalable.

Subsequently, Indian IT firms adopted a different model in which a significant part of their workforce was based offshore (primarily in India) and only those activities that required a greater understanding of the client's business were performed by a colocated onsite-based workforce. From having 100 % of the workforce onsite in the body shopping model, by 2003, with this new onsite-offshore model, only 50 % of the total workforce worked onsite. With the onsite workforce percentage continuing to go down, organizations began to recognize the importance and relevance of having a sound knowledge management (KM) system to manage what is increasingly becoming globally distributed work. In this model, which organizations hoped was scalable, low value-added activities like coding and testing were performed offshore, while activities like requirements management were performed onsite.

Over a period of time, IT firms started transitioning from low-end programming contracts to managing complete life cycle processes, gradually moving up the value chain. Many of them also simultaneously started offering Business Process Outsourcing services (also known as IT Enabled Services) which many refer to as moving down the value chain. This was accompanied by initiatives to get quality/ process maturity certifications like ISO 9001, CMM assessment. Organizations also focused on building long-term relationships with clients, gaining knowledge of the client's business domain and operating routines. Project managers began to develop strong project management skills which helped them in the coordination and engineering aspects of their jobs. Starting from offering discreet low-end services, today they are focused on offering services like end-to-end product development, business transformation and reengineering, and product innovation. More recently, due to changing global economic conditions and demands, these organizations have started adopting outcome-based pricing and other nonlinear initiatives to move away from the traditional headcount-based linear growth. There is a strong thrust to create intellectual property and also an attempt to shift from being a vendor to become a partner of the client organizations. These changes, however, require them to be very aware of the current and potential needs of their clients (NAASSCOM, 2011). Organizations not only require the development of knowledge that will meet the current and future needs of their potential clients, but they also have to ensure knowledge sharing among their employees so that they do not attempt to rebuild knowledge from scratch when it is already available in the organizations.

Given the scenario described above, many Indian IT firms recognized the importance of formal knowledge management systems and have invested heavily in repository-based KM to facilitate knowledge capture, retention, and sharing among their fast growing and globally distributed workforce. Despite these investments, many firms find it challenging to encourage knowledge sharing through these KM systems. It is in this context that our study was done. It seeks to understand the factors that encourage or inhibit the use of these KM systems for knowledge sharing. In the following sections we discuss the prior literature on knowledge sharing through KM systems, followed by a discussion of the design and findings of our study.

10.2 Organizational Knowledge Management

Organizational knowledge management is now considered an integral part of Indian IT firms' business process management. Marjanovic and Freeze (2012) propose a framework for the integration of knowledge with the business processes of an organization. Such an integrated framework has its own set of challenges. Foremost is the definition of knowledge itself and how much of which type of knowledge is embedded in a specific business process.

Knowledge has been described variously by scholars depending on their point of view. Emphasis is also given to the differentiation between data, information, and knowledge. A commonly held view is that data is raw numbers and facts, information is processed data, and knowledge is authenticated information (Alavi & Leidner, 2001). Another view is that information is data interpreted into a meaningful framework, whereas knowledge is information that has been authenticated and is thought to be true. According to Davenport (1997), only a continuum of data, information, and knowledge can be constructed and only broad "imprecise" statements about them can be made. Data, according to him, is simple observations of the state of the world. Information, as defined by Peter Drucker (1998), is "data endowed with relevance and purpose." Knowledge is information with the most value and consequently it is the hardest form to manage. It is valuable because it is a synthesis of multiple sources of information over time.

Davenport and Prusak (1998) define knowledge as a fluid mix of framed experiences, values, contextual information, and expert insights that provides a framework for evaluating and incorporating new experiences and information. It originates and is applied in the minds of knowers. According to them, knowledge in organizations often becomes embedded in documents, repositories, organizational routines, processes, practices, and norms. Most of the Indian IT services organizations that have implemented repository-based KM systems tend to follow this tenet and strive towards embedding organizational knowledge into various artifacts.

10.2.1 Knowledge Management Processes

Like many organizations worldwide, Indian IT services organizations have initiated knowledge management (KM) projects that systematically try to manage knowledge. Most of these knowledge management projects have as their primary aim one of the following (although they are not mutually exclusive): (1) to make knowledge visible and show the role of knowledge in an organization; (2) to develop a knowledge-intensive culture by encouraging knowledge sharing; and (3) to build a knowledge infrastructure (Davenport & Prusak, 1998). The importance of KM projects in Indian IT services organizations can be understood from the fact that many of them have been experiencing an annual growth rate of more than 30 % in the past 2 decades. Given that the dominant business model for these organizations has been a linear headcount-based growth model, the result was a significant increase in the number of new employees joining organizations over the same period. This, coupled with the fact that many of these organizations experienced high employee attrition rates, highlights the challenges faced by these organizations to ensure that large numbers of new employees are brought up to speed with the organizational knowledge. Many organizations have therefore invested heavily in building repository-based KM systems to facilitate knowledge capture, retention, and sharing among their fast growing and globally distributed workforce.

Knowledge management is generally regarded as a process involving four basic activities, viz., knowledge capture/creation (including knowledge maintenance and updating); knowledge storage and retrieval; knowledge transfer and distribution;

and knowledge application (using the knowledge) (Alavi & Leidner, 2001). These activities and sub-processes of knowledge management are briefly discussed in the following paragraphs.

10.2.1.1 Knowledge Capture/Creation

Knowledge capture/creation is a continuous process that involves interplay between the tacit and explicit dimensions of knowledge as the knowledge flows through individual, group, and organizational levels. Alavi and Leidner (2001) suggest that the flexible information systems and technologies can support various modes of knowledge creation. Computer-mediated communication, through e-mail, Intranet, online communities of practice, group support systems, and online repositories, supports multiple modes of knowledge creation. These systems and applications are capable of capturing knowledge at the point of origin and are therefore good starting points for the accumulation of knowledge. Computer-mediated communication provides an extended field for interactions among organizational members. It allows for sharing of ideas and perspectives and for establishing dialog that may enable individuals to arrive at new insights and/or more accurate interpretations than if they were left to decipher information on their own.

10.2.1.2 Knowledge Storage/Retrieval

The storage, organization, and retrieval of individual and organizational knowledge are important aspects of knowledge management. Organizational knowledge extends beyond the collective knowledge of all the individuals in an organization. Advanced computer storage technologies and sophisticated retrieval techniques could be effective tools for increasing the speed of access to organizational knowledge and for developing organization-wide knowledge repositories. Groupware tools and document management technologies enable organizations to store and retrieve knowledge in both structured and unstructured forms and to share this knowledge across time and space.

10.2.1.3 Knowledge Transfer/Distribution

An important aspect of knowledge management in an organizational setting is the transfer and distribution of knowledge to people/locations where it is needed and can be used. Since the organizational knowledge may be distributed across various locations, there is a need for strong mechanisms and systems to locate and retrieve this knowledge. Knowledge transfer can occur through multiple channels—formal, informal, personal, or impersonal. Information technologies can support all four forms of knowledge transfer. The formal ways of knowledge transfer are well established through automated workflows and organizational routines. The informal and impersonal means of knowledge transfer have been supported mostly through discussion databases, while the formal and impersonal means of knowledge transfer have been supported through knowledge maps and corporate directories. Though the personal knowledge transfer is heavily dependent upon an individual's preferences; this form of knowledge transfer is also supported by similar information technologies like discussion boards and chatrooms.

10.2.1.4 Knowledge Application

Although there are challenges associated with applying existing knowledge, information technologies can have a positive influence on knowledge application. The application of knowledge is achieved by embedding it in the organizational processes, procedures, and routines. Information technology can enhance organizational knowledge integration by facilitating the capture, updating and accessibility of organizational directives. They can also enhance the speed of knowledge application by codifying and automating organizational processes. Workflow automation systems and rule-based expert systems are means of capturing, embedding, and enforcing well-specified organizational routines and procedures.

10.2.2 Knowledge Management Strategies

Hansen, Nohria, and Tierney (1999) delineate knowledge management (KM) strategies, based on a study of knowledge management practices adopted by companies in several industries. According to them, organizations primarily (though not exclusively) employ one of the two dominant KM strategies—codification and personalization—which are linked to their competitive strategies. In codification strategy, knowledge is carefully codified and stored in databases and can be accessed and used easily by anyone in the organization. In personalization strategy, knowledge is closely tied to the person who developed it and is shared mainly through direct person-to-person contacts.

10.2.2.1 Codification KM Strategy

This strategy envisages a people-to-document approach, in which an electronic document system is developed that codifies, stores, disseminates, and allows reuse of knowledge. Organizations employing codification as the dominant KM strategy invest heavily in information technologies, with the aim of connecting people to the reusable codified knowledge. These organizations hire people who are well-suited to the reuse of knowledge and the implementation of solutions and reward them for using and contributing to KM databases. When the competitive strategy is to provide high quality, reliable, and fast systems implementation by reusing codified knowledge, the codification KM strategy is more appropriate. The economic rationale of this strategy is reuse, i.e., the aim is to invest once in a knowledge asset and then reuse it several times. It would imply that for project-driven IT services organizations, codification as the dominant KM strategy may be better suited for their internal knowledge management.

10.2.2.2 Personalization KM Strategy

Personalization KM strategy envisages a person-to-person approach, in which networks for linking people are developed so that tacit knowledge can be shared. Organizations adopting this as the dominant KM strategy invest only moderately in information technologies with the aim of facilitating conversations and the exchange of tacit knowledge. These organizations hire people who are well-suited to problem solving and who can tolerate ambiguity and reward them for sharing knowledge directly with others. When the competitive strategy is to provide creative, analytically rigorous advice on high-level strategic problems by channeling individual expertise, the personalization KM strategy is more appropriate. Many of the consulting organizations employ personalization as the dominant KM strategy as they rely heavily on the individual expertise of their personnel.

10.2.2.3 Choice of KM Strategy

The choice of the dominant KM strategy is not static, i.e., once chosen and implemented, it cannot simply be forgotten. Organizations need to revisit their dominant KM strategy over time in line with their market, business, and competitive strategies. At the same time, they need to build upon the alternative KM strategy to extract the maximum benefits from their KM initiatives. Choi and Lee (2002) recommend a dynamic KM strategy that varies depending on the knowledge characteristics and is a blend of both codification and personalization KM strategies.

When an organization is offering a customized or innovative product in a market segment and the employees rely more on their tacit knowledge to serve customers, personalization as the dominant KM strategy could be the right choice. However, as the organization learns and the products and markets mature and move towards standardized products, the dominant KM strategy of organizations also needs to be shifted to codification, wherein employees rely more on the explicit knowledge to serve the customer.

Organizations employing codification as the dominant KM strategy build sophisticated electronic repository-based knowledge management systems. Such systems enable better application, distribution, and management of knowledge across various entities within and outside of the organization. However, an organization should take this initiative only if it finds value in building an institutional memory or a comprehensive knowledge base. Kozubek (2012) cites the case of Intel, which has unified all of its legal resources under one portal.

A common problem encountered while implementing a repository-based KM system under the codification strategy is to achieve a critical mass of users and content. Another problem, referred to as "culture barriers," is that a repository-based KM system requires that employees be willing to share knowledge with others. It is obvious that a repository-based KM system must fit an organization's existing culture, norms, and incentive schemes to be successful. Liebowitz (2012) reports that cultural resistance to knowledge management still persists. Less than 40 % of the respondents in his study reported having a knowledge sharing culture in their organization, in contrast to over 60 % reporting a knowledge hoarding culture.

10.2.3 Knowledge Management Systems

Knowledge management (KM) systems refer to a class of information systems that are used for managing organizational knowledge. While not all knowledge management (KM) initiatives involve the implementation of information technology (IT), many of them rely on IT as an enabler. The common applications of IT to organizational knowledge management include the coding and sharing of best practices; the creation of corporate knowledge directories; and the creation of knowledge networks (Alavi & Leidner, 2001).

Knowledge management technologies may consist of filtering, indexing, classifying, storage, and retrieval technologies, coupled with communication and collaboration software (e.g., e-mail and groupware). In addition to knowledge directories and knowledge networks, a common application of KM technologies is the electronic knowledge repository, which stores documents, reports, memos, and other forms of organizational knowledge.

10.2.3.1 Knowledge Repositories

Knowledge repositories contain explicit information and knowledge that can be quickly retrieved by users through effective search procedures. Knowledge repositories are specifically suitable to codify descriptions of knowledge, experiences, and results of knowledge work and to identify the location of knowledge. However, knowledge repositories are not particularly suitable for sharing tacit knowledge, as these databases tend to capture only end results rather than interim learning (Weiss, 1999).

Technologically, a repository-based KM system contains a database with advanced search, retrieval, and indexing capabilities. Therefore, any set of technologies that would manage a database would also facilitate the creation and maintenance of a knowledge base. Gray and Durcikova (2006) elaborate on the role of knowledge repositories in the technical support environment where these repositories help to provide solutions to customers' problems.

10.3 Knowledge Sharing Through Repository-Based KM Systems

Researchers have widely studied individual acceptance and use of information systems employing Technology Acceptance Model (TAM), Theory of Reasoned Action (TRA), and Theory of Planned Behavior (TPB). TRA (Fishbein & Ajzen, 1975) and TPB (Ajzen, 1991) are general social psychology theories explaining and predicting a wide range of individual behaviors, including use of information systems (Davis, Bagozzi, & Warshaw, 1989; Taylor & Todd, 1995). These theories refer to a cognitive process through which beliefs and perceptions affect attitudes, which in turn affect behavioral intentions and eventually translate into actual behavior.

There have been consistent efforts to find an overarching theory to explain individual acceptance and use of information systems. Most of these efforts revolve around finding a better variant of TAM (Schwarz & Chin, 2007; Venkatesh & Davis, 2000) or TPB (Taylor & Todd, 1995) or a combination of the two (Venkatesh, Morris, Davis, & Davis, 2003; Wixom & Todd, 2005).

Venkatesh et al. (2003) reviewed eight competing theories employed to explain individual acceptance and use of information systems. They identified seven constructs that appeared to be significant direct determinants of intention or usage in one or more of the individual models.

In the context of repository-based KM system, the usage of this specific type of information system is deemed to be akin to sharing knowledge through this system. Thus, the purpose of implementing a repository-based KM system in an organization is to enhance creation, capture, distribution, and application of codified knowledge within the organization. But, if the KM system is not used by people in the organization, the basic objective of facilitating and enhancing knowledge sharing among the people would not be achieved.

10.3.1 Characteristics Affecting Knowledge Sharing

Individuals, as perceptive beings, are influenced by various contextual factors that affect their knowledge sharing behavior in an organization. These factors may be classified into five categories—characteristics of the individual, the organization, the technology, the task, and the knowledge itself. These categories are discussed briefly in the following paragraphs.

10.3.1.1 Individual Characteristics

An individual is the originator and user of knowledge existing in an organization who may be motivated to share this knowledge due to personal benefits, economic and noneconomic, or due to pro-social inclinations (Bock & Kim, 2002;

Constant, Kiesler, & Sproull, 1994, 1996; Constant, Sproull & Kiesler, 1996; Jarvenpaa & Staples, 2000, 2001; Schwarz & Chin, 2007; Venkatesh et al., 2003; Wixom & Todd, 2005). The specific characteristics of individuals that affect their knowledge sharing behavior through KM system are personal benefits, pro-social behavior, propensity to share, generalized reciprocity, expertise, self-esteem, computer comfort, and work experience. The literature indicates that the presence of these characteristics positively affects the knowledge sharing behavior of individuals and a higher concentration of these characteristics leads to more knowledge sharing.

Knowledge sharing through an impersonal medium such as a KM system does not offer direct extrinsic rewards. Thus, individuals must be motivated enough to share knowledge through the KM system. Knowledge sharing over computer networks is based on an individual's self-esteem, self-consistency, work experience, personal identification with the organization, feelings of commitment towards the organization, and the norms of generalized reciprocity.

10.3.1.2 Organizational Characteristics

Individuals work within the conceptual boundary of an organization. Thus, characteristics of a specific organization affect how individuals behave generally with their colleagues (Scholz, 1990; Wellman, 2007). Organizational factors affecting individuals' general behavior would also affect their knowledge sharing behavior. The specific organizational characteristics that may affect an individual's knowledge sharing behavior through KM system are structure, strategy, KM policy, culture, management support, measurement, and incentives (Mehta, 2008).

While organizational characteristics, like structure and strategy, affect the knowledge sharing behavior of employees, this affect is not homogenous and there is no single way to predict the knowledge sharing behavior of individuals. Also, organizational KM policy and management support for knowledge sharing affect an individual's knowledge sharing behavior positively. Most researchers in this field stress the need for a knowledge sharing culture, in the absence of such a culture individuals may not be inclined to share (Alavi et al., 2006; Liebowitz, 2012). Incentives for knowledge sharing, as well as the measurement of those activities, also affect knowledge sharing.

10.3.1.3 Technological Characteristics

In face-to-face knowledge sharing, technology may not assume much significance, but if knowledge sharing is mediated by technology, as it is with most KM systems, technological characteristics may significantly affect the knowledge sharing behavior of individuals in an organization. The specific technological characteristics that may affect knowledge sharing through KM system are knowledge infrastructure, search cost, and ease of use (Choi et al., 2010; Davenport & Prusak, 1998; Davenport et al., 2001). Owlia (2010) proposes a conceptual framework for KM system quality consisting of eight dimensions—functionality, completeness, reliability, usability, access, serviceability, flexibility, and security.

Knowledge infrastructure involves formal rules governing the exchange of knowledge over a computer network along with a set of cognitive resources (metaphors, common language) that help individuals to understand the mechanics of knowledge sharing (Gray & Durcikova, 2006). From an individual's perspective, technological architecture is not so important but the knowledge infrastructure is very important (Kozubek, 2012; Zack, 1999).

While sharing knowledge through electronic means ease of use is an important factor for an individual. With regard to knowledge sharing, especially with respect to seeking codified knowledge in knowledge repository-based KM system, the costs associated with and the time required to perform the search for that knowledge negatively affect knowledge sharing behavior. Similarly, for contributing knowledge to a knowledge repository-based KM system, the ease of use, in terms of the creation and classification of the knowledge artifact, would affect the knowledge sharing behavior of individuals.

10.3.1.4 Task Characteristics

Most of the work done in a knowledge-intensive organization possesses one or more of the following three characteristics: interdependence, complexity, and time pressure. Previous research suggests that the task performance, interdependence, complexity, and time pressure affect an individual's knowledge sharing behavior (Weiss, 1999).

Task interdependence affects knowledge sharing directly. If a task has high interdependence content, there is more likelihood of knowledge being shared. The complexity of a task implies that more information processing will go into performing this task (Goodman & Darr, 1998; Gray & Durcikova, 2006). Task uncertainty and equivocality can be reduced by sharing knowledge concerning that task. In project type work, the time pressure becomes important since performance also depends upon the time spent in completing the task. Thus, the time pressure on employees performing specific tasks negatively affects their knowledge sharing behavior.

If individuals are expected to work in teams and share knowledge with others, knowledge sharing is enhanced. However, if individuals are expected to perform only their individual tasks, knowledge sharing is lower and even, nonexistent in extreme cases.

10.3.1.5 Knowledge Characteristics

Since knowledge sharing through KM systems involves impersonal codified knowledge, the characteristics of this codified knowledge would also affect the knowledge sharing behavior of individuals. Knowledge characteristics that may affect knowledge sharing through KM system are shared context, availability, relevance, currency, usefulness, ownership, source, and trust (Bansler & Hav, 2003; Bera et al., 2011; Owlia, 2010; Wasko & Faraj, 2000).

The primary characteristic of any type of knowledge is the context in which it was generated and is most likely to be applicable. If individuals in an organization share the context of codified knowledge, its probability of being used increases many fold. But even if the knowledge is codified in knowledge repositories, an individual may not have access to this knowledge or it may not be available for use. In that case, one cannot gainfully employ that knowledge though it exists. Thus, the availability (or non-availability) of codified knowledge positively (or negatively) affects the knowledge sharing behavior.

The usefulness of codified knowledge depends on its relevance and currency. Even when an individual has access to knowledge repositories and knowledge is available there, it is rendered useless because it is not relevant to or current enough for the task in hand. Thus, the usefulness of the available knowledge, in terms of relevance and currency, positively affects the knowledge sharing behavior.

The knowledge sharing behavior of individuals also depends on who owns the knowledge. Some researchers suggest that perceived organizational ownership of knowledge leads to more knowledge sharing, though there is also contrary evidence (Jarvenpaa & Staples, 2000).

Authenticity of and trust in the source of the knowledge also affect knowledge sharing behavior. If the source is perceived to be authentic or trustworthy, individuals will seek more knowledge from these sources, which will lead to enhanced knowledge sharing.

10.3.2 Contributing Versus Seeking Knowledge

The above mentioned individual, organizational, technological, task, and knowledge characteristics are not independent of each other. For example, self-esteem, organizational incentives, and expected task performance imply personal benefits for an individual. Similarly search cost, search time, and time pressure in completing a task imply personal costs for an individual.

Besides, knowledge sharing by individuals in repository-based KM system may be better understood in terms of two distinct activities, contributing knowledge and seeking knowledge. Contributing and seeking knowledge are two complementary concepts, being part of the same higher order concept of knowledge sharing. For an individual, contributing and seeking knowledge in a repository-based KMS tend to be independent, discrete, and asynchronous activities.

Even though researchers have differentiated between the knowledge contributing and seeking activities conceptually, there are only a few studies that explicitly focus on one or the other activity. Goodman and Darr (1998) examine the role of computer-aided systems (CAS) in enhancing organizational learning in distributed environments. Their theoretical framework focuses on the decisions to contribute and adopt knowledge about best practices in a distributed environment.

10.4 Conceptual Model

Our study builds on the previous research and incorporates additional antecedents for the use of repository-based KM systems for knowledge contributing and seeking behaviors and examines them concurrently. The synthesized conceptual model (see Fig. 10.1) uses variables which are appropriate for understanding an individual's knowledge contributing and seeking behaviors in repository-based KM system and which have been identified through the review of information and knowledge sharing literature. Knowledge contributing and seeking as two discrete activities can exist independent of each other and for an individual, they may not occur simultaneously.

10.4.1 Antecedent Attributes

Out of the eight selected factors affecting knowledge contributing and seeking behaviors, four belong to personal characteristics category, viz., personal benefits, personal costs, propensity to share, and generalized reciprocity. Two belong to organizational characteristics category, viz., organizational knowledge ownership, and knowledge culture. Of the remaining, each one belongs to technological and knowledge characteristics, viz., knowledge repository characteristics and knowledge characteristics, respectively. In the context of repository-based KM system, task-related characteristics are subsumed in the knowledge repository characteristics and personal benefits and costs.

It can be argued that some of the antecedents may affect only the knowledge contribution or knowledge seeking behavior of individuals. For example, the variable perceived knowledge characteristics of the codified knowledge would affect only knowledge seeking behavior and not contributing behavior. It should also be

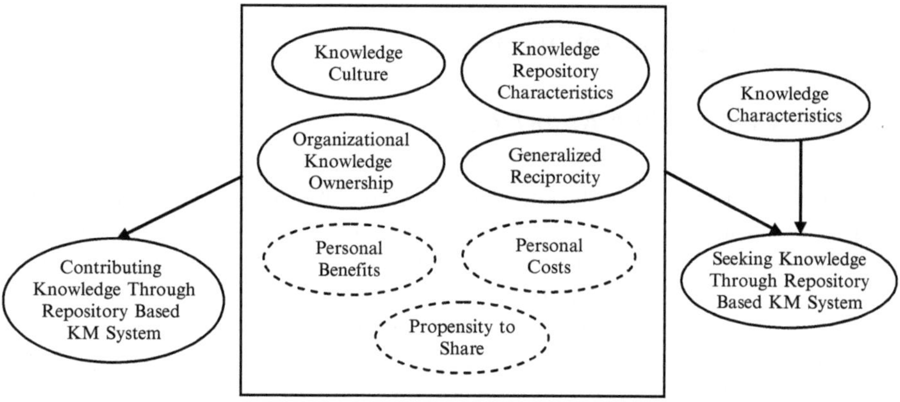

Fig. 10.1 The conceptual model

noted that though the three variables (dotted line ovals), personal benefits, personal costs, and propensity to share, affect both knowledge contributing and seeking behaviors, they are operationalized differently for the two activities.

Knowledge culture is a subset of organizational culture. It refers to the pattern of behaviors and attitudes that expresses an organization's orientation towards knowledge. Knowledge repository characteristics include access, navigation, and the interface of the knowledge repositories. Organizational ownership of knowledge refers to the prevalent norm that organizations own the knowledge created by their employees. Generalized reciprocity refers to an individual's pro-social inclination to contribute and seek knowledge through a computer network in the absence of expectations of a direct reciprocity.

Personal benefits are the tangible as well as intangible benefits accruing to an individual who engages in knowledge contributing and seeking activities. Personal costs represent the time and effort required to contribute and seek knowledge through knowledge repositories. Propensity to share is an individual trait which refers to an individual's willingness to share knowledge with others. Knowledge characteristics refer to an individual's perceptions of the codified knowledge in knowledge repositories.

10.4.2 Survey

The present study surveyed employees in the Indian IT services/BPO industry to understand their usage behavior in the context of repository-based KM system. The survey questionnaire included questions on demographics, and level of familiarity with KM systems, in addition to the questions on the variables in the conceptual model. A total of 104 usable responses were received from 22 organizations having a repository-based KM system for at least a year.

10.5 Findings and Discussion

10.5.1 Contributing Knowledge

During the course of the study, knowledge culture, knowledge repository characteristics, organizational knowledge ownership, and the propensity to contribute were found to be positively associated with the contributing behavior and contributing costs was found to be negatively associated with contributing behavior as envisaged. Contrary to anticipated relationships, contributing benefits was found to be negatively associated and generalized reciprocity was found to be weakly and negatively associated with contributing behavior. Table 10.1 lists the significance of antecedent variables for contributing knowledge through a repository-based KM

Table 10.1 Summary of significance of variables for contributing knowledge

Variable name	Significance	Remarks
Knowledge culture	Yes	
Knowledge repository characteristics	Yes	
Generalized reciprocity	No	Contrary relationship
Contributing benefits	Yes	Contrary relationship
Contributing costs	Yes	
Organizational knowledge ownership	Yes	
Propensity to contribute	Yes	

system and also flags those variables whose association was found to be contrary to the anticipated relationship.

A knowledge culture facilitating knowledge sharing was found to be positively associated with contributing knowledge through knowledge repositories, in agreement with prior studies that organizational culture affects knowledge sharing activities. CAS, like knowledge repositories, were found to be positively associated with contributing knowledge through these repositories, in agreement with previous studies that the quality of the KM systems affects knowledge sharing behavior. Consistent with some previous studies, organizational knowledge ownership was found to be positively associated with contributing knowledge through knowledge repositories. However it is contrary to Jarvenpaa and Staples (2000) finding that those individuals who believe that their knowledge belongs to organization are less likely to use electronic means, like knowledge repositories, to contribute knowledge. Consistent with findings of previous studies, the propensity to contribute knowledge was found to be positively associated with contributing knowledge through knowledge repositories.

The negative association of contributing costs with contributing behavior is consistent with previous studies which have found that the personal costs, in terms of time and effort, required are negatively related to the contributing behavior. Also, the pressure to complete projects on time, typical of a project-based scenario like the IT industry, results in a lack of time to contribute knowledge and adds to the contributing costs.

Contrary to the expectation, generalized reciprocity is found to be negatively though statistically insignificantly associated with knowledge contributing behavior. The relationship of generalized reciprocity to contributing behavior has not been explicitly studied before and requires further investigation.

The empirical results suggest that the personal benefits of contributing knowledge to knowledge repositories were negatively associated with actual contributing behavior. Previous studies show mixed results for providing incentives for knowledge sharing. Although many researchers and practitioners believe that incentives lead to more knowledge sharing, some studies show that incentives are negatively related to knowledge contributing behavior. Bock and Kim (2002) suggest that rewards have a punitive effect because they are manipulative like outright punishment. These authors suggest that individuals may feel that if they are being bribed to share knowledge, it must be something they would not want to do.

Table 10.2 Summary of significance of variables for seeking knowledge

Variable name	Significance	Remarks
Knowledge culture	Yes	Contrary relationship
Knowledge repository characteristics	Yes	
Generalized reciprocity	Yes	
Seeking benefits	Yes	Contrary relationship
Seeking costs	Yes	Contrary relationship
Organizational knowledge ownership	Yes	
Propensity to seek	Yes	
Knowledge characteristics	Yes	

In our post-study discussion with the participating organizations, the practitioners agreed and intuitively understood the importance of such a negative association of contributing benefits. One of them opined that as long as the contributing activity is informal, the benefits accruing to individuals are intrinsic and this may lead to high usage of knowledge repositories. But if the contributing activity is made formal by providing extrinsic benefits in the form of incentives, usage may decline because the rewards may have a punitive effect and individuals may feel that if they are being bribed to share knowledge, it must be something they would not want to do. Another practitioner concurred that the negative association of contributing benefits made sense and that their organizations did not provide extrinsic benefits such as incentives to individuals for knowledge sharing through knowledge repositories, instead they deliberately tried to stimulate intrinsic benefits like self-expression.

10.5.2 Seeking Knowledge

During the course of study, knowledge repository characteristics, generalized reciprocity, organizational knowledge ownership, propensity to seek, and knowledge characteristics were found to be positively associated with the seeking behavior. Knowledge culture and seeking benefits were found to be negatively associated with seeking behavior. Seeking cost was found to be positively associated with seeking behavior. Table 10.2 lists the significance of antecedent variables for seeking knowledge through repository-based KM systems and also flags those variables whose association was found to be contrary to the anticipated relationship.

CAS-like knowledge repositories were found to be positively associated with seeking knowledge through these repositories, in agreement with previous studies that the quality of the knowledge management systems affects knowledge sharing behavior of individuals. In agreement with previous studies, generalized reciprocity was found to be positively associated with the knowledge seeking behavior. Norms of generalized reciprocity imply that individuals seek knowledge over computer networks because either they had contributed knowledge earlier or expect to contribute knowledge in the future.

Organizational knowledge ownership was found to be positively associated with seeking knowledge through knowledge repositories which is consistent with some previous studies. However it contradicts Jarvenpaa and Staples (2000) finding that those individuals who believe that their knowledge belongs to organization are less likely to use electronic means, like knowledge repositories, for seeking knowledge.

The propensity to seek knowledge was found to be positively associated with actual seeking behavior. An individual's preference to seek knowledge from knowledge repositories rather than other sources implies a belief that knowledge repositories are more useful compared to other sources. Consistent with numerous other studies, the positive perceptions of the knowledge characteristics were found to be positively associated with the seeking knowledge through knowledge repositories.

Contrary to the proposed positive relationship of knowledge culture with seeking behavior, the knowledge culture was found to be negatively associated with seeking knowledge through knowledge repositories. Previous studies of the effect of knowledge culture on the knowledge sharing behavior also show ambiguous results. Jarvenpaa and Staples (2000) find that the information culture is negatively related to information sharing through collaborative electronic media. The authors rationalize that if there is an open culture, people tend to share information without the use of a medium, but if the culture is closed, people try to access information, which is not freely available, through electronic media. Their finding is similar to the finding of our study.

In the post-study discussion, practitioners seemed to agree and intuitively understood that in a facilitating knowledge culture, individuals would tend to seek knowledge directly from experts instead of seeking it from impersonal knowledge repositories. They perceived that with an open and supportive knowledge culture, individuals would search knowledge repositories only after they had talked to colleagues and experts and if they needed more knowledge and had been given pointers to additional knowledge in the knowledge repositories by these people.

The empirical results suggest that the personal benefits of seeking knowledge from knowledge repositories were negatively associated with actual seeking behavior. None of the previous research has studied seeking benefits in the context of knowledge repositories. Also, it may be the case that seeking knowledge from knowledge repositories is not akin to using the same knowledge for work-related activities, so the benefits of seeking knowledge may only be indirectly related to the work performance.

Seeking costs were found to be positively associated with actual seeking behavior. A few conceptual studies suggest that seeking knowledge through knowledge repositories entails search costs, which may be quite high, leading to disuse of knowledge repositories.

In the post-study discussion, the practitioners were not fully convinced by the arguments in connection with seeking benefits and seeking costs. After a great deal of brainstorming, one possible explanation emerged. It may be the case that for people with high seeking costs, the usage of knowledge repositories for seeking knowledge would be proportionately higher with low perceived seeking benefits, whereas for people with low seeking costs, usage of knowledge repositories for seeking knowledge would be proportionately low with high perceived seeking benefits.

A commonly expressed view was that it might be the "familiarity" with the repository-based KM system which could potentially explain the seemingly contradictory and counterintuitive results. Low familiarity would imply that individuals would spend more time and effort on searching the knowledge repositories leading to high usage of knowledge repositories and at the same time the corresponding benefits might be perceived to be low. Then, high familiarity would imply that the individuals would spend less time and effort on searching the knowledge repositories, leading to low usage of knowledge repositories and at the same time the corresponding benefits might be perceived to be high. But a counter opinion was that "familiarity" is too simplistic an explanation and is insufficient to explain the observed behavior, at least in the IT industry where people are familiar with databases and search engines. So, the underlying cause should be a more involved and discerning one.

A more compelling and discerning opinion did emerge. It was that even though high familiarity argument could be sustained on the ground that with low costs, usage of knowledge repositories for seeking knowledge could be low and corresponding benefits might be high. But the opposite view associated with low familiarity is counterintuitive in the sense that why anybody would keep searching and seeking knowledge from knowledge repositories when the associated costs are high and the corresponding benefits are low?

Finally, it was agreed that the familiarity argument was tenable only if people believed in the existence of useful knowledge in the knowledge repositories and believed in putting more time and effort into extract that knowledge. This view was partially corroborated by the results, where both seeking benefits and seeking costs were found to have a high correlation with knowledge characteristics and knowledge repository characteristics. Seeking benefits are positively and highly correlated with both knowledge characteristics as well as knowledge repository characteristics. Similarly, seeking costs are negatively correlated with both knowledge characteristics as well as knowledge repository characteristics. The negative correlation implies that if the perceptions about knowledge characteristics and knowledge repository characteristics go up, the perceptions about seeking costs would go down and vice versa.

10.5.3 Comparison of Factors Affecting Contribution and Seeking

In the previous section, we discussed the perceptions of individuals within the organizations in the context of knowledge contribution and seeking through repository-based KM systems separately. Now, let us compare and contrast how these perceptions stack up as the knowledge sharing perceptions. A comparison of individual variables across two activities for contributing and seeking knowledge is listed in Table 10.3.

Table 10.3 Comparison of significance of variables for contributing and seeking knowledge

	Contribution		Seeking	
Variable name	Significance	Remarks	Significance	Remarks
Knowledge culture	Yes		Yes	Contrary relationship
Knowledge repository characteristics	Yes		Yes	
Generalized reciprocity	No	Contrary relationship	Yes	
Personal benefits	Yes	Contrary relationship	Yes	Contrary relationship
Personal costs	Yes		Yes	Contrary relationship
Organizational knowledge ownership	Yes		Yes	
Propensity to share	Yes		Yes	
Knowledge characteristics	N/A		Yes	

10.5.3.1 Knowledge Culture

The findings related to knowledge culture are most significant in the sense that they address some of the ambiguity found in previous studies. The common perception among researchers and practitioners is that a knowledge sharing culture will lead to more knowledge sharing with or without the use of knowledge repositories. But this study has found that, at least in the context of repository-based KM systems, knowledge culture does not have a uniform impact on knowledge contributing and knowledge seeking activities. Empirical results suggest that knowledge culture has a negative association with seeking behavior, while it has a positive association with contributing behavior. Also, both the magnitude of path coefficient and its significance level are higher for the association with seeking behavior as compared to the association with contributing behavior. The implication of these findings is that in the presence of a supportive knowledge culture, knowledge sharing, especially knowledge seeking, may not occur through a repository-based KM system. There may be other mechanisms which enhance knowledge sharing in organizations that have a supportive knowledge culture.

10.5.3.2 Knowledge Repository Characteristics

As proposed, knowledge repository characteristics have a positive association with both knowledge contributing and seeking activities. Though the magnitude of the path coefficients varies across these two activities, the significance levels are high for both.

10.5.3.3 Generalized Reciprocity

This study found that generalized reciprocity is positively and significantly associated with seeking behavior, but not with contributing behavior. The insignificant negative association of generalized reciprocity with contributing behavior could have been the result of a measurement error, since generalized reciprocity was operationalized for the first time in this study. But, the significant positive association in the case of seeking knowledge, coupled with validity and reliability of the construct, suggests that there may be genuine differences in the affect of generalized reciprocity on knowledge contributing and seeking behaviors, which requires further investigation.

One of the important implications for the design of repository-based KM systems is that there should be more visibility for the contributions and contributors. When individuals perceive that others are also contributing to repository-based KM systems, they would be more inclined to contribute as well as to seek knowledge in repository-based KM systems.

Also, it may be the case that an individual may be contributing knowledge through other informal computer networks and so is not positively inclined to contributing knowledge in a repository-based KM system. The implication for the design of a repository-based KM system is that, either as an alternative or an addition, a less structured repository may be provided which may lead to enhanced knowledge contribution by such individuals.

10.5.3.4 Personal Benefits

The results of this study concerning personal benefits in both the cases of knowledge contributing and knowledge seeking behaviors are contrary to the proposed positive association. Personal benefits are found to be negatively associated with both knowledge contributing and seeking activities. The magnitude of the path coefficient in the case of contributing knowledge is more than double the path coefficient in case of seeking knowledge and both these path coefficients are highly significant. Also, even though personal benefits were differently operationalized for these two activities, both of these separate constructs show high reliability and validity.

10.5.3.5 Personal Costs

The findings of this study related to personal costs are interesting in the sense that they show differential affects on the knowledge contributing and knowledge seeking behaviors. As proposed, personal costs are found to be negatively associated with contributing knowledge, whereas, contrary to expected results, they are found to be positively associated with seeking knowledge. Also, the magnitude of the path coefficient is highest for contributing knowledge with a very high significance level, it is lowest for seeking knowledge with a low significance level. One possible reason for this result could be that personal costs were differently operationalized for these two activities, but still both of these separate constructs show acceptable reliability and validity, implying that the observed relationships may represent a real world scenario.

10.5.3.6 Organizational Knowledge Ownership

As proposed, organizational knowledge ownership has positive association with both knowledge contributing and seeking activities. The magnitude of the path coefficients for both activities is low, but they are comparable. Also, the significance level of the path coefficient is moderate for contributing knowledge, whereas it is low for seeking knowledge.

10.5.3.7 Propensity to Share

As proposed, propensity to share has a positive association with both knowledge contributing and seeking activities. The magnitude of the path coefficients is second highest for both these activities and their significance levels are very high. Also, even though propensity to contribute and propensity to seek were differently operationalized for the two activities, both of these separate constructs show high reliability and validity.

10.5.3.8 Knowledge Characteristics

As proposed, knowledge characteristics are found to be positively associated with seeking knowledge. The knowledge characteristics were not hypothesized to associate with contributing knowledge since knowledge repositories contain existing codified knowledge, which has already been contributed. Knowledge characteristics have highest path coefficient and significance level for knowledge seeking activity.

10.6 Conclusion

The present study reviewed and classified the literature pertaining to organizational knowledge management and individual knowledge sharing into conceptual and empirical research. Since there is a paucity of empirical research in the field of individual knowledge sharing, antecedents were identified based on the understanding of individual knowledge sharing gained from the review of extant literature.

In an evolving research domain, there will always be multiple viewpoints about the state of affairs and some of these viewpoints may even be contradictory. The knowledge management research domain is no exception. Though this study encountered varied and at times contradictory viewpoints on some of the factors studied, it was decided to be conservative and accept the majority opinion, though due note was taken of dissenting viewpoints.

The fact that independent variables have differential effects on knowledge contributing and seeking behaviors through knowledge repositories has implications for the design of repository-based KM system. Practitioners need to adopt a balanced approach in order to enhance knowledge sharing by individuals in the organizations and should not rely solely on knowledge repositories. The negative association of personal benefits with knowledge sharing behaviors implies that direct benefits in terms of incentives and performance gains may not always be sufficient motivators for sharing knowledge. This was further corroborated through discussions held with industry practitioners. Rewards, just like punishment, may sometimes actually undermine the intrinsic motivation (like self-expression, learning, etc.) that people may have for sharing knowledge (Bock & Kim, 2002). While implementing a knowledge management system, practitioners need to be consciously aware of the issues raised by this study and should address them explicitly.

10.6.1 Practical Implications

The findings of this study with respect to the antecedents of knowledge contributing and knowledge seeking behaviors have important implications for research as well as for practice. The findings related to knowledge culture are the most striking in the face of current literature and common perceptions among practitioners. It has always been opined that organizational culture is a barrier to enhanced knowledge sharing; therefore, it must be changed to make it more flexible and supportive of knowledge sharing activities. But the results of this study challenge this view and suggest that a more flexible and supportive knowledge culture may not be the best thing in the context of knowledge sharing through knowledge repositories. Indeed a flexible and supportive culture may lead to reduced knowledge seeking in repository-based KM system by individuals.

In the context of knowledge repositories, which are designed as formal channels for knowledge sharing, the research findings related to generalized reciprocity imply that they may lead to a decline in the knowledge contributing activities of even those individuals having high propensity to contribute knowledge. An important implication of this finding for the design of a KM system is that communities of practice might be a better way to motivate these individuals, since communities of practice are considered an informal channel for knowledge sharing. Incidentally, generalized reciprocity was conceptualized only in the context of communities of practice.

Incentives for knowledge sharing have been a contentious issue among researchers and practitioners alike. Empirical studies have found mixed results as to the efficacy of incentives in motivating individuals to contribute and seek knowledge. The findings of this study suggest that perceived personal benefits like incentives and improved performance may lead to a decline in the respective knowledge sharing activity. Practitioners seem to be more aware of the pitfalls of providing straightforward incentives to enhance knowledge sharing by individuals. They are devising multiple ways of providing rewards and recognition to motivate individuals to share their knowledge, to contribute and to seek through multiple channels.

In pure economic terms, individuals would be motivated to share their knowledge with others, if the associated benefits are more than the associated costs. But the results of this study provide a different interpretation. While individuals contribute their knowledge through knowledge repositories in spite of high costs and disregarding incentives, they seek knowledge through knowledge repositories incurring high costs despite there being almost no direct benefits. The implications of these research findings are important for practitioners, in the sense that individuals may not be contributing or seeking knowledge for economic benefits only. It might be the case that sharing knowledge fulfils their intrinsic urge for knowledge and learning and these individuals might have a very high intrinsic motivation to contribute and seek knowledge through knowledge repositories. This line of reasoning is supported by the research findings related to the propensity to share which is one of most important variables in explaining the variations in individual knowledge contributing and seeking behaviors through repository-based KM system.

The quality and currency of the knowledge of any source determine if individuals would seek knowledge from it. The research findings of this study corroborate the essential truth that perceived knowledge characteristics are the most important factor predicting use of knowledge repositories for seeking knowledge.

10.6.2 Learning Outcomes

We were able to glean multiple insights during the course of this research from the literature as well from practitioners. Although this study was done in Indian IT firms, these insights are valuable to everyone tasked with setting up repository-based KM systems. We learn that the purpose for implementing a KM system should be explicit and should always be kept in view. We understand that the design and implementation of a KM system should be appropriate for the competitive strategy of the organization; a straddling or mixed strategy may be a better choice depending upon the product and market mix. We realize that implementing a KM system for knowledge sharing is not just a technology initiative, it is also a change management initiative and should be handled accordingly.

We note that the features of a KM system should be intuitive and able to reduce the time and effort required to contribute and/or seek knowledge and the medium of communication through a KM system should be able to support rich information and knowledge. We realize that there should be multiple channels to contribute and seek knowledge through a KM system. Knowledge repositories are just one way of sharing knowledge through a KM system, other ways, like communities of practice, are available.

We learnt that the incentives for using a KM system and for sharing knowledge should be appropriate to the organizational context. Depending upon the organizational culture and how knowledge is being shared traditionally in the organization, a KM system should be configured to support those knowledge sharing processes, unless its implementation is a deliberate attempt to change the organizational knowledge sharing culture. And we understand that knowledge sharing should be a part of an individual's performance evaluation, whether it is done through KM system or through other means.

References

Ajzen, I. (1991). The theory of planned behavior. *Organizational Behavior and Human Decision Processes, 50*, 179–211.

Alavi, M., Kayworth, T., & Leidner, D. (2006). An empirical examination of the influence of organizational culture on knowledge management practices. *Journal of Management Information Systems, 22*(3), 191–224.

Alavi, M., & Leidner, D. (2001). Review: Knowledge management and knowledge management systems: Conceptual foundations and research issues. *MIS Quarterly, 25*(1), 107–136.

Bansler, J., & Hav, E. (2003). Building community knowledge systems: An empirical study of IT-support for sharing best practices among managers. *Knowledge and Process Management, 10*(3), 156–163.

Bera, P., Burton-Jones, A., & Wand, Y. (2011). Guidelines for designing visual ontologies to support knowledge identification. *MIS Quarterly, 35*(4), 883–908.

Bock, G., & Kim, Y. (2002). Breaking the myths of rewards: An exploratory study of attitudes about knowledge sharing. *Information Resources Management Journal, 15*(2), 14–21.

Choi, B., & Lee, H. (2002). Knowledge management strategy and its link to knowledge creation process. *Expert Systems with Applications, 23*(3), 173–187.

Choi, S., Lee, H., & Yoo, Y. (2010). The impact of information technology and transactive memory systems on knowledge sharing, application, and team performance: A field study. *MIS Quarterly, 34*(4), 855–870.

Constant, D., Kiesler, S., & Sproull, L. (1994). What's mine is ours, or is it? A study of attitudes about information sharing. *Information Systems Research, 5*(4), 400–421.

Constant, D., Sproull, L., & Kiesler, S. (1996). The kindness of strangers: The usefulness of weak ties for technical advice. *Organization Science, 7*(2), 119–135.

Davenport, T. (1997). *Information ecology*. New York: Oxford University Press.

Davenport, T., Harris, J., De Long, D., & Jacobson, A. (2001). Data to knowledge to results: Building an analytic capability. *California Management Review, 43*(2), 117–138.

Davenport, T., & Prusak, L. (1998). *Working knowledge*. Boston: Harvard Business School Press.

Davis, F., Bagozzi, R., & Warshaw, P. (1989). User acceptance of computer technology: A comparison of two theoretical models. *Management Science, 35*(8), 982–1003.

Drucker, P. (1998). The coming of the new organization. In: *Harvard business review on knowledge management*. Boston, Harvard Business School Press, pp. 1–19.

Fishbein, M., & Ajzen, I. (1975). *Belief, attitude, intention and behavior: An introduction to theory and research*. Reading: Addison-Wesley.

Goodman, P., & Darr, E. (1998). Computer-aided systems and communities: Mechanisms for organizational learning in distributed environments. *MIS Quarterly, 22*(4), 417–440.

Gray, P., & Durcikova, A. (2006). The role of knowledge repositories in technical support environments: Speed versus learning in user performance. *Journal of Management Information Systems, 22*(3), 159–190.

Hansen, M., Nohria, N., & Tierney, T. (1999). What's your strategy for managing knowledge? *Harvard Business Review, 77*(2), 106–116.

Jarvenpaa, S., & Staples, D. (2000). The use of collaborative electronic media for information sharing: An exploratory study of determinants. *Journal of Strategic Information Systems, 9*(2–3), 129–154.

Jarvenpaa, S., & Staples, D. (2001). Exploring perceptions of organizational ownership of information and expertise. *Journal of Management Information Systems, 18*(1), 151–183.

Kozubek, M. (2012). Knowledge repository: KM unifies a dispersed legal department's information base. *Inside Counsel*, 38-41.

Liebowitz, J. (2012). Cultural resistance to KM persists. *KM World*, 20–21.

Marjanovic, O., & Freeze, R. (2012). Knowledge-intensive business process: Deriving a sustainable competitive advantage through business process management and knowledge management integration. *Knowledge and Process Management, 19*(4), 180–188.

Mehta, N. (2008). Successful knowledge management implementation in global software companies. *Journal of Knowledge Management, 12*(2), 42–56.

NAASSCOM. (2011). *The IT-BPO sector in India: Strategic review 2011*. New Delhi: NASSCOM.

Owlia, M. (2010). A framework for quality dimensions of knowledge management systems. *Total Quality Management, 21*(11), 1215–1228.

Scholz, C. (1990). The symbolic value of computerized information systems. In P. Gagliardi (Ed.), *Symbols and artifacts: Views of the corporate landscape* (pp. 233–254). New York: Aldine de Gruyter.

Schwarz, A., & Chin, W. (2007). Looking forward: Toward an understanding of the nature and definition of IT acceptance. *Journal of the Association for Information Systems, 8*(4), 230–243.

Taylor, S., & Todd, P. (1995). Understanding information technology usage: A test of competing models. *Information Systems Research, 6*(2), 144–176.

Venkatesh, V., & Davis, F. (2000). A theoretical extension of the technology acceptance model: Four longitudinal field studies. *Management Science, 45*(2), 186–204.

Venkatesh, V., Morris, M., Davis, G., & Davis, F. (2003). User acceptance of information technology: Toward a unified view. *MIS Quarterly, 27*(3), 425–478.

Wasko, M., & Faraj, S. (2000). "It is what one does": Why people participate and help others in electronic communities of practice. *Journal of Strategic Information Systems, 9*(2–3), 155–173.

Weiss, L. (1999). Collection and connection: The anatomy of knowledge sharing in professional service firms. *Organization Development Journal, 17*(4), 61–77.

Wellman, J. (2007). Lessons learned about lessons learned. *Organization Development Journal, 25*(3), 65–72.

Wixom, B., & Todd, P. (2005). A theoretical integration of user satisfaction and technology acceptance. *Information Systems Research, 16*(1), 85–102.

Zack, M. (1999). Managing codified knowledge. *Sloan Management Review, 40*(4), 45–58.

Chapter 11
Ability to Share Knowledge of Doctors in Teaching Hospital in Indonesia

Oktri Mohammad Firdaus, Kadarsah Suryadi, Rajesri Govindaraju, and T.M.A. Ari Samadhi

Abstract The tacit knowledge held by physicians is rarely converted into explicit knowledge. The main challenge for doctors at teaching hospitals in Indonesia continues to be a high level of dependence on one doctor who has the knowledge. This study aims to conduct an analysis of the issues that can affect a physician's ability to share knowledge with peers in an effort to reduce the level of dependence on physicians. The method used is based on survey respondents using surveymonkey.com. The results of the processing and analysis of the data shows that there are four hypotheses identified ability to share knowledge with the indicator value of *t*-count greater than the value of *t*-table. The main conclusion of this study is that a physician's ability to share his knowledge with colleagues is strongly influenced by the ability to analyze the strengths and weaknesses of the knowledge and the ability to document the knowledge that is shaped into the form of tacit or explicit knowledge. Other factors affecting the physicians' ability to share knowledge are the frequency of interactions among them and the work environment where supporting a culture of sharing knowledge is expected as part of the organizational culture of teaching hospitals in Indonesia.

Keywords Ability • Knowledge sharing • Doctors • Teaching hospital

O.M. Firdaus, Ph.D (✉)
Department of Industrial Engineering, Widyatama University, Bandung, Indonesia

Department of Industrial Engineering, Bandung Institute of Technology, Bandung, Indonesia
e-mail: oktri.firdaus@gmail.com

K. Suryadi • R. Govindaraju • T.M.A.A. Samadhi
Department of Industrial Engineering, Bandung Institute of Technology, Bandung, Indonesia
e-mail: kadarsah@pusat.itb.ac.id; rajesri_g@mail.ti.itb.ac.id; asamadhi@mail.ti.itb.ac.id

K.-M. Osei-Bryson et al. (eds.), *Knowledge Management for Development*, Integrated Series in Information Systems 35, DOI 10.1007/978-1-4899-7392-4_11,

11.1 Introduction

In the field of medicine most cases remain at a practical level as tacit knowledge with individual doctors. The knowledge is not passed on to colleagues through documented sources and therefore cannot benefit them. Although there should be a sharing process that makes the knowledge of the cases known and understood by many doctors, it seems there is still a problem with the ability of doctors to share their knowledge with their colleagues as well as a reluctance to do so. Knowledge sharing (KS) is also affected by the availability of an effective mechanism to document the doctors' tacit knowledge in an explicit form. The use of media to document the tacit knowledge also plays an important role in the exchange of knowledge. It can be said that information and communication technologies (ICTs) now constitute one of the basic human needs; however, there are many people, including some in the field of medicine, who are reluctant to use ICTs as a tool in their daily activities. For example, despite the positive effects of Electronic Medical Records usage in medical practices, the adoption rate of such systems is still low and meets resistance from physicians (Boonstra & Broekhuis, 2010).

Similar problems of knowledge sharing exist in Indonesia. A classic situation often found in teaching hospitals in Indonesia is the high level of dependence on one senior doctor who has superior competence compared with his colleagues. This can have a direct impact on the quality of health services found at the hospital. One problem that can be foreseen is that when this doctor retires, moves out of town or abroad, or dies, his knowledge and expertise will disappear as well. A somewhat related issue, of which there are several examples, especially in teaching hospitals, is that senior doctors and professors who reach retirement have their tenure extended by the department or division in which they work. One consequence of this practice is that the succession and regeneration process is delayed. Another is that the senior doctors, who still belong to the active and productive age group, may feel awkward to introduce innovations or even make fundamental changes related to the pattern and quality of medical treatment.

Therefore, it becomes important to examine the factors that improve a physician's knowledge sharing capability. In this research we analyze results of a survey to determine the knowledge sharing practices in teaching hospitals in Indonesia. It was natural that any research into knowledge sharing among physicians in Indonesia should be conducted in these hospitals based on the assumption that teaching hospitals have doctors who are experts in their fields who constantly update their knowledge, thus making these hospitals the most effective places for the exchange of information and knowledge useful to the development of medicine in Indonesia.

11.2 Literature Review

11.2.1 Knowledge Sharing

Shin; Albino et al.; and Lee and Suliman (as cited in Yang & Chen, 2007) agree that knowledge sharing (KS) is represented as a set of behaviors in knowledge exchange involving actors, content knowledge, organizational context, appropriate media, and the social environment. Knowledge owners externalize their knowledge through skills development, codification, and presentation. This knowledge is then transmitted to the receiver (reconstructor) or through the appropriate media channels, and then the reconstructor integrates this knowledge through literacy, learning, interpreting, and absorbing. Therefore, knowledge sharing involves many complex factors and varied research is needed to determine those factors that foster it (Yang & Chen, 2007).

The study of knowledge sharing is experienced on different levels in a virtual community. Virtual communities allow users to interact and form relationships. Knowledge is recognized by integrating information, experience, and theory. Tacit knowledge can only be shared on an interpersonal level while explicit knowledge can be delivered through a structured process or technology base. People will participate in the virtual community to share and exchange knowledge if the perceived benefits exceed the perceived loss of valuable knowledge (Chang & Chuang, 2011).

Zarraga and Bonache (as cited in Lin, Lee, & Wang, 2009), who measured the knowledge sharing within a group environment through empirical analysis, explain that the factors that influence knowledge sharing are a sharing culture with organizational rewards, interpersonal trust, learning orientation, and an open leadership climate. Syed-Ikhsan and Rowland (as cited in Lin et al., 2009) explain that the factors influencing knowledge sharing in the implementation of knowledge management for community organizations are a shared culture, learning orientation, technology infrastructure, and knowledge networks. Other factors discussed by researchers include top management support, vision and goals, encouraged top management, database utilization, reciprocal benefits, reputation, knowledge self-efficacy, enjoyment in helping others, and social networks.

Lin et al. (2009) evaluated 16 factors that influence knowledge sharing using a fuzzy approach AHP (analytic hierarchy process). This resulted in the 16 factors being grouped into four major dimensions as follows:

1. Corporate culture

   - Social networks
   - Interpersonal trust
   - Sharing culture
   - Learning orientation
   - Organizational rewards

2. Employee motivations
   - Reciprocal benefits
   - Knowledge self-efficacy
   - Enjoyment in helping others
   - Reputation
3. Leadership
   - Vision and goals
   - Top management support
   - Encouraged top management
   - An open leadership climate
4. Information technology
   - Technology infrastructure
   - Database utilization
   - Knowledge networks

Of the four dimensions, corporate culture is the most dominant, and within that dimension, interpersonal trust is the most important factor affecting knowledge sharing. Thus interpersonal trust within an organization should be nurtured in order to encourage knowledge sharing; it may also affect other factors which can improve the quality of knowledge sharing in the organization and may lead to increased productivity.

Yang and Chen (2007) assumed that a working knowledge of an organization can affect the knowledge sharing behavior of its employees. They divide the factors that influence knowledge sharing into three dimensions, namely the organizational level (the subdimensions of culture, structure, people, and technology), the level of the individual, and the level of knowledge. The end result is that if a company can identify all of the dimensions, subdimensions then even the detailed factors, it can increase its efficiency in the process of knowledge sharing resulting in more time effective productivity.

Some researchers regard knowledge sharing to be dominated by the conventional process of direct (face to face) communication between the people in an organization. To further accelerate the process of knowledge sharing, the media have good skills especially in the development of ICT today. A concept of Web 2.0 is the answer to the problems that often arise where the media is not able to accommodate the needs of people in the process of knowledge sharing effectively (Cullen, 2008).

The identification of factors that influenced knowledge sharing by no means rules out the emergence of other factors, especially in some areas of study such as health that have unique characteristics. Job satisfaction, alignments between members of a group, individual performance, and other advantages of a group can also affect the perceived knowledge sharing process (De Vries, Hoff, & de Ridder, 2006).

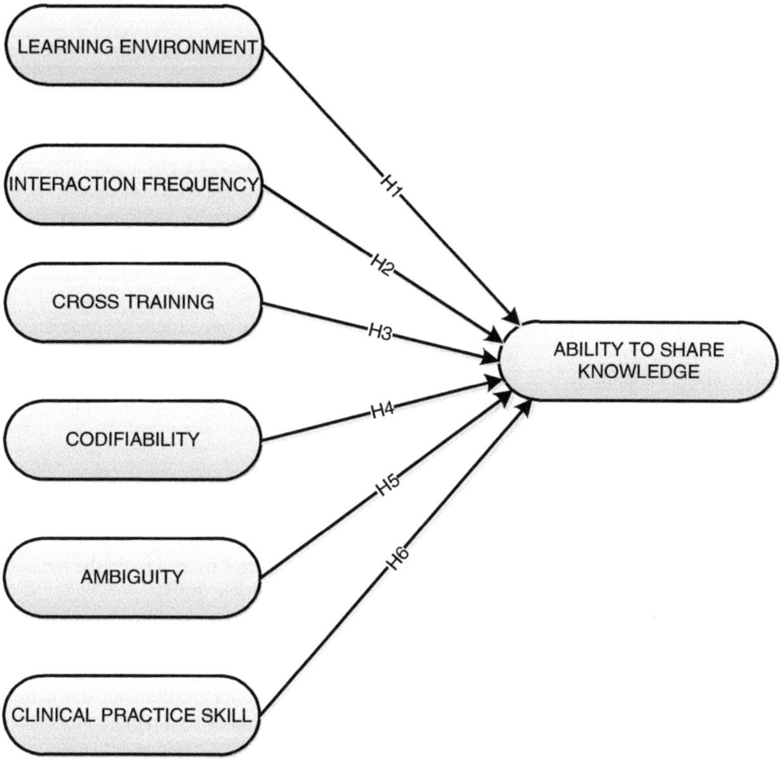

Fig. 11.1 Research model

11.2.2 Healthcare Knowledge Sharing

The level of skill and expertise of the giver of knowledge affects the ability to share knowledge with a recipient (Siemsen, 2005; Siemsen, Roth, & Balasubramanian, 2008). The study indicates that a person who possesses expertise, especially new knowledge, does not necessarily have sufficient ability to pass it on to someone else. Therefore it is important to examine the impact of the level of a person's ability to convey knowledge to others. Our study extends the direct antecedents the ability to share knowledge from Siemsen (2005) by adding clinical practice skill from the research model of Carnwell and Buchanan (2009) (Fig. 11.1). Six antecedents were identified and are as follows: (1) Learning environment, (2) Interaction frequency, (3) Ambiguity, (4) Codifiability, (5) Cross Training, and (6) Clinical practice skill (see Table 11.1).

The main reason for selecting Siemsen's model (2005) as the reference model for our research is that his study, produced insights into knowledge sharing which could be applicable to the field of health care. One thing that is quite interesting and

Table 11.1 Operationalization of research variables

Research variables	Operational definitions	Measurement dimension
Ability to share knowledge *Conceptual definition*: Level of skill and expertise necessary to share knowledge with the recipient (Siemsen, 2005; Siemsen et al., 2008)	Level of a physician's ability to perform activities of sharing knowledge	• Ability of a doctor to make knowledge known to his peers (Siemsen, 2005; Siemsen et al., 2008) • Facilities of a physician to share knowledge with colleagues (Siemsen, 2005; Siemsen et al., 2008) • Ability owned by a physician to share the knowledge with colleagues (Siemsen, 2005; Siemsen et al., 2008)
Learning environment *Conceptual definition*: The extent to which a conducive working environment supports effective communication (Siemsen, 2005; Siemsen et al., 2008)	The ability of a doctor's working environment to support ongoing knowledge sharing activities	• Ease to get a room to share knowledge with peers (Siemsen, 2005) • The availability of a place to share knowledge (Siemsen, 2005)
Cross training *Conceptual definition*: The degree to which the giver of knowledge can do the work directly receiving knowledge (Siemsen, 2005; Siemsen et al., 2008)	Depth of a physician's ability to perform activities of both medical and non-actions that are not medically main job	• A physician to easily replace the role of colleagues (Siemsen, 2005) • A doctor trained to do the job colleagues (Siemsen, 2005) • It is easier for a physician to switch jobs with his counterpart (Siemsen, 2005)
Interaction frequency *Conceptual definition*: The frequency with which the sender and receiver communicate in the workplace (Siemsen, 2005; Siemsen et al., 2008)	The frequency of interaction among physicians in medical and non-medical activities	• A physician communicates with his colleagues on a regular basis (Siemsen, 2005) • A doctor often interacts with his colleagues in the workplace (Siemsen, 2005) • A doctor often talks with his colleagues in the workplace (Siemsen, 2005)
Codifiability *Conceptual definition*: The degree to which tacit knowledge can be converted into explicit knowledge in a form of a document that is easy to use (Siemsen, 2005; Siemsen et al., 2008)	Depth of the ability of a physician to be able to document the knowledge he receives from colleagues	• Depth of ease for a doctor to save a knowledge into a form of manual (Siemsen, 2005) • Depth of knowledge to be able to clear a documented (Siemsen, 2005)
Ambiguity *Conceptual definition*: The degree to which the precise chain of cause and effect relationships that lead to an outcome when applying that knowledge is not understood by the sender (Siemsen, 2005)	Depth of a physician's ability to understand the advantages and disadvantages of a knowledge	• A doctor knows when the knowledge can be applied (Siemsen, 2005) • A doctor understands the circumstances in which the knowledge can be applied (Siemsen, 2005) • A doctor has a good understanding of the limitations of the knowledge (Siemsen, 2005)

(continued)

Table 11.1 (continued)

Research variables	Operational definitions	Measurement dimension
Clinical practice skill *Conceptual definition*: Hospital where a doctor did clinical practice at co-assistant phase or phase before being designated as physician (Carnwell & Buchanan, 2009)	Quality of the hospital where the doctor was based at the clinical practice co-assistant phase, the number of cases handled and the time intervals between sections	• The type of hospital where a doctor did clinical practice at the co-assistant phase • Facilities that support a physician in clinical practice at the co-assistant phase • The ratio of clinical practice activities at the main hospital compared to the support hospital • In the co-assistant phase the time gap when moving from one department to another

important that Siemsen was no longer limited to the use of the theory of reasoned action (TRA), the theory of planned behavior (TPB), and the technology acceptance model (TAM) in the process of building a model for research, but rather he used a motivation, opportunity and ability (MOA) framework to do in-depth synthesis and combined it with the TRA, TPB, and TAM. The other reason is that one of the final conclusions of Siemsen's work is that knowledge sharing attempts are directly influenced by motivation, opportunity and ability.

In this study, based on the status of knowledge sharing in health sector in Indonesia, it is reasonable that before going too far to attempt knowledge sharing, an in-depth exploration of the important variables that influence the ability to share knowledge is examined. The ability to share knowledge was selected for this research study based on interviews and preliminary studies that were conducted during 2010 and 2011 with doctors at a teaching hospital in Indonesia. From this preliminary work, it was assessed that it is not a lack of motivation or opportunity but inability that still hinders the process of sharing knowledge. A number of doctors expressed the view that although they were highly motivated and provided with opportunities to share knowledge these were not coupled with the ability to convey ideas and new knowledge because of fear—fear of being the only one to speak, or of delivering something too simple that would not necessarily add value to their particular field of medicine.

The addition of the variable, clinical practice skills, in our model is based on Carnwell and Buchanan (2009). In Indonesia doctors do not acquire their medical education in a single teaching hospital; a network of hospitals is used for training. Based on this, it was considered necessary to further assess the possible influence of clinical practice skills on a physician's ability to share knowledge with his colleagues. One of the interesting facts about medical education in Indonesia is the difference in the amount of hospital practice and also the number and complexity of cases handled by the Faculty of Medicine of State University and Faculty of Medicine of a private university. It simply cannot be generalized easily, because not a few doctors who have the educational background of the Faculty of Medicine, Private University, it has a number of unique cases and more impact on the level of confidence and ability to perform activities of sharing new ideas and knowledge its-new knowledge to their peers, even though the senior doctors, although an in-depth quantitative analysis of all the Faculty of Medicine in Indonesia, still statistically still shows that the State University graduates have the ability to slightly higher than graduates of private universities in terms of knowledge sharing.

11.2.3 Ability to Share Knowledge

Knowledge sharing can be considered an activity planned and managed systematically involving a group of like-minded people who are committed to sharing their knowledge resources, ideas, and experiences to achieve the goals set (Bali & Dwivedi, 2007). Sharing knowledge in health care can be characterized as an explanation and dissemination of health knowledge by and for healthcare stakeholders through a collaborative communication tool to advance the knowledge of the participating stakeholders. According to Abidi (2007), the purpose of healthcare knowledge sharing can be described as follows:

1. To provide efficient focus and access to evidence based knowledge sources, either by directing the user to the knowledge artifacts or by providing peer recommendations to help locate relevant knowledge artifacts.
2. To explicate and share "unpublished" intrinsic experiential know-how, insights, judgements, and problem-solving strategies of stakeholders to complement evidence-based knowledge.
3. To establish a culture of collaboration between like-minded stakeholders in order to stimulate collaborative learning, atypical problem solving, practice evaluation, critical appraisal of evidence, practices and outcomes, leveraging experiences and knowledge of colleagues, and feedback solicitation on practices and policies (p. 69).

11.3 Research Methodology

The main focus of this research is on the teaching hospitals that were committed to the process of communication and cooperation in carrying out their duties. We focused on four teaching hospitals just outside Dr. Cipto Mangunkusumo Hospital Jakarta. The four teaching hospitals are Dr. Hasan Sadikin Hospital Bandung, Dr. Kariadi Hospital Semarang, Dr. Sardjito Hospital Yogyakarta, and Dr. Soetomo Hospital Surabaya. Based on preliminary interviews conducted between January and April 2011, information was obtained that there are five departments within the hospitals that have a high level of interdependence. These departments are obstetrics and gynecology, pediatrics, radiology, anesthesia, and the clinical pathology laboratory.

The interviews in this study are intended as a first step in designing the study including an effective questionnaire. The first round of interviews was conducted at the beginning of the research and was addressed to the doctors who head the five departments identified the object of study in a hospital. Data of potential respondents and email addresses of researchers were also collected from Faculty of Medicine Padjadjaran University Bandung and Faculty of Medicine Gadjah Mada University Yogyakarta. Information was also obtained from professional organizations such as Ikatan Dokter Indonesia (IDI), Ikatan Dokter Anak Indonesia (IDAI), Perkumpulan Obstetri Ginekologi Indonesia (POGI), and Perhimpunan Dokter Spesialis Patologi Klinik Indonesia (PDS PATKLIN), as well as from the websites of the teaching hospitals.

The potential respondents were required to have a minimum of 2 years working experience and to be medical specialist candidates (residents), specialist doctors continuing as consultants, or specialists who are members of a Faculty of Medicine. The respondents were assumed to be representative of the actual population of doctors in terms of knowledge, skills, and experience in treating patients. In addition to these criteria, the physician is concerned with the doctors knowing each other well but also had a high level of interdependence especially in dealing with patient problems as part of the team.

The questionnaires could only be distributed after a certificate of ethical approval had been issued by the Health Research Ethics Committee RSCM/FKUI Jakarta. This is a major requirement in the field of health research in Indonesia. The certificate is valid once it passes the review of conduct during the period of 1 year and applied nationally in all hospitals located within the jurisdiction of the Republic of Indonesia.

We used a questionnaire as our data collection technique. The main part of the questionnaire consisted of closed questions with a list of possible responses. It was distributed to the 220 identified doctors using surveymonkey.com, the free online survey software and questionnaire tool. The main reason for the use of a computer-based questionnaire is that it is much easier than perceived, efficient, and also very effective particularly with regard to the processing and advanced data analysis. This is because descriptive statistical analysis of the responses received directly can be performed in real time, meaning that it is not directly to do the analysis and exploration of the tendency of respondents to reply and return the questionnaire study. It means that there is the possibility for further exploration of several other factors that might affect a person participating in the study, such as is there a relationship between time, space, speed of Internet access, user interface design and the layout, and the language used in the questionnaire.

The number of questionnaires returned by selecting the link provided in the email were 91 (41.3 % of the 220 questionnaires distributed), of which 65 were completely filled out (71.4 % of 91 questionnaires). Thirteen questionnaires were returned in PDF form directly by the respondents (5.9 % of the total of 220 questionnaires distributed) and of these questionnaires eight (61.5 % of the 13 questionnaires) were filled out perfectly. Not many questionnaires were returned via email, of the six that were, three or 50 % were completed perfectly. It can be said that 110

Table 11.2 Profile of respondents

Variables		Respondents Number	Percent
Age	≤30	13	17.10
	31–35	35	46.05
	36–45	0	0
	46–59	13	17.10
	≥60	15	19.74
Gender	M	39	51.32
	F	37	48.68
Level	Residents	16	21.05
	Staff	19	25.00
	Fellows	2	2.63
	Consultants	28	36.84
	Head of division	2	2.63
	Professors	6	7.89
Department	Clinical Pathology	18	23.68
	Pediatrics	23	30.26
	Radiology	8	10.53
	Anesthesia	16	21.05
	Obstetrics and Gynecology	16	21.05
Experience	2–6 years as doctor	25	32.89
	7–10 years as doctor	13	17.11
	11–15 years as doctor	5	6.58
	≥16 years as doctor	33	43.42

questionnaires were returned via the computer-based method (50 % of the total of 220 questionnaires distributed) and the number of questionnaires filled in perfectly was 76 (69.1 % of the total of 110 questionnaires returned).

Participation rates of respondents were quite good considering that 30 % of the respondents asked the researchers to further clarify the intent and purpose of this study before they completed and returned the questionnaire. This is because many of the researchers were not from the field of medicine and therefore their names were not recognized especially by senior doctors (consultant) and professors. Table 11.2 shows the profile of respondents.

11.4 Results

The first step in processing and analyzing the data is to test its reliability. The indicator widely used by the researchers for this is Cronbach's alpha. The size of Cronbach's alpha values can range from 0 to 1, where Nunnally (1978) explained that the minimum of a variable is said to be reliable 0.7 for the early stages, but in its development some researchers suggest that the minimum should be 0.8 or 0.9 with the aim to increase the confidence of researchers that the research instrument

Table 11.3 Indicator reliability

	AVE	Composite reliability	R^2	Cronbachs alpha	Communality	Redundancy
Ability	0.7981	0.9222	0.4006	0.8736	0.7981	0.2161
Ambiguity	0.8307	0.9363	0.0451	0.8976	0.8307	0.0320
Clincpract	0.5745	0.8157	0.0018	0.6860	0.5745	0.0004
Codifiability	0.8289	0.9064	0.0113	0.7938	0.8289	0.0146
Crosstraining	0.7269	0.8884	0.0089	0.8208	0.7269	0.0098
Interaction	0.7355	0.8927	0.0225	0.8190	0.7355	0.0113
Learning	0.8832	0.9380	0.0177	0.8697	0.8832	0.0172

Table 11.4 Discriminant validity

	Ability	Ambiguity	Clincpract	Codifiab	Cross	Interact	Learning
Ability	**0.8933**	0	0	0	0	0	0
Ambiguity	0.5381	**0.9114**	0	0	0	0	0
Clinpract	0.1379	0.3107	**0.7579**	0	0	0	0
Codifiability	0.3704	0.3687	0.2124	**0.9104**	0	0	0
Crosstrain	0.3425	0.3984	0.1509	0.2657	**0.8526**	0	0
Interaction	0.3290	0.3516	0.4689	0.2902	0.2699	**0.8576**	0
Learning	−0.0315	0.2084	0.3539	0.3058	0.1956	0.2311	**0.9398**

used is more reliable. Indicator test reliability used Cronbach's alpha a composite reliability or part called Dillon-Goldtein's Rho, its value is at least equal to Cronbach's alpha or perhaps greater (Chin, 1998). Indicator reliability for this study is described in Table 11.3.

After the reliability test, the next step is to test the validity. The validity test used in this study is discriminant validity. Fornell and Larcker (1981) explain that discriminant validity verification can be done by comparing the shared variances between factors with average variance extracted (AVE) of the individual factors. In principle, the square root of the AVE should be greater than the squared correlation between constructs and their variables in order to say that the new construct's variables are valid (Fornell & Larcker, 1981). In Table 11.4 the diagonal items (in bold) represent square root of the AVEs and the off diagonal items represent squared correlation between constructs. In this study no square roots for AVE variable were smaller than the squared correlation with other constructs. The greatest value is for learning environment (0.9398) and the smallest value is for clinical practice skill (0.7579). Therefore, for this study all the variables are valid.

Variable ability to share knowledge have six direct antecedents, namely learning environment, cross-training, codifiability, ambiguity, clinical skills practice, and interaction frequency. Testing the hypothesis on research used SmartPLS 2.0 software and the amount of bootstrapping run at 500. Research methods using computer-based questionnaire showed there are four direct antecedents of t value count on t-table where the interaction frequency with a value of t-count equals to 1.7237 (significant at $p<0.1$), ambiguity with t-count value of 3.7208 (significant at $p<0.001$), with a value codifiability t-count equal to 2.6221 (significant at $p<0.01$)

Table 11.5 Path coefficient and significance for the ability to share knowledge

	Computer-based questionnaire ($n=76$)	
Path/hypothesis	Path coefficient	t-value
Ambiguity → ability	0.4130	3.7208****
Clinpract → ability	–0.0515	0.3945
Codifiability → ability	0.2176	2.6221***
Crosstrain → ability	0.1286	1.4067
Interaction → ability	0.1630	1.7237*
Learning → ability	–0.2288	1.8305*

Note: *significant at $p<0.1$; **significant at $p<0.05$; ***significant at $p<0.01$; ****significant at $p<0.001$ (two-tailed)

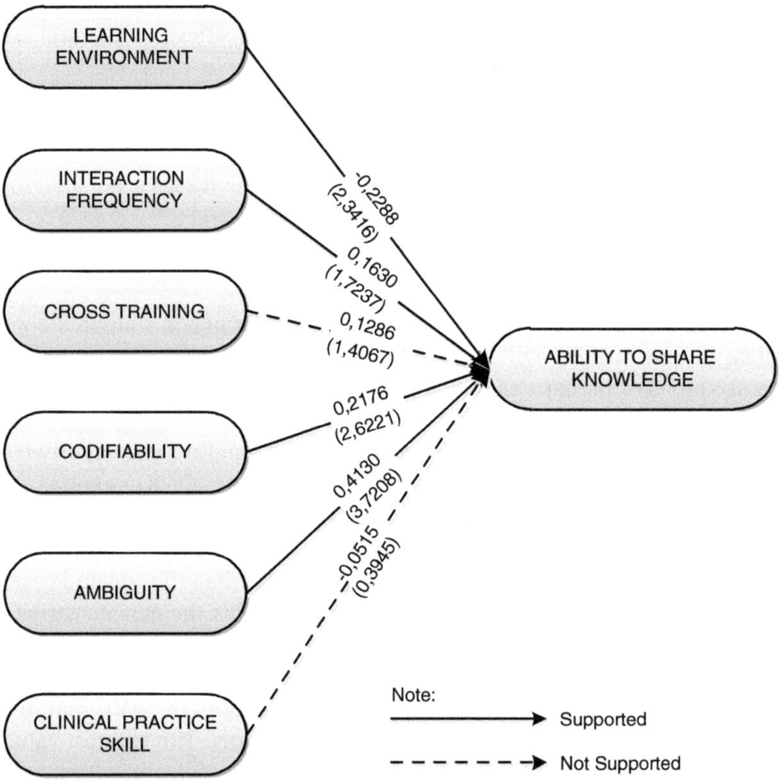

Fig. 11.2 Hypothesis testing result

and learning environment to the value of t-count equal to 1.8305 (significant at $p<0.1$). The explanation can be seen in Table 11.5. It shows that of the six research hypotheses, there are four that suggest the influence of the direct antecedent with the variable ability to share knowledge. A description of the hypothesis test results are described in Figure 11.2.

11.5 Discussion

The hypotheses test results indicate that four direct antecedents significantly influence the ability to share knowledge. They are learning environment, interaction frequency, codifiability, and ambiguity. When sorted by level of significance, ambiguity is the direct antecedent with the most significant influence. This suggests that clinicians understand the advantages and disadvantages of knowledge, and have the ability to analyze knowledge and decide which is appropriate to share with his colleagues. A physician's ability to understand the strengths and weaknesses of the particular knowledge that is still fresh is one of the keys to anticipating the occurrence of fatal errors in medical treatment caused by the weakness of knowledge or techniques for such treatments. This is connected to the awareness of the need to perform in-depth analysis prior to the acceptance of new knowledge that is directly applicable to the patient.

Another direct antecedent that has a significant effect is codifiability, meaning that most physicians already have the ability to document knowledge that is particularly tacit in nature. The ability to document tacit knowledge is motivated by an awareness on the part of the physician of the need to enhance the practical skills of of others particularly junior colleagues to reduce over-reliance on him because of his unique ability and knowledge. It was a challenge for the physician to document the knowledge given the selection of media and language options. This is quite important because the documentation process will work effectively when using media or language that is not only easy to understand and use by prospective users, but at the same time continuing to uphold the values of scientific knowledge.

Interaction frequency among the doctors in performing significant work also affects the ability to share knowledge. The frequency with which the doctors interact with peers of like mind, develops a sense of mutual trust. Interaction frequency that is quite high among doctors will indirectly help to improve their ability to share information and knowledge with their peers with the goal of improving the quality of medical treatment.

Work environment that supports knowledge sharing activities among doctors will encourage greater awareness of the need to share knowledge with colleagues. The availability of rooms which are specifically designed for doctors to share information and knowledge can help to develop good habits in of knowledge sharing. In the future this knowledge sharing will become part of the organizational culture that can serve as a distinct advantage and increase the competitiveness of a teaching hospital.

11.6 Conclusion and Future Work

The study concluded that the ability of physicians to share their knowledge with their peers is influenced by their ability to analyze the strengths and weaknesses of the knowledge, and the ability to document the knowledge that is in the form of tacit knowledge and explicit knowledge. Other factors that affect the ability of physicians to share knowledge are the frequency of interactions among them and a work environment that supports a culture of sharing knowledge.

The next step in this research is to inform the respondents of the results. More in-depth follow-up interviews and focus group discussions (FGD) are needed to examine the results of the statistical analysis. This purpose of this follow-up is to determine with the doctors if the interpretation of the outcomes of this statistical analysis conforms to their practices. These sessions will also be used to identify other factors that might influence the activities of sharing knowledge among physicians. The results of the study and the follow-up will be useful in designing mechanisms for more effective knowledge sharing among physicians at teaching hospitals in Indonesia.

References

Abidi, S. S. R. (2007). Healthcare knowledge sharing: Purposes, practices, and prospects. In R. K. Bali & A. N. Dwivedi (Eds.), *Healthcare knowledge management: Issues, advances and successes* (pp. 67–86). New York: Springer.

Aulawi, H. (2010). *Analisis Hubungan antara Knowledge Enablers, Perilaku Berbagi Pengetahuan dan Kemampuan Inovasi* [The Analysis of Relationship between Knowledge Enablers, Knowledge Sharing Behaviour and Innovation Capability]. Doctoral dissertation, Institut Teknologi Bandung, Bandung, Indonesia.

Bali, R. K., & Dwivedi, A. N. (2007). *Healthcare knowledge management: Issues, advances and successes*. New York: Springer Science.

Boonstra, A., & Broekhuis, M. (2010). Barriers to the acceptance of electronic medical records by physicians from systematic review to taxonomy and interventions. *BMC Health Services Research, 10*, 231. doi:10.1186/1472-6963-10-231.

Carnwell, R., & Buchanan, J. (Eds.). (2009). *Effective practice in health, social care and criminal justice: A partnership approach*. Maidenhead: Open University Press.

Chang, H. H., & Chuang, S. S. (2011). Social capital and individual motivations on knowledge sharing: Participant involvement as a moderator. *Information & Management, 48*, 9–18.

Chin, W. W. (1998). The partial least squares approach to structural equational modeling. In G. A. Marcoulides (Ed.), *Modern methods for business research* (pp. 295–336). Mahwah, NJ: Lawrence Earlbaum Associates.

Cullen, J. (2008). Professionalizing knowledge sharing and communications: Changing roles for a changing profession. *Business Information Review, 25*(1), 53–57.

De Vries, R. E., Hoff, B. V. D., & de Ridder, J. A. (2006). Explaining knowledge sharing: The role of team communication styles, job satisfaction and performance beliefs. *Communication Research Volume, 33*(2), 115–135.

Fornell, C., & Larcker, D. F. (1981). Evaluating structural equation models with unobservable variables and measurement error. *Journal of Marketing Research, 18*(1), 39–50.

Lin, H. F., Lee, H. S., & Wang, D. W. (2009). Evaluation of factors influencing knowledge sharing based on a fuzzy AHP approach. *Journal of Information Science, 35*(1), 25–44.

Nunnally, J. C. (1978). *Psychometric theory*. New York: McGraw-Hill.

Siemsen, E. (2005). *Essays on knowledge sharing*. Doctoral dissertation, University of North Carolina, Chapel Hill.

Siemsen, E., Roth, A. V., & Balasubramanian, S. (2008). How motivation, opportunity, and ability drive knowledge sharing: The constraining-factor model. *Journal of Operations Management, 26*, 426–445.

Yang, C., & Chen, L.-C. (2007). Can organizational knowledge capabilities affect knowledge sharing behavior? *Journal of Information Science, 33*, 95–109.

Chapter 12
Knowledge Sharing in the Health Sector in Jamaica: The Barriers and the Enablers

Gunjan Mansingh, Kweku-Muata Osei-Bryson, and Han Reichgelt

Abstract In knowledge sharing forums actors access each other's knowledge to assist in their own decision making process. However, in the absence of a formal knowledge management system, this knowledge may not be available for use/reuse. In this chapter we analyze different cases in the healthcare sector in order to identify the factors which either facilitate or impede knowledge flows while sharing knowledge. The barriers and enablers pertaining to knowledge access and retrieval and knowledge sharing are identified in the health sector. Furthermore, we theorize about the use and reuse of knowledge items and the issues related to accessing and retrieving them in knowledge-sharing forums. We examine the patterns of accessibility of a knowledge item in knowledge-sharing forums and their effect on perceived usability and perceived usefulness and relevance of the knowledge item.

Keywords Knowledge flows • Knowledge sharing • Knowledge items • Internal knowledge-transaction costs • Healthcare sector

---

G. Mansingh (✉)
Department of Computing, The University of the West Indies, Mona Campus, Jamaica
e-mail: gunjan.mansingh@uwimona.edu.jm

K.-M. Osei-Bryson
Department of Information Systems, Virginia Commonwealth University, Richmond, VA, USA
e-mail: kmosei@vcu.edu

H. Reichgelt
School of Computing and Software Engineering, Southern Polytechnic State University, Marietta, GA, USA
e-mail: hreichge@spsu.edu

K.-M. Osei-Bryson et al. (eds.), *Knowledge Management for Development*, Integrated Series in Information Systems 35, DOI 10.1007/978-1-4899-7392-4_12,

12.1 Introduction

The knowledge-based theory of an organization envisages capturing the cumulative knowledge of its employees, integrating it with the existing knowledge, and developing strategies to use knowledge for increased efficiency (Barney, 1991; Grant, 1996). Organizations must create an environment in which employees' knowledge can be converted into organizational knowledge, to be accessed by others for use in their decision making process. In an organization the different actors (sources and users of knowledge) who contribute to organizational processes are bound by knowledge flows (Zhuge, 2006). The prerequisite for developing a system which harnesses organizational knowledge to enable and improve organizational processes is to identify the sources and nature of knowledge and its flow from a particular source to a specific destination.

Since workers in the healthcare sector use knowledge from multiple sources, there is a need for knowledge management (KM) in the health sector (Sharma, Wickramasinghe, & Gupta, 2005; Wahle & Groothuis, 2005). In the sector there are multiple actors, including patients and their families, physicians, surgeons, epidemiologists, nurses, medical students, laboratory technologists, physiotherapists, researchers, educators, policy makers, and administrators. Knowledge sharing among the different actors in healthcare has been identified as an integral factor in creating a high-quality healthcare system (Richardson et al., 2001). Healthcare workers have acquired specialized knowledge and this knowledge has to be shared by the different actors to improve patient care. Moreover, the interaction between the actors also creates knowledge. Wahle & Groothuis (2005) emphasize that the management of knowledge in the health sector is essential as it can optimize the support to primary health processes, improve their efficiency and effectiveness, and improve the learning capacity of the organization.

In general, the healthcare industry in developing countries has not paid a great deal of attention to formally managing knowledge, and this is especially true of the healthcare sector in the English-speaking Caribbean. The current practice is limited to the manual recording of patient data in files, whereas the financial and demographic data is captured electronically in databases. There is no formal system for capturing knowledge from different actors and integrating it with existing knowledge even though knowledge-sharing forums exist. This may be due to the lack of awareness of the value of managing knowledge. Currently, the emphasis of the healthcare sector is primarily on transferring data not knowledge between actors. However, in order to improve healthcare decisions, actors may have to access each other's knowledge, and this knowledge may or may not be available in an appropriate format. Lacking also is a system which would enable the flow of knowledge.

Effective and efficient knowledge sharing among organizational members has been identified as a primary objective for KM research and practice (Shin, 2004). A KM system for sharing knowledge does not automatically lead to competitiveness and better products; researchers have presented both positive and negative correlations. Therefore, the different aspects of knowledge sharing need to be examined.

The objective of the present study is to understand the issues related to accessing, retrieving, and sharing knowledge in a Caribbean context. The emphasis is on identifying barriers which impede and enablers which facilitate the access and retrieval of knowledge in knowledge-sharing forums and the theoretical implications which affect access and retrieval of knowledge.

12.2 Literature Review

12.2.1 Knowledge: The Intellectual Capital

An analysis of the KM and KMS literature has led to the identification of several categories of knowledge, such as tacit (including cognitive tacit and technical tacit), explicit, individual, social, declarative, procedural, causal, conditional, relational, and pragmatic (Alavi & Leidner, 2001). These categories can be further classified into different dimensions, e.g., tacit-explicit, procedural-declarative, commonsense-expert, task-contextual, and social-individual (Ein-Dor, 2006; Nahapiet & Ghoshal, 1998). The most general differentiation, which has been the main focus of attention of researchers, is between tacit and explicit knowledge (Nonaka, 1994). Tacit knowledge is hard to articulate and is embedded in actions, commitments, and involvement within a particular context. Explicit knowledge, however, can be easily articulated, codified, or transmitted. All knowledge can be classified either as tacit or explicit. In the healthcare domain, declarative knowledge (know-what), procedural knowledge (know-how), social knowledge (know-who), and contextual knowledge (know-why) are considered to be important in managing knowledge (Wahle & Groothuis, 2005). Each of these knowledge items is embedded in different knowledge sources. These sources can be further examined based on a social-individual distinction. Social knowledge is accessible and sustained through social interactions and is inextricably located in social practices; it is not a simple aggregation of the knowledge of a set of individuals. Individual knowledge, on the other hand, exists in an individual's memory, personal records, and in his/her skills.

The sources of knowledge in an organization are termed knowledge retainers and the knowledge present in them is referred to as knowledge items (Rao & Osei-Bryson, 2007; Staab, Schnurr, Studer, & Sure, 2001). Knowledge retainers are the different locations of knowledge and possess knowledge of concepts and their instances (Nevo & Wand, 2005). In the healthcare sector a doctor is a human retainer with personalized knowledge about certain concepts, e.g. diseases, medical equipment, treatment protocols. Databases and documents are codified knowledge retainers which contain different concepts, e.g., information about patients, infections. Generally, personalized knowledge retainers contain tacit knowledge, whereas codified knowledge retainers contain the different types of explicit knowledge. To effectively manage knowledge in an environment, it is important to understand the relevant knowledge retainers and knowledge items, and the different aspects of knowledge embedded in the retainers.

Personalized retainers interact with each other to create organizational intellectual capital, which may also build social capital between retainers. Both organizational intellectual capital and social capital are important resources for an organization (Nahapiet & Ghoshal, 1998). Nahapiet and Ghoshal (1998) define social capital as goodwill that is produced by the fabric of social relations and that has the ability to facilitate action, while they define intellectual capital as knowledge which is socially and contextually embedded rather than a simple aggregation of the knowledge of a set of individuals. They argue that the coevolution of social capital and intellectual capital provides organizational advantage. To develop intellectual capital, organizations need to consider the different types of knowledge present within the organization and the levels of analysis of knowledge processes. The type of knowledge is determined based on the tacit-explicit dimension, while the level of analysis is based on examining the social-individual dimension.

Distinctions can be made between four types of organizational knowledge by forming a matrix of social/individual knowledge on one axis and tacit/explicit knowledge on the other (Spender, 1996). Individual tacit knowledge is the automatic knowledge that exists in different tacit forms, e.g. artistic or technical skills of individuals. Individual explicit knowledge is the conscious knowledge that exists in an individual's memory and personal records. Socially explicit knowledge is also referred to as "objectified knowledge" and is typically the type of knowledge that organizations are making significant investments to capture. Social tacit knowledge is embedded in social practice and might be hidden from individual actors, but is accessible and sustained through their interactions. According to Nahapiet and Ghoshal (1998) it is the social tacit knowledge that differentiates a high performance team from others. We will examine knowledge sharing as a phenomenon where both intellectual capital and social capital coevolve.

12.2.2 Knowledge Sharing

Knowledge sharing is regarded as a key enabler for KM (Lindsey, 2006; Shin, 2004). Knowledge sharing has two aspects, namely the supply side and the demand side (King, 2006). The supply side is concerned with motivating employees to share their knowledge and making clear its economic benefits to the employee and employer. The demand side, on the other hand, addresses the behavior and pattern of knowledge sharing among individual employees and the subsequent acquisition of the knowledge by the employer to enrich organizational knowledge. In this study we focus on the demand side by analyzing the access and retrieval issues that occur during sharing.

The healthcare sector requires the retention of critical knowledge as a primary requirement for managing knowledge in knowledge-sharing platforms (Dwivedi, Bali, & Naguib, 2003). Knowledge sharing requires the support of a KMS to help retain the shared knowledge. Organizations are using and developing technology-based KMS to facilitate the sharing and integration of knowledge. As sharing occurs between different actors, knowledge flows, thereby enabling the organizational processes. However, knowledge does not flow freely; therefore, it becomes essential to determine the barriers and enablers in knowledge-sharing forums.

12.2.3 Knowledge Flow

Knowledge flows involve several nodes, each delivering knowledge to their successors by either forwarding the knowledge gained from predecessors or by passing on their own knowledge (Zhuge, 2006). A node can also gain knowledge by interacting with other nodes. Knowledge flow analysis determines the flow of knowledge within an organization. It is important to understand the flow as it can be used to gain insights into "losses and gains" that occur during knowledge exchanges (Wiig, de Hoog, & van der Spek, 1997). A knowledge flow analysis helps to identify the barriers to knowledge flow, which can help explain the differentials in benefits that arise with knowledge sharing.

Knowledge flows have been defined as, "the sequences of transformation which are performed by agents on knowledge artifacts in support of specific actions or decisions" (Newman, 2002), where agents can be classified as either individual, automated, or collective. Knowledge artifacts are the inputs to and products of knowledge-enabled activities, while the transformations are the behaviors that agents perform on the artifacts. In defining knowledge flows, Newman differentiates between two types of behaviors within an organization. The first type is concerned with the organizational business processes, while the second enables business processes by supporting knowledge flows. In any domain where actions and decisions are enabled by knowledge, it is important to focus on the enablers of the business process rather than the sequences of task execution. Knowledge flows have been divided into four activity areas, they are knowledge creation, retention, transfer, and utilization (Newman & Conrad, 2000).

12.2.4 Constraints on Knowledge Workers

Any environment in which knowledge sharing occurs imposes limits on an individual's capacity to remember the knowledge of other group members. This creates a constraint on transactive memory within a group (Mohan, Jain, & Ramesh, 2006; Nevo & Wand, 2005), where transactive memory systems are defined as a set of individual memory systems and the communication that takes place between them (Wegner, 1995). When sharing knowledge, individuals not only form memories, but also meta-memories, i.e., memories about what other group members know. To extend transactive memory systems to build organizational memory two problems need to be addressed: the overwhelming size of the meta-memory needed and the uncertainty of ownership of the knowledge. In a small group it is easy for an individual to remember both his/her knowledge and what other group members know. However, as the group grows larger, it becomes impossible for an individual to remember what everyone else in the organization knows. In such situations knowledge that was shared may not be remembered by other group members. However, this problem can be alleviated by using technology-enhanced transactive memory systems (Nevo & Wand, 2005). Task-expertise-person (TEP) units have been used for transactive memory development in knowledge-sharing forums (Brandon & Hollingshead, 2004). TEP units are developed as individuals in the group form mental connections between the task requirements, expertise requirements, and the specific experts.

In the healthcare sector, doctors operate under well-recognized cognitive constraints, which are inherent to humans. Therefore, to improve decision making, efforts should be directed towards improving systems rather than individuals (Elson, Faughnan, & Connelly, 1997). The decision makers face cognitive constraints of errors in judgment and biases. To deal with complex, ambiguous, and uncertain decision making situations, they rely on cognitive simplification processes such as availability, adjustment and anchoring, prior hypothesis, and reasoning by analogy (Chen, Lee, Zhang, & Zhang, 2003). These biases can be reduced by creating and using a formalized KMS as facilitating knowledge flows to relevant actors helps to reduce the cognitive constraints.

12.3 Research Approach

The present study investigates the phenomena of knowledge sharing in a leading teaching hospital in the Caribbean. In order to understand the flow of knowledge in the healthcare sector a qualitative case study approach was undertaken whereby various actors, knowledge retention practices, access and retrieval of knowledge, and issues in sharing knowledge were identified and analyzed. The strength of the case study research method is its ability to perform in-depth investigations when the case being studied is broad and complex and cannot be studied outside its context (Yin, 2003). Furthermore, this approach also allows for the possibility of using flexible ways of collecting qualitative data.

Preliminary investigations revealed that the hospital had different forums for sharing knowledge among different actors in a particular discipline of medicine. Two case studies were selected, both of which are important for providing quality healthcare. The first case study is a weekly meeting between cardiologists and cardiothoracic surgeons to discuss cases. The objective of these meetings is to make the team members aware of certain cases, to discuss difficult cases and get feedback and suggestions about how to proceed or interpret findings, and to discuss the current evidence so that healthcare standards are being met. Data was collected by participant observation, by conducting interviews, and by examining archival records. During the interviews questions were asked to clarify the objective, motivation, and the details behind the meetings. Archival data and notes were examined to understand the recording procedures of these meetings. The study was conducted over a period of two months during which 30 cases were presented at 6 different group meetings.

The second case study concerns the management of the hardware supplies required for surgeries. The objective of this exercise is to ensure that the essential supplies are available through regular hospital sources or private sources. Surgeons and nurses were interviewed to obtain information regarding surgical supplies.

12.3.1 Case Study 1

12.3.1.1 Description

Cardiac meetings are held weekly in a leading hospital in the Caribbean. They provide a forum for sharing knowledge. The hospital does not mandate attendance and individual participation is therefore voluntary. Nevertheless, the meetings have been going on for 30 years. They are attended by doctors from different specialties (e.g., cardiologists and cardiothoracic surgeons), at different levels (e.g., consultants, residents, interns, and medical students) as well as cardiac laboratory technicians.

The meeting brings together cardiologists and cardiothoracic surgeons to discuss patients. The doctors at the meeting may be from different hospitals, both public and private. The objective of the meeting is to share knowledge about patients and to determine an appropriate course of action especially in those cases which, in the cardiologist's view, might require surgical intervention. The cardiologists select the cases and present them to the group. The outcome of the discussion is recorded in the patient's file by the junior doctors. However, the patient files may not be available if the patient is from another hospital or clinic. The responsibility for recording the major points of the discussion and for conveying information to the patient is left to the attending doctor. The cardiac lab technician keeps a register to track which of their cases were presented. Sometimes the surgeon takes notes during the discussion and stores them for future reference.

For each case that is presented, the patient's history is reported, including name, age, weight, gender, medication, symptoms, and tests done. The films of catheterization, echo cardiograms, and/or X-rays are discussed. While displaying the catheterization images, the cardiologist gives a commentary on the images.

12.3.1.2 Findings

The cases that were presented during the knowledge-sharing forum were analyzed and from these meetings we learnt several valuable lessons.

1. The clinical decision making process combines information and knowledge from both internal and external memory to make inferences that lead to decisions (Elson et al., 1997). The clinical information (i.e., the medical history, results of

physical examination, and laboratory findings) are combined with internal medical domain knowledge stored in individuals' memory or with some "external" memory. Therefore, clinical decision making requires access to knowledge from both internal and external sources. Often developing countries do not have electronic health records (EHR) and therefore the knowledge in an external source may not always be accessible and thus, in the process of decision making, several knowledge items may not be accessed. If knowledge items are not accessed for a period of time, it is likely that they will be in a state of non access and there is likelihood that these knowledge items will be devalued due to nonuse. The danger is that repeated devaluation affects the perceived relevance/importance and usefulness of a KI, as it could lead to the KI being in a state of permanent non-access, thus discouraging knowledge flows.

2. When knowledge sharing occurs within groups over a period of time, the individuals involved become memory aids for each other. The knowledge that is embedded within the group influences the performance and learning of its members. Transactive memories come into play as groups share knowledge and group members learn about the location and the subject of knowledge embedded in the group (Nevo & Wand, 2005). Research on transactive memory opines that mere participation is not enough in group sharing but that it is the interdependence between members that encourages the development of transactive memory (Moreland, 1999). In these forums often the knowledge items "know-who" and "know-what" are shared and these knowledge items become part of transactive memory. This memory develops over time as group members communicate and begin to rely on each other.

   In this case study, group members saw value in participation. They were aware of "who knows what" in their group. However, if this knowledge remains solely embedded in the group, individuals' memory can be overloaded as the group size increases. Therefore, to enable knowledge flows between groups, mechanisms to manage the transactive memory must be considered.

3. In the case study it was evident that the shared knowledge in these sessions remains as individual memories and is dependent on the record keeping efforts of individuals. Doctors relied more on their memory than on the written records of the proceedings. Absence of a particular doctor could affect the decision making process by either delaying it or by taking decisions without accessing his/her knowledge. Access to personalized knowledge is dependent on the accessibility of the human retainer (Rao & Osei-Bryson, 2007). Decision makers make decisions based on knowledge available to them; access to contextual knowledge can improve these decisions. The inability to access a retainer would not have been an issue if this shared knowledge had been in memory of the group members or documented.

   The value embedded in these discussions is lost, unless they are adequately recorded, stored, and then utilized. Therefore, if shared knowledge is only a transactive memory, it may not be retrievable at an appropriate time, and even knowledge that has been explicated may be lost. This is a barrier to accessing knowledge which prevents knowledge flows from occurring.

4. This case study demonstrated the importance of the process of retrieval. The actors share knowledge by articulating it, but they may not articulate how they got that knowledge. Other actors may have no interest in knowing how this knowledge was retrieved or the actor sharing the knowledge did not consider it necessary to state it. In instances when this process knowledge is not captured, other actors have to go through the knowledge creation cycle again, thus increasing the cost of applying the knowledge.
5. Developing countries often lack electronic health or medical records. Large filing rooms overflowing with patient files could lead to codified explicit knowledge not being retrieved which may affect the quality of the decisions. Due to the high costs associated with retrieval, actors may not try to access the required knowledge retainers especially since these forums are voluntary. This lack of retrieval capability results in knowledge being lost or devalued as it is not used. A knowledge item that is not used for a while is likely to lose its value and this could lead to its devaluation over a period of time. Devaluation occurs when the actors do not see any value is accessing a knowledge item or they disregard it as not being important.
6. Knowledge sharing can be both inter- and intra-group as actors may be from different functional areas. In the forum the actors were sharing "know-why" and "know-how," but not all actors were interested in knowing these aspects. The group members from different functional areas (i.e., inter-group) were building their "know-when" capability, while those from the same functional areas (i.e., intra-group) were building their "know-why" and "know-how." Hence, the types of knowledge flow between actors depend on their background and absorptive capacity. The transfer of knowledge between actors is dependent on source credibility, actors capability, and levels of communications between them (Joshi et al., 2007).

12.3.2 Case Study 2

12.3.2.1 Description

A preliminary survey of the practices of the purchasing and supplying equipment and implants revealed that the hospital has a central department for purchasing, storing, and supplying equipment and implants to different sections in the hospital such as laboratories, wards, out patients, and operating theatres. In an operating theatre the nurses keep an inventory of the supplies needed for a couple of days and regularly send requisitions for items to replenish the supplies to the central store. Hospital policy dictates that the hospital purchase and supply all the implants needed for specific surgeries but in practice it is not so because of a lack of funding. At times the hospital seeks and receives donations, which allow it to buy or receive some implants. Generally, however, the patients are expected to source their own implants.

To overcome this problem, different participants proposed strategies for acquiring implants from alternative sources (e.g., India) without compromising quality.

12.3.2.2 Findings

By analyzing this case study we learnt several lessons, they are as follows:

1. The absorptive capacity of individuals is influenced by their culture, value system and personal beliefs. In this case study we identified that the knowledge utilization of an individual is affected by intellectual colonization, which restricts individuals in societies that were previously colonies, from seeking and using knowledge sources from countries other than those considered to be developed. The subconscious intellectual submission that continues even after colonization ends, in which the societies evolve in a "neo-colonial" relationship with their colonizers (Pieter J. van Strien, 1997), leading to the belief that only certain countries can supply high-quality goods. This intellectual colonization has restricted certain countries from seeking and using knowledge from countries other than those considered to be developed. This barrier to knowledge utilization is often evident in developing countries which have colonization history.
2. Social capital is appropriable, i.e., social ties of one kind can be used for another purpose (Adler and Kwon, 2002). Doctors in developing countries often try to use this social capital to enter into relationships to ease their workflows. However, the administrators, due to lack of understanding of the common objectives, may not see these as appropriate. This often causes tension even though doctors are trying to improve the process and the knowledge flows. To facilitate knowledge flows, it is important for the actors to have an understanding of the common objectives.

12.4 Discussion

In the case studies we identified potential barriers and enablers to accessing and retrieving knowledge (see Tables 12.1 and 12.2). These barriers and enablers have been identified in the context of healthcare and may be applicable to other knowledge-sharing forums where the actors are working towards a common objective. By removing the barriers and ensuring that the enablers are well managed, the efficiency of the knowledge-sharing process can be improved.

12.4.1 Practical Implications

Based on the case studies, we have identified issues that need to be addressed for appropriate knowledge flows to occur. The cases analyzed exhibited behaviors which support patient care; as such, they do not address the actual business processes. Rather, they concern behaviors that enable the business processes. Analysis of behaviors helps practitioners determine the activity areas in which knowledge needs to be managed for decision makers to use it efficiently. It thus allows the practitioners to identify the knowledge flows that need to be improved. Further, this analysis will help KMS design as it addresses the knowledge needs of different actors and the barriers that

Table 12.1 Barriers in the case studies

Barrier to	Reason for barrier	Outcome
Accessing knowledge	Repeated deliberate devaluation of a knowledge item	A relevant knowledge item is not retrieved. Not only was it not used but its value was debased. This affects the perceived quality of the knowledge item in terms of usefulness and degree of importance/relevance (Rao & Osei-Bryson, 2007)
Accessing shared knowledge	Shared knowledge is not stored	Duplicating the knowledge-sharing process reduces its efficiency
Sharing all aspects of knowledge	Process knowledge is not shared	Due to lack of knowledge about the process or the "best practices," the shared knowledge will get lost
Accessing codified knowledge	Improper procedures in capturing knowledge	Codified knowledge is lost. This affects the decision quality
Retrieval and utilization of knowledge	A neo-colonial relationship between countries (i.e., countries that were colonized and their colonizers) taints the perception about the knowledge item and thus affects individuals' behavior	Knowledge that exists in the sector is not used for organizational purpose
Knowledge creation	Lack of social capital between actors	Knowledge that exists in the sector is not used for organizational purposes

Table 12.2 Enablers in the case studies

Enablers	Reasons	Outcome
Knowledge-sharing forums enable creation of workaround knowledge	Sharing experiences builds task-expertise-people (TEP) links in group member's memory	The (TEP) units are developing in this knowledge-sharing forum
Knowledge transfer across functional boundaries	The images are helping the actors who are from different specialties share their mental models	Facilitates different aspects of knowledge to be shared. Each actor is interested in certain aspects of knowledge which the images are facilitating

must be overcome; this will enable actors to exhibit behaviors which facilitate utilization of knowledge. Mapping such behaviors is important if organizations want to develop and use knowledge management systems effectively.

12.4.2 Theoretical Implication

In the first case study, healthcare professionals share knowledge for better patient care management. While sharing, certain knowledge items (KI) are used. From a theoretical perspective it is important to understand how accessibility affects

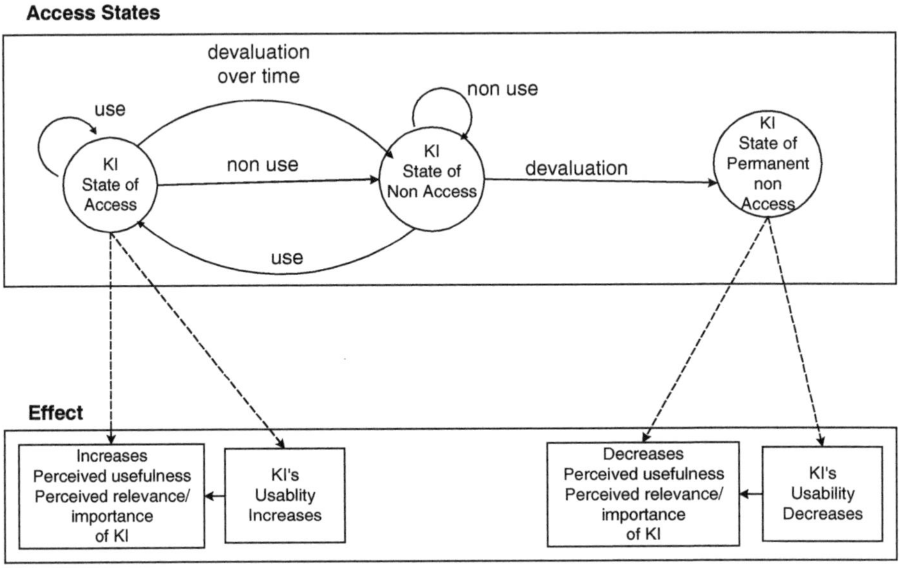

Fig. 12.1 Access states and their effect on a knowledge item

usability, perceived usefulness, and perceived relevance/importance of a KI. We have identified 3 different states of access, access state, non access state, and permanent non access state (see Fig. 12.1). There are different triggers which move a KI from one state to another. When a KI is in the access state and it is being used, its value is increased. However, when it is repeatedly devalued or not used, it becomes less likely to be retrieved and it moves to a state of non access. A knowledge item that is not accessed and whose value is undermined without the group inspecting it results in its devaluation. Repeated devaluation of this kind can lead to the item being in a non access state. We hypothesize that future retrieval is negatively affected when knowledge items are not accessed and/or are devalued.

If a KI is accessed and used frequently it is in the access state, but infrequent use can move it to non access state. A KI in the non access state does not affect factors such as, usability, perceived usefulness, and perceived importance/relevance. It is important to note that infrequent use does not put the KI in a state such that it cannot be retrieved. Usage can switch the state to access state. As a result, the KI, which was in non access state, moved to the access state. However, a KI in a non access state which is further devalued may move to a permanent non access state. In this state a KI is not used and this decreases usability, perceived usefulness, and perceived importance/relevance of the KI.

In case study 2 the knowledge that is being shared is not being used by the relevant actors in their decision making process. The case study emphasizes the importance of social capital as it affects the absorptive capacity of actors. The study identifies a barrier to the absorptive capacity of an actor which influences the ability of knowledge creation and transfer. This barrier has not been previously identified in the knowledge-sharing literature (Lindsey, 2006; Shin, 2004). We propose that in certain societies that have a history of colonization, it is difficult to break away from shackles of colonization. We hypothesize that in neo-colonial societies it is harder for individuals to embrace knowledge which is not from traditional sources and this reduces their absorptive capacity as all options are not considered.

12.5 Conclusion

The case studies have helped to better understand the issues which are at play in knowledge-sharing forums. The study explores the behavior of actors in a knowledge-sharing forum; more precisely, we examine the effect of patterns of access to different knowledge items on the perceived usability, perceived usefulness and perceived relevance of these knowledge items. From analyzing the case studies, the barriers which impede and enablers which facilitate knowledge flows have also been identified.

Our case studies show that knowledge is not being re-used as often or as effectively as it could be to improve patient care. There are several issues that need to be resolved before knowledge can be accessed, retrieved, and shared by the different actors and thus enable them to provide quality health care. Therefore, it is important to understand the factors that facilitate knowledge flows within an organization.

We examined different forums where actors interact to fulfill their organizational roles. In one forum, actors are willing to share knowledge as they feel that they have something to contribute. All actors willingly contribute but some of the value in sharing knowledge is lost as relevant KIs are either not captured, retrieved or stored, or they are devalued. The barriers that hamper knowledge flow and the resulting losses are identified in this paper.

There was no knowledge sharing in the second case study and it is important to understand why the knowledge that existed within the organization was not used in the decision making process. Understanding these barriers is an important precursor to actually designing an appropriate KMS.

The chapter also presents another perspective in knowledge management literature by proposing states of accessibility. As more and more knowledge is being used in decision making, it becomes important to identify the relevant knowledge items and determine their access state. The different patterns of accessibility can affect the retrieval and the usage patterns of a KI. The findings of this study can be used to explain the use and reuse of knowledge in organizations. Even in cases where actors or agents are willing to share knowledge for a common goal, there are factors which impede use/reuse. It is important for organizations to understand these factors so as to minimize them and improve the knowledge communication structure.

Information systems development (ISD) paradigms are considered to be the wrong starting point for developing KMS (Moteleb & Woodman, 2007). For KMS development it is important to have mechanisms that incorporate both the nature and flow of knowledge in an organization. Understanding the knowledge flows will be essential in determining the knowledge management strategy which will facilitate knowledge use and reuse.

Acknowledgment Material in this chapter has appeared in "Issues in knowledge access, retrieval and sharing—Case studies in a Caribbean health sector," Expert Systems with Applications, vol. 36, 2009.

References

Adler, P. S., & Kwon, S. -W. (2002). Social capital: Prospects for a new concept. *The Academy of Management Review, 27*(1), 17–40.

Alavi, M., & Leidner, D. E. (2001). Review: Knowledge management and knowledge management systems: Conceptual foundations and research issues [theoretical]. *MIS Quarterly, 25*(1), 107–135.

Barney, J. B. (1991). Firm resources and sustained competitive advantage. *Journal of Management Information Systems, 17*, 99–120.

Brandon, D. P., & Hollingshead, A. B. (2004). Transactive memory systems in organizations: Matching tasks, expertise, and people. *Organization Science, 15*(6), 633–644.

Chen, J. Q., Lee, T. E., Zhang, R., & Zhang, Y. J. (2003). Systems requirements for organizational learning. *Communications of the ACM, 46*(12), 71–78.

Dwivedi, A. N., Bali, R. K., & Naguib, R. N. (2003). Organization current knowledge design (OCKD): A knowledge management framework for healthcare institutions [empirical] (pp. 1236–1239). *IEEE.*

Ein-Dor, P. (2006). Taxonomies of knowledge. In D. G. Schwartz (Ed.), *Encyclopedia of knowledge management*. Hershey, PA: IDEA Group.

Elson, R. B., Faughnan, J. G., & Connelly, D. P. (1997). An industrial process view of information delivery to support clinical decision making: Implications for systems design and process measures. *Journal of the American Medical Informatics Association, 4*(4), 266–278.

Grant, R. M. (1996). Toward a knowledge-based theory of the firm. *Strategic Management Journal, 17*(Winter), 109–122.

Joshi, K. D., Sarker, S., & Sarker, S. (2007). Knowledge transfer within information systems development teams: Examining the role of knowledge source attributes. *Decision Support Systems, 43*(2), 322–335.

King, W. R. (2006). Knowledge sharing. In D. G. Schwartz (Ed.), *Encyclopedia of knowledge management* (pp. 493–498). Hershey, PA: Idea Group.

Lindsey, K. L. (2006). Knowledge sharing barriers. In D. G. Schwartz (Ed.), *Encyclopedia of knowledge management* (pp. 499–506). Hershey, PA: Idea Group.

Mohan, K., Jain, R., & Ramesh, B. (2006). Knowledge networking to support medical new product development [empirical]. *Decision Support Systems*. doi: 10.1016/j.dss.2006.02.005.

Moreland, R. L. (1999). Transactive memory: Learning who knows what in work groups and organizations. In L. L. Thompson, J. M. Levin, & D. M. Messick (Eds.), *Shared cognition in organizations: The management of knowledge* (pp. 3–31). Mahwah, NJ: Lawrence Erlbaum Associates.

Moteleb, A. A., & Woodman, M. (2007). Notions of knowledge management systems: A gap analysis. *The Electronic Journal of Knowledge Management, 5*(1), 55–62.

Nahapiet, J., & Ghoshal, S. (1998). Social capital, intellectual capital and the organizational advantage. *Academy of Management Review, 23*(2), 242–266.

Nevo, D., & Wand, Y. (2005). Organizational memory information systems: A transactive memory approach. *Decision Support Systems, 39*, 549–562.

Newman, B. (2002). Agents, artifacts, and transformations: The foundations of knowledge flows. In C. Holsapple (Ed.), *The knowledge management handbook* (Vol. 2). Berlin, Germany: Springer.

Newman, B., & Conrad, K. W. (2000). *A framework for characterizing knowledge management methods, practices, and technologies.* Paper presented at the Third International Conference on Practical aspects of Knowledge Management (PAKM2000) 30–31 October, Basel, Switzerland.

Nonaka, I. (1994). A dynamic theory of organizational knowledge creation [article]. *Organization Science: A Journal of the Institute of Management Sciences, 5*(1), 14–37.

Pieter, J. v. S. (1997). The American "colonization" of northwest European social psychology after World War II. *Journal of the History of the Behavioral Sciences*, 33(4), 349–363.

Rao, L., & Osei-Bryson, K. M. (2007). Towards defining dimensions of knowledge systems quality. *Expert Systems with Applications, 33*(2), 368–378.

Richardson, W. C., Berwick, D. M., Bisgard, C., Bristow, G. R., Buck, C. R., Cassel, C. K., et al. (2001). *Committee on quality of health care in America, Institute of Medicine. Crossing the quality chasm: a new health systems for the 21st century*. Washington, DC: The National Academic Press.

Sharma, S. K., Wickramasinghe, N., & Gupta, J. N. D. (2005). Knowledge management in healthcare. In N. Wickramasinghe, J. N. D. Gupta, & S. K. Sharma (Eds.), *Creating knowledge-based healthcare organizations*. Hershey, PA: IDEA Group.

Shin, M. (2004). A framework for evaluating economics of knowledge management systems [article]. *Information & Management, 42*(1), 179–196.

Spender, J. C. (1996). Making knowledge the basis of a dynamic theory of the firm. *Strategic Management Journal, 17*(S2), 45–62.

Staab, S., Schnurr, H.-P., Studer, R., & Sure, Y. (2001). Knowledge processes and ontologies. *IEEE Intelligent Systems, 16*(1), 26–34.

Wahle, A. E., & Groothuis, W. A. (2005). How to handle knowledge management in healthcare: A description of a model to deal with the current and ideal situation. In N. Wickramasinghe, J. N. D. Gupta, & S. K. Sharma (Eds.), *Creating knowledge-based healthcare organizations*. Hershey, PA: IDEA Group.

Wegner, D. M. (1995). A computer network model of human transactive memory. *Social Cognition, 13*(3), 319–339.

Wiig, K., de Hoog, R., & van der Spek, R. (1997). Supporting knowledge management: A selection of methods and techniques. *Expert Systems with Applications, 13*, 15–27.

Yin, R. (2003). *Case study research—Design and methods* (Vol. 5). Thousand Oaks, CA: Sage.

Zhuge, H. (2006). Knowledge flow network planning and simulation. *Decision Support Systems, 42*(2), 571–592.

Chapter 13
The Ulwazi Programme: A Case Study in Community-Focused Indigenous Knowledge Management

Niall McNulty

Abstract Prevailing ideas about knowledge management in post-apartheid South Africa have been marked by notions of redress, the recognition of previously marginalized narratives and categories such as intangible heritage and indigenous knowledge. Key to these developments has been a democratizing turn, a participatory approach to the development and management of knowledge resources. Born of changes in the broader political context and the policy environment, the Ulwazi Programme is a new South African heritage initiative that has been set up by the eThekwini Municipal Library's Libraries and Heritage Department to preserve and disseminate indigenous knowledge of local communities in the greater Durban area. The Programme, in the form of a localized Wiki, functions as a collaborative online archive of local knowledge and histories that are collected from the community by volunteer fieldworkers and then shared via the Internet and on cell phones. This utilization of a combination of open-source and social media applications for archival and heritage purposes is unique in South Africa. The chapter presents the structure and the implementation details of this indigenous knowledge preservation system.

Keywords Indigenous knowledge • Localized wiki • Ulwazi • Community engagement

13.1 Introduction

African contributions to the current global information economy have been limited due to a lack of infrastructure and access in most African countries, with minimal local content available online and little production and dissemination capability

---

N. McNulty (✉)
McNulty Consulting, Cape Town, South Africa
e-mail: niall.mcnulty@gmail.com

K.-M. Osei-Bryson et al. (eds.), *Knowledge Management for Development*,
Integrated Series in Information Systems 35, DOI 10.1007/978-1-4899-7392-4_13,

among communities (Greyling, 2009). This lack of local online content means that the African public in general has little reason to use the Internet, hindering access to important digital resources and limiting the development of much-needed Information and Communication Technology (ICT) skills (Greyling & McNulty, 2011).

Historically, there has been a low level of access to the Internet in South Africa. However the African Telecommunication/ICT Indicators of 2008 place growth in Africa's mobile sector at close to a quarter of a billion subscribers with mobile phone penetration at one in three people (International Telecommunications Union, 2008), many of these with access to the mobile web. Working on the premise that communities in the region now have access to the Internet in some way, the Ulwazi Programme (www.ulwazi.org) was developed as a localized wiki using the concept of a user-generated library of local histories and indigenous knowledge in the greater Durban area.

This chapter examines the structure of the Ulwazi Programme, analysing it as a potential model for indigenous knowledge management in Southern Africa. It explores ways in which the Ulwazi Programme contributes to ongoing transformation in the heritage sector in terms of cultural representation, access to knowledge resources (of local relevance and in the vernacular) and public participation in the constitution of the archive. It considers the extent to which a municipal initiative can collect and disseminate the "people's knowledge" through supposedly democratizing technologies and what the limitations of the project are.

13.2 Background

Indigenous knowledge has been defined as "the local knowledge that is unique to a given culture or society. It is the basis for local-level decision making in agriculture, health care, food preparation, education, natural-resource management, and a host of other activities in rural communities" (Warren, 1991). There are several challenges confronting indigenous people as they attempt to maintain control over, and benefit from, the digitization of their cultural heritage (Brown & Nicholas, 2012). The authors emphasize that this knowledge is seen as public domain representing vanished or vanishing cultures. Therefore digitizing this knowledge in databases provides a powerful and an effective tool for promoting and protecting it.

Storytelling has been used successfully for knowledge transfer (Swap, Leonard, Shields, & Abrams, 2001) and is considered to be an effective mechanism for conveying tacit knowledge (Bidwell, Winschiers-Theophilus, Koch-Kapuire, & Chivuno-Kuria, 2011). Local indigenous knowledge in Africa has historically been transmitted orally from one generation to the next. Therefore storytelling provides an excellent mechanism to capture tacit knowledge and databases of stories are technologies that can be used in transferring tacit knowledge (Davidavičienė & Raudeliūnienė, 2010). Also there is a trend in developing digital libraries as a public social service for cultural development through the use of social web technologies. Wenger's survey of community-oriented technologies proved the critical importance of a community-supporting platform in community-building programmes (Wenger, 1998). He highlighted the importance of the type of technologies used and the positioning of the programme as an extension of social services offered through the public library. Web 2.0 technologies are the key, allowing potential participants to communicate with one another in a community-specific way, enriching social interaction processes and outcomes (Stanoevska-Slabeva, 2002), thereby building social capital (Bidwell, 2010). This social capital is of importance to the continued growth of the project, with community engagement and ownership of the programme vital to its success. This kind of community-oriented development is also called the grass roots approach.

Libraries are in an ideal position to assist with the discovery and recording of the knowledge, and its organization and promotion (Lor, 2004). Also the skills of librarians allow them to assist with data management and other forms of content management (Lor, 2008). A public library operates as a custodian of the knowledge resource created through the preservation of context-related local knowledge in a digital library that is of relevance to local communities.

Based on the literature, we undertook the development of indigenous knowledge preservation system in the form of localized Wiki. In this chapter we highlight the benefits of using the bottom-up approach where the community is involved in the creation of the system and a public library is used as the custodian of managing this knowledge resource.

13.3 Overview of the Ulwazi Programme

Established in 2008, the Ulwazi Programme is based in the eThekwini Municipality in the province of KwaZulu-Natal on the east coast of South Africa and operates in urban, peri-urban and rural areas within municipal boundaries. The demand for ICTs and digital media literacy among rural communities in the eThekwini Municipality is high and increasing (Averweg & Greyling, 2008). Hughes and Dallwitz (2006) argue that through the use of ICT, indigenous groups and marginalized local communities can be empowered to overcome the barriers to entry into the global information society, but on their own terms (Hughes & Dallwitz, 2006).

The Ulwazi Programme operates as an integral part of local public library and information services, using conventional desktop computers, the Internet and the latest mobile technologies to collect indigenous knowledge and local histories. The Programme's Community Memory website has been developed in the form of a Wiki, an open-source webpage designed to enable contributions and modifications from multiple users. This is achieved by training volunteer community journalists in digital media production and oral history skills, which enables them to collect stories from their own communities and input them into the Ulwazi Programme's website using the computers at any of the public libraries in the eThekwini Municipality. Each of the 90 public libraries has at least one public-access, Internet-enabled PC.

Local knowledge in Africa has historically been transmitted orally from one generation to the next. In South Africa, various factors, like urban migration and the AIDS pandemic in younger generations, have contributed to a disruption of these chains of cultural transmission. Digital technologies, in particular mobile phones, offer some ways in which this information can be recorded and circulated by facilitating the preservation and dissemination of local knowledge through digital audio recordings, photographs and articles. The Ulwazi Programme is a unique example of this, using the public library infrastructure, the communities it serves and Web 2.0 technology to record and share their knowledge and histories. The technology allows for multiple contributions from a variety of perspectives, male, female, young and old. A focus of the project is to record the knowledge of the older generation and make it available to the younger generation. This includes the history of local areas, details of traditional practices and ceremonies and the ways people lived in the past.

The participatory role that local communities play in generating content for the Ulwazi Programme enriches the website through the multiple perspectives it presents. The technologies used facilitate the social interaction necessary for the expression of identity, creating social capital in the community through a network of human relations (Mbaya, 2010). Social media and Web 2.0 technology give the local communities a variety of ways to interact with their own heritage and contribute their perspectives on the website resources. Web 2.0 technologies such as blogs, online forums and wikis can enable interaction and collaboration in heritage projects, as well as an exponential growth in user-generated content (Bowen, 2008).

13.3.1 Policies and Plans Guiding Development

The eThekwini Municipality's Integrated Development Plan (IDP) is a long-term strategy document for the Municipality. The IDP is an eight-part plan and the Ulwazi Programme is linked directly to Plan Five, which focuses on empowering citizens by "enhancing skills, providing easily accessible information" and bridging the "digital divide" by making Durban a "Digitally Smart City". It also relates to Plan Six, which deals with cultural diversity and "the promotion and conservation of heritage through local history projects and the use of gallery and museum spaces".

The Library and Heritage Department of the Municipality has its own strategic plan, which calls for equitable information service to all residents of the eThekwini Municipality. The Ulwazi Programme provides a framework for the collection and sharing of local histories and cultures through a digital library of content created by the community. Through the Programme, sustainable preservation and dissemination of local knowledge of rural and communities is enabled and a digital knowledge resource of local relevance is also developed. Community engagement results in capacity building in digital and information literacy skills, and empowerment in terms of knowledge and ICT skills.

As a library outreach programme, the Ulwazi Programme is in line with global goals in the African Charter for Popular Participation (United Nations, 1990), the United Nations Social Development Plan (United Nations, 1995) and the United Nations Millennium Development Goals (United Nations, 2000), as well as the plans of action of the World Summit on the Information Society (WSIS) (WSIS, 2003, 2005), in particular the goal of providing equitable access to information and knowledge (Greyling & McNulty, 2011). The Geneva Plan of Action (WSIS, 2003) states:

- Access to information and knowledge. This concerns policies relating to public domain information, community access points (including such access in libraries) as well as alternative software models (open-source and free software). One of the actions envisaged is the development of digital public library services.
- Capacity building. This covers skills needed for the Information Society, including literacy and "ICT literacy", the use of libraries in e-literacy work and the empowerment of local communities to use ICTs.
- Cultural diversity and identity, linguistic diversity and local content. This action plan focuses on the promotion of respect for cultural identity, traditions and religions and dialogue among cultures as a factor in sustainable development. Libraries feature prominently in this plan, most notably with regard to their role in providing access to content and indigenous knowledge though the promotion of cultural heritage, supporting local content development and enhancing the capacity of indigenous peoples to develop content in their own language.

The Ulwazi Programme thus fulfils a number of the aims of WSIS action plans.

13.4 Elements of the Ulwazi Programme

The project consists of three interrelated elements; the community, the technology and the public library. Each is vital in the creation and running of the Ulwazi Programme and key to its success.

13.4.1 Community

For the purposes of the project, the community is defined as being the residents of the eThekwini Municipality. Connections with the communities in the Municipality are primarily through community journalists (who actively collect and submit stories), members of the public (who can register an account and submit a story on a more ad hoc basis) and through direct engagement with local residents often through community groups. Contributions to the Ulwazi system consist of personal and community histories, customary practices, living circumstances and historical environments.

13.4.1.1 Community Engagement

The Ulwazi Programme actively encourages participation from diverse cultural groups in the eThekwini Municipality, while also functioning as a tool for social cohesion in the city. The website has sections on, inter alia, the local Zulu population, European colonial history and the Indian population in the city of Durban. The Programme adopts a bottom-up philosophy in its structure, with the community as the most important member in the partnership (Coetzee, 2001), as both generators of the Programme's content and its primary audience. This continuous community engagement and ownership increase the Programme's success.

Outreach programmes are also run at schools in the Municipality. Target groups in the community include the elderly, cultural groups (including artists and crafters), professionals and technologists. Prominent members of the community are invited to contribute to the project with an appropriate member of the community, suggested by community members, to conduct the interview.

13.4.1.2 Community Journalists

Community journalists are actively recruited. They are generally younger people with some ICT skills, an interest in heritage and culture and a desire to acquire new skills and gain work experience. The community journalists have an intimate knowledge of the areas in which they operate and already established relationships with their interviewees. This ground-level approach generates a much richer quality of content than external researchers could collect. These journalists already have a relationship of trust with members of the community and provide a valuable link to the older generation and its store of local knowledge and histories. The community journalists collect stories through personal interviews, in the form of audio recordings and video interviews. The oral practice of storytelling, which the Programme encourages, conveys tacit aspects of the narrative better than a mere electronic report of spoken words (Bidwell et al., 2011).

Community journalists are trained in oral history research and protocols, digital media production (digital photography, audio recording and web-based content management) and Internet literacy skills. Their submissions consist of short journalistic style reports, but can be supplemented with oral histories and stories recorded as audio or video files. Community journalists are required to submit at least three stories a month and attend the monthly feedback meetings. This structured work plan ensures continuity, while incentives such as stipends and cellular phone airtime retain volunteer's enthusiasm for the Programme.

13.4.1.3 Contributions

Leavy (2006) developed a set of ten protocols to provide guidelines for consultation with custodial owners in indigenous communities in Australia. This model is useful as a framework for recording the heritage of local communities. The framework recommends that communities make their own decision on which stories they want to have recorded as part of their digital heritage. All contributions are made on a voluntary basis, and from a personal perspective, i.e. the interviewees decide what information they want to part with and describe events from their own personal experience. As can be expected, oral histories are highly contextual (Grele, 1991). All interviewees sign a release form, allowing the information to be used for educational purposes only, including publications, exhibitions, presentations and the web, without relinquishing copyright or performance rights. The content is licensed online through a Creative Commons License, with full acknowledgement of the owner of the knowledge. The result is that the community retains ownership of knowledge resource created, with the library as custodian, and active participation ensures sustainability.

13.4.2 Technology

13.4.2.1 Ulwazi on the Web

The recent emergence of Web 2.0 technologies has allowed for large-scale collaboration in the creation of online, user-generated data (Farkas, 2007). In the Ulwazi Programme, the preservation of indigenous knowledge and local histories takes place through a community-managed web portal using open-source, social software technologies (see Fig. 13.1). This use of social software technologies tries to mirror the dynamic aspects of the community's organizational structure and can be used to support community activities (Stanoevska-Slabeva, 2002; WSIS, 2003). This utilization of a combination of open-source and social media applications for archival and heritage purposes is unique in South Africa.

From the outset, the team behind the Programme made a conscious decision to use open-source, as opposed to proprietary, software. This type of software is developed by a group of volunteers and released for public use with little or no restrictions. Key to this decision was the desire not to be hampered with yearly subscription fees for proprietary software but also, on another level, to align with the aims of the open-source community—openness, sharing and collaboration. A similar decision to make use of open-source software was also the case with the Dulwich OnView, a community-run museum website that focuses on the development of user-generated content to engage the visitors with the museum's collections. Much like the Programme, they explain their use of open-source software as a means to "minimise costs and maximise the free use of local people as volunteers" (Beazley, Bowen, McDaid, & Liu, 2010). The Programme operates its own LAMP server. LAMP is an acronym for Linux, Apache, MySQL and Php, four popular open-source server technologies (Dougherty, 2001).

The Programme uses two open-source content-management systems to develop and run its website. The first is a content-management system that allows a website

Fig. 13.1 Front page of Ulwazi digital library

to be built that can be administered by non-technical users. This section of the website consists of the blog and informational part of the website. The Programme blog has been created using WordPress (www.wordpress.org), a popular blogging framework. The second is the Community Memory component of the website that has been developed as a wiki, using the MediaWiki framework—the same software used to run Wikipedia (http://mediawiki.org). A wiki is a "browser-based collaborative writing environment, in which a community can create and exchange information without having web programming skills" (Rahman, 2007). This means that the community journalists, and even the general public, can easily add articles to the website, using a browser on a PC or mobile phone (see Fig. 13.2). These frameworks are both large, open-source projects with active developer communities, which means updates and improvements to the frameworks are made available on a regular basis. Both these frameworks are freely available for download and can be installed on a local server, which is the approach taken by the Ulwazi Programme. The Programme also uses social media technologies that the target audience may already be familiar with. These include a Facebook fanpage and the Twitter account, as well as a photo-sharing group on Flickr and a video channel on Vimeo.

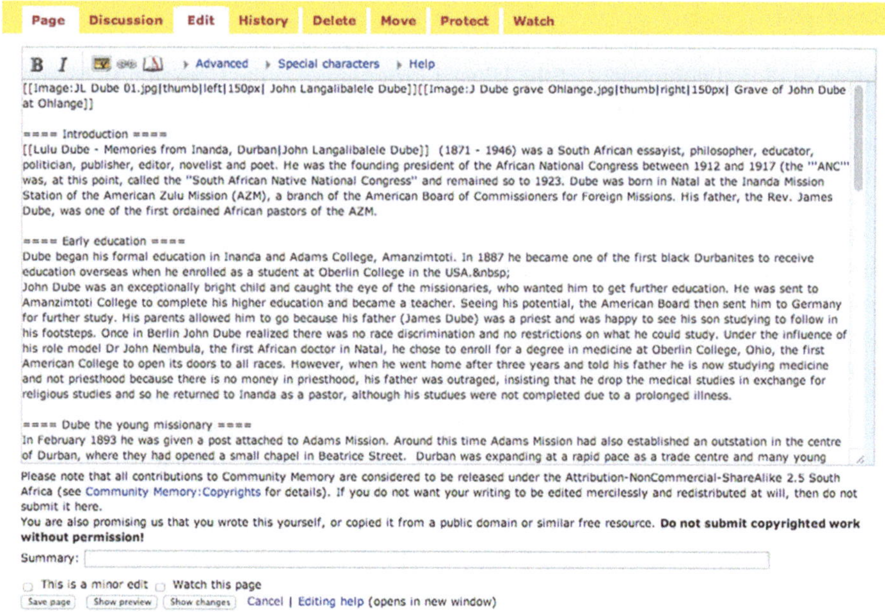

Fig. 13.2 Editing window for community journalists and general public

Blog and Social Media

The Ulwazi Blog publishes community news, notification on recent submissions and information on new features as well as general Programme news. Blog posts are displayed in reverse-chronological order, with a built-in comment function. The blog is multilingual with posts and comments accepted in English and Zulu. Administered by the content-manager, submissions are also encouraged from the community journalists and the general public. This is facilitated through a unique email address (post@ulwazi.org) allowing users to email through blog posts, which are automatically added to the blog stream, once checked by the content-manager. Linked from the blog are the Facebook fanpage and the Twitter account, which users can follow to stay updated on the latest activity from the Ulwazi Programme. Not activated yet, but under discussion, is the use of social media platforms to collect content (stories, images and video) from the community.

Blogs are also used to manage content around specific projects. An example of this is the Ulwazi Schools' Project (http://ulwazi.org/school), run in conjunction with the Goethe Institute. The blog holds information on the project and was actively used by participants to share their experiences and content collected.

MediaWiki

The main digital component of the Ulwazi Programme is the Community Memory website, with the blogs and social media accounts used to both support and promote the Programme's activities. Information on the Programme, including submission procedures and contact details of team members, are made available through the website. The MediaWiki framework is ideally suited to the aims of this project. It allows anyone with access to the Internet and a browser to register an account. Once logged in, users can edit existing articles or add new articles to the website. Crucially, the MediaWiki framework keeps a record of all changes made, allowing the content-manager to track activity on the site and revert to an early version of a page if necessary. This has proved useful in countering spammers, who attempt to add commercially focused pages or links. Content is primarily submitted in English and Zulu, the local vernacular, but other languages such as Afrikaans are used in the Community Memory website, ensuring representation from all sectors of the local geographic community. The MediaWiki framework also has an advanced user management system. This allows users to be grouped together with permissions, such as the ability to delete content, added to specific groups, creating a hierarchy of authority. Users who abuse the website or who fail to follow the submission guidelines can also be blocked. Content is organized using a flexible taxonomy, consisting of a number of categories and subcategories, which can be expanded to accommodate all content submitted.

13.4.2.2 The Mobile Web

There has been a steady increase in mobile phone usage in Africa, with popular statistics suggesting penetration close to 70 %, while the desktop-based Internet population is still only 10.9 % (Miniwatts Marketing Group, 2010). This disproportional relationship can be attributed to issues of affordability and inaccessibility preventing the uptake of the conventional desktop PC in South Africa (Ford & Botha, 2009). The lack of stable electricity supply also inhibits the uptake of desktop technology. With this in mind, the easy maintenance and ease of use of audio and text interfaces of mobile phones make them more attractive to communities who do not have access to established forms of ICT, allowing them to connect with people and information.

Most mobile phones today are sold with a web browser pre-installed. This, combined with the fact that all mobile service providers in South Africa have migrated to the 3G network, means that ordinary South Africans are accessing the Internet from their phones in ever-increasing numbers. The success of Internet-based mobile applications, such as MXit (an instant messaging service for mobile phones developed in South Africa) and M-PESA (a mobile phone-based money transfer service developed in Kenya, but now available in South Africa), also means that the average users now associate their phone with more than just the calls they make and text messages they send. The convenience of use of the mobile phone means it is now a tool to "amplify and enable decentralized interaction" (Donner, 2010).

Based on these developments, and following current trends in South Africa, the Ulwazi Programme adapted the existing digital components, Community Memory website and blog, for use on mobile phones.[1] Taking into account the restrictions inherent in designing interfaces for mobile devices, notably the screen size and cost of mobile data, a mobile interface was developed for the Programme in 2010. This interface uses a simple hyperlinked menu, linking to main sections of the website, with body copy and images underneath. The cascading style sheet (CSS) template design of the desktop interface was replaced with simple HTML and all embedded video content, resource-heavy scripting and unnecessary functionality were removed. The stripped-down version of the Community Memory site still has all essential functionality including the ability to quickly navigate to pages or sections, full searching features and the ability to comment on blog posts. It can be used on the simplest of Internet-enabled mobile devices. A script on the server recognizes when users are accessing the website from a mobile device, automatically presenting the mobile interface. Since the development of the mobile interface, access via mobile devices has increased dramatically, now accounting for 20 % of all visitors.

13.4.3 The Library

The Programme is run through the multi-branch public library system, currently comprising 90 urban, peri-urban and rural libraries, all with free Internet available through public-access desktop PCs. The public library exists as the anchor partner for the Ulwazi Programme, utilizing its existing infrastructure and resources, with community journalists and the public using the Internet-enabled public-access computers to submit content as well as to access existing content.

The public library provides stability for the Programme, in terms of its position, both within the community and within local government structures. As part of their social services, public libraries should be responsible for providing free and equal access to information and knowledge (Hedelund, 2006). Branch libraries provide a direct link to the communities and assist in raising awareness of the Ulwazi Programme, also hosting outreach programmes, distributing promotional material and assisting in coordinating data collection. These branch libraries are also submission points for the community journalists as well as access points for the general public.

Librarians have expertise in information management, and support the community by assisting with this aspect of the project. The technology used—in the form of the open, social platform the Programme is built upon—preserves the dynamic

[1] For more on the Ulwazi Programme and the mobile web see "The number in my pocket: the power of mobile technology for the exchange of indigenous knowledge", Elizabeth Greyling and Niall McNulty, Knowledge Management for Development Journal 7 (3), 2011.

nature, social embeddedness and shared character of community knowledge. The Community Memory website, following Mosimege (2005), uses a folksonomic categorization system as opposed to controlled vocabularies, with categories created according to the content collected by the community journalists and contributions from the general public. Contributors are free to use traditional names for concepts unique to their community. They can also be added in English or Zulu. The advantage of folksonomies, in contrast to a controlled vocabulary, is that it is open-ended and can respond quickly to changes in the way users categorize content (Hartman, 2006). The website is a living document, a "work in progress" to which anyone can add to or edit, to keep the knowledge updated, while at the same time providing a historical window. All changes are tracked and older versions of a page can be referenced or reverted to. Embedded in this process is the ability to "understand the cultural and historical value of information shared and curated in a socially distributed fashion" across various technologies (Liu, 2010).

13.5 Implementing Ulwazi Programme Findings

The Ulwazi Programme has been institutionalized by the eThekwini Municipality as part of regular library services and receives an annual budget. Financial costs for the Programme are kept to a minimum through the use of open-source software, existing government infrastructure and volunteers. The core team managing the project consists of the project leader (the system librarian in the eThekwini Municipality's Library and Heritage Department), a part-time digital manager responsible for server and website maintenance and a part-time content-manager, who is responsible for light copy editing of submitted articles as well as Zulu translations.

The Programme is coordinated from a central programme office, where training, data management and other functions are performed, including assistance with transcriptions and translations, and image processing and archiving. The community journalists are given, and trained in the use of, digital audio recorders and digital cameras. They are required to submit three articles a month, each with a minimum of 400 words and with a photograph. The audio files of interviews with community members are considered a primary source, and are occasionally distributed online where they add value to the article, e.g. they could consist of a song or musical instrument that is mentioned in the article. Articles are submitted at the nearest public library to the community journalist, through one of the public-access computers and loaded directly to the website, or at the monthly meetings held at the central programme office. They can also be submitted via email directly to the content-manager.

The core team holds monthly programme meetings where new submissions are discussed and debated and issues covered. These also serve as continual training and support sessions for the community journalists with the digital manager providing assistance with loading articles, images and audio clips to the Community Memory website and the content-manager assisting in article construction. The content-manager assists with proofreading, translations and categorization.

Regular review of the Programme is conducted by the core team with key indicators of progress including:

- Number of entries in the various categories
- Number of images and video created
- Number of times the site is visited
- Number of people contributing to the website
- Number of community journalists trained to collect and capture stories and information
- Community surveys and opinion polls

13.6 Findings

13.6.1 Content Analysis

The Ulwazi Programme website has (at last count) 791 user-generated articles in total. Of these, 356 are written in Zulu, with the remaining 435 in English. There are also 514 images, including photographs taken by the community journalists as well as images scanned in from the local history museum. The Programme has also produced a number of video and audio clips. The articles are organized into 176 different categories. Three broad categories—Environment, Culture and History—form the organizing structure, with other categories created organically, depending on the content submitted by the community. The most popular of these categories (based on number of articles) are People & Personal Histories; Children's Stories & Legends; Clan Praises; Indigenous Games; The History of Surnames; Traditional Ceremonies; and Traditional Customs. These categories give a good indication of the type of content available through the Ulwazi Programme website but also the information that the community feels is important to preserve and share (see Fig. 13.3).

Since the Ulwazi Programme's inception, Google Analytics has been used to track usage statistics. This is a tool made available by Google to monitor and report on user-interactions with the content of a website. A small script, supplied by Google and added to every page of the website to be tracked, sends data back to the site's Analytics account. This includes data on where the website users are located, what sources they use to access the website and what content they are interested in. For the purposes of this analysis, we extracted a report for the period 01 Jan 2011 until 31 Dec 2011. This period is the third year in the Ulwazi Programme's existence. By this point, the Ulwazi Programme was well-known in the areas in which it operates and the user-base was constant. For the total period under examination, the Ulwazi Programme's website received 91,817 visitors.

If we change the focus from content collected by the Ulwazi Programme, to content accessed by its users, we see an interest in uniquely regional and cultural content. Seventy-five percent of all visitors to the Ulwazi Programme arrive through

Fig. 13.3 Subcategories of the category history

search engines (such as Google, Yahoo! and Bing) with the remaining users accessing the Ulwazi Programme website directly; from social media networks and links from referring websites. Google Analytics tracks this data, including the search-engine keywords used to find the Ulwazi Programme website. These keywords indicate the type of content people are actively searching for. Popular search terms include umemulo (a traditional 21st birthday celebration), umembeso (a type of traditional clothing), izaga (Zulu proverbs), izinganekwane (traditional folk tales), umbondo (a traditional marriage agreement), umhlonyane (a puberty ceremony for females), impepho (a spiritual herb) and izithakazelo (clan names). Notably, most of the top search terms are in the Zulu language. This is an indication of the desire for but lack of local language content online. The Ulwazi Programme—with a critical mass of Zulu articles, in particular of a cultural nature—has become a key resource for search engines. Popular pages on the Ulwazi Programme website (again also tracked by Google Analytics) include Isaiah Shembe (a Zulu religious leader), Umemulo, Traditional Wedding, Imicimbi Yesintu (a traditional ceremony), Ukuqala Komemulo (a coming of age ceremony), Umembeso, Ukuthwasa (a spiritual healer's training), Umhlonyane (a traditional ceremony), Izinganekwane, Zulu Clothing and Recipe for Steam Bread. The most-accessed articles on the Ulwazi Programme website are linked to traditional ceremonies and customs of the Zulu people. This data reiterates that local users are searching for local content online, and finding it through the Ulwazi Programme website.

13.6.2 User Demographics

In 2011, the Ulwazi Programme attracted visitors from 182 countries. The global reach of the Internet and the effectiveness of search engines mean that once content is published online it is available worldwide. Countries in the top ten of Ulwazi Programme users include the United States, the United Kingdom, India, Germany, Canada, Australia, France and Netherlands. However, the majority of visitors—close to 60 % of the total—come from South Africa, suggesting an interest in local content by local users. On a national level, the regional spread is split evenly between the provinces of KwaZulu-Natal and Gauteng. KwaZulu-Natal is the province where the eThekwini Municipality and the Ulwazi Programme are located while Gauteng (the economic centre of South Africa) has a large proportion of Zulu-speaking residents. The other seven provinces in South Africa all send visitors to the Ulwazi Programme website, albeit in considerably smaller numbers. This trend is reinforced when looking at visitor demographics at a city level. Durban (the main city in the eThekwini Municipality and the largest city in KwaZulu-Natal) and Johannesburg (the largest city in the Gauteng province) are the top urban locations for Ulwazi Programme web-users. In the list of top ten cities, Cape Town is the only city that is not located in the provinces of KwaZulu-Natal or Gauteng. Therefore, while the project generates interest from around the world, it is South Africa, and in particular the two provinces with the majority of Zulu-speakers, that are the major users of the website. These statistics uphold one of the Ulwazi Programme's assumptions—the need for relevant online local content in local languages.

13.6.3 Limitations

Some limitations to the Ulwazi Programme have also been discovered. These include a high turnover of community journalists, who, because sourced from an unemployed sector of the community, leave the Programme once employment opportunity arises. This places additional stress on the recruitment and training aspects of Programme. While the decision to embrace a multilingual approach towards content has been successful, this has also meant that selective translations have been required. Content management takes time and requires a certain set of skills and relevant experience. Training and development of volunteers and community journalists has proven to be time-consuming with the development of ICT skills generally slow among rural communities in the Municipality. The training of small groups and one-on-one support, while effective, is labour-intensive.

13.7 Conclusions

Current ICT and mobile technology have the potential to empower communities to preserve and manage their own local knowledge. By creating an online platform that they can engage with and providing access to their indigenous knowledge, communities start participating in the global information society and bridging the digital divide. Initiatives like the Ulwazi Programme also provide valuable opportunities for skills development, knowledge provision and social networking, with the potential for job creation and poverty alleviation. Collaboration and knowledge sharing using Web 2.0 technologies and social media tools allow for the context of the knowledge to be preserved. Making this information more widely available assists in cross-cultural understanding and tolerance and could improve social cohesion in the community. Technology empowers communities to record what they feel is important in a way that makes sense and is logical to them. Through the Ulwazi Programme, the capacity of the local communities of eThekwini to develop and access content in their own language has largely been proven. Previously marginalized communities now have online access to local knowledge, along with the prospect of participating in the global information society and bridging the digital divide. A reading of the Google Analytics data further indicates that while the Ulwazi Programme website has global interest, the majority of users come from South Africa, in particular provinces in which Zulu is spoken. The content these users are interested in—as shown through search terms that bring users to the Ulwazi Programme website and the articles they access—is regionally and culturally specific and, for the most part, in the local vernacular. As the Internet becomes more pervasive in all aspects of society, through the development of mobile and geolocation technologies, it also has the potential to become more relevant locally. The Ulwazi Programme is an example of this with local users interested in local content in local languages. The Programme provides a model to be replicated in other African countries, bearing in mind the local contexts, languages and political environments in which it will function.

References

Averweg, U. R., & Greyling, E. H. (2008). Survey of information and communication technologies and information needs in the eThekwini Municipality in South Africa. In M. Leaning (Ed.), *Issues in information and media literacy* (pp. 227–256). Santa Rosa, CA: Informing Science Press.

Beazley, I., Bowen, J. P., McDaid, S., & Liu, A. H. Y. (2010). Dulwich OnView: An art museum-based virtual community generated by the local community. In A. Seal, J. P. Bowen, & K. Ng (Eds.), *EVA London 2010: Visualisation and the arts* (pp. 79–86), London, UK, British Computer Society.

Bidwell, N. J. (2010). Ubuntu in the network: Humanness in social capital in rural South Africa. *Interactions, 17*(2), 68–71.

Bidwell, N. J., Winschiers-Theophilus, H., Koch-Kapuire, G., & Chivuno-Kuria, S. (2011). Situated interactions between audiovisual media and African herbal lore. *Personal and Ubiquitous Computing, 15*(6), 609–627. doi:10.1007/s00779-010-0337-1.

Bowen, J. P. (2008). Wiki software and facilities for museums. In D. Bearman & J. Trant (Eds.), MW2008: Museums and the Web 2008, Montreal, Canada. *Archives & Museum Informatics*. Retrieved from http://www.museumsandtheweb.com/mw2008/papers/bowen/bowen.html

Brown, D., & Nicholas, G. (2012). Protecting indigenous cultural property in the age of digital democracy: Institutional and communal responses to Canadian First Nations and Māori heritage concerns. *Journal of Material Culture, 17*(3), 307–324.

Coetzee, J. K. (2001). A micro foundation for development thinking. In J. K. Coetzee, J. Graaff, F. Hendricks, & G. Wood (Eds.), *Development theory, policy and practice* (pp. 118–139). Cape Town: Oxford University Press.
Davidavičienė, V., & Raudeliūnienė, J. (2010). *ICT in tacit knowledge preservation*. Paper presented at the sixth international scientific conference business and management 2010, Vilnius, Lithuania.
Donner, J. (2010). Framing M4D: The utility of continuity and the dual heritage of "mobiles and development". *Electronic Journal on Information Systems in Developing Countries, 44*(3), 1–16. Retrieved from http://www.ejisdc.org/ojs2/index.php/ejisdc/article/view/746/342
Dougherty, D. (2001). *LAMP: The open source web platform*. Retrieved from http://www.onlamp.com/pub/a/onlamp/2001/01/25/lamp.html
Farkas, M. G. (2007). *Social software in libraries: Building collaboration, communication, and community online*. Medford, NJ.: Information Today.
Ford, M., & Botha, A. (2009). MobiLed—Mobile-Led and leading via mobile. In P. Cunningham & M. Cunningham (Eds.) *Proceedings of the IST-Africa 2009 conference* (p. 13), Kampala, Uganda.
Grele, R. (1991). *Envelopes of sound: The art of oral history*. New York: Praeger.
Greyling, E. H. (2009). Content development in an indigenous digital library: A model for community participation. In P. Cunningham & M. Cunningham (Eds.), *Proceedings of the IST-Africa 2009 Conference* (pp. 6–8), Kampala, Uganda.
Greyling, E. H., & McNulty, N. (2011). The number in my pocket: The power of technology for the exchange of indigenous knowledge. *Knowledge Management for Development Journal, 7*(3), 256–273.
Hartman, K. (2006). Knowledge management using Weblogs, Wikis and RSS. In *Proceedings of the 17th standing conference of eastern, central & southern African Library & Information Associations* (pp. 401–412), Dar es Salaam, Tanzania.
Hedelund, L. (2006). Community Center Gellerup from everyday practice to method development: A Danish Public Library case. In *Proceedings of the 17th standing conference of eastern, central & southern African Library & Information Associations* (pp. 219–244), Dar es Salaam, Tanzania.
Hughes, M., & Dallwitz, J. (2006). Ara Irititja: Towards culturally appropriate best practice in remote indigenous Australia. In L. E. Dyson, M. Hendrik, & S. Grant (Eds.), *Information technology and indigenous people* (pp. 146–158). Hershey, PA: Information Science Publishing.
International Telecommunications Union. (2008). *African telecommunication/ICT indicators 2008*. Retrieved from http://appablog.wordpress.com/2008/05/12/itu-telecom-africa-2008-opens-in-cairo/
Leavy, B. (2006). Digital songlines: Digitising the arts, culture and heritage landscape of Aboriginal Australia. In L. E. Dyson, M. Hendrik, & S. Grant (Eds.), *Information technology and indigenous people* (pp. 159–169). Hershey, PA: Information Science Publishing.
Liu, S. B. (2010). Trends in distributed curatorial technology to manage data in a networked world. *Upgrade Journal, 11*(3), 18–24.
Lor, P. J. (2004). Storehouses of knowledge?: The role of libraries in preserving and promoting indigenous knowledge. *Indilinga, 3*(1), 45–56.
Lor, P. J. (2008). Digital libraries and archiving knowledge: Some critical questions. *South African Journal of Libraries and Information Science, 74*(2), 117–128.
Mbaya, H. (2010). Social capital and the imperatives of the concept and life of Ubuntu in the South African context. *Scriptura, 104*, 367–376.
Miniwatts Marketing Group. (2010). *Internet world stats*. Retrieved from http://www.internetworldstats.com/stats.htm
Mosimege, M. (2005). *Indigenous knowledge systems policy in South Africa: Development of digital libraries and implications for benefit sharing and intellectual property*. Paper presented at the Commons-Sense Conference, Johannesburg. Retrieved from http://www.commons-sense.org/presentation/mosimege/Mosimege.pdf
Rahman, M. (2007). *MediaWiki administrator's guide*. Birmingham, UK: Packt Publishing.
Stanoevska-Slabeva, K. (2002). Toward a community-oriented design of Internet platforms. *International Journal of Electronic Commerce, 6*(3), 71–95.

Swap, W., Leonard, D., Shields, M., & Abrams, L. (2001). Using mentoring and storytelling to transfer knowledge in the workplace. *Journal of Management Information Systems, 18*(1), 95–114.

United Nations. (1990). The African charter for popular participation in development and transformation. In *Proceedings of the international conference on popular participation in the recovery and development process in Africa*, Arusha, Tanzania.

United Nations. (1995). World Summit for Social Development: A new agenda for social development. In I. Davids, F. Theron, & K. J. Maphunye (Eds.), *Participatory development in South Africa: A development management perspective* (pp. 223–233). Pretoria: Van Schaik.

United Nations. (2000). *United Nations millennium development goals*. Retrieved from http://ddp-ext.worldbank.org/ext/GMIS/home.do?siteId=2

Warren, D. M. (1991). *The role of indigenous knowledge in facilitating the agricultural extension process*. Paper presented at the international workshop on agricultural knowledge systems and the role of extension, Bad Boll, Germany.

Wenger, E. (1998). *Communities of practice: Learning, meaning and identity*. Cambridge: Cambridge University Press.

World Summit on the Information Society. (2003). *The Geneva declaration of principles and plan of action*. Geneva: World Summit for the Information Society Executive Secretariat.

World Summit on the Information Society. (2005). *Tunis agenda for the information society*. (WSIS-05/TUNIS/DOC/6/rev.1.) Retrieved from http://portal.unesco.org/ci/en/files/20687/11327453881tunis_agenda_En.doc/tunis_agenda_en.doc

Chapter 14
Knowledge Management for Programs on Information and Communications Technologies for Development (ICT4D) in South Africa

Sue Conger

Abstract The Living Labs in South Africa (LLiSA) projects have been introducing telecommunications and Internet technologies to remote rural South African municipalities for over 7 years. The projects have exhibited mixed success, with some quite successful in assisting schools and health clinics to use the Internet for obtaining and sharing information and others enjoying initial success only to fall into disuse. Knowledge management for technology expertise, Internet and computer usage, and software tools has required a transfer of knowledge to local interested individuals. However, knowledge management is typically not an explicitly named aspect of the projects. Rather, projects cite a need for training and development of skills for maintainability, but no explicit knowledge management. This research describes knowledge management characteristics, then analyses information and computer technology for development (ICT4D) projects around the world to develop best practices and their knowledge management components. The Siyakhula Living Lab, a part of LLiSA, is evaluated with attention to the extent to which knowledge management best practices are applied. The knowledge management used is simple and somewhat effective in developing a growing base of technology users in the project's supported locations, but does not address documentation of project information for use in local maintenance and support. Recommendations for knowledge management in ICT4D and, specifically the LLiSA projects, are developed.

Keywords Information and communications technology • ICT • Knowledge management • Community involvement

S. Conger (✉)
University of Dallas, Irving, TX, USA

Rhodes University, Grahamstown, Eastern Cape, South Africa

UNISA, Johannesburg, Gauteng, South Africa
e-mail: sconger@udallas.edu

K.-M. Osei-Bryson et al. (eds.), *Knowledge Management for Development*, Integrated Series in Information Systems 35, DOI 10.1007/978-1-4899-7392-4_14,

14.1 Introduction

The significant body of research on information and communications technologies for development (ICT4D) gives us guidelines on conduct and expectations of outcomes for such work. The Living Labs in South Africa (LLiSA) is a long-running program of remote rural ICT4D projects in South Africa that have both impressive successes and disappointments. The question guiding this research is what knowledge management (KM) practices for remote South African rural projects might improve their outcomes?

From an academic perspective, this research is important because past KM research in ICT4D projects is sparse. The existing research does not look at specific project use of KM and deals primarily with the government policy level of recommendations (cf. Ferguson, Mchombu, & Cummings, 2008; Jain, 2006). This research evaluates cases for which knowledge management is important to sustainability. Thus, this research begins to fill a gap in KM research by discussing specific issues relating to project sustainability that can be dealt with through a KM effort.

Another contribution is the development of a set of best practices for KM and for ICT4D projects that might be applied to other analyses of project successes and failures. There are other attempts at ICT4D best practices (e.g., Unwin, 2009), but they do not include explicit knowledge management practices.

One area that appears to have general applicability to project work, specifically in ICT4D projects, is knowledge management (KM). KM applies to ICT4D because projects implement technology that requires on-going support and maintenance without the aid of the original development team. This paper seeks to first develop a summary of knowledge management to develop best practices that should be part of any ICT4D project to optimize its probability of success. ICT4D research from many developing countries then is examined to identify the practices are key to success to be emulated or key to failures and to be avoided. These are evaluated to determine their KM content. South Africa's LLiSA projects and their outcomes are summarized with the Siyakhula Living Lab (SLL) discussed in detail in terms of its KM practices. This analysis identifies areas for changing the way knowledge needs are managed that should improve the potential for outcome sustainability. This paper is not meant to criticize the LLiSA projects, which are successful in helping remote rural peoples adopt wireless technologies, including primarily cell phones and health clinic and school-based Internet. The projects have accomplished some feats of technological innovation in the field. This research seeks to provide LLiSA projects with the benefit of KM successes around the world that, when applied in their own work, might improve their successes' sustainability.

14.2 Knowledge Management Theory Best Practices

Knowledge management (KM) is the systematic process of acquisition, organization, and communication of organizational member knowledge for reuse by others in the community (Alavi & Leidner, 2001). Knowledge relates to an individual's ability to take an action and can relate to declarative (know-what), procedural (know-how), causality (know-why), conditional (know-when), or relational (know-with) types of knowledge (Zack, 1998 as cited in Alavi & Leidner, 2001). Each knowledge type needs to be examined to determine the extent to which the project being documented needs the type of information and the extent to which the information can be codified. Some organizations only code the fact of the information and identify the person to contact, providing a directory of subject matter experts for their knowledge repository (Alavi & Leidner 1999, 2001). Recording of both searchable information and a directory of information sources are considered best practices.

For instance, for a project-based KM system, the directory might include key characteristics of the projects, such as hardware, software, company size, etc. and for each, contact information about the characteristics (Alavi & Leidner, 1999). In addition, the searchable information might contain a summary of the project and the difficulties it faced and how they were overcome, project staffing, project conduct, and so on. Such a directory combines both searchable information and contact information.

Knowledge is categorized as tacit or explicit. Tacit knowledge is held in an individual's mind and relates to an individual's experiences with technical aspects in terms of skills or procedural knowledge (Nanaka, 1994). Explicit knowledge is known, codified, and shareable (Nanaka, 1994).

Tacit knowledge poses the larger challenge to KM as expertise and reasoning processes are difficult to clearly identify. Professionals are often not able to articulate their reasoning processes (Davenport, De Long, & Beers, 1998). Plus, when solutions are constantly tailored to situations, pre-defining situational needs may not be possible. Explicit knowledge, on the other hand, is more simply the codification of relatively well-understood knowledge into a reusable format.

An example of both types of knowledge can be seen in a help desk situation. Explicit knowledge on past computer outages is codified into a "known errors database" (KEDB), which is a searchable, online database accessible by all help desk support staff (Conger & Probst, in press; Van Bon, 2005). When an outage occurs and is recorded, the KEDB is checked to determine if a solution or work-around already exists. When found, the solution is applied and verified as working. When no solution is found, the expertise of the help desk staff worker in the form of tacit knowledge takes over. Then, the worker reviews his past experience to determine similar situations and tries to resolve the issue based on that past experience. Alterations and improvised solutions based on experience may result (Conger & Probst, in press; Verjans, 2005). Ideally, then, the new solution should be able to be codified and added to the KEDB but often, the circumstances are so unique that the solution is unlikely to ever be used again. An example might be an outage due to a vendor engineering change. The reasoning used to find the root cause is interesting but the solution is mundane, rarely applicable, and not worth the effort to put into a KEDB. Separating those tacit situations of interest from those that are not is a subjective, difficult prospect.

Challenges to KM relate to all aspects of its information life cycles, including identification and acquisition, storage and retrieval, and dissemination (Alavi & Leidner, 2001; Teece, 1998,). Identification and acquisition relate to the ability of the person with the experience recognizing a need to share his expertise and their ability to codify it in some useful way. The storage and retrieval aspects relate to creating a digital, shareable record of some type and also defining search terms or file names to allow easy recognition of the shared content. As different individuals have different mental models and names for tasks and artefacts, creating the search terms and file names become difficult intellectual tasks. Then, dissemination is the sharing of information across a community of users such that they are all apprised of the new information and how to access it. The larger the organization, the more likely the number of shareable knowledge items would be large and the more often items would be added to the digital cache. The challenge in this environment is not only to overwhelm users with information on new knowledge items, but also to keep them informed about the items that are available. Thus, information about the information, that is, meta-data, becomes necessary.

The human adjunct to digitally recording information is the development of a community of practice, also called a knowledge cluster (Brown & Duguid, 2001; Evers, Nordin, & Nienkemper, 2010). Knowledge is only important when applied or shared. Sharing does not always come naturally because of culture, organization, geography, or many other reasons (Bowen, Edwards, Cattell, & Jay, 2010; Evers el al., 2010; Gottschalk, 2007). Encouraging the target user community to become not just users, but contributors to the knowledge store, can motivate them to continue to use the project products (Evers et al., 2010). Thus, part of the project purpose becomes knowledge production.

While proximity is desirable, to remote rural people, Internet access removes distances between villages. Further, the individuals who actively contribute to knowledge stores can be recognized and rewarded for their participation as encouragement not just to them but to incite others to participate (Gottschalk, 2007). Sites that create their own community of practice become more sustainable as they rely less and less on the project originators and more on local expertise to conduct the project's work (Brown & Duguid, 2001; Evers et al., 2010; Robinson, Anumba, Carrillo, & Al-Ghassani, 2006).

To summarize, key aspects of knowledge include knowledge type, definition of key knowledge in a project, the life cycle for KM, development of a knowledge cluster, and development of processes for knowledge productions. These should be considered in all projects, but particularly in remote rural projects because the experts change from time to time and communities that continually rely on the remote experts for key maintenance activities tend to be less successful (Geldof et al., 2011). The creation of a community of practice that is based in sharing knowledge through an automated knowledge store is important to reducing reliance on project originators (Brown & Duguid, 2001; Evers et al., 2010).

14.3 Knowledge Management in Remote Rural Technology Implementation

In this section, we discuss ICT4D project research all over the world to discern the types and outcomes of KM in those projects. Ultimately, the two main goals of all projects are success of the initial project, usually in the form of working technology, and sustainability of the initiative. Different activities are required for initial start-up versus sustainability, which is the focus here. For sustainability, many key activities need to take place, and somewhere in those processes, knowledge transfer needs to take place and spread. First, we discuss key activities and how they might impact KM. Next, key shortcomings of ICT4D projects that inhibit sustainability and how they relate to KM are developed and analysed to identify KM components. Then, knowledge outcomes, to the extent they exist, to develop best field practices relating to KM are identified to provide the basis, along with KM theory for evaluating the South African LLiSA projects.

14.3.1 Key Activities in ICT4D Projects

Remote rural projects can be initiated as part of a governmental, NGO, academic, or private corporate initiative. India, a country with hundreds of remote rural initiatives, has all types, including some that seek to develop entrepreneurial skills among locals who would "own" the final products (Best & Kumar, 2008; Toyama, 2011; Vaughan, 2011; Walsham, 2010). Other countries evaluated include Brazil, Indonesia, Nepal, India, China, Sri Lanka, Mozambique, and Nigeria. Table 14.1 lists the requirements for project success, summarizing findings of these projects.

While ICT4D authors all have their own, unique, "best practices" lists for the particular project under study, all seem incomplete by themselves. Even the combination of all of the lists would be incomplete as the ephemeral aspects of success are often in the personalities and abilities of the individuals involved (Robinson et al., 2006; Turner & Müller, 2005). In fact, Unwin (2009) lists 260 principles for effective ICT4D implementation. The importance of Table 14.1 lies in hints at KM needs that should be addressed by a project that can be associated with each item on the list.

As Table 14.1 shows, there is little agreement across authors on what constitutes "required" activities for ICT4D project success, even when they are in the same country. This often relates to cultural differences, which, even in the same country, can have failure projects even though previously successful approaches were used (Ferguson, Huysman, & Soekijad, 2010). All of the items in Table 14.1 appear to be important. The list highlights that researcher perspective is necessarily constrained and that the guidelines from the Project Management Institute's (PMI) Project and Program Management Bodies of Knowledge might be just as useful (or more useful, being more regularized) as a list of needed activities (Levin, 2013; Project Management Institute [PMI], 2004, 2008). Although analysis of PMBOK is beyond the scope of this research, this might be a future area for research.

Every item on the list has a knowledge component that could explicitly be identified. A few of the items are expanded on here, chosen because of the far-reaching implications to choices made early in the ICT4D project's life.

One key area for discussion is the selection of a local champion. A champion is a cheerleader, and an active advocate for a project. Often there are both technical and business champions (Mason, McKenney, & Copeland, 1997). In remote villages, there is a chief, king, or other potentate who rules the area. The approval of these individuals is always

Table 14.1 Key requirements for remote rural ICT4D success

Key requirements for success	Author
A local champion, preferably who can take over management and maintenance; draw on the strengths of multiple actors for project governance; leverage local capabilities; eventually give locals control over daily operations; train and work with locals, eventually give them control over daily operations; invest time in partnership building and networking	Cunningham et al. (2012), Geldof et al. (2011), Heeks and Molla (2009), Kanya and Good (2012), Thapa and Saebo (2011)
Address issues of accessibility	Unwin (2009)
Attend to cultural differences in gaining trust and cooperation but also not changing the culture; treat locals in such a way that their traditional "social fibre" remains intact; researchers come with or lose preconceptions to become effective at cultural interpretation	Geldof et al. (2011), Krauss and Turpin (2010)
Balance between demand and supply of resources	Geldof et al. (2011)
Committed, enthusiastic, competent leaders	Geldof et al. (2011), Heeks (2009)
Communicate trust, openness, mutual respect, and understanding through all communications	Geldof et al. (2011)
Design appropriate technology; needs-based projects, adapted to local context; new approaches—flexibility, improvement, iterative learning in situ and from the past; provide working, appropriate technology; develop contextual understanding should be the basis for project design; local community involvement with attention to local politics; evaluation of local needs, bottom-up projects; output-based focus; ensure that project designs are aligned to local realities	Bidwell et al. (2011), Cunningham et al. (2012), Geldof et al. (2011), Heeks (2009), Heeks and Molla (2009), Krauss and Turpin (2010), Thapa and Saebo (2011), Unwin (2009)
Emphasis on sustainability (e.g., life of project), include economic and socio-political sustainability	Cunningham et al. (2012), Geldof et al. (2011), Heeks (2009), Heeks and Molla (2009), Unwin (2009)
Ensure that all problems are remedied	Unwin (2009)
Have project team study ICT4D in school to better understand	Kanya and Good (2012)
Manage expectations	Cunningham et al. (2012)
Monitoring and evaluation	Heeks (2009), Unwin (2009)
Strategy with long-term and short-term goals	Kanya and Good (2012)
Transparent, ethical basis for partnership; trust and shared vision among partners who understand the scope of each other's roles and activities	Geldof et al. (2011), Heeks (2009), Unwin (2009)

gained before a project begins. However, the ruler is almost never a champion or the "manager" of the on-going project and rarely is a user of the technology or capability being provided. According to Diffusion of Innovation Research, this is a mistake (Rogers, 1994). Success is more likely when the most senior manager, or Chief, is the client and a user of the project, and when the person reporting to the Chief is the manager of the on-going efforts. Thus, the Chief would serve as a ceremonial, advocate role for the project. Local commitment at the chieftain level sends a message not only to project participants but to potential users of the technology that it is sanctioned within the cultural boundaries of the village or unit. By only gaining approval for project conduct, success or failure is not associated with the Chief, and by not using the technology, the Chiefs send the message that it is accepted but not promoted. This kind of passive aggressive stance is common in rural projects and the populace may partially use the technology but is less likely to embrace it by seeking innovative or adaptive uses.

In addition, KM requirements of a champion and manager need to be considered. Both champion and manager need constant updating with project status, successes, issues, and so on, to deal with local conditions relating to the project. This may require training in managerial techniques since local management may be largely inherited and ceremonial. On-going KM needs include access and knowledge about how to access policies, procedures, processes, etc. relating to the project, and then, what to do with the knowledge once it is known. These are non-trivial managerial requirements for whomever takes on the job, but may invite particular resistance from a Chief not often challenged in his (yes, they are almost always male) ability to manage.

The requirements "output-based focus," committed leaders, investment of time in partnership building, and sustainability all relate to project success (Geldof et al., 2011; Heeks, 2009). These best practices also have a KM component. For instance, in having an output-based focus, many technology projects focus on the technology (Geldof et al., 2011). It must be functional, simple, intuitive, and work. This set of characteristics is technical and is able to be completed with the technology running when the experts leave. In addition, the ability of locals to maintain equipment; add and change access rights, users, and technology; and manage the facility to ensure security, accessibility, and safety. Further, technology also needs to be understood, startable, stoppable, interruptible, troubleshot, modifiable, and adaptable. These characteristics, while having a design component, are expertise-based and require local, on-going support with growth of expertise for untethered management of the technology once the experts leave. These all require different understanding and skills—engineering and mechanical, administrative computing, building and grounds custodial skills, and technology design and use. Thus, identification of a single manager to continue the work is unlikely. Rather several people, plus their backups, need to be identified early in the project's life and trained both in class and on-the-job to take over the work. As soon as trained, these people should take over all maintenance so they can be coached and mentored by the project team while they are on site (Thapa & Saebo, 2011).

For each question raised during training and mentoring, it is important to define aspects of project information required for immediate and on-going support, which information are optional, and which information are needed only when there is an outage. Then, for each answer, a KM strategy should be developed to match the capability needed. In addition, capabilities for continued remote contact to the project team, preferably with remote access to the computers, should be defined to ensure proper escalation of problems for resolution should they occur. These project roles require different types of knowledge, all of which should be provided for in a KM data store for use. Often KM data stores are thought to be a searchable database, but they could be multi-media with indices for document physical and digital locations, DVDs or CDs, videos, audio presentations, or other media. For instance, DVD

Table 14.2 Key reasons for remote rural ICT4D failure

Key reasons for failures	Author
Design was not context-appropriate technology, insufficient bandwidth	Thapa and Saebo (2011), Toyama (2011)
Local organizations were not partners; participation of community was not invited as a group; relationship with local government was not developed	Toyama (2011)
Project did not adhere to socio-cultural norms	Toyama (2011)
Services did not meet local needs	Toyama (2011)
Finances were insufficient, lack of business model for sustainability (i.e., relied on donations)	Toyama (2011), Thapa and Saebo (2011)
Stakeholders were not incented to support the project	Toyama (2011)
Low literacy inhibited participation	Thapa and Saebo (2011)
High age of local community inhibited participation	Thapa and Saebo (2011)
Inconsistent electricity	Thapa and Saebo (2011)
Lack of trained maintenance people	Thapa and Saebo (2011)

hardware maintenance videos or other aids might demonstrate finding the problem then show step-by-step instructions for the fix.

In summary, the list in Table 14.1 illustrates that there are a significant number of areas on which to focus managerial attention for building enduring local skill sets. Each area needs to be analysed for its knowledge components and its method of management. Ideally, this planning would predate the project but often, the issues are revealed as project work is conducted. As a result both planned and ad hoc methods for identifying and designing KM needed for sustaining ICT4D are required.

14.3.2 Key Shortcomings of ICT4D Projects

In general, KM is not an explicit part of remote rural projects. The terms training, learning, and skills development often appear in project documentation, but the term "KM" is sparsely found to date (cf. Ferguson et al., 2008, 2010; Jain, 2006; Kleine & Unwin, 2009). In this section we analyse key reasons for ICT4D project failures to identify practices to be avoided.

As the list in Table 14.2 shows, many of the reasons for project failures are the opposite of items in Table 14.1. Often the project initiators believe they have attended to a needed area, but their actions are insufficient or misguided and ultimately fail (Toyama, 2011). For instance, if the problem is low literacy, means to deal with the problem are required. Use of handsets for mobile phones with simple, iconic instructions would be required for any use. Reading programs that begin at an elementary level and are designed for adults might be added to the project tasks (Thapa & Saebo, 2011). Further, typing or other skills classes for learning how to deal with a keyboard may be needed. Similarly, with inconsistent electricity, some means for solar panels, wind-up equipment, or other electrical substitute might be required.

The issue of not attending to local norms is a knotty one (Krauss & Turpin, 2010). Just defining local norms is challenging. It is clear that technology cannot overcome existing inequalities in an environment; rather, it often magnifies them (Toyama, 2011). In many remote villages, for instance, women's roles are caregiver, teacher, and homebody (e.g., cooking), but in many ICT4D projects women enthusiastically embrace the opportunity to enlarge their worlds and seek to participate in ways that violate local norms of behaviour (Grunfeld, 2011). Similarly, introverted, marginalized individuals might embrace technology as a way of connecting with like-minded souls; such connections can violate norms, for instance, by providing a forum for unrestricted interaction (Bidwell et al., 2011).

ICT4D projects almost always result in new language and cultural changes relating to understanding and use of the technologies (Bidwell et al., 2011). As a result, projects can become exclusive and divisive (Heeks, 2009). Changes in local culture, such as women increasingly voicing their opinions, also occur (Grunfeld, 2011). Women, in particular, who become involved as users of ICT4D projects work more in the community, talk more, share ideas, and are viewed as more similar to the men in the village as a result of ICT4D project involvement (Grunfeld, 2011). As a result the culture does change and is not always viewed as a positive change by locals. These changes are viewed as minimal by many ICT4D initiators because, in their world, the changes are minimal (Pade, Mallinson, & Sewry, 2008). However, with sensitivity to local conditions these issues can be made a positive outcome for the project (Grunfeld, 2011; Krauss & Turpin, 2010). For instance, having a mobile phone makes users "feel more connected to the world," thus overcoming isolation (Grunfeld, 2011). Technology can be oriented toward improving the lot of the entire community by providing, for instance, information about jobs, farming techniques, animal concerns, and so on (Grunfeld, 2011). These are framing issues. Best practice is for locals to decide on their own projects and uses of technology without prompting (Geldof et al., 2011). But, to initially "sell" a project, positive outcomes for the community appear most likely to gain fast, wide-reaching acceptance (Grunfeld, 2011; Heeks, 2009).

14.3.3 Relating ICT4D Best Practices and Shortcomings to Knowledge Management

In this section, the contents of best practices and key failure components are summarized to determine the extent to which KM development activities might be developed to address the activity. Items stated negatively in table 14.2 are restated as positive steps that should be part of best practices so all of the items included should be done.

As Table 14.3 discusses, KM in ICT4D could play various integrating roles as well as the traditional KM role of providing documented accessibility to project information. The integrating roles could include cultural aspects of projects such that information becomes available to indigenous people in their own language, through iconic presentations, or even in audio native language versions. By making

Table 14.3 Best practices summary and their knowledge management components

Key requirements for success	Relationship to KM
Develop a project strategy with long-term and short-term goals	A project strategy needs to include KM for sustainability and to reduce, over time, the need for original developer involvement. Without the development of local skills, supported by KM efforts, sustainability becomes questionable (Chuang, 2004; Marais, 2011; Masiero, 2011)
Emphasize sustainability (e.g., continued life of project), including economic and socio-political sustainability; provide sufficient financing; develop business model for sustainability (i.e., do not rely on continuing donations)	A KM facilitates sustainability and, without a KM, sustainability becomes less probable (Robinson et al., 2006). Each ICT4D project needs to develop local talent to eventually take over project management and on-going support. Without a KM, and without a KM that spans multiple projects, such sustainability is unlikely without continued technical management by the original developers
Develop committed, enthusiastic, competent leaders; incentivize stakeholders to support the project; invest time in building partnerships with all stakeholders—politicians, NGOs, local community, etc.	Commitment and enthusiasm usually wane as project sustainability becomes an issue. By developing local competence in a variety of ways, one of which would be KM, can help sustain the commitment and enthusiasm (Jeon, Kim, & Koh, 2011). However, the development and continuance of these leadership characteristics is a complex problem that goes far beyond what can be accomplished by KM
Attend to cultural differences in gaining trust and cooperation but also not changing the culture; treat locals in such a way that their traditional "social fibre" remains intact; Adhere to socio-cultural norms; researchers come with or lose preconceptions to become effective at cultural interpretation	These culture recommendations are very different ways of looking at the same issue, none of which is a KM issue and none of which may be completely possible with any change effort. At best, a project should be sensitive to cultural norms and a KM might also seek to maintain indigenous knowledge through the KM facility as a way to recognize cultural importance (Bidwell et al., 2011; Ferguson et al., 2010). Indigenous needs might be translation to local language that is spoken, not typed. Both of these require some form of KM to be accomplished
Define a local champion, preferably who can take over management and maintenance; draw on the strengths of multiple actors for project governance; train and work with locals, eventually give them control over daily operations; train maintenance people	This individual needs multiple types of declarative, process, causal, conditional, and relational knowledge that may be both tacit and explicit (Alavi & Leidner, 2001). Thus, this may be more than one person, for instance, one person for educational content and one person for hardware/software support
	A project strategy needs to include KM for sustainability and to reduce, over time, the need for original developer involvement (Robinson et al., 2006). A KM facilitates this turnover. Without a KM, the burden of being a local controller for a project may cause burnout or turnover without adequate training of replacements. With a KM, the local controller can train backups and share the burdens of growth in number of users supported. Without the development of local skills, supported by KM efforts, sustainability becomes questionable (Marais, 2011)

(continued)

Table 14.3 (continued)

Key requirements for success	Relationship to KM
Communicate trust, openness, mutual respect, and understanding through all communications; invest time in partnership building and networking	This issue transcends KM but has a small KM component in that communication requires some understanding of local culture, past decisions, and transparency to develop trust, which can be facilitated through explicit KM (Bidwell et al., 2011) A KM facilitates the needed partnership building and networking, especially if a KM can be shared across many similar projects
Balance demand and supply of resources	Supply of resources, particularly human resources (HR), is always scarce in ICT4D projects. By treating both knowledge and HR as assets to be managed, KM can facilitate this management (Davenport et al., 1998). In addition, improving local HR capabilities seems required to loosen ties to project developers over time; KM can facilitate this development
Design appropriate, fully-working technology that is based on local needs, adapted as needed, involves the local community, partners local organizations, develops relationships with local governments, attends to local politics, contains output-based focus, applies new approaches with flexibility of design, uses iterative development, is context-appropriate, includes sufficient bandwidth, with services that meet local needs, and includes infrastructure, such as consistent electricity, as needed	This includes the development of an appropriate mechanism for KM, designed with the users in mind, and preferably, with their participation. The KM component to a project must also be sensitive to needs, adapting to local grammar, vocabulary, and language as needed to ensure use and continued development (Bidwell et al., 2011; Marais, 2011; Masiero, 2011; Tow, Venable, & Dell, 2011) IT projects require a certain amount of improvisation (Barrett, 1998; Verjans, 2005). While the issue of new approaches transcends KM, a KM that documents decisions, problems-solutions, capability development, etc. can facilitate learning across projects and across time (Conger & Probst, in press) A goal orientation, output-based focus transcends KM; however, KM should be a goal of the project as part of sustainability planning In addition, to address political concerns, the "what's in it for me" issue should be addressed explicitly for each person with a political stake in a project's success. A KM might be able to help address those concerns
Ensure that all problems are remedied	A KM, like a KEDB in a help desk, can be used to document problems and their resolutions so that if they recur, they can be remedied efficiently and quickly
Have project team study ICT4D in school to better understand	This is a KM problem in two senses. First, a team will be productive sooner if they have understanding of ICT4D context. Since each context is different, general education might be supplemented with KM on specific locales. Second, project teams should also have at least basic understanding of KM, needs, techniques, tools, and so on in order to be able to develop a KM that is sensitive to local needs but also provides the needed support

(continued)

Table 14.3 (continued)

Key requirements for success	Relationship to KM
Manage expectations	This is a KM problem to the extent that sustainability is questioned. A KM will not guarantee sustainability but should be a component for facilitating knowledge growth of local participants over time (Best, Thakur, & Kolko, 2009; Nanaka, 1994)
Monitoring and evaluation	Like other aspects of an ICT4D project, evaluation of the KM should be conducted and used to provide continuous improvement
Transparent, ethical basis for partnership; trust and shared vision among partners who understand the scope of each other's roles and activities	This issue transcends KM but has a small KM component in transparency to develop trust, which can be facilitated through explicit KM (Geldof et al. 2011; Heeks, 2009)
Address issues of accessibility; low literacy or high age of potential participants inhibited participation	The access requirement typically relates to hardware access. However, once that access is gained, access to information and/or how to obtain information are also required (Toyama, 2011). These often take the form of FAQs, a rudimentary KM. In addition, training in typing or basic computer use is likely required and could be made part of a KM capability. To the extent that age, literacy, or other impediments exist, they should be considered in development of the project plan and recognized as limitations (Donner & Toyama, 2009)

KM information accessible to more than computer and English literate people, the problems of accessibility are partially alleviated.

Making all of the technology available via smart devices, such as phones, may also expand the reach of KM efforts by allowing the rural people to access the KM data store via cell phones, which have about >80 % penetration in South Africa, about half of which is rural accessibility (Telecoms boom, 2013).

14.4 LLiSA Remote Rural Research

The prior sections develop concepts relating to best practices for ICT4D projects around the globe to define best practices and the extent to which KM practices can be applied to them. With this backdrop of ICT4D projects throughout the world, the South African government created and sponsors the LLiSA program, a collective of projects conducted through universities that provides networks, computers, and applications for use in remote rural villages (Pitse-Boshomane et al., 2008). Most of the projects also have NGO and industry partners, for instance the Meraka Institute and Nokia under the Cooperation Framework on Innovation Systems between Finland and South Africa (COFISA) (Eliasz & von Staden, 2008; Pitse-Boshomane et al., 2008). Six labs are currently active with three others in planning stages (Cunningham, Herselman, & Cunningham, 2012). The active labs are briefly described below to provide an understanding of the diversity of projects and also the potential for KM sharing across the projects. All projects operate through different aspects of tribal life, but all include some telecommunications implementation along with PC labs and Internet access.

14.4.1 Siyakhula Living Labs

The SLL started as a single project to provide computers and telecommunications in the Mbhashe province village of Dwesa (Dugmore, 2012). The village school and health clinic, the initial projects, have evolved to a program of 24 projects currently spanning over 13 villages. SLL is the most sophisticated and successful of the LLiSA labs, enjoying 15 years of stability in leadership from the academic and local communities (Dugmore, 2012). As a result several projects through COFISA, the SA government, Nokia, and other entities have successfully concluded. Community involvement has become more active over time (Coetzee, du Toit, & Herselman, 2012) with co-creation of content and community members providing researchers with knowledge of possible markets and products, entrepreneurial desires, etc. SLL is run out a Dwesa village school and is supported by several of the teachers (Dugmore, 2012).

While the SLL has had great success in implementing information and communication technology in the Mbhashe Municipality, a missing link exists between the ICTs available and the potential for use in daily community livelihoods (Pade et al., 2008). The technology that has been implemented in the targeted rural communities has not always been adopted as actively by local Mbhashe residents (Pade et al., 2008). In general, many remote village technology implementation projects suffer from a lack of understanding of local communities and their needs (Pade-Khene, Mallinson, & Sewry, 2011). As a result some information and communication technologies (ICT) are implemented and not used, and no impact analysis is done to determine either why adoption fails or what the impact on the community is for adoptions that succeed (Pade-Khene & Sewry, 2011). Thus, the sustainability of ICT change is an issue. Further, some technology is implemented and left in the hands of local caretakers but without continued development. For instance, some school assignments using the Internet were created early in the SLL projects. Teachers in the school are champions of the SLL research, but have not substantively added to the lesson plans and assignments; thus, there *is* transfer of knowledge and skills but the continuation of skills' use is inconsistent.

14.4.2 Limpopo Living Lab

Limpopo Province Living Lab (LLL) was not successful until it was folded into the Limpopo Economic Development Enterprise, an organization wholly owned by the provincial government. The lab is run out of the community center with the main goals of supporting local government initiatives (Coetzee et al., 2012). While having many ambitious programs, the LLL is less successful than it would like as efforts are abandoned as they face obstacles to meeting government goals.

14.4.3 North-West Living Lab

North-West Living Lab (NWLL) is a non-profit arm of a for-profit organization, Research Logistics. Originally a research project, the effort expanded to community "interventions" that include a toolkit for healthy community development that is in a testing stage (Coetzee, 2011). The goal of the project is positive customer satisfaction and profit from the venture. This project is on-going.

14.4.4 SAP Living Labs (SAP-LLs)

Mpumalanga and Gauteng Provinces have three LLs to support health care, mobile business services, and innovative socio-economic development. These are discussed together because they all use the same methodology and are programs of the research arm of SAP AG. Using local focus groups to identify opportunities, SAP Research convenes a team of academic, professional, business, and local groups to implement a local-requested initiation (Coetzee et al., 2012). With attention to technology infrastructure, usage patterns, applications, and economics of projects, SAP seeks to develop models for micro, small, and midsize enterprises that might be propagated throughout other regions. These labs have had sustainability issues with two of three projects discontinued (Cunningham et al., 2012). For instance, a patient health system spread successfully throughout several clinics and a regional hospital only to be discontinued when the municipal health department did not take responsibility for running the system (Cunningham et al., 2012).

14.4.5 Reconstructed Living Lab

Athlone's Reconstructed Living Lab (RLL), in the Western Cape, seeks to address social issues such as gangs and drug abuse (Coetzee et al., 2012). This lab, too, has started and stopped operation over the last 10 years as funding or other resources became too scarce to continue (Cunningham et al., 2012). As a social experiment, RLL currently is successful in developing and employing over 30 local staff (Cunningham et al., 2012; Parker & Parker, n.d.). RLL has many positive aspects but less success in the social reforms it seeks; for instance, only about 25 % of students complete classes (Cunningham et al., 2012).

The labs all do some form of monitoring and evaluation and all adjust activities based on the findings. All have different relationships with the LLiSA programs, using it for support (SLL, NWLL), collaboration (LLL), research partner (SAPLLs), and knowledge sharing (RLL) (Cunningham et al., 2012). Several of the labs have had interrupted activities when there was insufficient community involvement or resources, or there was a change of academic or business partners (Parker & Parker, n.d.). All rely on funding from various sources and, therefore, are also prone to shrinkage in a poor economy (Cunningham et al., 2012). The South African labs all have some economic motivation, but also focus on community development and socio-cultural involvement (Cunningham et al., 2012). Thus, all are vulnerable to capital availability and economic downturns.

While much more modest in their goals than European living labs, the African LLiSA network has shown increasing success over the last 7 years as the usefulness of the Internet, need to communicate with family members via cell phones, and other needs for services using ICTs surface (Cunningham et al., 2012).

14.4.6 SLL and Knowledge Management

The SLL is used as an example for in-depth analysis of project compared to best practices and their knowledge management aspects as summarized in Table 14.3. The SLL was created to deploy a "simple, cost-effective and robust, integrated ebusiness [and] telecommunication platform ... in marginalized ... communities in South Africa" (Dugmore, 2012, p. 3). The Dwesa-Cwebe community, where the SLL implementations have taken place, has 15,000–20,000 residents in the overall area (Dugmore, 2012; Gumbo, Thinyane, Thinyane, Terzoli, & Hansen, 2012). The "current user base is approximately 200 community members and 4,500 learners ... from 17 schools" (Dugmore, 2012, p. 4). Over the 7+ years of existence, SLL projects have deployed telecommunication networks with solar and electrical connectivity and computer labs in the 17 schools of the Dwesa-Cwebe area of Mbhashe Municipality in the Eastern Cape (Dugmore, 2012; Gumbo et al., 2012).

Training for local residents included basic computer literacy as well as specific technology training (Pade-Khene & Sewry, 2011). Teachers in the schools are encouraged to obtain ACE training and accreditation. Once teachers are trained, they in turn seek not only to train their students and other community members, but also to raise awareness of the SLL initiatives (Pade-Khene & Sewry, 2011).

Software functionality, in addition to MS Office, includes among others customized applications for mobile phone information lookup, and PC software for managing finances. Basic Internet access and MS Office remain the most consistently used software, along with the default games that come with Windows. One project developed assignments for teachers to use in school programs for every grade level; these too have remained successful but have not been added to significantly.

Needs analysis for other applications was conducted using "traditional" techniques that were found to be insufficient in the rural context because users were unable to predict what they might want from a technology they had no knowledge of (Gumbo et al., 2012; Pade-Khene et al., 2011). As a result, new techniques were

Table 14.4 KM best practice in SLL

KM Best practice for project success	Siyakhula Living Lab practices
Understanding of type, definition, and key knowledge in a project	This understanding, such as it exists in SLL, is casual and typically confined to the CS implementers of the technology. There is no explicit discussion of KM in SLL documents or practices
Understanding and application of a KM life cycle process that continues after project implementation	There is no explicit discussion of KM in SLL documents or practices
Development of a knowledge cluster or community of practice	There is no explicit discussion of or development of knowledge clusters in SLL documents or practices. A knowledge cluster has emerged in the 200 or so adults who use the technology and have become closer and are aware of each other. Of that 200, about 20 of the people are the key sources of information for everyone else
Development of processes for knowledge production	There are no explicit KM processes in SLL documents or practices

developed that posed possible problems faced by the local people and their requirements became the methods they would use to deal with the hypothetical problems (Gumbo et al., 2012). In addition to mobile telephony, applications for Xhosa interfaces and portability from one environment to another (e.g., PC to phone) have been developed. Local medical practices and remedies have been codified into a type of KM capability to complement modern medical practices (Gumbo et al., 2012). Other implementation efforts focused on facilitating government interactions, connecting local to country judicial systems, and developing local content (a form of KM) (Gumbo et al., 2012). The most successful projects have been phone access and those in the schools and health clinics (Pade et al., 2009; Pade-Khene et al., 2011).

SLL is the most successful and longest-running LLiSA project in South Africa (Dugmore, 2012). As the most successful project, it is more likely to have incorporated knowledge management than the other projects.

As Table 14.4 summarizes, there is no conscious attention to KM in the SLL projects. According to Dr. Alfredo Terzoli, the principal investigator for SLL, KM has not been a conscious part of the project activities to date (Personal communication with Dr. Terzoli, June 12, 2013). The pressure on the SLL has been to be as efficient with time as possible. Thus, time spent at Dwesa, about 7 h by car from Grahamstown, is defined to be as hands-on and goal-oriented in terms of completing technology infrastructure installation and maintenance, as possible.

Dr. Terzoli admits that KM could play an important role in the SLL project in terms of documenting decisions, issues and their resolutions, and other pertinent project information. However, he also feels that the money provided is more for infrastructure development than for KM about the infrastructure.

Although there was no specific attention to KM, the project sought to develop "prosumers," that is, local users who both produced and consumed their ICT resources (Gumbo et al., 2012). This was to be accomplished by both implementing the technology for use, but also training the local users to develop their skills to the point where they, too, could produce new information and uses from the technological resources provided (Gumbo et al., 2012). While there has been success in the training and overall telephony use, some of the applications have fallen into disuse, e.g., judicial and government outreach. Efforts are on-going to create more Xhosa-interface applications with translation capabilities for them to interface to other apps. It is believed that this will be a key to sustaining and building use in the parents and older populations in the Dwesa-Cwebe area (Osah & Pade-Khene, 2013).

Another SLL researcher at Rhodes University, Dr. Caroline Khene, conducted her dissertation research on the development of a method for baselining a project and performing needs-based project requirements analysis (Pade, Palmer, Kavhai, & Gumbo, 2009). Dr. Khene's method was used for one part of the SLL projects but not for all. The portion of the SLL projects based on the baseline report and using needs-based project requirements analysis was considered by all stakeholders to be successful. However, other parts of the SLL project, while technical successes, have failed to generate the desired user base. In general, the telecommunications, PC labs, and educational aspects of SLL are the most successful (Pade et al., 2008; Pade-Khene & Sewry, 2011).

Table 14.5 evaluates the SLL projects from the perspective of ICT4D best practices and their related KM components and identifies opportunities for improving the probability of project successes.

Drs. Terzoli and Khene were asked about the potential for KM in the SLL projects (Personal communication with Dr. Terzoli, June 12, 2013 and Dr. Khene, June 18, 2013). She believed that KM could be an important contributor to SLL sustainability, but she also reiterated that providing needs-based solutions to local problems was also key in developing users. KM alone is not likely to develop a user base. Dr. Terzoli was interested in trying a KM sub-project, but was not optimistic about the potential of funding for work not directly related to installing new capabilities.

The SLL project, like all of the LLiSA projects, faces challenges relating to funding continuity, development of the human capital in the Dwesa community to begin to reduce the need for university or NGO involvement, and the need to continuously prove the usefulness of the technology to continue to grow the user base. In addition, knowledge of the projects and the ability of local residents to participate still remains limited with many possible users lacking awareness of the project (Osah & Pade-Khene, 2013).

These challenges also relate to Toyama's three areas of technology amplification—differential access, capacity, and motivation (Toyama, 2011). Access, though provided through projects such as SLL, may not relate to needs of Dwesa natives. Capacity relates to education, social skills, and relationships of influence that all can be used to develop personal capital. However, remote rural natives may not understand how to use technology to improve their social capital and, further, may view their local social capital could suffer (Personal communication with Kirstin Krauss, June 14, 2013). Thus, the human capacity to develop and understand global social

Table 14.5 ICT4D best practices and SLL KM

Project key requirements for success	Siyakhula Living Lab practices
Develop a project strategy with long-term and short-term goals	"Long" is defined as several years into the future and is not explicitly defined. "Short" term relates to the immediate project and is elaborated to the extent that work can be assigned and performed from the schedule There is no specific discussion of sustainability. Training was conducted for the first project and those taught have taught other support staff
Emphasize sustainability (e.g., continued life of project), including economic and socio-political sustainability; provide sufficient financing; Develop business model for sustainability (i.e., do not rely on continuing donations)	There is no explicit KM plan or implementation. Local talent was developed through training and was conducted for the first project. Those taught have taught other support staff There is no KM specifically addressed for either single or multiple projects in a single location
Develop committed, enthusiastic, competent leaders; incentivize stakeholders to support the project; Invest time in building partnerships with all stakeholders—politicians, NGOs, local community, etc.	Training was conducted for the first project and those taught have taught other support staff. There is no on-going development of local support staff to deepen their expertise. There is little to no local support for the hardware or operating software
Attend to cultural differences in gaining trust and cooperation but also not changing the culture; treat locals in such a way that their traditional "social fibre" remains intact; adhere to socio-cultural norms; researchers come with or lose preconceptions to become effective at cultural interpretation	Since there is no formal KM, there are no identified Indigenous KM needs. There is some translation of material into Xhosa and some interfaces are presented in Xhosa (Gumbo et al., 2012) Typed input typically requires mostly English
Define a local champion, preferably who can take over management and maintenance; draw on the strengths of multiple actors for project governance; train and work with locals, eventually give them control over daily operations; train maintenance people	Such knowledge as exists relates to mostly declarative about the operation of software used in the site networks There is no formal KM strategy or formal KM effort. The KM performed was a by-product of implementation to "train the trainers" in software use Training provided after the first sessions is by the individuals trained during those sessions but without benefit of a KM to ensure complete, accurate training There is no formal development of local skills beyond that developed through the initial usage training
Communicate trust, openness, mutual respect, and understanding through all communications; Invest time in partnership building and networking	Since there is no formal KM, the type of trust that might be developed as a result of KM capabilities is missing from this project
Balance demand and supply of resources	There is no formal KM and no KM data store relating to SLL projects

(continued)

Table 14.5 (continued)

Project key requirements for success	Siyakhula Living Lab practices
Design appropriate, fully-working technology that is based on local needs, adapted as needed, involves the local community, partners local organizations, develops relationships with local governments, attends to local politics, contains output-based focus, applies new approaches with flexibility of design, uses iterative development, is context-appropriate, includes sufficient bandwidth, with services that meet local needs, and includes infrastructure, such as consistent electricity, as needed	There is no formal KM and no KM data store relating to SLL projects. A problem-based method of eliciting requirements has been developed to help residents think in terms of capabilities they cannot envision; there is an attempt to use a needs-based approach to development (Gumbo et al., 2012)
Ensure that all problems are remedied	There is no formal KM and no KM data store relating to SLL projects. However, there is a help desk service that seeks to remedy problems (Gumbo et al., 2012)
Have project team study ICT4D in school to better understand	Rhodes University, the home school for SLL, does have an ITC4D course that is optional for MIS students but not for CS students. Both types of students work on SLL projects but on different aspects
Manage expectations	SLL expectations management is done verbally and through project plans
Monitoring and evaluation	There is little monitoring and evaluation of finished projects other than to support up-time of the network
Transparent, ethical basis for partnership; trust and shared vision among partners who understand the scope of each other's roles and activities	KM is not used for this aspect of SLL project work. In terms of partnering, there is felt to be a good partnership between the SLL team and the local support team. After working together for over 7 years, many relationships have matured into trusting friendships
Address issues of accessibility; low literacy or high age of potential participants inhibited participation	FAQs are provided and training is expected to provide accessibility. Neither literacy nor age are explicitly evaluated or incorporated into project designs

capital may need to be developed before remote rural communities have a need to actively embrace the Internet and much that it offers (Toyama, 2011). The last issue is motivation. Dwesa natives have been observed most often playing games on the computer (Personal communications with Dr. Caroline Khene, June, 2013). Such computer play is viewed as indicating a less successful ICT4D project. However, as Toyama points out, as most people stop working, they tend to play at something (Toyama, 2011). In this computer play, the Dwesa natives are no different than anyone else. But these three amplifications point to the need for development of the individuals involved in the project, for them to develop in the way envisioned by project funders and initiators. In a modest way, KM associated with SLL might reduce the problems amplified by technology projects.

14.5 LLISA Knowledge Management

None of the LLiSA projects is organized or managed in the same way. As a result, all planning and project activities are unique to each living lab. This uniqueness allows response to local conditions, but provides a challenge to KM information sharing across LLs. The LLiSA projects are somewhat insular sharing information within the LLiSA projects at annual conferences. Conference attendees have not included the locals who take up maintenance responsibilities and there is no evidence that the conference information sharing has any impact on how any of the projects are conducted, although there is a desire to leverage available resources and use existing infrastructure for knowledge sharing (Pitse-Boshomane, 2009).

Each LL is operated differently. For instance, the Limpopo lab is run out of the Care Center by healthcare professionals, while the Siyakhula lab is run out of the school, and another out of the community center (Pitse-Boshomane, 2009). Because the background, interests, and education of the support staff varies widely across each living lab location, the availability of a joint KM store with accessibility to all South African lab partners would seem to have great potential to ease the support burdens of the local staff.

Ideally, the KM activities would be managed cohesively and would relate to all aspects of the information life cycle, including identification, acquisition, storage, retrieval, and dissemination (Alavi & Leidner, 2001; Probst, 2010; Teece, 1998). First, identification is difficult. For instance, in a remote rural project, knowledge about the project governance and processes, its technology artefacts, and technology use are all clearly understood and usually well-documented. However, knowledge about how-to information on small things, such as changing a fuse, wiring computer connections, where to get computer connection wires, where to find how-to information, are all important to sustainability of a project, but is less well understood as critical to the project's success. Further, where an individual from a developed part of the country might say, "look it up on the Internet," that thought may not occur to a novice Internet user. Even if the thought did occur, knowing the right search terms, how to evaluate the information presented, and then applying that information to the particular situation may be beyond the resources of a remote rural user.

Similarly, KM acquisition in terms of identifying that knowledge needs to be shared and that individuals intimately involved in a project need to provide their information presents challenges. Much of the technology innovation is on-the-spot improvisation to create success under changing conditions. Such improvisation is often recognized as application of expertise, but not recognized as an expertise that needs to be shared as the situation may appear to be singular.

Similarly, KM storage offers challenges in that documentation of some type, with identifying information about the knowledge and provider, is needed. This may take the form of paper, intranet documents, podcasts, databases with key search terms, or some other manifestation (Grimshaw & Gudza, 2010). Literacy, access, and language barriers all present issues relating to the forms of storage chosen.

KM retrieval requires methods of identification, cataloguing, advertising, and so on to first support the ability of community members to know that some information exists, and then to provide accessible retrieval of the information. These are not small hurdles as bandwidth, accessibility, and irretrievability all can inhibit knowledge use.

Finally, KM dissemination is the act of sharing information about information availability throughout a group of users. When projects are similar, ideally a central repository of common project KM information would be desired. In addition, similar projects might share significant amounts of information across all LLiSA projects. However, local geography, weather, and so on may preclude the direct application of techniques from one part of the country to another. The culture of both the projects and the tribes may inhibit the use of expertise not generated in the local context. Political discussions over where this is and how project KM information should be administered might overwhelm the project. In a less ideal situation, local organization could create their own KM stores but these, too, require administration, some sort of directory to advertise the data available, and possibly a gate-keeper to evaluate the value, accuracy, and usefulness of knowledge items.

In summary, sharing knowledge stores across all living labs projects and programs seems desirable. To do so may encourage differentiation of expertise, removing the burden to know everything about everything from one or a few people in each location. By sharing knowledge across programs, project success may become more sustainable.

14.6 Discussion

KM appears to have potential as a valuable contributor to remote rural ICT4D projects by contributing to project sustainability, continuing development of local staff skills, and educational and skills support for local participants. In addition, KM appears to have potential for cross-LLiSA project management of similar information with synergies across the group of projects and less work for those involved in creating and maintaining the KM data stores.

However, there are hurdles and barriers to the success of cross-project KM efforts that may lead to its best being deployed in a local setting. First, while the Xhosa tribe predominates in the Eastern Cape, each area governed by a chief has its own idiosyncratic culture, some distinctive language, and skills and capabilities (Personal communication with Dr. Caroline Khene, June 13, 2013). These are common differences across cultures that inhibit exact replication of change efforts across cultures (Bidwell et al., 2011; Ferguson et al., 2010; Krauss & Turpin, 2010).

In addition, skills and capabilities can differ widely across villages in Dwesa and across projects spread across the country. This, too, is a common difference that requires contextual adjustment of techniques and approaches across locales (Thapa & Saebo, 2011). From a KM perspective, this could mean iconic and native language capabilities that are accessible from smart devices.

Toyama's (2011) amplifiers—differential access, capacity, and motivation—all differ from even one village to the next (Osah & Pade-Khene, 2013). Each of the amplifiers may require differences, for instance, in how KM is structured, implemented, or used to appeal to users across contexts. Further, there is a persistent focus on *use* (cf. Dugmore, 2012) rather than a measure of *usefulness* that confuses the important issue in the adoption of novel technologies (Donner & Toyama, 2009). Usefulness would seem to be the more useful measure that is then followed by use and would be consistent with all innovation and adoption research, such as technology acceptance.

All of the differences listed above contribute to the list of key factors of successes and failures in Tables 14.1 and 14.2 that is partial and divergent across projects and settings. As a result of these unique characteristics, every project becomes a one-off that requires careful contextualization, customization of approach, and development of local resources. A KM capability could facilitate the uniqueness required of these design issues.

14.7 Summary and Conclusions

This paper sought to develop recommendations for knowledge management for the LLiSA projects. To develop these, first, best practices from knowledge management theory were identified. These included attention to KM life cycle, knowledge types, definitions, structure, presentation, and media. In addition, use of local language should be considered.

Next, ICT4D projects around the globe were analysed to determine key required practices to be emulated and key reasons for failure to be avoided. Key among these was contextualizing all aspects of the work and involvement of all stakeholders with trust-building, transparency, and development. From these we apply cultural sensitivity, needs-based projects, high involvement of local community, preferable with the Chief or King as the main project champion and user, and the active development of local talent to carry on the work once the initiators have left.

Then we evaluated the active LLiSA and their individual activities' successes to date, focusing on the most successful lab, the SLL, and abstracting to all of the LLiSA labs. In general, there is little learning from one project to another and no discernible day-to-day operational information. As a result, each lab stands alone in its ability to provide sustained success. This isolation makes the KM burden on the individual locations significant. Also, because KM does not appear to be a recognized, planned activity in any of the projects, many opportunities to develop skills, codify knowledge, and develop KM resources that might be shared are lost.

Even with these challenges, the LLiSA ICT4D projects have enjoyed significant successes and continue to grow and proliferate. In future, the projects could be improved by specific attention to knowledge management and the benefits this activity could provide to the local support teams.

References

Alavi, M., & Leidner, D. E. (1999). Knowledge management systems: Issues, challenges, and benefits. *Communications of the Association for Information Systems, 1*(7), 1–37.

Alavi, M., & Leidner, D. E. (2001). Review: Knowledge management and knowledge management systems: Conceptual foundations and research issues. *MIS Quarterly, 25*(1), 107–136.

Barrett, F. J. (1998). Managing and improvising: Lessons from jazz. *Career Development International, 3*, 283.

Best, M. L., & Kumar, K. (2008). Telecenters: Challenges from the sustainable access in rural India (SARI) project. *Information Technologies and International Development, 4*(4), 31–45.

Best, M. L., Thakur, D., & Kolko, B. E. (2009, April). The contribution of user-based subsidies to the impact and sustainability of telecenters-the ecenter project in Kyrgyzstan. *2009 International Conference on Information and Communication Technologies and Development (ICTD)* (pp. 192–200). IEEE.

Bidwell, N. J., Lamas, M., Marsden, G., Dlutu, B., Jones, M., Tucker, B., et al. (2011). *Please call ME.N.U4EVER: callback & social media sharing in rural Africa.* Retrieved from http://pubs.cs.uct.ac.za/archive/00000715/01/CallBack-Final.pdf

Bowen, P., Edwards, P., Cattell, K., & Jay, I. (2010). The awareness and practice of value management by South African consulting engineers: Preliminary research survey findings. *International Journal of Project Management, 28*(3), 285–295.

Brown, J. S., & Duguid, P. (2001). Knowledge and organization: A social-practice perspective. *Organization Science, 12*(2), 198–213.

Chuang, S. H. (2004). A resource-based perspective on knowledge management capability and competitive advantage: An empirical investigation. *Expert Systems with Applications, 27*(3), 459–465.

Coetzee, H. (2011, June). *Sustainable community development in the North West province of South Africa.* Paper presented at the 3rd Annual LLiSA Workshop, Rhodes University, Grahamstown, South Africa.

Coetzee, H., du Toit, I., & Herselman, M. (2012). Living labs in South Africa: An analysis based on five cases studies. *The Electronic Journal for Virtual Organizations and Networks., 14*, 1–30.

Conger, S., & Probst, J. (in press). Knowledge management in service desk decision making. In M. Mora, (Ed.), *Engineering and management of IT-based service systems: An intelligent decision-making support systems approach.* London: Springer.

Cunningham, P., Herselman, M., & Cunningham, M. (2012). *Supporting the evolution of sustainable Living Labs and Living Labs networks in Africa* (Version 1.8). Dublin, Ireland: International Information Management Corporation.

Davenport, T. H., De Long, D. W., & Beers, M. C. (1998). Successful knowledge management projects. *Sloan Management Review, 39*(2), 43–57.

Donner J., & Toyama, K. (2009, June). *Persistent themes in ICT4D research: Priorities for intermethodological exchange.* Paper presented at the 57th Session of the International Statistics Institute, Durban, South Africa.

Dugmore, H. (2012). *The Siyakhula Living Lab: An important step forward for South Africa and Africa.* Grahamstown, South Africa: Rhodes University.

Eliasz, T., & von Staden, R. (2008). *Dwesa village connection business modeling: Feasibility analysis.* Ungana, Africa: Cooperation Framework on Innovation Systems between Finland and South Africa (COFISA).

Evers, H. D., Nordin, R., & Nienkemper, P. (2010). *Knowledge cluster formation in Peninsular Malaysia: The emergence of an epistemic landscape* (Working Paper Series 62). Bonn, Germany: University of Bonn, Center for Development Research. Retrieved June 24, 2013, from http://mpra.ub.uni-muenchen.de/25845/1/WP62_Evers-et_al-K-cluster_Malaysia.pdf

Ferguson, J., Huysman, M., & Soekijad, M. (2010). Knowledge management practice: Pitfalls and potentials for development. *World Development, 28*(12), 1797–1810.

Ferguson, J. E., Mchombu, K. & Cummings, S. (2008). *Management of knowledge for development meta-review and scoping study*. (IKM Working Paper No. 1). Bonn, Germany: IKM Emergent Research Programme, European Association of Development Research and Training Institutes (EADI). Retrieved June 24, 2013, from http://wiki.ikmemergent.net/files/080421-ikm-working-paper-no1-meta-review-and-scoping-study-final.pdf.

Geldof, M., Grimshaw, D. J., Kleine, D., & Unwin, T. (2011). *What are the key lessons of ICT4D partnerships for poverty reduction? Systematic review report.* Egham, England: Royal Holloway, University of London. Retrieved June 24, 2013, from http://r4d.dfid.gov.uk/PDF/Outputs/SystematicReviews/DFID_ICT_SR_Final_Report_r5(2).pdf

Gottschalk, P. (2007). *Knowledge management systems: Value shop creation*. Hershey, PA: IGI Global.

Grimshaw, D. J., & Gudza, L. D. (2010). Local voices enhance knowledge uptake: Sharing local content in local voices. *The Electronic Journal of Information Systems in Developing Countries, 40*, 1–12.

Grunfeld, H. (2011). *The contribution of information and communication technologies for development (ICT4D) projects to capabilities, empowerment and sustainability: a case study of iREACH in Cambodia.* (Doctoral dissertation, Victoria University, Wellington, NZ).

Gumbo, S., Thinyane, H., Thinyane, M., Terzoli, A., & Hansen, S. (2012). Living lab methodology as an approach to innovation in ICT4D: The Siyakhula Living Lab experience. In P. Cunningham & M. Cunningham (Eds.), *Proceedings of the IST-Africa 2012 Conference*. Retrieved June 24, 2013, from http://www.siyakhulall.com/sites/default/files/ISTAfrica_Paper_ref_18_doc_4809_0.pdf

Heeks, R. (2009). Where next for ICTs and international development? *ICTs for development* (pp. 29–74). Paris: OECD.

Heeks, R., & Molla, A. (2009). *Impact assessment of ICT-for-development projects: A compendium of approaches*. Manchester, England: University of Manchester, Institute for Development Policy and Management (IDPM).

Jain, P. (2006). Empowering Africa's development using ICT in a knowledge management approach. *The Electronic Library, 24*(1), 51–67.

Jeon, S., Kim, Y.-G., & Koh, J. (2011). An integrative model for knowledge sharing in communities-of-practice. *Journal of Knowledge Management, 15*(2), 251–269.

Kanya, R., & Good, A. (2012, September). ICT4D: A case study of Jigawa state government in Nigeria. In *Proceedings of the IPID Annual Symposium 2012, Kristiansand, Norway.*

Kleine, D., & Unwin, T. (2009). Technological revolution, evolution, and new dependencies: What's new about ICT4D? *Third World Quarterly, 30*(5), 1045–1067.

Krauss, K., & Turpin, M. (2010, March). Towards the emancipation of the ICT4D researcher: Reflecting on a case study in deep rural South Africa. *Proceedings of the ICT and Development—Research Voices from Africa IFIP TC9 Relationship Between Computers and Society Workshop at Makerere University, Uganda.*

Levin, G., & Green, A. (2013). *Implementing project management: Templates and forms aligned with the standard for program management* (3rd ed.). Boca Raton, FL: Auerbach Publications.

Marais, M. (2011). *Analysis of the factors affecting the sustainability of ICT4D initiatives*. Pretoria, South Africa: Meraka Institute.

Masiero, S. (2011). Financial vs. social sustainability of telecentres: Mutual exclusion or mutual reinforcement? *The Electronic Journal of Information Systems in Developing Countries, 45*(3), 1–23.

Mason, R. O., McKenney, J. L., & Copeland, D. G. (1997). Developing an historical tradition in MIS research. *MIS Quarterly, 21*(3), 257–278.

Nanaka, I. (1994). A dynamic theory of organizational knowledge creation. *Organization Science, 5*(1), 14–37.

Osah, U. J. & Pade-Khene, C. (2013). A process assessment of the Siuakhula Living Lab: Assessing service utilization. Unpublished manuscript, Rhodes University, Grahamstown, South Africa.

Pade, C., Mallinson, B., & Sewry, D. (2008). An elaboration of critical success factors for rural ICT project sustainability in developing countries: Exploring the Dwesa case. *The Journal of Information Technology Case and Application, 10*(4), 32–55.

Pade, C., Palmer, R., Kavhai, M., & Gumbo, S. (2009). *Baseline study report.* Grahamstown, South Africa: Rhodes University Siyakhula Living Labs Project.

Pade-Khene, C., Mallinson, B., & Sewry, D. (2011). Sustainable rural ICT project management practice for developing countries: Investigating the Dwesa and RUMEP projects. *Information Technology for Development, 17*(3), 187–212.

Pade-Khene, C. & Sewry, D. (2011, April). Towards a comprehensive evaluation framework for ICT for development evaluation—An analysis of evaluation frameworks. *Proceedings of the 2nd International Conference on Information Management and Evaluation.* Toronto, Canada, Reading, UK: Academic Publishing International.

Parker, M., & Parker, R. (n.d.). Reconstructed living labs: Reconstucting communities through innovation. Meraka Institute. Retrieved June 24, 2013, from http://llisa.meraka.org.za/images/b/b5/RLabsInnovationApproach.pdf.

Pitse-Boshomane, M. (2009, July 1–3). *Report on SAFIPA/LLiSA provincial event in Mpumalanga, Nelspruit.*

Pitse-Boshomane, M., Marais, M. A., Morris, C., Roux, K. van Rensburg, R., Herselman, M., et al. (2008, October 27–30). *Catalysing innovation: The promise of the Living Lab approach in South Africa.* In 5th Prato Community Informatics & Development Informatics Conference: ICTs for Social Inclusion: What is the Reality? Prato, Italy: Monash University.

Probst, J. (2010). Knowing me, knowing you...ah ha: A knowledge management primer. *Proceedings of Pink Elephant Annual Conference, Las Vegas, NV, February 21-23.*

Project Management Institute. (2004). *A guide to the project management body of knowledge.* Newton Square, PA: Author.

Project Management Institute. (2008). *The standard for program management* (2nd ed.). Atlanta, GA: Author.

Robinson, H. S., Anumba, C. J., Carrillo, P. M., & Al-Ghassani, A. M. (2006). STEPS: A knowledge management maturity roadmap for corporate sustainability. *Business Process Management Journal, 12*(6), 793–808.

Rogers, E. M. (1995). Diffusion of Innovations, 4th edition, New York:Free Press.

Teece, D. J. (1998). Research directions for knowledge management. *California management review*, 40(3), 289.

Telecoms boom leaves rural Africa behind. (2013, February). *BusinessTech.* Retrieved from http://businesstech.co.za/news/telecommunications/30954/telecoms-boom-leaves-rural-africa-behind/

Thapa, D., & Saebo, O. (2011, January). Demystifying the possibilities of ICT4D in the mountain regions of Nepal. *Proceedings of the 44th Hawaii International Conference on Systems Science (HICSS-44 2011), Koloa, Kauai, Hawaii* (pp. 1–10). IEEE.

Tow, W. N. F. H., Venable, J., & Dell, P. (2011). Toward more effective knowledge management: an investigation of problems in knowledge identification. *Proceedings of the Pacific-Asian Computer Information Systems Conference*, Paper 191, Retrieved February 19, 2013, from http://www.pacis-net.org/file/2011/PACIS2011-191.pdf.

Toyama, K. (2011). Technology as amplifier in international development. *Proceedings of the 2011 iConference* (pp. 75–82). New York, NY: ACM.

Turner, J., & Müller, R. (2005). The project manager's leadership style as a success factor on projects: A literature review. *Project Management Journal, 36*(2), 49–61.

Unwin, T. (2009). *ICT4D: Information and communication technology for development.* Cambridge, England: Cambridge University Press.

Van Bon, J. (2005). *Foundations of IT service management based on ITIL* (2nd ed.). Zaltbommel, Netherlands: Van Haren Publishing.

Vaughan, D. M. (2011). *ICT4D—Linking policy to community outcomes*. Partners in micro-development. Retrieved February 18, 2013, from http://www.microdevpartners.org/documents/ICT4DLinkingPolicytoCommunityOutcomesPDF.pdf

Verjans, S. (2005). Bricolage as a way of life: Improvisation and irony in information systems. *European Journal of Information Systems, 14*, 504–506.

Walsham, G. (2010). ICTs for the broader development of India: An analysis of the literature. *The Electronic Journal of Information Systems in Developing Countries, 41*, 1–20.

About the Authors

Kweku-Muata Osei-Bryson is Professor of Information Systems at Virginia Commonwealth University in Richmond, VA, where he also served as the Coordinator of the IS Ph.D. program during 2001–2003. Previously he was Professor of Information Systems & Decision Sciences at Howard University in Washington, DC. He has also worked as an Information Systems practitioner in industry and government. He holds a Ph.D. in Applied Mathematics (Management Science & Information Systems) from the University of Maryland at College Park.

His research areas include Data Mining, Knowledge Management, IS Security, e-Commerce, IT for Development, Database Management, Decision Support Systems, IS Outsourcing, and Multi-criteria Decision Making. He has published in various leading journals including *Information Systems Journal, Knowledge Management Research & Practice, Decision Support Systems, Information Sciences, European Journal of Information Systems, Expert Systems with Applications, Information Systems Frontiers, Information & Management, Journal of the Association for Information Systems, Journal of Information Technology for Development, Journal of Database Management, Expert Systems with Applications, Computers & Operations Research, Journal of the Operational Research Society*, & *the European Journal of Operational Research*. He serves as an Associate Editor of the INFORMS Journal on Computing, as a member of the Editorial Boards of the Computers & Operations Research journal and the *Journal of Information Technology for Development*, and as a member of the International Advisory Board of the *Journal of the Operational Research Society*.

Gunjan Mansingh is a Lecturer and Undergraduate coordinator in the Department of Computing at the University of the West Indies (U.W.I.), Mona, Jamaica. She obtained a Ph.D. in Information Systems and an M.Phil. in Computer Science from U.W.I. and a B.Sc. from Bombay University, India. She worked for a few years in the IT industry in Jamaica before moving to academia.

Her research interests are Data Mining, Decision Support Systems, Knowledge Management and Knowledge Management Systems, Expert Systems, and Technology Adoption. In her research she has worked in different domains in

K.-M. Osei-Bryson et al. (eds.), *Knowledge Management for Development*, Integrated Series in Information Systems 35, DOI 10.1007/978-1-4899-7392-4,

Jamaica such as healthcare, crime, agriculture, and e-commerce. In her research her focus has been on harnessing data, information, and knowledge in the various sources to assist in the decision making process. She has publications in refereed journals such as *Decision Support Systems, Information Systems Frontier, Knowledge Management Research and Practice, Information Sciences, Expert Systems with Applications, and British Journal of Sports Medicine*. She also has papers published in the proceedings of IEEE Communications Conference Jamcon, e-business workshop, SIG GlobDev workshops, SIGDSS workshops, IRMA, Conf-IRM, AMCIS, and IASTED. She teaches various courses at the undergraduate and the graduate level in Computer Science and Information Systems.

Lila Rao is the Deputy Executive Director (Acting) and a Lecturer in Information Systems at the Mona School of Business and Management, The University of the West Indies. She holds a Ph.D. in Information Systems from The University of the West Indies and an M.Sc. in Computer Science from the University of Waterloo, Canada.

She currently does research in various areas including Data Warehousing and Mining, Data, Information, and Knowledge Quality, Decision Support Systems, and Technology Adoption. She has a strong interest in addressing some of the issues related to improving the quality of information systems (e.g., data and information and design quality). She has published in a number of international journals including *Decision Support Systems, Knowledge Management Research and Practice, Data and Knowledge Engineering, International Journal of Information Systems for Crisis Response Management, Expert Systems with Applications,* and *Information Systems Frontiers* journal. She also has papers published in the proceedings of FLAIRS Research Symposium, e-business workshop, IRMA, AMCIS, and ICEIS.

Ricardo Anderson is an Assistant Lecturer in the Department of Computing at the University of the West Indies (U.W.I. Mona-WJC). His research interests include Knowledge Management Systems, Knowledge Discovery in Database, and Data Mining. Ricardo holds a Bachelor's degree in Computer Science and a Master's in Computer-based Management Information Systems both from the U.W.I. He has a paper in the proceedings of SIGDSS conference.

Francis Kofi Andoh-Baidoo is Assistant Professor, Department of Information Systems & Quantitative Methods, College of Business Administration, University of Texas—Pan American, USA. He obtained his Ph.D. in Information Systems from Virginia Commonwealth University, Richmond. He has an M.B.A. and an M.S. in Information Technology Management from University of North Carolina, Greensboro, and Bachelor of Science in Materials Engineering (Honors) from the Kwame Nkrumah University of Science & Technology, Kumasi, Ghana. His research areas include Data Mining, Knowledge Management, IS Security, e-Commerce, IT for Development, Database Management, Decision Support Systems, and ICT use in developing nations. He has published in journals such as *Expert Systems with Applications, Information Systems Frontiers, IEEE Security & Privacy, Journal of Information Technology Theory and Application, Information*

Resources Management, International Journal of Services and Standards, and *International Journal of Electronic Finance*. He serves on the editorial board of several journals including the *Journal of Information Technology Theory and Application, International Journal of Electronic Finance*, and *Journal of Information Technology Education*.

Rajendra K. Bandi is an Associate Professor (Information Systems) at the Indian Institute of Management Bangalore, India. He received his Ph.D. in Business Administration (computer information systems) from the Robinson College of Business, Georgia State University, Atlanta, USA. His research interests are in technology adoption, enterprise systems implementation, knowledge management, social impacts of computing, and software engineering. He has guided multi-country research on ICT-enabled relocation of work, coordinating researchers from several Asian and European countries. He has published several research papers in international journals and presented papers at many international conferences.

Sue Conger, Ph.D., is on the faculty of University of Dallas as Director, Information & Technology Management program. She publishes extensively, speaks at conferences globally, and is a Visiting Professor at Rhodes University in South Africa, which is the source of her interest in the Living Labs programs. Dr. Conger is active in academic and industry associations. She is on five editorial boards and the program and planning committees for several conferences. Her research interests are IT service management, IT-related privacy, emerging technologies, and innovative uses of IT. She authored *The New Software Engineering* (1994) and *Planning & Designing Effective Web Sites* (1997), and *Process Mapping & Management* (2011). She is presently at work on a book on IT Service Management.

Oktri Mohammad Firdaus is a lecturer in Industrial Engineering Department at Widyatama University, Bandung, Indonesia. He earned his Master of Engineering in Industrial Engineering from Bandung Institute of Technology, Indonesia. Currently he is a Ph.D. candidate in Industrial Engineering & Management, Bandung Institute of Technology, Indonesia, with focus on Medical Knowledge Management.

Rajesri Govindaraju is an Associate Professor at the Faculty of Industrial Technology, Bandung Institute of Technology, Indonesia. She completed her bachelor in informatics from Bandung Institute of Technology, Indonesia, and Ph.D. in Enterprise Information Systems Implementation from University of Twente, The Netherlands. Her current research areas include information systems implementation, ERP systems, e-business systems adoption and implementation, and Knowledge Management Systems. She currently serves as the Chairman of the Industrial Systems and Techno Economic Research Group, Bandung Institute of Technology. Her email address is rajesri_g@mail.ti.itb.ac.id.

Virgilio Lopez-Morales obtained his Ph.D. in Engineering Sciences from the Ecole Centrale de Nantes, France. Currently he is a full time researcher at Universidad Autonoma del Estado de Hidalgo, Mexico. His research interests include decision support systems in modeling and control, intelligent distributed systems, and multi-agent systems. He has published more than 35 papers in journals and conferences in these areas.

Patricia Nalwoga Lutu is a Senior Lecturer in the Computer Science department at the University of Pretoria in South Africa. She obtained the Ph.D. in Computer Science from the University of Pretoria in 2010. She obtained the M.Sc. Computer Science in 1981 and B.Sc. Computer Science in 1979 both from the University of Manchester in the United Kingdom. Since 1981 she has lectured in Computer Science and in Informatics at various universities in Nigeria, Lesotho, and South Africa. She has lectured in database systems for more than 20 years. Her current research interests include machine learning, data mining, decision support systems, and business intelligence.

Niall McNulty is a digital media consultant at the forefront of using new technologies to record and share African content, in particular local knowledge, histories, and cultural practices. Amongst other community-oriented projects, working with the eThekwini Municipality in Durban, he launched and manages the Ulwazi Programme (www.ulwazi.org), an initiative that uses social technologies like blogs, wikis, and mobile phones, the public library infrastructure, and community participation to collect and disseminate indigenous knowledge and local history. In 2011, with the support of the Goethe Institute, Niall extended this program to township schools surrounding Durban where Grade 10 students were taught digital literacy, oral research skills, and digital media production. This has made an enormous contribution to the collection of local histories and culture, and to the amount of Zulu language content available on the Internet. In 2012, in recognition of his work, he travelled to Kenya as an invited expert, presenting at the Standing Conference of Eastern, Central and Southern Africa Library and Information Associations (SCECSAL). As an added accolade, on behalf of the Ulwazi Programme, he collected the runner-up award at the 2012 Telkom Highway Africa New Media Awards, in the "Community Engagement Through Technology" category. Niall's work offers outstanding examples of how social technologies intersect with local culture, history, and language and shows one way libraries can remain relevant in the digital age. These technologies can be used as a democratizing tool allowing everyday people to record and access information about their area or community, in their own language.

Vikas Mehra is an IS researcher and a business consultant. He obtained his doctoral degree in Information Systems from the Indian Institute of Management Bangalore. His areas of research are information systems, knowledge management, technology acceptance, and organizational strategy. His areas of consulting are decision sciences, knowledge management, information systems management, and leadership development. He has presented and published his research in various international conferences. He has also prepared multiple cases for research and class discussion. He is a reviewer for international academic journals and conferences. He has more than 12 years of experience as a practitioner in the manufacturing, automotive, financial services, analytics, and learning and development domains.

Babajide Osatuyi is an Assistant Professor of Computer Information Systems & Quantitative Methods at the University of Texas—Pan American. His research interests include decision support systems for emergency management, knowledge management, social network analysis, and information and communication technologies for development. He serves as reviewer for Information Systems Journals and Conferences. His research has appeared in journals such as *Computers in Human Behavior, Information Processing and Management, International Journal of Innovation and Learning, International Journal of Data Engineering, International Journal of Knowledge, Culture and Change in Organizations, Journal of Information Technology Theory and Application*, and *Electronic Journal of Information Systems for Developing Countries*.

Yacine Ouzrout is a Computer Scientist in the Supply Chain & Product Lifecycle Management group of the DISP Laboratory at the University Lumiere Lyon2 (ULL). He obtained his Ph.D. in Computer Engineering from the National Institute of Technology of Lyon (INSA), and his HDR (Habilitation Thesis) in 2012 from the University Lyon2. Currently, he is an Associate Professor at ULL. He is the Director of the Institute of Technology of his university. His research interests include multi-agent systems, simulation, decision support systems, and distributed information systems. Dr. Ouzrout has been involved in several European projects including Asia-Link East–west project, Erasmus Mundus eLink, and Sustainable eTourism and is currently the ULL coordinator of the Erasmus Mundus eLink project. He is co-chair and member of program committees of International conferences (PLM, SKIMA, AICIT, ICTIS, etc.), member of Scientific Commissions (DISP Laboratory, Computer Science Commission ULL, etc.), and reviewer for several international journals and conferences.

Han Reichgelt is the Dean of the School of Computing and Software Engineering, Southern Polytechnic State University, Georgia, USA. Prior to that, he held appointments at Georgia Southern University in Statesboro, Georgia; the University of the West Indies, Mona Campus, Jamaica; the University of Nottingham, England; and the University of Edinburgh, Scotland. He received his Ph.D. in Cognitive Science from the University of Edinburgh in Scotland and his B.Sc. and M.Sc. from the University of Nijmegen in The Netherlands. His research interests include IT Service Delivery Quality, Computing Education, and Health Information Technology. Han is the (co-)author of over 100 journal and refereed conference papers, as well as a textbook on Knowledge Representation in Artificial Intelligence. He also co-edited books on Expert Systems Development and on Information Systems Delivery Quality. His research interests include IT and economic development, IT application delivery quality, Health Information Technology, and computing education. Han currently serves on the Advisory Committee for the Georgia Regional Extension Center at Morehouse School of Medicine, and is a commissioner for the ABET Computing Accreditation Commission.

Koen Rossel-Cambier is a Belgian development economist who, over the last 20 years, has worked on overseas long-term assignments in amongst others Senegal,

Italy, Morocco, and Barbados with international organizations such as the ILO, the World Bank, UNICEF, and the European Union. Dr. Rossel-Cambier has managed projects and undertook technical assistance missions in more than 40 developing countries, in particular in Africa and in Latin America and the Caribbean. He has authored numerous articles in peer-reviewed journals, working papers, and textbooks tackling a wide range of applied economic challenges taking into account social development dimensions. Koen Rossel-Cambier was academic assistant with an M.B.A. program for the HUB in Brussels in the beginning of his career and is now also senior Associated Researcher with the universities of Mons (UMONS) and Brussels (ULB), Belgium. He holds a Doctoral Degree (Ph.D.) in Applied Economic Sciences (UMONS) for his innovative research on combined microfinance schemes. He also completed Master's Degrees in respectively Applied Economic Sciences (KUL), International Trade (HUB), and International Relations (KUL-Université Fribourg).

T.M.A. Ari Samadhi is an Associate Professor and Head of Department of Industrial Engineering, Bandung Institute of Technology, Indonesia. He earned his doctorate from The University of New South Wales, Australia. He joined the Manufacturing Systems Research Group.

Kadarsah Suryadi is a lecturer in Department of Industrial Engineering, Bandung Institute of Technology, Indonesia, and is also a Professor of Decision Support Systems. He earned his doctorate from Universitae d'Aix Marseille III, France. He joined the Industrial Management Research Group. He currently serves as the Vice Rector for Academic and Student Affairs, Bandung Institute of Technology, Indonesia.

Index

K.-M. Osei-Bryson et al. (eds.), *Knowledge Management for Development*, Integrated Series in Information Systems 35, DOI 10.1007/978-1-4899-7392-4,

L

M

MIX
Papier aus verantwortungsvollen Quellen
Paper from responsible sources
FSC® C105338

If you have any concerns about our products,
you can contact us on
ProductSafety@springernature.com

In case Publisher is established outside the EU,
the EU authorized representative is:
Springer Nature Customer Service Center GmbH
Europaplatz 3, 69115 Heidelberg, Germany

Printed by Libri Plureos GmbH
in Hamburg, Germany